The Handbook of
ECOLOGICAL MONITORING

The Handbook of
ECOLOGICAL MONITORING
A GEMS/UNEP publication

Edited by

ROBIN CLARKE

CLARENDON PRESS · OXFORD
1986

Oxford University Press, Walton Street, Oxford OX2 6DP

Oxford New York Toronto
Delhi Bombay Calcutta Madras Karachi
Petaling Jaya Singapore Hong Kong Tokyo
Nairobi Dar es Salaam Cape Town
Melbourne Auckland

and associated companies in
Beirut Berlin Ibadan Nicosia

Oxford is a trade mark of Oxford University Press

Published in the United States
by Oxford University Press, New York

British Library Cataloguing in Publication Data
The Handbook of ecological monitoring.
1. Environmental monitoring 2. Ecological
surveys.
I. Clarke, Robin
363.7 TD193
ISBN 0-19-854590-8

Library of Congress Cataloging in Publication Data
The Handbook of ecological monitoring.
"A GEMS/UNEP publication."
Bibliography: p.
Includes index.
1. Environmental monitoring. 2. Ecology—Technique.
I. Clarke, Robin.
QH541.15.M64H36 1986 574.5′028 85-29744
ISBN 0-19-854590-8

Set by Cotswold Typesetting Limited, Cheltenham
Printed in Great Britain by St Edmundsbury Press,
Bury St Edmunds, Suffolk

Through ignorance or indifference we can do massive and irreversible harm to the earthly environment on which our life and well-being depend. Conversely, through fuller knowledge and wiser action, we can achieve for ourselves and our posterity a better life in an environment more in keeping with human needs and hopes.

United Nations Conference on the Human Environment, Stockholm 1972

Foreword

M. K. Tolba, Executive Director,
United Nations Environment Programme

The Earth's biosphere is under attack. As we struggle to wrest from it a decent living for ever more people, signs of strain are beginning to appear. Planners are thus faced with the problem of devising strategies for development which provide for the needs of the human population without damaging the fabric of its existence. The art and science of doing this is called environmental management.

Regrettably, environmental managers still know surprisingly little about the biosphere. What is happening to this precious resource, which supports not only man but all other living things? How fast are new deserts being created? Where is the tropical forest disappearing most rapidly? How are land-use patterns changing?

Answers to these, and many other more detailed questions can be provided by ecological monitoring—a system of surveying the Earth's resources that can provide planners with the data they so badly need. Although decision makers are increasingly aware of the potential of ecological monitoring, detailed knowledge of the techniques involved is less common.

The *Handbook of ecological monitoring* is designed to fill this information gap. It will be of use to planners who wish to know something of the range of techniques that are now available to obtain environmental data, the variables that can be analysed, and the precision that can be obtained. It will also be of use to the specialist designing or managing a monitoring programme. While today's specialists are often required to be experts in many fields, none can be expected to encompass the range of knowledge needed to obtain data on the ground, from the air and from space. This book seeks to integrate such knowledge, providing for the first time a detailed account of the whole system of ecological monitoring under one cover.

Its publication stems directly from the work of UNEP's Global Environmental Monitoring System (GEMS). For more than a decade now, GEMS has been actively developing the techniques of ecological monitoring and ensuring that planners in both developing and developed countries are aware of their potential.

Publication of the *Handbook of ecological monitoring* is timely because it coincides with the latest and most adventurous step to be taken by GEMS: the establishment of GRID, the Global Resource Information Database. Information on GRID is presented in the Postscript to this book (Chapter 5).

Currently, environmental data are scattered in many different places. They are stored in a variety of formats that are not easily comparable. As a result, decision-makers are often forced to duplicate previous work to obtain information which differs in nature only slightly from that which already exists.

The Global Resource Information Database is designed to put an end to this state of affairs. It is designed to bring all kinds of existing environmental data into one place, and make them easily accessible to decision-makers all over the world. This is an exciting prospect, and one which will surely hasten the day when all decisions that affect the environment can be taken wisely, from a position of knowledge, and with due regard to the future generations who must live with the results of these decisions.

The United Nations Environment Programme, and the Global Environmental Monitoring System which is a part of it, are thus working actively towards a better future for the environment. Safeguarding the biosphere is UNEP's first priority. I hope that this book will play a part in providing a better future for the inhabitants of this planet, both those alive today and those who will succeed us.

Contents

(Plates fall between pp. 240 and 241 of the text)

Contributors   xv

1. Habitat monitoring theory   1
  1.1 Ecological monitoring and the environment   1
  1.2 What is ecological monitoring?   2
  1.3 The uses of ecological monitoring   3
  1.4 The history of ecological monitoring   3
  1.5 Ecological monitoring in practice   4
  1.6 Ecological monitoring data   6
  1.7 Ground, aerial and satellite monitoring   7
      1.7.1 Ground monitoring   7
      1.7.2 The aerial survey   9
      1.7.3 Satellite monitoring   14
  1.8 The ecological monitoring unit   15
  1.9 The costs of ecological monitoring   16
  1.10 Developing an ecological monitoring programme   20
  1.11 Towards a global system   20
  References   21

2. Ground monitoring   22
  2.1 Climate measurements   23
      2.1.1 Meteorological methods and equipment   23
      2.1.2 Types of station   24
      2.1.3 Rain-gauge distribution and type   25
      2.1.4 Other climatic factors   25
            2.1.4.1 Evaporation and transpiration   25
            2.1.4.2 Solar radiation   26
      2.1.5 Statistical techniques   26
            2.1.5.1 Limitations of conventional statistics   26
            2.1.5.2 Possibilities of stochastic approaches   27
      2.1.6 Rain-gauge network design: a case study   28
  2.2 Preparation of a base map   29
  2.3 Soil mapping and interpretation   31
      2.3.1 How the environment affects soil formation   31
      2.3.2 The soil profile   34
      2.3.3 Describing the soil profile   35
      2.3.4 Soil sampling   36
      2.3.5 Soil analysis   37
      2.3.6 Field methods in soil survey   38

2.4 Land-form classification   40
  2.4.1 Landscape morphometry   44
  2.4.2 Surveys along hillslope transects   46
2.5 Soil erosion and sediment yields   48
  2.5.1 Catchment or drainage-basin studies   48
    2.5.1.1 Methods: monitoring of sediment loads   49
    2.5.1.2 Methods: suspended load   49
    2.5.1.3 Methods: bedload   50
    2.5.1.4 Methods: reservoir sedimentation surveys   51
    2.5.1.5 Experimental design for catchment studies   53
  2.5.2 Process studies   53
    2.5.2.1 Short-term field observations   54
    2.5.2.2 Landslides and debris flows   54
    2.5.2.3 Biological activity   54
    2.5.2.4 Rill and gully erosion   55
    2.5.2.5 Surface erosion   56
    2.5.2.6 Monitoring surface erosion   57
    2.5.2.7 Monitoring rill, gully, and streambank erosion   59
2.6 Vegetation monitoring   60
  2.6.1 The vegetation survey   62
  2.6.2 Sampling vegetation   65
  2.6.3 Vegetation sampling methods   67
    2.6.3.1 Plot sampling   67
    2.6.3.2 Intercept methods   69
    2.6.3.3 Plotless sampling   71
  2.6.4 Summarizing and analysing community composition data   72
  2.6.5 Biomass and productivity measurements   73
  2.6.6 Permanent study plots   75
  2.6.7 Standardizing data collection   76
2.7 Large mammal herbivores   77
  2.7.1 Use of primary production by wild and domestic herbivores   81
  2.7.2 Population ranges and the use of vegetation types   82
    2.7.2.1 Counting the occurrence of animals   83
    2.7.2.2 Removing or adding known numbers of animals   87
    2.7.2.3 Methods involving animal sign   89
    2.7.2.4 Use of vegetation types   90
  2.7.3 Herbivore diets   91
    2.7.3.1 Diet components   91
    2.7.3.2 Units of measurement   92
    2.7.3.3 Methods of obtaining samples   92
    2.7.3.4 Analysis   96
    2.7.3.5 Impact of herbivores on the vegetation   102
2.8 Nutrition and population dynamics   104
  2.8.1 Body condition   104
    2.8.1.1 General body condition   105
    2.8.1.2 Fat reserves   106
    2.8.1.3 Protein reserves   106
  2.8.2 Nutritional value of the diet   107
    2.8.2.1 Protein–energy nutrition   108

     2.8.3 Analysis of population dynamics   108
          2.8.3.1 Ageing animals   108
          2.8.3.2 Reproduction   110
          2.8.3.3 Disease, parasitism, mortality, and life tables   110

  2.9 Social and economic surveys   111
     2.9.1 Survey design   113
     2.9.2 Sampling methods   114
     2.9.3 Data-gathering techniques   117
     2.9.4 Organization of the survey   123
     2.9.5 Data analysis   129
     2.9.6 Conclusion   130

  References   131

3. Aerial monitoring   141

  3.1 The use of light aircraft   141
     3.1.1 Introduction   141
     3.1.2 Major applications   142
          3.1.2.1 Long-term monitoring of animal populations   142
          3.1.2.2 Regional resource inventories   144
          3.1.2.3 Environmental impact assessment   145
          3.1.2.4 Vegetation monitoring   146
          3.1.2.5 Monitoring land-use changes   147
     3.1.3 The systematic reconnaissance flight   147
          3.1.3.1 General concepts   147
          3.1.3.2 Visual observations   148
          3.1.3.3 Vertical 35-mm photography   148
          3.1.3.4 Ancillary data   149
          3.1.3.5 Data integration   149
          3.1.3.6 Data recombinations   150
          3.1.3.7 Data analysis   150
     3.1.4 Stratified random sampling   159
          3.1.4.1 The concept of stratification   159
          3.1.4.2 Data collection   161
          3.1.4.3 Data integration and analysis   161
          3.1.4.4 Comparison between the SRF and STRS methods   161
     3.1.5 Block and total counting   164
          3.1.5.1 Block counting   164
          3.1.5.2 Total counting   164
     3.1.6 Important publications   165

  3.2 Operational procedures for aerial surveys and monitoring   166
     3.2.1 Aircraft and equipment   166
          3.2.1.1 Basic considerations   166
          3.2.1.2 Aircraft   166
          3.2.1.3 Avionics   166
          3.2.1.4 35-mm cameras   167
          3.2.1.5 Ancillary equipment   167
     3.2.2 Crew duties   168
          3.2.2.1 Pilot   168
          3.2.2.2 The front-seat observer (FSO)   168

3.2.2.3 The rear-seat observers (RSO)   169
3.2.3 Section of data variables   169
    3.2.3.1   Introduction   169
    3.2.3.2   Land-form   170
    3.2.3.3   Climate   170
    3.2.3.4   Hydrology   172
    3.2.3.5   Erosion   173
    3.2.3.6   Vegetation   173
    3.2.3.7   Agricultural land-use   174
    3.2.3.8   Livestock and wildlife   174
    3.2.3.9   Settlements and population   175
    3.2.3.10 Administration, infrastructure, and services   176
3.2.4 Survey planning   176
    3.2.4.1 Maps   176
    3.2.4.2 Survey-timing   176
    3.2.4.3 Designing a systematic sample   177
    3.2.4.4 Stratification   182
    3.2.4.5 Subunits   183
    3.2.4.6 Pre-survey flights   184
3.2.5 Piloting and navigation   185
    3.2.5.1 Control of height above ground level   185
    3.2.5.2 Control of ground speed   185
    3.2.5.3 Navigation without the GNS   186
    3.2.5.4 Navigation with OMEGA/VLF   186
    3.2.5.5 Other operational procedures   189
    3.2.5.6 Geo-referencing the subunits   190
3.2.6 The front-seat observer records   191
    3.2.6.1 Flight parameters   191
    3.2.6.2 Camera operation   191
    3.2.6.3 Qualitative observations   192
3.2.7 The rear-seat observations   192
    3.2.7.1 Defining the counting strip   193
    3.2.7.2 The observations   193
    3.2.7.3 Recording and transcribing   194
3.2.8 35-mm vertical sample photography   196
    3.2.8.1 Cameras and mounts   196
    3.2.8.2 Film   197
    3.2.8.3 Photo-scales   197
    3.2.8.4 Set-up for photo-interpretation   199
    3.2.8.5 Count and area data   199
    3.2.8.6 Interpretation procedures   200
3.2.9 The aerial survey data base   201
    3.2.9.1 Data base structure   201
    3.2.9.2 Collation and integration of ancillary data   203
    3.2.9.3 Data transformations   205
    3.2.9.4 Data manipulation   205
    3.2.9.5 The survey estimates   207
    3.2.9.6 Precision of the survey estimates   208
    3.2.9.7 Applications for thematic mapping   210
    3.2.9.8 Applications for resource inventories   210

3.2.9.9 Data base analyses 211
3.2.10 The control of bias 212
    3.2.10.1 General considerations 212
    3.2.10.2 Bias from survey design 212
    3.2.10.3 Bias from aircraft operation 213
    3.2.10.4 Observer counting bias 214
    3.2.10.5 Bias from photo-scale 214
    3.2.10.6 Bias from photo-interpretation 216
3.2.11 Conclusion 218

Bibliography 219

4. Remote sensing 222

4.1 Principles of remote sensing 222

4.2 The history of remote sensing 223
    4.2.1 Remote sensing from space 226

4.3 Photographic sensors and applications 228
    4.3.1 The metric camera 228
    4.3.2 Photographic resolution 229
    4.3.3 Black-and-white panchromatic aerial photography 230
    4.3.4 Black-and-white infra-red film 231
    4.3.5 Colour film 231
    4.3.6 Colour infra-red film 231
    4.3.7 Multiband photography 232
    4.3.8 The large-format camera 234
    4.3.9 Filters used in photography 234

4.4 Imaging with non-photographic sensors 235
    4.4.1 TV cameras or image tubes 235
    4.4.2 Optical-mechanical scanners 237
    4.4.3 Thermal infra-red scanners 238

4.5 Multispectral scanners (MSS) 243

4.6 Active microwave systems 245
    4.6.1 The history of microwave imaging 245
    4.6.2 Principles of active microwave imaging 245
    4.6.3 Radar resolution 247
    4.6.4 Performance of SAR systems 247
    4.6.5 SAR availability 249
    4.6.6 SAR monitoring applications 249
        4.6.6.1 SAR in agriculture 250
        4.6.6.2 SAR in forested land 250
        4.6.6.3 SAR in rangelands 252
        4.6.6.4 SAR in wetlands 252
    4.6.7 Spaceborne SAR 252
    4.6.8 Conclusions 255

4.7 Space systems useful for ecological monitoring 255
    4.7.1 Automatic satellites 258
        4.7.1.1 Landsat: the programme 259
        4.7.1.2 Landsat: the multispectral scanner system 262
        4.7.1.3 Landsat-1 and -2: the return beam vidicon system 265

4.7.1.4 Landsat-3: the return beam vidicon system 266
4.7.1.5 The data-collection system 266
4.7.1.6 The Thematic Mapper (TM) Landsat-4 and -5 267
4.7.1.7 Landsat and ecological monitoring 269
4.7.1.8 SPOT (Système Probatoire d'Observation de la Terre) 270
4.7.2 Meteorological satellites 271
4.7.3 Manned satellites 271
4.7.4 Applications 272
4.7.4.1 Processing the data 274

Bibliography 276

5. Postscript: GRID: a tool for environmental management 283

5.1 National, regional, and global environmental data 283

5.2 Utility of existing environmental data 284

5.3 Towards a global data base for the environment 285
5.3.1 The organization of GRID 286
5.3.2 The functions of GRID 286
5.3.3 How GRID will work 287
5.3.3.1 The hardware 287
5.3.3.2 The software 288

5.4 The future of environmental data management 288

Index 291

Contributors

This book is based on contributions from the following authors:

Dr M. Abdel-Hady, Remote Sensing Centre, Academy of Science, Research and Technology, 101 Kasr El-Eini Street, Cairo, Egypt.

Dr Peter M. Ahn, Head, Farming Systems Division, IDESSA (Institut des Savanes), B.P. 604, Bouake, Ivory Coast.

Dr David J. Campbell, Assistant Professor, Geography and African Studies, Michigan State University, 315 Natural Science, East Lansing, Michigan 48824-1115, United States.

Mr Robin Clarke, Consultant writer and editor, Maltshovel House, Eynsham, Oxford, OX8 1HF, United Kingdom.

Dr H. Croze, GEMS, United Nations Environmental Programme, P.O. Box 30553, Nairobi, Kenya.

Dr Patrick Duncan, Station Biologique, Tour du Valat, Le Sambuc, 13200 Arles, France.

Dr Thomas Dunne, Department of Geological Sciences, AK-20, University of Washington, Seattle, Washington 98195, United States.

Dr Allan Falconer, Regional Centre for Services in Surveying, Mapping, and Remote Sensing, P.O. Box 18118, Nairobi, Kenya.

Dr M. D. Gwynne, GEMS, United Nations Environmental Programme, P.O. Box 30553, Nairobi, Kenya.

Dr J. S. G. McCulloch, Institute of Hydrology, Crowmarsh Gifford, Wallingford, Oxon, OX10 8BB, United Kingdom.

Dr S. J. McNaughton, Professor of Botany, Syracuse University, Department of Biology, 130 College Place, Syracuse, New York 13210, United States.

Dr M. Norton-Griffiths, Ecosystems Ltd, P.O. Box 30239, Nairobi, Kenya.

Dr J. O. Palgen, Sun Station, P.O. Box 43816, Tucson, Arizona 85733, United States.

Dr L. M. Reid, Department of Geological Sciences, AK-20, University of Washington, Seattle, Washington 98195, United States.

1. Habitat monitoring theory

1.1. Ecological monitoring and the environment

Ecological monitoring is a systematic method of collecting information about the Earth's natural resources. As a technique, it dates from the late 1960s when widespread concern was first expressed about many of today's current environmental problems. The United Nations Conference on the Human Environment, held in Stockholm in 1972, later recommended that the United Nations set up a global environmental monitoring system designed to provide the world's nations with the information they needed about the state of the environment.

The Global Environment Monitoring System (GEMS) has now been in existence for nearly a decade. Its administrative headquarters were first set up by the United Nations Environment Programme (UNEP) which was established in Nairobi as a direct result of the Stockholm conference. Over the past two decades, GEMS has provided much valuable information about the state of the environment: observation networks have been set up to measure many of the parameters with which environmental scientists are today most concerned: carbon dioxide levels in the atmosphere, heavy metal pollution in rivers and oceans, ozone concentrations in the upper atmosphere, and acid rain precipitation, for example. However, the relationship between human beings and their environments extends far beyond pollution. The Global Environment Monitoring System is also involved in monitoring the climate, the marine environment, renewable resources in arid and semi-arid lands, forest cover and soil degradation; it will soon be concerned with monitoring genetic resources and food production as well.

Human populations depend for their existence on the Earth's natural resources. The minerals in the Earth's crust and the soil which covers most of it are the primary resources which determine the pattern of human settlements over the globe. Of course, other factors – including land-form, soil, climate, the distribution of natural flora and fauna, and the presence of water – also play key roles in the complex system known as the biosphere. The ways in which these factors interact to produce an ecosystem, of which the human population is but one part, are complex and immensely varied, stretching all the way from the slash-and-burn agriculture of tropical forest populations to the highly industrialized farming techniques of the central plains in the United States.

Ecosystems are constantly changing. In the developed countries, they are modified mainly by changes in technology designed to increase agricultural production and improve the human environment. In the developing countries, changing technology is disturbing patterns of existence which have been little altered for many centuries. But development, almost by definition, means deliberately altering the nature of existing ecosystems, a process which is fraught with danger unless it is carefully planned and account is taken of all the factors involved.

Until recently, it has not been possible to plan land-use development in an entirely rational manner. The data which planners need have not been available and the issues involved have often appeared too complex and numerous to be the subject of entirely rational decision making. Ecological monitoring is the technique which has evolved over the past decade which promises to make the lives of decision makers and planners, particularly in the developing countries, a great deal easier.

1.2. What is ecological monitoring?

Ecological monitoring is a combination of techniques which enables data to be collected, relatively cheaply, on the life-support capacities of large areas of land. The data concern people, animals, plants and the Earth itself, and are collected in one of three main ways:

- on the ground, either from fixed stations or by mobile teams of observers;

- from the air, by human observers flying in light aircraft at very low altitude (augmented by aerial photography); and

- from space, using information and visual images supplied by orbiting satellites such as Landsat.

Data are collected systematically by relating the information to a grid system superimposed on the terrain to be surveyed. A single survey will reveal only a static situation, frozen in time. While this may be all that is required, continuous monitoring over time is usually a great deal more useful, revealing changes which occur in an ecosystem as a result, for example, of human intervention or climatic change. The grid system allows a series of maps to be prepared which often exposes interesting relationships between the variables being surveyed – the relationship between movements of pastoralists and grass cover, or soil type and water availability, for example.

The three monitoring levels are complementary. Ground techniques are the most expensive but provide a great deal of detail. Aerial surveys are cheaper and quicker but the information they produce is less detailed. The use of satellite information is becoming more and more important, and the cost involved and the detail supplied are now increasingly competitive with other techniques. However, nearly all ecological monitoring programmes eventually require the use of all three techniques. One important reason is that the information they provide can be compared and correlated, ensuring that the survey is conducted with as much precision as possible. As information on these correlations builds up, and confidence in the reliability of the data grows, the cheapest technique can be progressively substituted for the more expensive ones.

1.3. The uses of ecological monitoring

Initially, an ecological monitoring programme may be designed to answer very specific questions. Development planners need a great deal of information about what is happening on the ground now before they can make decisions about what could or should happen in the future. How many cattle do their rangelands support? What crops are being grown and in what quantities? Where is the dividing line between what is essentially desert and what is semi-arid land? How much of the area is covered in woodland? And where do soils exist which are suitable for irrigation? These are a few of the questions that can be answered by ecological monitoring.

If the programme extends over time, the range of questions is greatly increased. The speed of desertification and deforestation, for example, can be measured accurately. The sociological, economic, and ecological effects of an irrigation scheme can be analysed. The effects of a drought on livestock numbers and species mix can be evaluated.

This kind of information is of use to many more people than planners. For example, the managers of large areas of land − whether they are farmers, the superintendents of wildlife parks, or consulting engineers to irrigation projects − are provided with a means of checking the effectiveness of their management techniques. Ecological monitoring can not only provide information to produce an action plan but can also provide feedback on the effects of the action taken.

1.4. The history of ecological monitoring

The first ecosystem to be systematically studied from the ground was probably Marley Wood on the Wytham Estate near Oxford in the United Kingdom. There, in 1947, Charles Elton began to lead generations of researchers through the intricacies of a temperate woodland ecosystem, research which has been continued now for more than three decades. In the United States, Van Dyne began similar work on a much larger scale, using teams of researchers to investigate the ecology of temperate grasslands (Van Dyne 1969 and 1972). All this research depended essentially on highly detailed ground studies.

These techniques are not applicable to the problems of most developing countries, where finance is limited, the areas to be surveyed are vast and answers are required extremely quickly. Tropical ecology is a new science and few background data are available. But what is known is that the stability usually associated with temperate systems may not exist in the tropics, where vast areas of land are currently undergoing rapid change.

Aerial surveying has a longer history. The first aerial photographs of east African countries were taken by the Royal Air Force in the 1920s, and provide a valuable record of the conditions which existed at that time. After the Second World War, light aircraft began to be used in the same region to gather ecological data – mainly on wildlife and poaching. By the late 1950s, the economic and strategic importance of arid and semi-arid land in east Africa was beginning to be realized, and governments turned to ecologists and rangeland management specialists for more data. The technique of aerial sampling was soon developed which, by replacing the need for a total count with more limited but statistically valid sample counts, greatly reduced the expense and time involved in data collection. To add greater detail, data collected from aircraft soon began to be supplemented by ground observations. Data on habitats and animal populations began to be gathered simultaneously and repetitive data collections were made to reveal more details of how the picture changed with time, over seasons and over the longer term. In 1969, scientists at the Serengeti Research Institute in northern Tanzania began a systematic monthly coverage of the 30 000 km^2 Screngeti ecosystem. The concept of ecological monitoring was born.

A new level of data acquisition was introduced in 1972 when Landsat-1 (then called ERTS-1) was launched in the United States. This was the first of the Earth-resource assessment satellites and several more members of the Landsat series have since become operational. In addition, Earth-resource data are available from the United States National Oceanic and Atmospheric Administration's satellites, NOAA-6, NOAA-7, and now NOAA-8.

At first, the information provided from satellites offered only a very broad view of events on the Earth – useful, for example, mainly for demarcating self-contained land systems. But resolution was rapidly increased and biologists in east Africa began to add satellite data to their other information to produce a more complete picture. One direct result of all this activity was that the government of Kenya decided to set up the world's first ecological monitoring unit: the Kenya Rangeland Ecological Monitoring Unit (KREMU).

1.5. Ecological monitoring in practice

The KREMU was established in 1975 as a bilateral project between Kenya and the Canadian International Development Agency, with technical expertise being provided by the United Nations Food and Agriculture Organization. Its initial purpose was to determine the numbers, distribution and seasonal movements of domestic animals – mainly cattle, sheep, goats, camels, and donkeys – and about fifteen species of wildlife herbivores. It is now also monitoring climate, habitat, and changes in human land use.

The need for this information arises from the fact that more than 80 per cent of Kenya has a rainfall of less than 750 mm a year, and most of the population lives in three small but relatively well-watered areas. The government is determined upon increasing the productivity of the arid and semi-arid areas, and intends eventually to replace the traditional pastoralism of the area with commercial stockraising. However, these areas also support large numbers of wild herbivores, including such animals as the gazelle, wildebeest, impala, and zebra. Not only is there a need to protect these species, but they have commercial value both as a source of income from tourists and as a potential livestock resource, which could be farmed either alone or in combination with conventional domestic livestock. Clearly, there is some conflict of interest involved in developing rangeland farming further, and sound data are needed on which to base future management strategies.

Routine sampling began in 1976 and 500 000 km² of the low-potential, semi-arid pastoral areas of Kenya have now been repeatedly surveyed – an area twice the size of the United Kingdom. The estimated running cost is approximately US$200 000 a year (excluding capital costs). The average cost of surveying 1000 km² of ground (averaging out the costs of all three monitoring levels) works out at about US$400, but the cost of Systematic Reconnaissance Flights (SRFs) alone is substantially lower: only about US$50/1000 km². Ground surveys, of course, are by far the most expensive.

Ecological monitoring has already been useful elsewhere in Kenya. One project has identified those areas in Kenya where wildlife and domestic livestock are either highly concentrated or particularly thinly spread, allowing planners to decide where to allocate effort in developing enterprises based on both types of fauna. Elsewhere, dangerous rates of decline in those forms of wildlife which are important in Kenya's tourist industry have been identified. Grevy's zebra and elephants, for example, have declined by 60 per cent since 1972. Another study has shown that Landsat 'false-colour' images can be inexpensively analysed to provide a better predictor of where both domestic livestock and wildlife are likely to be found than can be provided by conventional measures of rainfall and evaporation rates (Gwynne 1977).

In southern Tanzania, 30 000 square kilometres of the Rukwa region of the country have been surveyed from the air to determine the current distribution of infrastructure, domestic livestock, and wildlife. This allowed a preliminary land-use plan to be prepared for the area in only six months from the time the data was gathered (Rodgers 1978). In Saudia Arabia, aerial photographs have been used to outline the seasonal ranges of livestock. The information was needed in the design of a water scheme network (Ecosystems 1978). And in Kenya again, a combination of ground and aircraft data has been used to identify areas where primary production is being used in different ways and where the seasonal dispersal of livestock and wildlife differs. The data enabled land-use zones to be created and pin-pointed locations for watering points needed to increase the grazing available for the herds of pastoralists (Western and Croze 1977).

1.6. Ecological monitoring data

The data which are collected during ecological monitoring can be listed and analysed in a number of different ways. The most obvious, and simplest, classification is threefold:

- habitat;
- fauna;
- economic/social.

From the point of view of the land-use planner, in the long run the object of monitoring is to improve conditions for the human population. But in most developing areas, and particularly in arid and semi-arid regions, human lifestyle is highly dependent on the animals which the territory can support. And the animals, in their turn, depend on the primary production – grass, shrubs, and trees – of the habitat in which they live.

Ecological monitoring therefore begins with a survey of the habitats involved. Though a vegetation survey is an important constituent of habitat monitoring, much more is also involved: the growth of vegetation, and the species mix most likely to survive, depends on such factors as soil type and depth, the nature and efficiency of natural drainage systems, climatic factors such as rainfall, wind, and insolation, and the types of land-form involved – steep slopes, broad valleys, rocky outcrops, and undulating plains, for example. As is made clear later in this book, the classification of land-form types is, in practice, a complicated and important component in the description of habitat.

Fauna surveys must encompass both domestic livestock and wildlife. Simple number-counts can be used in the first instance to estimate total populations, and their locations and densities. Such data can be most efficiently collected by aerial survey. However, to be of much practical use the information required about animal populations must be much more subtle: migration patterns must be measured, seasonal changes in animal numbers estimated and long-term trends analysed. Aerial survey techniques for the collection of data on fauna have advanced rapidly over the past few years. It is now possible, for example, to deduce information about population dynamics, age structure, total biomass, and habitat utilization from aerial survey (see, for example, Norton-Griffiths and Pennycuick 1973; Croze 1972).

The collection of data on economic, social and political issues is perhaps the least advanced of the three main areas. Census data, of course, provide the background but is rarely adequeate for thorough land-use planning. Current land-use patterns must be accurately known and aerial survey techniques can be used to map data on the location and density of human settlements. Correlation of these data with land-form features, soil types, faunal distribution, and climatic variations can lead to a much improved understanding of the preferred locations of villages, hamlets, and farms. In fact, the subtle ways in which human population distribution relates to environmental factors are important considerations in most types of planning. Land-use development is of little use if inappropriate terrain is allocated to people in an attempt to improve their standard of living.

The actual data which can be collected during ecological monitoring are most conveniently divided into three groups: permanent attributes, such as data on soils and drainage; semi-permanent attributes, such as data on plant cover, the distribution of non-migratory animals, and the location of human settlements; and finally, ephemeral or seasonal attributes such as climatic factors, plant productivity, and the location of surface water. A full list of these attributes is given in Table 1.1 (see Croze and Gwynne 1975).

1.7. Ground, aerial, and satellite monitoring

The three levels of monitoring – from the ground, from aircraft and from satellite – are the subjects of Chapters 2, 3, and 4 of this book, where they are described in detail. A short summary of their usefulness and limitations is included here in order that the reader can progress to the detailed descriptions with a broad overview of what is involved.

1.7.1. Ground monitoring

Ground sampling techniques are those which are traditionally used by ecologists. Today, they are important for three reasons: for supplying fine detail; for supplying 'ground-truth' measurements which can be used to establish the precision of more 'remote' data supplied by aircraft and satellite; and to help in the interpretation of such data. There are still some attributes which are best monitored from the ground. These include

Table 1.1. Habitat attributes assessable by ecological monitoring

1. *Permanent attributes*
   topography
   soils
   drainage
   water holes
   static animal features, such as termite mounds

2. *Semi-permanent attributes*
   plant physiognomy
   (cover, vegetation type, etc.)
   plant community composition
   zoogenic features
   (wallows, salt licks, etc.)
   distribution of non-migratory large mammal species
   human settlements
   (villages, farms, ranches, and roads)

3. *Ephemeral or seasonal attributes*
   rainfall
   insolation
   soil moisture
   evapotranspiration
   plant phenology (greenness)
   plant productivity
   (biomass, part composition, chemical composition, energy content, etc.)
   distribution of migratory large mammal species
   large mammal productivity
   (biomass, reproductive state, condition, food off-take, etc.)
   large mammal population structure
   fire
   surface water

rainfall, soil moisture (now normally measured with a neutron probe) and a number of other environmental factors.

The Systematic Ground Survey (SGS) is probably the most expensive weapon in the ecological monitoring armoury. It also provides the finest detail. Survey lines are laid down, though they can rarely be entirely regular due to the nature of the terrain and the inevitable inaccessability of some areas. Generally, SGS sample site lines tend to follow existing features such as roads, tracks, railway lines, and livestock paths. Recording sites are placed in the relatively undisturbed habitat to one side of these features. In East Africa, site intervals of 0.5 and 1.0 km have been used for SGS monitoring transects. The data recorded at sample points include the vegetation phenology, height, species, species density, and cover of grasses, and the growth stage, density, and cover of woody plant species (as well the browsing and grazing intensity of large mammals). Samples are also collected for chemical and energy content analyses.

Ground surveys to check aerial data on the numbers and location of large mammals are not normally necessary, unless the vegetation is so dense that animal concealment introduces serious errors in the aerial data. However, data on smaller mammals must usually be gathered from the ground, and ground-level checks on the herd structure and composition of even the larger mammals are usually useful. Ground surveys are essential for determining sex ratios in both wild and domestic stock. Samples of slaughtered animals may be needed to check on food consumption patterns, to estimate health, condition and reproductive state of the animals, and to establish growth/age relationships for most species.

Though the expense of ground surveys means that they are rarely carried out more often than is strictly necessary, experience has shown that they are essential in checking data obtained both from the air and from satellite unless there is a substantial historical data set available. After two or three years' work, many investigators have come to regret that they did not originally spend more time in devising ground sampling techniques, for example for vegetation growth stage, and for animal population structure. Ground surveys are also essential for the initial calibration of satellite data.

1.7.2. The aerial survey

The aerial survey is currently the most cost-effective of the three monitoring techniques. The basic technique, which has been evolved in East Africa but is widely applicable elsewhere (Croze and Gwynne 1980), is known as the Systematic Reconnaissance Flight (SRF).

The first step is to overlay the area which is to be studied with a grid pattern, typically of 10×10 km (see Fig. 1.1). This grid is used for systematically recording position while flying, and for presenting and analysing the data obtained. The grid is drawn on a 1:250 000 topographical map or on a Landsat image. The most useful such grid for areas between 80 degrees north and south is the Universal Transverse Mercator because it features on many national map series at scales of 1:10 000 to 1:500 000.

Flights are normally made in the morning and late afternoons – those made earlier or later are hampered by poor light conditions and excessively long shadows, while those made during the middle of the day may produce unreliable data because many animals rest in the shade during the hottest parts of the day.

Typically, an SRF involves a crew of four, flying at about 150 km/h and at a height of some 100 m. The pilot is responsible for navigation

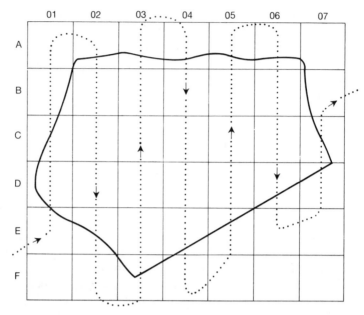

Fig. 1.1. The study area shown with the SRF grid system imposed, together with the aircraft flight tract (*dotted line*) for an SRF.

and informs his or her crew of the numbers of the transects as they are flown. A Very Low Frequency navigation system allows the pilot to fly over the transect with great accuracy, even if the terrain is featureless. Two rods or 'streamers' are attached to the wing struts on either side of the aircraft, forming a 'frame' inside which the two rear observers can count the numbers of animals or other features which are being monitored. This frame typically covers a strip of ground about 250 m wide. Its exact width, of course, depends critically on the pilot's holding a measured altitude with as much accuracy as possible (see Fig. 1.2). If animal groups or other features are too numerous to be accurately counted, a simple solution is to photograph the group, and make an accurate count from the photograph. Data are normally recorded every minute thoughout the flight and then arranged onto the grid squares by a computer which is fed details of the aircraft's flight path and ground speed.

The other observer, sitting next to the pilot, uses a tape recorder and camera to monitor information on habitat: topography, drainage, greenness of vegetation, grass height, and the presence or absence of water, for example. Permanent features, of course, need only be monitored on the first flight over an area. In the future, this technique is likely to be increasingly supplemented by the use of high-resolution, colour video tape recorders (VTR) which provide an almost ideal record of conditions

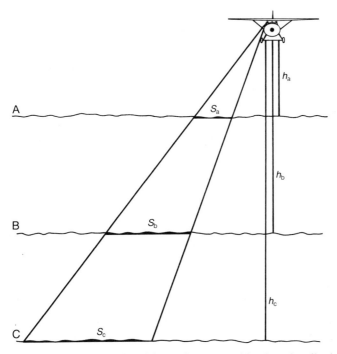

Fig. 1.2. The effect of changing flying altitude above ground level on the effective sample strip width. A, B, and C represent different ground surfaces over which the aircraft is flying at heights $h_{a,b,c}$ respectively. The strip width ($S_{a,b,c}$) varies proportionally with change in h. Thus in:

A. The aircraft is flying too low, resulting in a decrease in strip width. Animal population estimates will be biased downwards, leading to an underestimate of animal numbers.

B. The aircraft is flying at the correct altitude for the required strip width.

C. The aircraft is flying too high, resulting in an increase in strip width. Animal population estimates will be biased upwards, leading to an overestimate of animal numbers.

on the ground. Because the tape can be stopped at will when being viewed on the ground, individual 'freeze frames' can be used at base to provide animal counts, eliminating the fatigue and inaccuracies which are an inevitable part of in-flight observation. The VTR is still an expensive piece of equipment. An alternative is to use a small cine camera, controlled to expose one frame every five to seven seconds, or an automatic 35-mm camera mounted on the aircraft belly. The disadvantage of this is the time which elapses while film is being developed before the results can be analysed.

An SRF can be flown as often as desired – monthly, bi-monthly, every six months, or once a year. The current cost of an SRF is surprisingly low: in the region of US$50/1000 km^2, depending on the country involved and excluding the cost of equipment, observer time, and capital cost of the aircraft.

There are many different ways of plotting the data. The simplest, of course, is to transfer them manually to a map. However, data can also be punched on to computer cards, or keyed on to a computer disc or a magnetic tape. Computer programs now exist which will file the data, plot them on distribution maps and make estimates of animal populations and biomass (see Norton-Griffiths and Pennycuick 1973). While a computer is not essential in this work, it does speed the process and eliminate much tedious manual effort. In the Serengeti Research Institute monitoring programme, for instance, no less than 34 pieces of information were collected for each of 300 grid squares.

An SRF programme, using very little sophisticated equipment, can provide a broad range of information. At a minimum, this might include:

1. Estimates of numbers and densities of major domestic and wild herbivores.
2. A picture of the seasonal movements of major herbivores.
3. A vegetation map expressed in terms of plant physiognomy and/or plant cover.
4. A soil map expressed in terms of soil colour types.
5. An outline of the areas which are important for wildlife which could be used to locate possible parks and reserves.
6. An outline of the areas important for livestock which could be used in the planned control of stock numbers and in rangeland development.
7. A land-use map showing human settlements, rangeland, agriculture, forestry, etc.
8. If the programme is continued over several years, it would also be possible to delineate productive and non-productive areas.

The ways in which the SRF is used to provide this kind of information are summarized in Table 1.2.

Table 1.2. Some results from systematic reconnaissance flights

Type of flight	Distance between flight lines	Periodicity	Type of result
Inventory	5–10 km	*Once only,* or once every few years	Estimation of size of domestic or wild animal populations
			Permanent data-base from which to draft maps of soil, vegetation or topography

Table 1.2.—*continued*

Type of flight	Distance between flight lines	Periodicity	Type of result
			Distribution of infrastructure (roads and villages)
			Verification of ecozone boundaries determined from aerial photos or Landsat imagery
			Determination of stock routes
Specific objective	20–50 km	*Annual* Beginning of annual rains	Advanced information on beginning of 'green wave'
		At peak of rains	Estimation of annual primary production
		End of dry season	Distribution and type of burns
Monitoring	5–30 km	*Seasonal*	Increasingly precise estimation of animal population sizes
			Distribution and phenology of vegetation cover
			Seasonal animal distribution
			Distribution of primary and secondary production
			Correlations between biotic and abiotic factors
			Establishment of boundaries of ecological management units
			Correlations between animal distribution spectral signatures from Landsat imagery

1.7.3. Satellite monitoring

Satellites are now being used to monitor such things as weather, crop conditions, forest diseases, air, sea, and freshwater pollution, and primary production. As far as ecological monitoring itself is concerned, information can currently be collected from the Earth Resources Technology Satellites, now known as Landsat, which have been operational since 1972, and from the NOAA series of satellites. The Landsat satellites orbit the Earth at a height of 900 km and pass over the same spot on the Earth's surface every 18 days. Landsat is equipped with sensors which monitor reflected radiation from the Earth's surface in several bands of the electromagnetic spectrum with a resolution of 80×80 m. The latest in the series, Landsat-4, is equipped with a thematic mapper with a resolution of 30 m.

Landsat output comes in two forms: photographic images which are produced by computer integration of the spectral data; and the digital data themselves. The 'photographs' are of lower resolution than the data from which they are obtained, each photo covering an area of 185×185 km. They are produced as both black-and-white negatives and positives, and as 'false-colour' images in which colour is used artificially to pick out differing features in the image. Correlation of these false-colour images with data obtained from ground or aerial surveys can be very valuable; once the false-colours have been equated with known features on the ground, the satellite imagery can then be reliably used as a source of information, without the need for further ground or aerial surveys, except when further correlations are required.

One of the great advantages of using Landsat data is that the information is repeated at frequent intervals – twice a day every 18 days. This means, for example, that variations over time of such factors as the greenness of grassland (which appears red in the false-colour images) can be followed as it varies with seasons, or even with shorter-term bursts of primary productivity, providing information which is potentially valuable, for instance, for pastoralists searching for improved grazing.

The NOAA meteorological satellites cover an even wider swath of the Earth – 1200 km wide with overflights of the whole planet twice every day. The spectral data provided by the Advanced Very High Resolution Radiometer which they carry is comparable to that of Landsat, especially in the red and near-infra-red regions of the spectrum. However, the price for increased coverage is a much more coarse resolution: picture elements of 1×1 km.

So far, satellite information has been most valuable in exploratory soil surveys of large areas of semi-arid rangelands and in evaluating seasonal productivity over very large areas. The technique is also becoming invaluable in monitoring productivity and in predicting productivity

Table 1.3. Results obtainable from visual Landsat data

Type of image	Results
1:1 000 000 mosaic of colour composites	Preliminary definition of ecological zones
1:1 000 000 colour composite transparencies (in a seasonal series)	Identification of ephemerally green areas
	Identification of zones with a high production potential
	Estimation of occupancy by pastoral peoples, domestic stock, and wildlife (given correlations with SRF data)
	Soil humidity (given correlations with ground studies)
1:500 000 and 1:250 000 colour composites, paper positives, or transparencies	Preliminary topography, soils, or vegetation maps

failures caused by drought. Table 1.3 summarizes the kind of information which can currently be obtained from satellite observations.

A number of new resource satellites is due to be launched in the future, including the US SPOT and the Japanese ERS. SPOT was due to be launched in 1985 and included a capacity for stereoscopy and increase resolution to 10 m.

1.8. The ecological monitoring unit

The operational body needed to run an ecological monitoring pro-gramme consists essentially of a project manager, technical experts, and field staff. Together, they comprise an ecological monitoring unit (EMU). Experts need qualifications in such fields as ecology, soil science, agri-culture, botany, economics, sociology, remote sensing, and data analysis. Clearly, an EMU can be a large unit if it includes experts in all relevant fields. However, this is not strictly necessary; indeed, if budgetary con-straints are very severe, the EMU can be reduced to what is essentially a two-man team – a project manager, who is a pilot and ecologist, and a botanist who can also deal with remote sensing and data anlysis.

An EMU may or may not be a part of government. If it is, it can belong to a single ministry and be run by a steering committee with representatives from several ministries. In Kenya, the KREMU was originally inter-ministerial but now operates from what is perhaps a sounder base within the Ministry of Finance and Planning. It is steered by a committee of experts and planners from the Ministries of Agri-culture, Wildlife and Tourism, and Finance and Planning.

An EMU does not require very sophisticated equipment, with one possible exception: the advanced analysis of satellite data is relatively expensive and involves computing facilities which may not be easily available. Although the results which can be obtained in this way can be of excellent value, this technique is not vital to an ecological monitoring programme.

The rest of the equipment, with minimum costs in brackets, is listed below:

- a 4–6 seater, high-wing single-engine, light aircraft (second-hand, US$50 000)
- two 4×4 vehicles (US$20 000)
- desk-top, micro- or mini-computer (US$5000)
- two 35 mm cameras (US$1500)
- field equipment: camping gear, rain gauges, neutron probes, etc.
- office equipment: stereoscope, mapping equipment, etc.

The KREMU, which is now one of the largest EMUs in the world, has 10 senior expatriate and counterpart staff, about 20 support staff, two aircraft, and five vehicles. With a team of this size, it is able to monitor the entire 500 000 km² of Kenya's rangelands for a cost which amounts to about 0.5 per cent of what Kenya earns from tourism.

1.9. The costs of ecological monitoring

The costs of the information supplied by ecological monitoring can vary very widely. A detailed ground survey may produce information at a cost of as much as US$100/km² while simple analysis of data from Landsat images can be provided at about US$0.01/km². Not only do the costs vary widely, but so does the level of detail provided with each technique. The secret of optimizing the cost/detail ratio is clearly to use the cheapest technique which will provide the right level of resolution for the job.

The costs of ecological monitoring data are not static but vary with time (see Fig. 1.3). Initially, in the early days of an EMU, ground work can provide detailed information but only at a cost which is inappropriate for large-scale application. Data obtained by SRF and satellite can be used over much larger areas but the level of detail supplied is relatively poor.

However, as data begin to accumulate, it becomes possible to correlate the results from the intensive method (ground survey) with the more extensive methods (SRF and satellite data analysis). Providing these correlations continue to hold good (and ground surveys must still be made from time to time to check that there has been no ecological

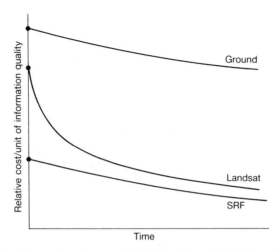

Fig. 1.3. Relative changes in cost per unit of information collected from the ground, from Landsat imagery and from SRF.

change), the extensive methods can then begin to replace the intensive one. Finally, the quality of information from the extensive methods becomes so good that the more expensive techniques can be almost phased out. By this time, high-quality information can be cheaply obtained over very large areas.

In many ecological monitoring programmes, SRF holds the key to cost-effectiveness. For example, an SRF conducted over a 10-km grid, covering an area of 100 000 km² (three times the size of the Sahelian area of Upper Volta), has been estimated to cost only US$13 000. Table 1.4 shows a comparison of costs for SRFs conducted at differing intensities.

Table 1.4. Costs of systematic reconnaissance flights

Intensity	Optimum area (km²)	Daily coverage (km²)	Proportion coverage animal habitat (percentage)		Cost (US$/1000 km²)
5 km	500–10 000	5000	10	40	250
10 km	1000–50 000	10 000	5	20	130
20 km	more than 10 000	20 000	2	10	70
50 km	more than 100 000	50 000	1	5	40

These figures are estimates only and may vary by as much as 25 per cent according to local conditions. They include the cost of pilot, crew, and data analysis.

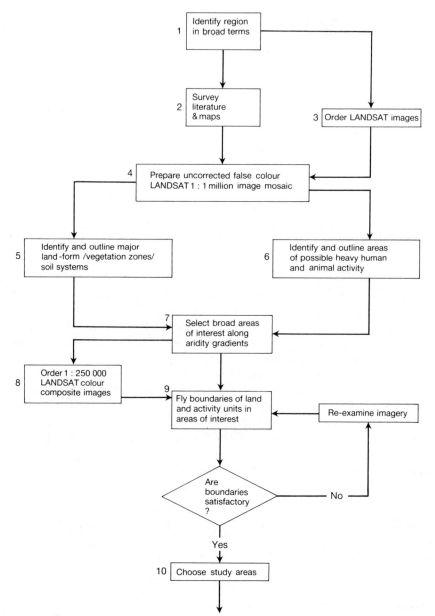

Fig. 1.4. Flow chart for ecological monitoring.

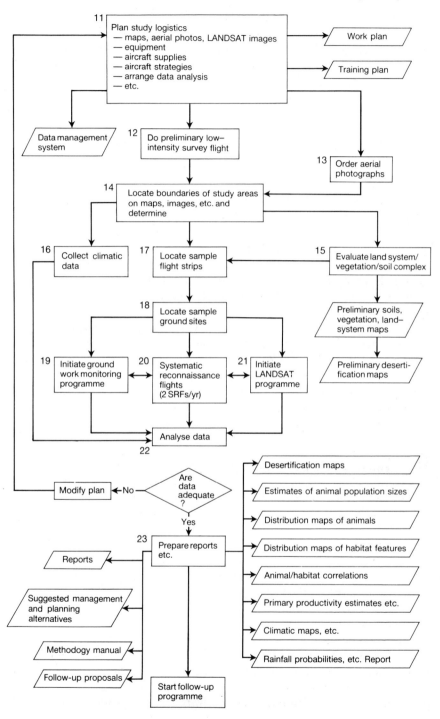

Total costs, of course, are another matter. The KREMU, which monitors about four-fifths of Kenya, costs about US$ 1 million a year to run; this includes all operating expenses, capital outlay, and staff salaries. If only operating and maintenance costs are considered, however, this figure reduces to US$ 200 000 per year or about US$ 400/1000 km^2 surveyed (of which SRFs account for US$ 50/1000 km^2).

1.10.   Developing an ecological monitoring programme

The basic steps involved in developing an ecological monitoring programme are illustrated in the flow chart in Fig. 1.4 (GEMS 1977). Essentially, they involve planning the approach, executing the initial stratification from a low-intensity survey flight, fixing preliminary operational boundaries over the study area, beginning data collection from the three levels (ground, air, and space), analysing the data, producing preliminary results, reviewing the depth and scope of the information obtained, preparing reports for operational units (management and planning), and starting follow-up programmes while routine monitoring is being continued.

Results can be obtained relatively quickly. There is no reason why the review stage ('Are data adequate' in Fig. 1.4) cannot be reached within eighteen months of setting up the EMU. Users should therefore be able to have initial reports in their hands within two years of the beginning of the project. Where necessary, it is possible to cut corners to such an extent that first reports can be produced within six months, as indeed happened in a Tanzanian project (Rodgers 1978).

1.11.   Towards a global system

So far, the number of operational ecological monitoring programmes is limited – although the technique itself is providing increasingly valuable information in response to specific demands from many governments in developing countries. As ecological monitoring becomes more popular, we can begin to look forward to a time when most of the Earth's surface – and all its arid and semi-arid areas – are regularly and systematically monitored by the techniques described in this book.

This will bring numerous advantages. Correlations which currently exist only within certain national programmes can then be continued across national frontiers, making it easier to set up new programmes when they are required. As the numbers of ecological monitoring units grow, so too will pressure for them to co-operate within a much broader context, that of international ecological monitoring. Satellites already perform international monitoring and, with some exceptions a few years ago, the fact that they do so has not produced insuperable political difficulties. It will be surprising if the international nature of ecological monitoring does not assume paramount importance over the next two decades.

By then, of course, it is likely that a global environmental data system will be in existence. Today, environmental data on the Earth are widely scattered between dozens of different data banks, all recording data in different ways and at different resolutions. These data are not comparable, and the additions which are constantly being made to them can rarely be used for truly interdisciplinary studies. It is a matter of some urgency that this be put right. A global environmental data system, into which national environmental monitoring units can feed information and from which they can extract it equally easily, would provide the soundest basis imaginable from which to effect lasting improvements to the human environment.

References

Croze, H. (1972). A modified photogrammetric technique for assessing age-structures of elephant populations and its use in Kidepo National Park. In *E. Afr. Wildl. J.* **10**, 91–115.

—— and Gwynne, M. D. (1975). East African habitat monitoring practice: a review of methods and applications. *Proc. int. Livestock Centre for Africa seminar on the evaluation and mapping of tropical rangelands.* Bamako, Mali. ILCS, Addis Ababa.

—— —— (1980). The concept and practice of ecological monitoring over large areas of land: the systematic reconnaissance flight. *Selected works on ecological monitoring of arid areas.* United Nations Environment Programme, GEMS/PAC Information Series No. 1, Nairobi.

Ecosystems (1978). *Aerial census of domestic stock in the Arabian Shield south.* Consultant report to Macharen International, March 1978.

GEMS (1977). *Model project proposal document for a rangeland monitoring project.* UNEP, Nairobi.

Norton-Griffiths, M., and Pennycuick, L. (1973). Trend surface analysis (MX23). In *Tech. Pap. Inst. Dev. Stud.,* Nairobi **8**, 1–10.

Rodgers, W. A. (1978). *A draft report encompassing recommendations for the improvement of wildlife conservation in Rukwa Region, Tanzania.* Report to the Bureau of Resource Assessment and Land-Use Planning, Dar-es-Salaam.

Van Dyne, G. M. (1969). *The ecosystem concept in natural resources management.* Academic Press, New York.

—— (1972). An integrated ecological research programme. In *Mathematical models in ecology* (ed. J. N. A. Jeffers). Blackwell Scientific Publications, Oxford.

Western, D., and Croze, H. (1977). Monitoring rangeland resources in Kenya. *International environmental monitoring,* a Bellagio Conference, *Rockefeller Foundation Report,* pp. 64–71.

2. Ground monitoring

A complete ecological survey of a region in a developing country would have to include, as a minimum, data on climate, soils, land-forms, water, vegetation, and animal and human populations. This is the order in which these things are dealt with in Chapter 2 of this book, which is concerned with ecological monitoring from the ground.

When data can be collected so much more quickly and cheaply from aircraft and satellites, it is important to be clear about the reasons for ground monitoring. They are twofold: first, there are still a number of ecological attributes which can be measured satisfactorily only from the ground; and, second, many airborne and spaceborne techniques depend for their accuracy on calibrations which can be made only from observations on the ground. Among the first category would be included such things as rainfall, soil moisture, detailed soil analysis, rates of soil erosion, the details of vegetation cover such as crop mix, the preferred diets of herbivores, condition of animal populations and, of course, many of the cultural practices of the human populations which inhabit the area.

Ground monitoring, though critical to the success of any major programme, is slow and expensive. Constraints on money and time, and the logistical difficulties of deploying experts in remote locations, mean that techniques have to be devised for extracting the maximum possible amount of data from the minimum number of observations. For these reasons, ground monitoring depends far more than air or spaceborne monitoring on the development of sophisticated statistical techniques of sampling. While these may appear complex in some of the accounts that follow, their importance to successful ground monitoring cannot be over-estimated. In fact, they enable the researcher to cut by a factor of at least ten – and in some cases much more – the time and effort that must be deployed to gather essential data.

This is clear from the first account of ground monitoring which follows and which is concerned with climatic data. In one area of the United Kingdom, for instance, statistical techniques have been used to reduce the number of rain-gauges from 379 to only 220, with no loss to the many different users of the network. Such is the power of modern statistics. Similar economies in measurement can be effected in every area of ground monitoring. Researchers in ecological monitoring units, therefore, have no choice but to become competent statisticians and to familiarize themselves with the now well-documented techniques of sampling.

22

2.1. Climate measurements

Vegetation grows on the Earth's surface only when climatic and hydrological conditions allow it. But although most plants depend on rainfall or snow to survive, some can exploit other forms of water. Foresters are well aware of the importance of occult or mist precipitation in promoting plant growth, and of the ability of certain riverine species to profit from their position by a watercourse, perhaps in an otherwise arid environment. Roots of some forms of vegetation, including grasses such as *Pennesitum clandestinum* (Kikuyu grass), can extract water from depths of 10 m in deep lateritic soils in Kenya.

Thus, although the survival of certain species might provide a very rough indication of climate, such techniques are not practical on a global scale. It therefore behoves environmentalists to heed Lord Kelvin's admonition:

When you can measure what you are speaking about and can express it in numbers, you know something about it; but when you cannot measure it, when you cannot express it in numbers, your knowledge is of a meagre and unsatisfactory kind.

2.1.1. Meteorological methods and equipment

The primary objective of the meteorologist is to provide a synoptic picture or overview of the weather at a single point in time and over a large area of the Earth's surface, probably covering several countries. The hydrologist's need for accuracy in determining rainfall in a catchment area leads him to be even more exacting than the meteorologist; in addition, his world is dominated by extremes such as flood and drought.

The environmentalist, on the other hand, is likely to be less concerned with accuracy and more concerned with the continuity of measurements over time and space. Extreme phenomena – although critical at the time – are but brief interludes in a long series of data, of which the mean values are the most important.

To measure rainfall, the hydrologist would, in an ideal world, specify that it be measured in depth of water received per unit area at ground level in a standard meteorological gauge sunk in the ground with a surround which is designed to prevent splashback into the gauge. (Rainfall and snow measurement are extensively covered in the World Meteorological Organization's *Guide to hydrological practices*, WMO, No. 168, 1983.) It might be thought that more sophisticated forms of rainfall measurement could now be used. One such technique, used in forecasting and in assessing rainfall in reservoired catchments, is radar. This can clarify the rainfall pattern over a catchment area but actual gauges must still be used to provide some 'ground-truth' or calibration of the radar pattern.

2.1.2. *Types of station*

Most national networks of meteorological and hydrological stations were established in response to national requirements. Just as rain-gauges are rarely sited in unpopulated areas (the uplands of the United Kingdom, for example, have very few rain-gauges, while the lowlands possess perhaps the densest network of rain-gauges in the world), so full meteorological and hydrological stations tend to be sited at places where there are pressing national reasons for them – at airports and strategic river crossings, for example.

These networks should be exploited to the fullest possible extent in environmental monitoring. Additional equipment should, where practical, use the standard national instrumentation in the conventional national way. Yet national resources are rarely available to install many additional stations for global environmental monitoring. Where there are obvious gaps in national networks it is advisable to consider automatic devices, such as the UK Institute of Hydrology's Automatic Weather Station (AWS) which is capable of operating unattended for either two-week or four-week periods. These devices do not depend on local observations and the analysis of the magnetic tape cassettes and solid-state memories used to record the data can be made at base. Although there is a danger that if the equipment goes wrong the fault will be detected only after extensive travel and weeks of waiting for the computer analysis, there is a facility for conducting spot checks on the operation of the weather station, though not necessarily of the logging devices used to record the data.

Substantial differences occur between 'standard' observations in different national networks. These may be due to differences in the instrumentation or in the way it is used; these may be environmental (the height at which an instrument is placed may be determined on the basis of the frequency of heavy snowfalls, for example) or historical, reflecting only the policy of a previous colonial power. Despite years of effort by the World Meteorological Organization, it has proved difficult to persuade nations to use standard equipment in standard ways. While it is generally undesirable to make major changes to observations to reduce a continent's climatological diversity to realistic levels, the use of additional gauges can make it possible to attain more meaningful comparisons between data from different countries. If comparison reference gauges, as well as standard national gauges, are introduced, the effects can be very beneficial.

2.1.3. Rain-gauge distribution and type

Each country has its own standards of rain-gauges, both for those read daily and for those read monthly. These gauges are simple collectors which store accumulated rainfall over periods of from 1 to 31 days. In the latter case, in hot climates, it is usual to maintain a film of oil over the collector surface to minimize evaporation. Details of these gauges are contained in the WMO *Guide to hydrological practices*. More complex gauges, which record rainfall at successive 10- or 15-min intervals, are also used in hydrological practice. These are also described in the WMO *Guide*.

Recently, computer microchips have begun to be exploited in simple, solid-state recording equipment such as the Institute of Hydrology's Simple Instrument System (SIS) Raingauge. This plastic, tipping-bucket device can record on any suitable logging equipment; the basic SIS logger provides daily rainfall totals for up to 86 days and a more sophisticated version provides 10- or 15-min totals for up to 7 or 10 days respectively. The daily recording form of the SIS rain-gauge requires only an observer with a notebook to transfer the totals from the logger store; the output of the 10- or 15-min device must be produced as either a paper tape record or a magnetic tape for subsequent computer interpretation.

Whatever type of gauge is used, allowance must be made for the possibility of theft, damage or destruction. This is best done by designing a network with a certain amount of redundancy so that any loss of data can be offset by the interpolation of data from the remainder of the network. There is also obvious merit in using equipment which provides the information needed as simply and cheaply as possible; the day of throw-away rain-gauges may not yet have come, but some modern equipment certainly includes too many sophisticated, yet unnecessary, built-in features.

2.1.4. Other climatic factors

Rainfall is the single most important variable to be measured in a global monitoring programme, partly because it is the dominant component in the hydrological cycle, and partly because it varies over time and space much more widely than the other climatic factors. The production of statistically valid national and regional maps of rainfall probabilities may require some 30 years of daily rainfall records.

2.1.4.1. Evaporation and transpiration Evaporation also plays an important role in the hydrological cycle. As a climatic or hydrological variable, it is difficult to measure directly: devices such as evaporation pans and instrumental evaporimeters really provide only an indication of the evaporative power of the atmosphere rather than a precise measurement of it. While they can be used for many hydrological purposes, there is more merit in recording the individual agricultural meteorological variables which control evaporation. These are solar radiation, which supplies most of the energy for evaporation; air temperature, which affects the efficiency of transfer of incoming solar energy into latent heat of evaporation of water; and air humidity and wind speed, which together provide a measure of the ability of the atmosphere to remove water vapour from the evaporating surface.

All these variables can be combined into an estimate of potential evaporation using one of several equations, of which Penman's is the best known. Considerable expertise now exists in using estimates of open-water evaporation or transpiration to deduce estimates of the water requirements of different crops in different seasons. The basic data for these calculations are best obtained locally, even though they all vary less dramatically than rainfall. Thus, for many environmental monitoring purposes, adequate data on solar radiation can be obtained from a very sparse network and sometimes even from world insolation maps, and regional air temperature and humidity maps. These variables are, of course, affected by altitude, but the ways in which temperature and dew point vary with height are readily available in the literature.

2.1.4.2. Solar radiation Incoming short-wave radiation can be recorded on a horizontal surface by a solarimeter or pyrheliometer such as the Kipp or Eppley with a suitable recording millivoltmeter or logger. In the past, integration of daily totals of short-wave radiation was complex, time consuming and expensive so that radiation was recorded in only a few centres the world over. Modern microchip technology has enabled radiation measurements to be integrated much more simply and cheaply, even where there is no mains power supply. A Kipp solarimeter is an integral part of the AWS which, using rechargeable batteries and solar cells, records solar radiation, net radiation, air temperature and humidity at a height of 1.5 m, windrun and direction at 2 m, as well as rainfall. The measurements are recorded on magnetic tape for later computer retrieval, but other logging systems can also be used.

2.1.5. Statistical techniques

2.1.5.1. Limitations of conventional statistics The climatic analyst uses meteorological data to make inferences or predictions relevant to his particular problem. Probability theory and statistics are indispensable in this work and also offer the possibility of conveniently summarizing large quantities of data. Progress has been closely linked with advances in digital computing; in the early days of data analysis, analysts were limited to calculating simple statistics of sets of observations such as means, variances, and coefficients of variation, skewness, and correlation, and perhaps to fitting standard probability distributions to allow probabilistic statements to be made about the behaviour of individual variables.

Such basic statistical tools did not allow the analyst to identify and to model the spatial and temporal structure of his data – an important area because, for example, the degree of spatial coherence characterizing measurements of a climatic variable will greatly influence the number of sampling points and their location in a monitoring network. Such work has now become common, putting the design of monitoring networks on a sounder scientific basis. Paradoxically, however, if a network is to be scientifically designed in this way, a network must already be in existence, providing the data required to produce the design. Consequently, in those parts of the world where little or no data exist, rain-gauge networks, for example, must still be designed on the basis of the gauge spacings recommended in the WMO *Guide to hydrometeorological practices* (1983), which are derived from the judgements of experienced experts. This does not detract from the merits of the quantitative design methods just mentioned. Once sufficient data are accumulated in a new network, its performance can now be critically assessed; in time, this work will improve the initial design of monitoring networks.

2.1.5.2. Possibilities of stochastic approaches It is frequently necessary to estimate quantities which are not measured directly by a monitoring network, such as spatial averages and interpolated values at points within the network area which are not gauged. For rainfall, the simplest and most commonly used way of deriving interpolated values has been to use the measurement at the nearest gauge as the interpolated value. Methods of deriving averages have ranged from using a simple arithmetic average of schemes in which topography and relief as well as the spatial configuration of the gauges is taken into account.

While methods which incorporate a priori information on the variation of the quality of interest over space have distinct intuitive appeal, they share with other empirical methods one disadvantage: they do not provide any estimate of accuracy. As a result, the performance of different methods cannot be objectively assessed, and the user of the data cannot know whether the estimated quantites are sufficiently accurate for his purposes. However, if the spatial statistical structure of the variable can be modelled, then precision (in terms of mean square error) for quantities estimated by applying any sets of weights linearly to the measurements can be calculated; further, the weights can be chosen to minimize the mean square error. A case study of the design of a rain-gauge network in the south-west of England is described below.

2.1.6. Rain-gauge network design: a case study

There is an extensive network of rain-gauges in the United Kingdom, consisting mainly of storage gauges which are read daily. In 1977, some 7000 of these gauges conformed to a standard of construction, observation practice and site specified by the British Meteorological Office. The records of these gauges are stored on a computer-based archive after thorough quality control. Concern was expressed in the mid-1970s about the cost-effectiveness of collecting so much data from a network which had never been formally designed but which had evolved over time in response to many different demands. Accordingly, in 1977, research was commissioned at the UK Institute of Hydrology to develop methods of redesigning the network, and, in 1978, a case study was undertaken with the British Meteorological Office and the Wessex Water Authority to redesign the network in the Authority's region which covers an area of some 10 000 km^2 in south-west England.

Initially, a cost–benefit approach to the problem was considered. However, rainfall frequently represents but one input to complex decision-making processes (for example, in water-resource management) which makes economic benefits difficult to assess. Instead, the accuracy requirements of users (principally in agriculture, water resources, and meteorological research) were assessed by interview; these requirements were stated as root mean square errors not to be exceeded for a specified percentage of time, taken as 95 per cent. This technique was recognized to be difficult since users could not always specify the accuracy they needed. However, the performance of the network, quantified using the procedures previously described, was used as a baseline check on questionable accuracy requirements, and the network then redesigned to give, as far as possible, the overall accuracy provided by the existing network.

At the beginning of the study, there were 333 daily-read gauges and 46 monthly-read gauges in the area, making a total of 379 gauges. Records for 232 of these were available in the Meteorological Office archive. A data-base consisting of daily data in a number of categories for a 5-year period, and monthly totals for a 15-year period, were assembled for analysis. Spatial correlation functions were fitted to the data in various categories for gauges lying within overlapping squares of 35 km side. This ensured that the rates of correlation decay over the region were allowed to vary, but smoothly, so as to avoid discontinuities in the maps of optimal point interpolation error (on a 1-km grid) which were subsequently prepared. The choice of the grids for fitting and mapping depends on the scale of the area, on the local variation in correlation structure and on computational considerations. For specific areas, where areal averages were required by users, the accuracies of these were also calculated by carrying out the necessary numerical integrations.

This work placed the redesign of the network on a quantitative basis. But the system could not be redesigned on the basis of only a statistical analysis; account had to be taken of the quality of the observations provided by individual gauges to ensure that, if gauges which contributed to redundant accuracy were deleted, a base of high-quality gauges was still maintained. Individual gauges were assessed for quality by surveying each site in the network before undertaking the design study.

It was decided that the new network should provide the same level of interpolation accuracy as the old one over 90 per cent of the region and that local requirements for accuracies in areal averages should be met. This enabled redundant gauges in the area to be eliminated and the effect of this to be assessed quantitatively. In some areas of deficient accuracy, sites for new gauges could be identified. The result was a new network of 220 gauges, which represented a significant reduction in data collection and processing costs with no identifiable loss to the users. As a check, the gauges in the existing network were deleted randomly and comparisons made with the redesigned network of 220 gauges in terms of overall accuracy; the methodology described above produced a significant improvement in accuracy, underlining its usefulness as a tool for designing monitoring networks of rainfall as well as other environmental variables. Rain-gauge networks in other areas of the United Kingdom are currently being redesigned.

2.2. Preparation of a base map

Base maps are usually required for the display of ecological information, such as the distribution of plant and animal species. Sometimes there is interest in the spatial association between individual species, or groups of species, and other attributes of the landscape such as soil type, rock type, or land-form. A monitoring programme designed to investigate such matters must sample a range of these variables, which therefore need to be mapped from field observations or aerial photographs onto a base map at a useful scale.

Another reason for needing maps of soils, geology, or land-forms is to help choose ground monitoring sites that represent extensive, homogeneous areas. It is important to know the extent of each area represented, and how it is distributed through the landscape. These matters affect the extrapolation of data from monitoring sites to large areas, and the integration of variables such as primary production over a whole landscape or ecosystem. The ecologist with limited resources may need to restrict measurements to sites that are representative of large areas, rather than to sites that are more convenient but representative of only a small fraction of the landscape.

The cost of preparing national or regional maps is very high, and consequently base maps must normally be prepared from maps that already exist. Topographic maps are available for almost all countries at scales of at least 1:250 000. This is adequate for most ecological monitoring programmes but not necessarily for the correlation of biological attributes with some of their controls or for the display of the intricate spatial patterns which can exist along watercourses or similar features. In these cases, maps with a 1:50 000 scale may be necessary, and they are available in some developing countries.

Stratification of the landscape into units on the basis of major abiotic controls can be useful. In some cases, a geological map can be the easiest and most obvious base on which to design an ecological monitoring programme. However, such maps are not designed for this purpose and usually contain a great deal of information on subtle geological differences or ages of rocks that do not influence ecological factors.

Soil maps are usually a more useful base on which to design an ecological sampling programme, because soils reflect to some degree the interaction of the major abiotic controls – climate, hydrology, geomorphology, and rock type – and they are the substrate for primary production. The cost of producing a soil map can often be justified in an ecological monitoring programme. Before such expense is undertaken, however, there should be detailed consultation between the soil surveyor and potential users of the information. There have been many examples of laborious, expensive, and slow surveys that generated detailed maps too late to be used in the planning or even the elucidation of an ecological survey. For many ecological monitoring programmes, a map with a level of detail that can be obtained during a reconnaissance soil survey is adequate.

If a suitable base map does not exist, it may be necessary to construct one from aerial photographs or Landsat imagery. Overlapping sequences of vertical photographs can be assembled into a mosaic, which can be photographed or traced to produce a map. The photographs are laid out so that the overlapping features are superimposed. The centre point of each photo is marked and also transferred to the neighbouring prints. Lines are drawn between the centre point of each photo and the transferred centre points of neighbours. Adjacent photographs are then superimposed so that lines joining each pair of centres are coincident. This procedure places each photograph in its approximately correct orientation relative to others. Various techniques for improving the orientation are described in standard texts on photogrammetry (see Miller 1961; Kilford 1966; Thomas 1966). Features can then be traced from the photographs, either directly onto a transparent overlay or through special plotting machines. Elevations can also be measured and the maps contoured, if this is necessary, but fixing elevations on aerial photographs requires slow, expensive ground survey.

Aerial photographs are particularly useful in the design of an eco-logical monitoring programme. They contain much more detail than standard maps, making it easy to identify features. They often show subtle patterns of topography, soils, and vegetation that do not appear on maps. Because the ecologist can examine a three-dimensional image of overlapping prints with the aid of a stereoscope, aerial photographs can be valuable both in the early stages of the design of a monitoring scheme and throughout the study as understanding of subtle patterns and their interrelationships increases. The value of aerial photography has been greatly increased during the past decade by the widespread availability of false-colour photographs which express the reflectance and thermal emission of soils and vegetation (Reeves 1975). Vegetation types, and changes in their density or condition, can be mapped from the subtle variations of colour discernible in these photographs. In some cases, the simultaneous recording of two or more wavelengths of the electro-magnetic spectrum yields more information than the monitoring of a single wavelength.

2.3. Soil mapping and interpretation

The soil is part of the natural environment and can be understood only in relation to geology, relief, vegetation, and climate, while in many cases it has also been much modified by human activities. Soil mapping is based on the detailed examination of soil profiles in the field, supported to some extent by soil sampling and analysis, but has recently been made quicker and more accurate by the use of air photographs and, to some extent, satellite images. The methods which can be used in soil mapping depend on the purpose for which soils are mapped, and the scale of the map produced.

2.3.1. How the environment affects soil formation

The characteristics of a soil can be conveniently related to the influence of five environmental soil-forming factors:

1. The parent material from which the soil is developed.
2. The climate, past and present, of the area.
3. The vegetation supported by the soil, and the soil fauna which live in it.
4. The relief.

   5. Time, i.e. the length of time for which other factors have been influencing soil formation, as shown by the degree of profile development.

   Soil parent material refers to any material from which, or in which, a soil profile develops. Some soils are derived from the underlying parent rock, and are known as sedentary soils. Others are developed in transported material, such as colluvium or alluvium, or even in a deposit of organic material.

   The chemical and physical properties of the soil are usually closely related to the nature of the parent material, as modified by the climate. In the case of soils developed from rocks, for example, the soil scientist would be particularly interested in the ease with which the rock weathered, and the products were released. The texture of the soil (the relative percentages of sands, silt, and clay) is also closely related to the parent material. With increasing soil weathering, weatherable minerals such as felspars are converted into clay but the resistant minerals, of which the most common and important is quartz, remain as the sand fraction. As a general rule, basic rocks (which contain no quartz) weather relatively quickly to give clay soils, whereas acid rocks weather more slowly and give rise to soils which contain quartz sand. An extreme case would be provided by a rock consisting of little except quartz, such as a quartzite or quartz sandstone, which would weather slowly to give a relatively poor sandy soil. Parent rocks also differ widely as to the plant nutrients they release on weathering.

   Climate, past and present, has both direct and indirect influences on soil formation. The indirect influence is on the nature of the vegetation and the direct influence is on the soil itself, since rainfall and temperature influence the speed and way in which materials weather and the subsequent development of the soil profile.

   The fastest and most thorough weathering occurs in hot, wet climates. Warmer temperatures speed up the rate of chemical reactions, while water is the main agent of chemical weathering, being involved in such processes as solution, hydration, hydrolysis, reduction, and the removal of the soluble products liberated. For this reason, the soils of the hot, wet tropics consist mainly of kaolinitic clay minerals, quartz sand, and sesquioxides (Al_2O_3 and Fe_2O_3). The chemical weathering of rocks and soils is slower or even non-existent in colder or drier climates.

   Rainfall may also cause soil leaching, particularly when rainfall exceeds the rate of evapotranspiration. If the soil profile is already saturated, further water will pass through the profile and drain away. It is this water washing downwards through the soil profile which causes leaching. Very fine soil particles may move downwards (as when clay moves from the topsoil to the subsoil over a period) but the main effect of leaching is to remove soluble products. The ions mostly affected are calcium and magnesium, and their progressive removal from the soil results in it becoming more acid. Thus, soils in very wet areas tend to be acidic. In dry areas or dry seasons, the opposite occurs: water may evaporate at or near the soil surface and the topsoil is enriched in the ions left behind when the water evaporates. In extreme cases, in some arid and semi-arid areas, a crust of soluble salts may be left at the surface.

Rainfall, and the movement of water in the soil, thus exerts a fundamental influence on soil formation and explains why soils are closely related to climate.

Vegetation is itself related to climate and to the soil. It influences the soil in two main ways: by adding raw organic residues which decompose to form the humus in the soil, and by recycling nutrients from the lower soil layers to the topsoil.

The amount and distribution of humus in the soil is related to the nature of the raw organic residues derived from the vegetation, and to a lesser extent to the contribution of dead soil fauna. In temperate areas, some grassland soils contain large quantities of organic matter. So do tropical forest soils, which often contain leaves, flowers, fruits, and branches which decompose at or near the surface, resulting in a dark, humus-rich topsoil overlying a subsoil which is often relatively low in organic matter. In tropical savannah areas, vegetation is typically much sparser, and the amounts of residues left to decompose and add humus to the soil are further reduced by grazing and often by annual dry-season burning. The result is a topsoil which is low in humus and light in colour. There may be a relatively gradual transition to the subsoil in which humus is derived mainly from the decay of grass roots.

Plants also influence soil development by extracting nutrient ions from the root zone, including – in the case of deeper rooted plants – the lower soil horizons, and by concentrating them through leaf-fall and decomposition in the topsoil. Trees and shrubs are often particularly effective in concentrating nutrient ions in the upper soil layers.

In the tropics, shifting cultivation involves leaving the land fallow under natural vegetation. The beneficial effects of this are related to the two main effects of vegetation discussed above: the increase in humus content of the topsoil, which improves its chemical and physical properties, and the bringing up of nutrient ions from the lower soil layers.

Relief influences soil formation partly because of its influence on water movement and soil drainage. In many parts of the tropics, there is a more or less regular sequence of soils related to relief. In the 1930s, Geoffrey Milne, working in East Africa, gave the name 'catena' (Latin for chain) to such sequences, and the term 'soil catena' has been widely adopted and used. A typical soil catena may consist of red, well-drained soils on the summits and upper slopes, brown and yellow, less well-drained soils on the middle and lower slopes, and gray or mottled, poorly-drained soils in the valley bottoms. Additional complications may arise because different sites may be associated with different local parent materials: the upper soils may be sedentary, the lower-slope soils may be developed in colluvium which has moved down the slope under the action of gravity, and the valley-bottom soils (and soils of some alluvial terraces) may be developed in alluvium deposited by the stream or river. In the case of large rivers, the alluvium may have come from an area of different geology and climate. Both the relief and the geomorphological history of an area thus influence the nature and distribution of its soils.

Time is an additional soil-forming factor in the sense that it, too, causes differences between soils. The soil scientist is not particularly concerned with the chronological age of a soil in years, but with the degree of profile development. A young or immature soil is one which has had no time to develop or, more commonly, one which has not developed because of a steep slope or resistant parent material: the result in both cases is a profile consisting of only a topsoil overlying little-changed parent material. Mature soils have a fully developed profile reflecting the local environment.

Man, of course, profoundly modifies soils, for better or worse, when he clears or burns vegetation, and cultivates, drains, and fertilizes the soil. He may be regarded as a sixth soil-forming factor.

2.3.2. The soil profile

A soil profile is a vertical cross-section of the soil showing the horizons or layers of which it is composed. Soil horizons usually run more or less parallel to the surface, and differ in some important respect from the horizons above or below them.

The soil scientist or surveyor is not usually satisfied with looking at the upper part of the soil but takes as his basic unit for description and classification the whole soil profile. In practice, however, some soils are very deep, as when rock weathering has gone down to 20–30 m, or when soils are developed in very deep alluvium. In such cases, examination of the soil profile may be confined to the upper few metres.

Although soil profiles differ widely, soil scientists frequently recognize three major horizons: the topsoil (A horizon), the subsoil (B horizon) and the underlying unconsolidated material or weathered substratum (C horizon) which may in turn merge into or overlie hard rock.

The topsoil or A horizon is usually the soil horizon of maximum biotic activity. Roots may be relatively frequent, and the humus may make the topsoil darker than the subsoil. Topsoils may lose clay, iron or aluminium which may then accumulate in the B horizon below, so that topsoils are sometimes described as horizons of eluviation, as opposed to the B horizon of illuviation below it.

The subsoil or B horizon is the horizon below A in which an illuvial concentration of clay (or iron, aluminium or humus) has occurred, or in which soil weathering and development have resulted in the formation of a soil horizon which has a structure and in which original rock fragments have been decomposed; colour is often different from that of the topsoil and more pronounced. Texture is often somewhat heavier than the topsoil, and organic matter and biotic activity typically much less. B horizons vary considerably in their nature and properties.

The A and B horizons together are sometimes referred to as the solum. The C horizon, or weathered substratum, is a mineral horizon (other than bedrock) which underlies the solum. It is relatively little affected by soil-forming processes but may have been subjected to weathering, salt accumulation, some forms of cementation and other processes. The C horizon may or may not be the material from which the solum is assumed to have developed.

Underlying consolidated bedrock (R), such as gneiss, schist, granite, or limestone may underlie these horizons and be included in the description of the profile.

2.3.3. Describing the soil profile

Careful, standardized soil-profile descriptions are an essential part of most soil survey work. Soil profile descriptions tend to follow a standardized format, as set out in the FAO handbook *Guidelines for soil description*. This handbook was based on the procedures set out in the earlier US Department of Agriculture *Soil Survey Manual* (US Department of Agriculture Handbook 18).

Individual soil-profile descriptions should include:

(a) information on the site, including its location, elevation, physiographic position in relation to the land-form, the slope (gradient), the vegetation or land-use and the climate;

(b) a brief general description outlining the essential characteristics in two or three sentences; and

(c) a detailed horizon by horizon description, giving the depth in centimetres, the colour, texture, structure, consistency, pores, content of coarse material (such as rock fragments, quartz gravel, or ironstone nodules), roots, the nature of the boundary with the horizon below, and the soil pH.

The colour of the soil is defined, usually when moist, by using the

Munsell soil-colour chart. If there is a marked difference between moist and dry colours, both should be given.

The texture of the soil refers to the relative percentages of sand, silt, and clay. Soil surveyors usually estimate texture by moistening the soil and feeling it; for detailed profile descriptions this estimate may be confirmed by laboratory analyses.

The structure of the soil refers to the natural aggregation of the individual soil particles to form such structural units as crumbs, granules, blocks, and plates. In profile descriptions, the degree of structural development (or grade) is given (structureless, weak, moderate, or strong), together with the size of the units and their type.

The consistency of the soil refers to its handling qualities at different moisture contents. Wet soil is described in terms of its stickiness and plasticity, a moist soil in terms of its friability or firmness, and a dry soil in terms of its hardness.

Soil pores are usually described in terms of their abundance (few, common, or many) and size, and additional information may be included on their continuity, orientation, distribution, and morphology.

2.3.4. Soil sampling

An old saying has it that the analysis is no better than the sample. In other words, it is no use carefully analysing a sample which has been taken carelessly and is not representative of the soil it is meant to represent. Analyses are generally expensive, and often the soil surveyor, agronomist, or ecologist has far fewer analyses than he would like. He must make certain, therefore, that if soil samples are taken and analysed, the sites are selected with care and the samples taken correctly.

There are two main types of soil sample: the sample of a soil profile, horizon by horizon, down to a required depth; and the bulk sampling of an area, usually of the topsoil only. The latter is useful for agricultural advisory purposes or other research and involves the taking of a relatively large number of small samples (preferably 25–40 or more) down to a fixed depth (such as 15 cm) which are then thoroughly mixed and subsampled to give a representative bulk sample.

In normal soil survey work, a representative soil profile is selected, divided into its natural horizons, and each horizon sampled. When sampling, the site of the profile (its position in relation to the relief and gradient) is recorded, as are observations on the vegetation or land-use. The structure of the soil, number of pores and roots, and other properties are examined and described.

A careful profile description with accompanying analyses is the basis for most soil classification work but a soil profile represents only a very small area – virtually a point. For other types of investigation involving, for example, the influence of a particular crop, tree, or type of vegetation, or agronomic treatment on the soil, then bulk sampling of an area or of contrasting areas may yield more appropriate results.

2.3.5. *Soil analysis*

The types of soil analysis required, and the number of soil profiles that need to be analysed depend on the purpose of the survey, its scale, and the money available.

For general ecological studies, the characteristics of greatest importance, apart from soil depth, are:

Soil texture: this is estimated in the field and may be confirmed for selected samples in the laboratory by measuring the percentage by weight of sand, silt, and clay in the fine earth fraction of the soil.

Soil organic matter content: can be estimated in the field, but confirmation is needed in the laboratory, at least for the upper horizons.

Soil pH: can be measured in the field by using colour indicators or portable battery-operated pH meters, and can be confirmed for selected samples in the laboratory.

Soil salinity or alkalinity: can be detected in the field by the presence of salts or from the nature of the vegetation, and determined in the laboratory by measuring the conductivity of a saturation extract of the soil and/or by direct determination of ions present (such as sodium).

Soil moisture holding capacity: this is influenced by soil organic matter content, texture, structure, depth, and content of coarse material such as gravel and stones, since these reduce the proportion of fine earth. The available water held by a soil can be measured in the laboratory, preferably on undisturbed core samples.

For agricultural purposes, additional analyses or tests may be carried out to give a better idea of the chemical characteristcs of the soil and its ability to supply nutrients to the plant in balanced amounts. These data may then be interpreted to result in fertilizer recommendations. The following routine analyses are often carried out, in addition to those mentioned above, to characterize profiles selected as typical: cation exchange capacity; exchangeable cations (Ca, Mg, and K, sometimes Na, Mn); and extractable phosphorus.

The cation exchange capacity of soil is a fundamental soil property related to the organic matter content, and type and amount of clay. It indicates the ability of the soil to retain cations for plant use.

The percentage base saturation represents the extent to which the cation exchange capacity of the soil is actually occupied by the exchangeable cations listed above, and is calculated as follows: sum of cations $\times 100$/cation exchange capacity.

The percentage base saturation is broadly related to soil pH. A soil with a saturation of 100 per cent often has a pH of neutral or somewhat above. A soil with a percentage base saturation of less than 20 per cent is generally rather acid in reaction (pH 5.5 or less) but the precise relationship between base saturation and soil pH depends on a number of factors, including the nature of the colloids (organic matter and clays) present.

To determine the amount of available phosphorus, a number of different extractants have been used. The aim is to remove only part of the total phosphorus present, and from this to estimate the phosphorus-supplying power of different soils. Commonly used extractants include weak acids such as acetic, dilute solutions of strong acids, and weak solutions of sodium bicarbonate. When large numbers of agricultural soils are analysed on a routine basis, the results can be correlated with crop responses to phosphatic fertilizers.

For soil classification purposes, the analyses needed depend on the system of classification used. In the French system of classification, widely used in French-speaking Africa, for example, highly weathered soils are separated from less weathered ones by measuring the silica/alumina ratio (SiO_3/Al_2O_3) of the clay fraction. This is an example of an analysis which is carried out relatively seldom, and only for the purpose of soil classification.

For the US Soil Taxonomy, the following analyses are normally necessary:

soil texture (particle size distribution)
organic carbon
total nitrogen
cation exchange capacity
exchangeable cations (Ca, Mg, Na, K)
hydrogen ions
pH in water
aluminium
extractable Fe_2O_3.

2.3.6. Field methods in soil survey

Field methods employed in soil survey work vary considerably according to the purpose of the survey, the time and money available and, above all, the scale of the final map.

Small-scale maps at 1:500 000, 1:1 000 000 or smaller, can show only broad groups of soils, often related to physiographic features such as plateaux, footslopes, or large valleys. If exploratory surveys of this type are being carried out where little soil information is available, the soil map will be based on a study of all available environmental information.

Medium-scale soil maps at 1:500 000 to 1:250 000 are widely used and have been produced by many countries. They cannot usually show individual soil series, but can map groups of soils. In some areas the mapping unit may consist of a soil catena or sequence of soils related to relief.

Large-scale maps at 1:20 000 or larger are usually prepared for particular purposes, for limited areas. They may be required for feasibility studies for agricultural development schemes. For irrigation schemes, or soil reclamation work, scales as large as 1:5000 or 1:2500 may be required. Large-scale maps show individual soil series, and even subdivisions of individual soils based on minor profile differences.

For the preparation of medium-scale maps, the use of air photographs is now widespread: it allows soil maps to be prepared more quickly and accurately than would otherwise be the case. Air photographs are often available in steroscopic pairs so that the user can obtain an impression of the relief. Air photographs, apart from allowing the soil surveyor to locate himself accurately on the ground, give him information on vegetation, relief, and land-use. The normal technique is for the soil surveyor to study the air photographs, as well as all available information on climate, relief, geology, and vegetation, as part of the pre-field work. This enables the surveyor to make a preliminary separation into areas which appear to have different soils. This is then checked by fieldwork. Thus air photographs allow the soil surveyor to locate a limited number of observations more effectively and give him valuable help in interpolating the nature of the soils between observations.

On large-scale maps, the number of observations in relation to the area mapped is greatly increased, so that the map is based less on interpolation and more on relatively detailed fieldwork. As a rule, there should be approximately one soil observation for each cm^2 of the final map. A soil 'observation' can be any relevant examination of the soil in a soil pit or with a spade or auger, but is commonly an auger observation down to a depth of at least 1 m. Soil observations for large-scale maps are often carried out on a regular grid. For example, a regular parallel grid with lines 100 m apart on which observations were made every 100 m would give one observation per cm^2 of a final map published at a scale of 1:10 000. In practice, the density of observations can be increased or decreased according to such factors as the complexity of the soils and the purpose of the survey.

In some cases, soil surveys involving a combination of mapping scales have been successfully carried out. In Ghana, relatively large areas (usually river basins) were mapped at a scale of 1:250 000, the mapping units at this scale showing soil associations (usually soil catenas, or a mixture of soil catenas, related to the dominant local parent material). The maps were supplemented by detailed information obtained from sample strips, usually one mile long and a quarter of a mile wide, sited across the relief so as to show the soil sequence from summit to valley bottom. The strips were mapped at a scale of 1:7920 (eight inches to the mile). Six parallel traverses 88 yards apart ran the length of the strip, and observations on the soils were made at 88-yard intervals along the traverses, thus giving 126 preliminary soil observations.

Because the soils were often gravelly in the upper 50–80 cm, a hole was dug with a locally-made soil chisel (similar to the chisels used for felling oil palms) to a depth of about 90 cm and the layers below, to about 1.5 m, examined with a soil auger. Extra soil observations were then made as required to check soil boundaries, and when the soils had been mapped in this way soil pits were then dug on typical sites for detailed profile descriptions, sampling, and analysis.

At the same time as the soils were examined and mapped, maps were made of (a) relief, using an Abney level; (b) vegetation; and (c) current land-use. It was thus possible to compare the soil distribution with the topography, and the sample strips also provided detailed information on the same scale on vegetation and land-use. Sample strips or sample areas on which soils, relief, and vegetation are mapped at the same scale can be very useful in ecological studies, provided that care is taken to ensure that the small area chosen for detailed study is typical of the larger area it is meant to represent.

2.4. Land-form classification

The need to choose ground monitoring stations that represent important fractions of the landscape or to explain differences observed along transects frequently requires that a landscape be separated into a relatively small number of homogeneous units. A popular method of classification is based on land-forms. The method has value because there is often a close relationship between land-forms and other factors of more direct ecological interest such as soil properties, abundance and form of water supply, or plant and animal distributions. A land-form classification often allows soil or vegetation types that characteristically occur in juxtaposition or that typically grade into one another to be lumped together. Thus, a smaller number of classes is usually used if the ecosystem is subdivided on the basis of land-forms than if it is based on soil or vegetation alone.

A particularly clear and simple example of a hierarchical land-form classification is shown in Fig. 2.1. The landscape portrayed in the lower

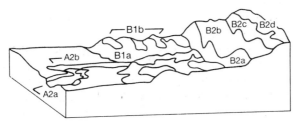

Level 3: The Step 2 units are separated into:

A2a – Bottom lands	B2a – Front slopes	B2c – Upper ridge slopes
A2b – Break lands	B1b – Ridge tops	B2d – Crest lands
B1a – Side slopes	B2b – Canyon lands	

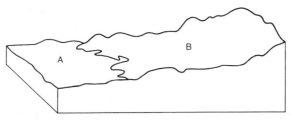

Level 2: The units of Step 1 are further divided into A1, lowland surface; A2, drainageway: B1, foothills: and B2, mountain lands.

Level 1: Two units are delineated – A, lowlands: B, uplands.

Fig. 2.1.

block diagram can be subdivided to various degrees, depending on the level of detail needed for the particular purpose. In some cases, only the difference between lowlands and uplands may be significant, and the classification need be continued only as far as Level 1. For other purposes, more detail may be required and the original two classes may be further separated.

The most sophisticated expression of this approach is the technique, developed by the Australian CSIRO, of dividing a landscape into land systems and land units. Ollier (1974) gives a well-documented review of this and other methods of terrain classification. A land system is defined as 'an area or group of areas throughout which a recurring pattern of topography, soils and vegetation can be recognized'. Land systems are convenient mapping units for broad reconnaissance surveys. If necessary, they can be subdivided into land units, which are small homogeneous areas of simple form, with a particular rock type, soil, and water regime. For example, a certain land unit may consist of steep, convex ridge tops underlain by sandstone with bare rock or thin gravelly soils and a vegetation cover of xerophytic bush.

Helmut Epp classified the landscape of Serengeti National Park into land systems for the purposes of planning ecological surveys and park management. One of his land systems is illustrated in Fig. 2.2. Other examples are illustrated by Ollier (1974).

The usual method of initiating a land-system classification is to delineate areas which appear distinct on aerial photographs. All this requires is aerial photographic coverage of the landscape at a scale of between 1:20 000 and 1:60 000, a large mirror stereoscope (cost approximately US$2000) and some training in air-photo interpretation. This part of the

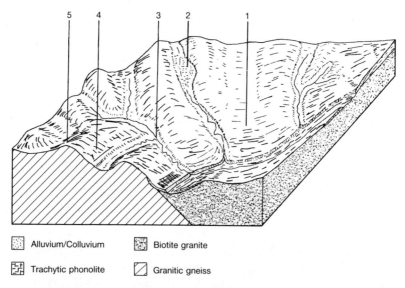

Alluvium/Colluvium		Biotite granite	
Trachytic phonolite		Granitic gneiss	

Fig. 2.2. Njaramau land system.

Fig. 2.2. (*cont.*)

Animal habitat: Dry-season holding area for migratory ungulates; local habitat for large herds of buffalo: topi, impala, kongoni, and predators limited, due to a large human population in the area.

Geology: Biotite granite and granitic gneiss with a thin cover of trachytic phonolite in the northern section.

Geomorphology: Dissected undulating terrain with narrow drainage floors and inliers rising up to 30 m above the surrounding surface.

Njarumau Land System

Unit Area	Morphology	Soils	Vegetation
1 Medium	Footslope, planar, up to 2.0°; 25% cover of flakes, chunks	Moderately deep dark reddish brown sandy loam to sandy clay pH 6.0	*Acacia gerrardii, Acacia robusta,* 20% cover, up to 4 m high; *Themeda triandra, Loudetia kagerensis,* 65% cover, up to 0.7 m high; *Mearua edulis, Phyllanthus spp.,* up to 10% cover, up to 0.3 m high
2 Small	Drainage area (swamp) planar, up to 0.3° slope	Very deep black clay; pH 6.5–9.0	*Leersia hexandra, Sporobolus consimilis,* 85% cover, up to 1.5 m high
3 Small	Drainage line, steep side, near planar, up to 2.0°, 25–50% flakes chunks, blocks	Moderately deep to very deep brownish black to black sandy clay to clay; pH 6.0–7.5	*Teclia trichocarpa, Croton dichogamus,* 50% cover, up to 7 m high; *Setaria chevalieri, Panicum maximum,* 75% cover, up to 1.5 m high
4 Medium	Mid-side slope of interfluve crest, planar to near planar, up to 3.5°, 25–50% cover of flakes, chunks; debris mantle with rock outcrop	Shallow to moderately deep dark brown to brownish black loam to sandy loam to sandy clay; pH 6.0	*Acacia senegal, Acacia hockii, Rhus natalensis,* 20% cover, up to 4 m high; *Teclea trichocarpa, Tarenna graveolens, Teclea nobilis* (in thickets), 75% cover, up to 6 m high; *Setaria chevalieri, Themeda triandra, Loudetia kagerensis,* 65% cover, up to 1.0 m high; *Vigna frutescence,* 5% cover, up to 0.2 m high
5 Medium	Rocky interfluve crest, convex, up to 4°, rock outcrop with debris mantle, 50–75% cover of chunks, blocks	Shallow to very shallow dark reddish to dark brown sandy loam; pH 6.0	*Teclea trichocarpa, Tarema graveolens, Teclea nobilis* (in thickets), 75% cover, up to 7 m high; *Setaria chevalieri,* 20% cover, up to 0.3 m high; *Acacia gerrardii, Acacia hockii, Acacia senegal,* 20% cover, up to 3 m high; *Themeda triandra,* 75% cover, up to 1m high.

exercise produces a provisional set of land units grouped into land systems, traced onto a transparent overlay.

The next step ideally involves co-operative fieldwork by a geomorphologist, pedologist, and plant ecologist – although one person with some knowledge of all three sciences often has to do the work alone. The fieldwork consists of systematic description of the land-forms, soils, and vegetation along transects chosen to test the reality of boundaries between the provisional land units and systems. The provisional classification will usually be modified as a result of this fieldwork which often collects a great deal of information on soil characteristics and erosion, geological and hydrological processes, and botany. However, the published description of each land system is usually brief. For more information, see Ollier (1974) and the sources to which he refers.

2.4.1. Landscape morphometry

Most land-form descriptions are still couched in rather vague terms, such as 'gently undulating plains' or 'steep, intricately dissected ridges'. While these are usually adequate for most ecological surveys of a single region or ecosystem, the definition of classes is so vague that the results are often not reproducible by other analysts, and cannot be used as a basis for comparison with other regions. In a search for more objective methods, a number of different land-form parameters have been used, but there is no consensus about the best approach. The technique usually involves the measurement or systematic observation of a few landscape characteristics, such as maximum valley-side angle, slope profile, valley width, and valley depth. Class boundaries are then defined for each attribute (see Table 2.1). The class intervals are not necessarily uniform. They are ideally chosen with reference to some important ecological threshold, such as the critical gradient for accelerated soil erosion, gullying, soil cover, landslides, or soil waterlogging but at the beginning of a survey it may not be possible to define class boundaries in this manner.

Some work has been done on quantifying various aspects of landscape form that could influence productivity. For example, hill gradient can affect the local rate of soil erosion and therefore soil properties. The drainage density (total length of stream channels per square kilometre of

Table 2.1. Examples of classifications of land-form parameters

Maximum valley-side angle (%)	2	2.0–3.9	4.0–7.9	8.0–15.9	16
Slope length (m)	10	10–49	50–99	100–199	200
Slope profile form	Rectilinear	Convex	Concave	Convex–concave	Complex
Valley width (m)	100	100–199	200–399	400–799	800

land) indicates the average distance between water supplies and, in some regions, the amount of water-margin habitat per unit area of landscape. Elsewhere, the drainage density may be a useful relative index of the rate of erosion. Relatively little research has been done on the correlation between these indices and ecological characteristics and processes, but the measures could be used more widely for objective, quantitative description and separation of a landscape into homogenous units.

Particular morphometric indices are occasionally used in ecological research for testing hypotheses. For example, Fig. 2.3 shows the frequency distribution of gradients on a ridge occupied by Masai settlements in southern Kenya. No settlements are located on gradients steeper than 8 per cent, in spite of the fact that gradients of up to 27 per cent were available. This work produced some insights into the factors that affect decisions about settlement sites among the Masai (Western and Dunne 1979). See also Strahler (1964) for a valuable review of landscape morphometry.

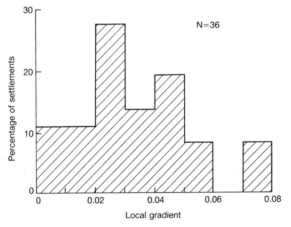

Fig. 2.3. Frequency distribution of Masai settlements in relation to hillslope gradient on Eremito Ridge along the northern margin of Amboseli National Park.

Because the average slope of a landscape is often a useful descriptor for ecological surveys and planning, it is worth mentioning the simple technique developed by Wentworth (1930) for obtaining this parameter from topographic maps. First, a number of transects (usually about 10) is laid out in each of two directions perpendicular to one another. The number of contours intersected by each line is then measured and the average calculated. Average percentage slope is then given by the expression:

average no. of contour intersections $\times$ contour interval (m per km)/63.3

Many planning or ecological studies of rivers have incorporated measures of channel characteristics. These include qualitative classifications (such as those listed in Table 2.2), as well as the straightforward quantitative descriptions of channel width, mean flow velocity, sinuosity (ratio of channel length to valley length), and gradient. Dunne and Leopold (1978) provide details of how to collect, analyse, and use quantitative information on channel characteristics in planning. Hynes (1963) has reviewed the value of documenting channel parameters in studies of aquatic ecology.

Table 2.2. Example of a qualitative classification of river channel pattern

Channel pattern	Channel characteristics of interest in planning and ecology that are frequently associated with channel pattern.
Rock bound	Narrow, deep, rough channel with a steep or irregular gradient, rapids or waterfalls common. Bed is rocky with some large boulders. Flow is highly turbulent and often fast. Channel is immobile. Views along and away from the channel are usually restricted by rock walls.
Alluvial – straight	Sinuosity (channel length divided by valley length) less than 1.3. Straight reaches are rare and short in most rivers, and occur most frequently in steep, bouldery reaches. Bars of coarse sediment usually occur on alternating sides of the channel.
– meandering (can be sub-divided into sinuosity classes)	Smoothly curving bands with deep pools on the outside of each band and shallow ripple sections in the straighter portions of the channel between bends. Diverse, but regularly repeated set of habitats defined by flow depth and velocity. Shifting occurs by erosion of the outer, concave bank and deposition of sediment on the inner, convex bank. Slight irregularities in the shifting process can isolate ox-bow lakes and other habitats in the flood-plain.
– braided*	Irregular channel form with large spatial and temporal changes in depth and velocity. Great diversity of habitats. Many braided channels have weak, sandy or gravelly banks, and high rates of sediment transport so that they migrate rapidly and irregularly across the flood-plain.

*A braided channel is one that is separated into two or more channels by bars or islands. See Fairbridge (1968) for more detail on channel patterns.

2.4.2. Surveys along hillslope transects

For many ecological purposes, data are collected along transects. It is often useful to conduct geomorphological surveys in the same manner, with the transect aligned downhill and/or along the contour.

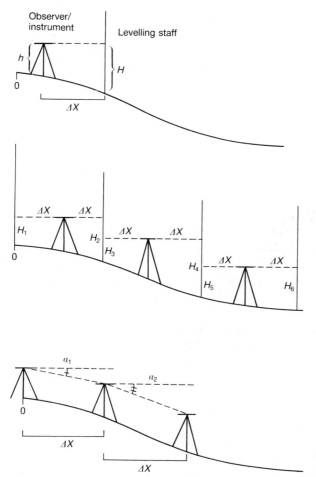

Fig. 2.4. Three methods for measuring a topographic profile, using a tape and a hand-level or Abney level.

A typical hillslope description in such a survey would involve measuring a topographic profile with a tape and a hand-level (or Abney level). Three methods of doing this are illustrated in Fig. 2.4.

Other data can be collected at chosen intervals along the transect. For example, in a study of settlement-site distribution among Masai pastoralists in southern Kenya, Western and Dunne (1979) measured: ground cover; canopy density; distance to settlements and the diameter and age of settlements; and colour and particle-size frequency of the surface soil. Detailed information on the surveying of hillslope profiles can be obtained from the manual by Leopold and Dunne (1972).

2.5. Soil erosion and sediment yields

The ultimate source of the sediment eroded from slopes is weathering of bedrock. The weathered material is incorporated into the soil and transported by erosion and 'tree-throw' until it enters a stream or river which eventually removes it from the drainage basin. Changing climatic conditions, vegetation, and land-use can affect the relative rates of weathering, transport downhill, and introduction of sediment into streams, resulting in effects such as enhanced local deposition, erosion, and sediment loading in streams. Field analysis of these problems must therefore be planned with a specific goal in mind, and strategies and techniques must be selected which are appropriate to those goals.

Erosion-related topics of recent concern have included: the effects of changing land-use on rate of soil loss; downstream enlargement of flood-plains; the amount of silt and sand deposited in stream gravels used by fish during spawning; stream turbidity and water quality; and rates of sediment deposition in lakes and reservoirs. Several approaches have been developed for the documentation and analysis of these problems. Analyses can be carried out on the scale of an entire drainage basin, in which case they generally involve measurements of stream sediment loads or deposition rates at sediment traps such as reservoirs at the mouths of basins. In other cases, attention is focused on a single process such as the effect of forest-felling on frequency of landslides or the effect of cultivation on gully erosion. Here the analysis will centre on the monitoring of the distribution and rate of that process. A third approach involves combining the results of a number of studies into a quantitative account of rates of sediment production and transport in a basin. Ideally, such an approach could provide information on sediment yield that would be directly comparable to the results of whole-basin studies. Such an approach, which involves the construction of sediment budgets, is outlined by Dietrich and Dunne (1978) and Dietrich, Dunne, Humphrey, and Reid (1981).

2.5.1. Catchment or drainage-basin studies

Catchment studies are designed to make use of indices of basin conditions which are measureable at the mouth of a basin. Measurements thus represent an integration of conditions or responses over the entire catchment. The index generally chosen for evaluating sediment-related problems is the annual basin sediment yield, or quantity of sediment leaving the basin during a year. This can be measured by monitoring sediment transport from the basin or can be reconstructed from measurements of infill rates of catch-basins at the basin mouth. In either case, the data can be used to provide information on sediment yields under either stable or changing conditions or to compare different basins experiencing different conditions.

2.5.1.1. Methods: monitoring of sediment loads Sediment is transported by water either in suspension or by traction along a stream or river bed. Both mechanisms must be evaluated if total sediment yield is to be determined. Suspended sediment may be monitored to evaluate the effects of changing land-use or because high turbidity is itself often of concern in aquatic ecology. Suspended sediment loading is a relatively easy-to-measure index of the magnitude of other changes in a basin. Suspended sediment usually comprises at least 90 per cent of the total load.

2.5.1.2. Methods: suspended load Suspended sediment samples are usually collected with a depth-integrating sampler such as the DH-48 (see Fig. 2.5); water is passed into the sample bottle at precisely the flow velocity, so by lowering the sampler into the flow at a constant speed, each portion of the flow is sampled in accordance with its proportion of the total discharge. Samplers of this type can be either hand-held or lowered on cables. Others, called point-integrating samplers, are designed with a release that allows sampling at a particular depth. Both types, and their usage, are described in detail by Guy and Norman (1970).

The samples are analysed either by filtering and weighing to determine sediment concentration (Guy 1969) or by measuring turbidity using a turbidity meter. In the latter case, care must be taken to confirm that there is a well-defined relation between sediment concentration and turbidity for the sampling location (Kunkle and Comer 1971). Occasionally, in-stream turbidity meters are used. These can provide a continuous

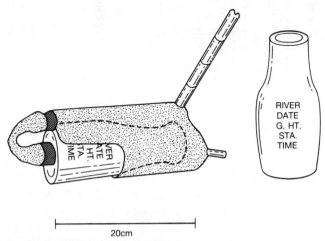

20cm

Fig. 2.5. The DH-48 depth-integrating sampler for the collection of suspended sediment samples.

record of stream turbidity at a single depth which can be used as an index
of water quality or of light penetration for ecological studies.

Annual sediment yield can be calculated as follows. The measurements
of suspended sediment discharge are plotted against water discharge to
construct a sediment-rating curve for the site (see Fig. 2.6). A record of
water discharge or a flow-duration curve then allows the sediment yield
to be calculated for the period of record. The water discharge for each
day (or hour, or any other time period available) is used to enter the
abcissa of the rating-curve graph. Reading upwards reveals the appropriate sediment transport rate for the period. These values are summed
for each day of a year to obtain the annual yield.

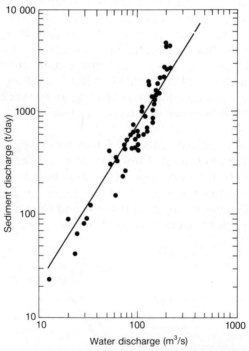

Fig. 2.6. Sediment rating curve for the Tana River, Kenya (from Ongweny 1978). Erosion
and sediment transport in the Upper Tana catchment, with special reference to the Thika
basin.

2.5.1.3. Methods: bedload Bedload refers to the sediment that hops, or is
dragged and rolled along the streambed by fluid drag. Because it is difficult to sample, bedload is rarely monitored. Two types of samplers are in
use. The most common is some variation of a heavily-weighted basket
lowered to the bed and held in place for a measured time. Such samplers
usually perturb the local transport rate, however, because they retard the

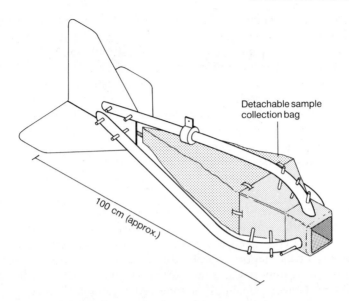

Detachable sample
collection bag

100 cm (approx.)

Fig. 2.7. The Helley-Smith sampler, used for monitoring bedload.

flow, and measured transport rates are thus uniformly low. The Helley–
Smith sampler (see Fig. 2.7) represents an improvement on the basic
design which largely overcomes this problem (Helley and Smith 1971). It
consists of a heavy metal frame with a forward opening which is flared in
such a way as to force water through the mouth at exactly the flow
velocity in the surrounding fluid. The orifice is placed on the streambed,
and bedload particles pass into the mouth of the sampler unhindered.
There they are trapped in a net attached to the downstream end of the
frame. The trap efficiency for a sampler with a 7.6 cm orifice has been
shown to be near 100 per cent for particles smaller than fine gravel.
Larger samplers have been used successfully to sample gravel transport.

Bedload transport measurements are expressed as the sediment
volume or mass passed in a unit of time (for example, tonnes/m/day).
Samples are needed at each of five to ten stations across the channel to
define the cross-sectional variation at a single sampling time. Integration
of the averages across the stream produces the total instantaneous rate of
bedload transport. This value is then plotted against the simultaneous
water discharge. Repetition of the procedure at different discharges
yields a bedload-rating curve, similar to the suspended sediment rating
curve in Fig. 2.6. It is used with a water discharge in the manner just
described to calculate annual bedload yield.

2.5.1.4. Methods: reservoir sedimentation surveys Total load (the sum of
bedload and suspended load) can be obtained by repeated surveys of the

beds of reservoirs, lakes, artificial sediment catch basins or stockponds. The measurements are made at least several years apart (and usually a decade or more), and the total sediment accumulation provides only a long-term average for the period between measurements. Ideally, the site of an artificial reservoir is always surveyed before the reservoir is created. Then, if the reservoir is periodically drained, the bed elevation can be surveyed with an engineer's level along lines between permanent bench-marks. If the lake is not drained, the changes in bed elevation can be surveyed periodically from a boat or raft (Rausch and Heinemann 1977; Murray-Rust 1972).

Repeated topographic surveys give only the volume of accumulated deposits, which may be all that is required for reservoir design. However, for assessing the amount of soil erosion represented by the deposit or for comparison with sediment transport measurements in streams, the volume must be converted to mass. This can be done by estimating the bulk density of the deposits, preferably by collecting cores of measured volume from the deposits and measuring the dry weight of sediment per unit volume. Geiger (1965) gives some average bulk density values for various sediments which are useful for preliminary estimates.

Small water-bodies do not trap all the sediment entering them. The proportion of the influx that settles onto the bed is called the trap efficiency of the lake. It can be measured by sampling sediment loads above and below the lake. In the absence of such local data, a preliminary estimate of trap efficiency can be obtained from Fig. 2.8. Once the trap efficiency has been obtained, it is divided by 100 and divided into the measured change of sediment volume between surveys to obtain the amount of sediment entering the water-body.

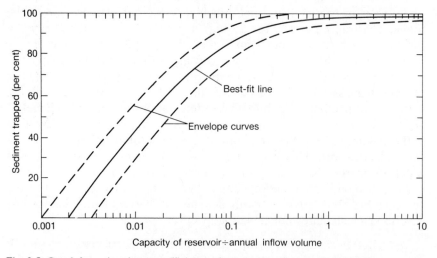

Fig. 2.8. Graph for estimating trap efficiency of water body. (Source: Brune 1953.)

2.5.1.5. Experimental design for catchment studies Application of baseline studies is straightforward: measurements of average sediment yield from catchments under stable conditions can be applied to estimate yields from other basins under similar conditions. For example sediment yields from undisturbed highland forests in Kenya average about 20–30 t/km^2/year (Dunne 1979).

Often, however, the goal of a study is to determine the effects of changing conditions. In such cases, the paired basin approach is frequently applied. Sediment yields are measured at the mouths of similar basins undergoing different levels of disturbance, and differences in yield are attributed to the differences in disturbance. Other studies compare sediment yields in a catchment before and after disturbance, again making the assumption that measured changes are a direct result of disturbance.

Paired-basin studies are useful in outlining the general relationship of sediment yields to changing basin conditions. Such studies, for example, have demonstrated that disturbances associated with logging increase sediment yields over those from undisturbed forests (Brown and Krygier 1971). In addition, sediment-yield data exist for many basins, allowing comparisons to be made of the variables which affect sediment production (Wallis and Anderson 1965; Dunne 1979).

Such studies, however, have major drawbacks as far as application and interpretation are concerned. Rarely can more than a few basins be monitored during a study, so that results are not replicated. Only the coarsest of controls can be recognized. Variation between basins is undefined. Results are extremely sensitive to the occurrence of large, rare events such as landslides and major floods. The results cannot be applied quantitatively to other basins. In addition, a long record is necessary either to determine the dependence of sediment yield on weather conditions or to calculate an average yield over the distribution of weather conditions. Where the disturbance is brief, measurements may not be continued for long enough to characterize adequately the effects of the change. Finally, measurements made at the mouth of a catchment can provide information only about the net response of a basin; they are merely indices of basin conditions and can provide little information on how sediment is being generated within the basin.

2.5.2. Process studies

Concern over changing conditions is often centred on their effect on a single erosion process. Heavy grazing, for example, can lead to accelerated soil erosion and road building can increase the incidence of landslides. Evaluating such changes requires analyses of individual processes. The time available for the analysis generally determines the approach to be taken. If only a short study is possible, information must be gathered by short-term field observations and proxy measurements of rates, while longer studies can make use of a number of monitoring techniques and different study plots.

2.5.2.1. Short-term field observations Rates of erosion can sometimes be inferred from a single period of observation. For instance, evidence of a discrete process may persist for long enough to represent the range of conditions controlling the erosion rate. Landslide scars, for example, are usually visible for a decade or more; an estimated landslide frequency calculated by dividing the number of scars of 10 years' age or less by 10 would thus represent an average rate for the range of weather conditions experienced in that 10-year period. Alternatively, the overall rate may be considered to be constant over time, particularly when the period of activity is rapid or well-defined (for example, a count of burrow mounds at the end of a season can provide an estimate of the downslope move-ment of soil caused by a stable population of burrowing animals if their burrowing habits are known).

2.5.2.2. Landslides and debris flows Landslides and debris flows (land-slides which have entered a stream, generating a liquid-like flow of sediment and organic debris which continues downstream) leave long-lasting evidence of their occurrence. These scars or deposits can often be dated by determining the age of vegetation growing on them. A survey of landslide scares, with associated measurements of slide volumes and ages, thus allows the average rate of sediment transported by slides to be calculated. Where forest canopy is sparse or landslide scars are large, aerial photographs can provide an efficient means of mapping slide distribution and measuring surface areas. Field measurements of slide depth and vegetation age can then be used to calculate the rate of influx of sediment to channels by these processes (Swanson and Dyrness 1975).

The same methods can be used to evaluate erosion from debris flow, though in this case the depth of erosion is often difficult to measure. Erosion depths on stream or river banks can be determined from measurements of scarp height, root exposure, or possibly by comparing the remnant soil thickness with soil thickness on similar undisturbed valley walls. The volume of sediment removed from a stream or river can also be estimated from deposits in neighbouring channels. Often, much of the transported sediment is trapped in a debris fan, providing a minimum estimate of sediment moved if the proportion of organic debris in the fan can be estimated.

2.5.2.3. Biological activity In some areas, processes such as animal burrowing and tree-throw transport large amounts of soil downhill. Tree-throw mounds, like landslide scars, are persistent and datable, and so can be evaluated using techniques similar to those for landslides, though care must be taken to determine transport direction and displacement (Denny and Goodlett 1956).

The effects of burrowing on erosion have also been evaluated using a single survey in cases where the period of burrowing is well-defined. In the Pacific North-west of the United States, for example, mountain beavers stop burrowing in late summer, so a survey of unvegetated mounds in early autumn covers the year's activity. If the population of burrowers is relatively constant, then a single survey can provide an estimate of the average annual volume of soil moved by burrowing animals. However, once again transport direction and displacement may not be obvious; a knowledge of burrow layout is necessary to calculate a net transport rate (Reid 1981).

2.5.2.4. Rill and gully erosion Rills and gullies usually occur in association with disturbed areas such as roads, cropland, pasture land, and excavated areas. Local populations can often provide information about the location of gully headwalls over time. Measurements of gully volumes can then be used in conjunction with anecdotal information to estimate gully erosion rates. If aerial photographic coverage is available, sequential photographs can be used to calculate the rate of headwall retreat and to measure gulley widths. Field measurements can then be used to define a relation between gully width and cross-sectional area, thus allowing the volume of material eroded over time to be calculated.

These methods are adequate for large, rapidly retreating gullies but for smaller ones, and those expanding at rates of less than 5–10 m/yr, it is usually possible only to map the absence or presence of the gullies from aerial photographs.

Rills are not as noticeable as gullies, so anecdotal information may not be as useful; neither are they visible on aerial photographs. If rills date from a known disturbance, then rill volumes can be measured and the volume of sediment lost can be averaged over the period since the disturbance. In this way, a minimum estimate can be made of the average rate of erosion from rills, assuming no lowering of the inter-rill surface. This technique can often be used for rills associated with roads with a known construction or resurfacing date and for those associated with landslides of known age.

Rills, by definition, are features which can be ploughed over. Where they are found in a ploughed field, they can be assumed to have formed since the field was last ploughed. A survey of rills at the end of the wet season can then provide a minimum estimate of annual rill erosion. Rill volumes can be measured by level surveys along the contour. If no bench-marks are installed before the wet season, such a survey provides a minimum estimate of rill erosion (Fig. 2.9(a)), but if bench-marks are

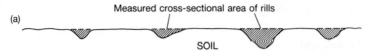

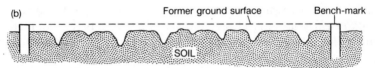

Fig. 2.9. Measuring rill volume by means of level surveys along a contour. If no bench-marks are installed (a) a minimum estimate only of the rill erosion can be obtained. If bench-marks are installed (b) the total volume of erosion can be measured.

installed after ploughing, the total volume of erosion can be measured (Fig. 2.9(b)). In the latter case, it is necessary to ensure that soil compaction is not responsible for the general lowering of the surface, or to correct for such settling by taking soil cores and measuring soil density at the time of each survey, but such a level of detail is not necessary for the documentation of most erosion problems because the compaction effect is usually small.

2.5.2.5. Surface erosion Many of the most widespread forms of erosion take place slowly but almost continuously – in contrast to the rapid and discontinuous effects of landslides and gully formation. These more gradual processes occur most commonly when the soil is left bare and is therefore exposed to the action of wind and rain, and to disturbance by vehicles and animals. Because this type of erosion occurs almost uniformly over a surface, it may be difficult to detect. Some of the signs that it is occurring include the presence of mounds of earth around plants, pedestals of soil beneath stones, and accumulations of sediment uphill from individual plants.

Surface erosion processes often occur so gradually that vegetation survives on the eroding surface. But as the roots become exposed, the crowns of plants are either left above the new ground level or on pedestals where the original ground surface has been protected by the plant's crown and held in place by roots. In many areas, the ages of woody plants can be determined by counting growth rings in the stem, though the number of rings set down each year may depend on species and climate. By measuring the height of the residual mounds underneath woody plants and determining the age of the plants, the average rate of surface lowering can be determined over the lifespan of the plants (see Fig. 2.10).

The measurement of erosion pedestals is subject to several pitfalls, however. Mounds formed by erosion of the surrounding surface must be

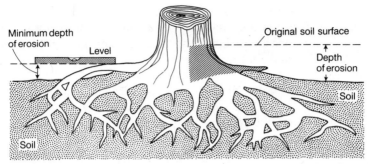

Fig. 2.10. Measurement technique. On the left, the top of the root (on appropriate species) indicates the minimum elevation of the original soil surface. On some plants, a morphological feature or a change in bark texture or colour indicates the original ground elevation (right-hand side). The carpenter's level is set on a survey rod to extend measurement beyond a wide canopy.

carefully distinguished from those due to aggradation around the plants caused either by transport of soil into the area protected by the canopy or by termite activity. It is usually possible to recognize when this is happening by examining the soil texture, structure and organic content of the mound and the surrounding soil. Species which raise the soil surface as their roots and bole grow must also be avoided. Finally, unless plants of different ages are used, the measurements may provide only an average lowering rate, since erosion may have accelerated since the plant was established. Measurements of surface lowering are made by setting up a large carpenter's level parallel to the contour. A vertical line is then measured to determine the depth of lowering (Lamarche 1968). Dunne *et al.* (1978, 1979) have described the use of the technique in the Kenya rangelands and some of the applications to which the results may be put.

2.5.2.6. Monitoring surface erosion If sufficient time is available, erosion rates can be measured more accurately by monitoring the erosion processes. This approach is particularly useful for widespread, frequent processes such as sheet erosion, and for gully and streambank erosion. Infrequent, large-scale events such as landslides are better analysed by mapping and dating.

Surface erosion rates can be monitored either by measuring the rate at which the surface is being lowered or by measuring the amount of sediment coming from the surface. In both cases, monitoring should be carried out for long enough for a mean value for sediment loss to be statistically sound (an average annual rate, for example, must be based on many years' data) or for a relation to be defined between the loss rate and the controlling factors such as rainfall intensity or wind velocity. If such a relation can be defined, then an average annual loss rate can be calculated from climatic records.

The rate of lowering is measured by making repeated measurements of the ground surface elevation relative to a datum. The most common techniques used are measurements along fixed erosion-pins, measurements from a fixed line and repeated surveys with tape and level from a fixed bench-mark.

Erosion-pins are stakes or nails inserted perpendicular to the ground surface (see Fig. 2.11). The top of the pin then provides a bench-mark from which the disturbance to the ground surface can be measured with a millimetre rule. Pins must be long enough to ensure that they remain stationary, and should be thin enough to avoid extensive disruption of surrounding soil; 25 cm nails or wire spikes are frequently used. In areas where aggradation is expected, the nail can be inserted through a washer lying on the ground surface; later accumulation can then be measured as the thickness of sediment lying on top of the washer. Both washers and the heads of the nails, however, may protect the ground surface below and result in the formation of erosion pedestals, which must be removed before measurement. In areas subject to frost heaving, elevations of the nail heads with respect to a fixed bench-mark should be measured with a surveying level to preclude fictitious measurements caused by heaving of the nails. Erosion-pin networks are inexpensive and easy to install and monitor, permitting the use of large networks (Leopold, Emmett, and Myrick 1966).

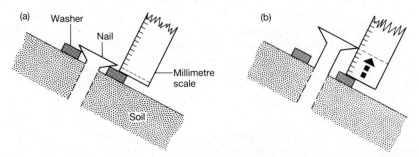

Fig. 2.11. Measurement of erosion (or deposition) at stakes: (a) installation; (b) remeasurement.

Surface lowering can also be monitored using point gauge measurements from a rigid frame supported on fixed posts. The advantage of this method is that the measurement technique does not affect the ground surface at all. Surface profiles can also be repeatedly surveyed using a tape and level from a fixed-elevation bench-mark, also resulting in minimal surface disturbance.

Surface erosion can also be monitored by measuring the amount of sediment leaving a plot of known size. Small plots can be defined by installing metal siding, and larger ones by surveying the hillslope above the collecting area. In either case, sediment and runoff from the plot are collected in a trough at its base (see Fig. 2.12) and channelled into a holding tank.

Care must be taken to avoid disturbing the soil lip while installing the trough, and once installation is complete the lip must be protected from accelerated erosion. This can be done by laying a concrete apron immediately above the trough, and moulding the uphill edge to match the soil surface. The trough itself must be installed with sufficient gradient to transport all sediment entering it to the collecting tank.

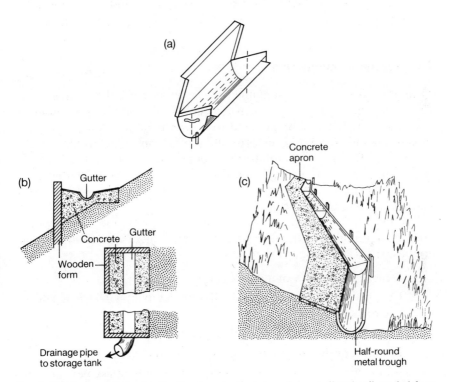

Fig. 2.12. Various kinds of collection troughs for measuring runoff and soil eroded from plots: (a) Gerlach trough; (b) concrete gutter; (c) trough for collecting large amounts of debris, including coarse particles from large plots.

2.5.2.7. Monitoring rill, gully, and streambank erosion Although aerial-photo interpretation and anecdotal accounts may be adequate to reconstruct gross changes in gully morphology, much sediment may be generated by very small changes in channel length and cross-sectional area. The more precise techniques described in this section are necessary to resolve these small-scale changes.

Repeated measurements of erosion pin networks can be used to monitor erosion on gully walls and stream banks. Networks can also be used effectively to monitor changes in rill cross-section. Measurement techniques are the same as those used for monitoring surface erosion. The retreat of streambanks, gully sidewalls and headwalls, and the linear growth of rills, can be monitored by repeated measurements of the distance between the feature of interest and a series of fixed bench-marks above the streambank or around the gully or rill perimeter. Precise definition of gully erosion and aggradation, however, requires repeated level surveys across bench-marked cross-sections and along the gully profile.

2.6. Vegetation monitoring

Vegetation is one of the fundamental classes of natural resources. Two principal goals of any comprehensive ecological monitoring programme must therefore be, first, to characterize the vegetation of the region being monitored and, second, to incorporate a procedure for periodic vegetation surveillance into the monitoring programme. The collective plant life of a region acts as an ecological integrator of all aspects of the environment which, if properly interpreted, can serve as both a record of the past and a window to the future.

The most frequently described properties of vegetation are its species composition plus various functional attributes, often expressed on a per species basis. The most common are:

1. Density, or number of individuals per unit area.
2. Frequency, or proportion of all samples within which a species occurs.
3. Standing crop, or total dry weight per unit area.
4. Biomass, or dry weight of living tissue per unit area.
5. Productivity, or change in standing crop or biomass per unit area per unit time.
6. Average individual size.

If it is to be effective, vegetation monitoring must be organized to reflect the goals of the monitoring programme and, in addition, must incorporate sufficient flexibility to accommodate changing goals in the future. Three decisions must be made early on which will determine the types of information to be collected and how that information is analysed:

1. What spatial scale is appropriate for the objectives of the programme?
2. What temporal frequency is appropriate for the objectives of the programme?
3. How quantitative should vegetation monitoring be to provide sufficient information, consistent with the spatial and temporal scales deemed appropriate?

Consider two different programmes that will require different types of information. One is designed to monitor the woody vegetation of regions adjacent to towns and villages in areas where charcoal is a major fuel. The objective is to determine the rate of tree depletion associated with charcoal-making. The other is designed to monitor grassland vegetation in regions utilized by the domestic stock of pastoral peoples. The objective is to monitor rangeland conditions to determine whether the vegetation is being used efficiently or is being overgrazed. The first study must monitor a total area of 500 000 km^2, but within this region only the woody vegetation near human settlements need be monitored. The second study encompasses a total area of 10 000 km^2, but the whole region must be monitored, since it is all used, at certain times of the year, by the pastoralists' livestock.

These two projects present two quite different problems of spatial scale. In the charcoal project, a large area must be covered but only isolated locales within it need by monitored. Moreover, changes in the woody vegetation are quite conspicuous so that visiting each locale by ground transport would not be necessary. In the grazing project, by contrast, a much smaller total area requires monitoring, but the monitoring must be more continuous over the whole area and many of the changes will be less conspicuous because of the small size of the plants being studied. So programme one would concentrate monitoring around settlements while programme two would study sites scattered throughout the area.

Now to the second decision that must be made: what is the appropriate temporal frequency for these studies? This depends on adequate information from past experience about how rapidly the vegetation is likely to change. In some cases, previous studies can provide the necessary information but in others only educated guesses will be available. Suppose personnel working on the charcoal project have information from a previous study indicating that the rate of tree depletion due to charcoal-making in a similar type of woody vegetation averages about 1 per cent per year. They therefore decide that monitoring every two years is sufficient. But suppose personnel on the rangeland project have no direct information except a general understanding that changes from palatable to unpalatable plants can occur quite rapidly if the range is overstocked. They may in such circumstances decide that monthly monitoring is necessary.

Personnel on each project must now decide what sort of data are to be collected and how they can be collected most efficiently. Since trees are large enough to be visible in low-level aerial photography, members of the charcoal project decide that aerial photographic monitoring will provide the necessary data for them to determine the rate of deforestation associated with charcoal-making. Use of aircraft also allows them to cover the large area of little interest rapidly, while photography can be concentrated in areas of importance to project goals. The rangeland monitoring project, in contrast, requires that areas to be monitored be visited by ground transport, since the plants are too small to show up in aerial photographs.

Moreover, changes in species composition will be even less conspicuous than the gross changes in tree cover to be monitored by the charcoal project. Members of this project therefore decide to establish 50 permanently marked plots throughout the study area and to visit each site monthly. They will record species composition of the vegetation. It is also recognized by members of the rangeland team that some estimate of the intensity of grazing must be obtained. So fenced plots are also established at each of the 50 sites and the amount of forage present is regularly measured.

These examples show how important it is to deal with the three critical planning decisions at the beginning of a programme. The charcoal project has minimal manpower requirements, but requires expensive investments in an aircraft and photographic equipment. The rangeland project has more modest equipment requirements, but must have sufficient trained personnel to provide accurate monitoring of grassland species composition and forage utilization.

This section proceeds from low-resolution methods of vegetation monitoring to increasingly detailed and numerical methods that require more manpower. It initially considers survey methods that are based on classification of vegetation by remote sensing. These classifications require a skilled photo-interpreter but can be completed largely from existing sources of aerial photographs which are now available for virtually all areas of the Earth. The next degree of resolution is obtained by reconnaissance on the ground using rapid, semi-quantitative methods. We then consider quantitative sampling methods, and the information needed to design a sampling programme. And, finally, methods for measuring vegetation productivity are considered.

2.6.1. The vegetation survey

Aerial surveys from aircraft and satellites have made wide regions of the

Earth's surface accessible for vegetation monitoring by trained inter-preters. Interpretation of much of this remote imagery requires highly technical training and its implementation is beyond the scope of this book. Nevertheless, any monitoring programme that must survey large or remote areas should consider availing itself of the multispectral scanner imagery available from the US National Aeronautics and Space Admin-istration's Landsat programmes.

Photographic images in the visible spectrum (black-and-white pan-chromatic and true colour) and near infra-red (false-colour and infra-red panchromatic) are more generally available. At a scale of 1:50 000, these images are excellent for preliminary survey, and at a scale of 1:25 000 can be combined with field surveys on the ground to develop vegetation maps with sufficient resolution for most ecological monitoring programmes. Oblique aerial photographs are of limited value because of distortion from foreground to background.

Vertical photographs are much more useful since they are usually taken with a 60 per cent overlap along the flight line and a 10 per cent overlap from side to side. They can then be used in stereoscopes to provide a three-dimensional view of the vegetation photographed. This survey method should be an essential part of any monitoring programme covering an extensive or remote area that cannot be easily traversed by ground transport. Definition is good enough to allow taxonomic identifi-cation of many trees and shrubs and to estimate the size of individual trees with knowledge of the appropriate scaling factor. Every monitoring programme should, when initially planned, give serious consideration to utilizing existing aerial photographs to provide a baseline of initial infor-mation, and to implementing a regular programme of photography to provide a permanent, semi-quantitative record of change.

A taxonomic reconnaissance of the vegetation by ground transport should also be completed. This will serve as the baseline for further, more quantitative monitoring methods. It should list the three or four most abundant species in each vegetation layer and note their topo-graphic location, landform associations and whatever properties of the underlying soil are apparent. This type of survey is best performed by a skilled plant taxonomist, often in co-operation with a geomorphologist. Such a team can traverse an area quite rapidly, developing an initial qualitative description of the vegetation that can then be used in more intensive programmes.

One of the most widely used means of making an initial, semi-quantitative classification of vegetation types is the Braun-Blanquet method (see Table 2.3), named after its originator (Braun-Blanquet 1964). The method requires considerable experience but, once learned, it can provide a rapid means of describing vegetation that is often com-parable to methods based on more intensive data collection.

Table 2.3. Vegetation attributes collected for Braun-Blanquet analysis

FIELD DATA

Score	*Species characteristics*
Cover-abundance class (an importance estimate)	
1	One or a few individuals.
2	Less than 5% of sample area.
3	Abundant but with low cover or less abundant but with higher cover; less than 5% of total cover.
4	Very abundant but less than 5% cover.
5	5–12.5% of total cover.
6	12.5–25% of total cover.
7	25–50% of total cover.
8	50–75% of total cover.
9	75–100% of total cover.
Sociability (a pattern estimate)	
1	Growing as solitary individuals.
2	Growing in small groups or tussocks.
3	Small patches of individuals.
4	Extensive patches.
5	Extensive mats, mostly pure populations.
Vitality and fertility (a vigour-reproduction estimate)	
●	Vigorous, commonly completing life cycle.
●●	Vegetative propagation, little sexual reproduction.
○	Feeble, little reproduction.
○○	Occasionally germinating, little growth.

SYNTHESIS AWAY FROM THE FIELD:

Constancy-presence	*Frequency* (percentage of sample plots)
I	1–20
II	21–40
III	41–60
IV	61–80
V	81–100

Fidelity class	
1 (Accidentals)	Species with abundance maximum outside of community.
2 (Companions)	Species without abundance maximum in any particular community.
3 (Preferentials)	Present in several communities, but most abundant in a particular one.
4 (Selectives)	Clear distribution centre in a particular community.
5 (Exclusives)	Completely or almost completely restricted to a certain community.

2.6.2. *Sampling vegetation*

Since it is impossible to sample the vegetation in an area of meaningful size by counting and measuring the size of every plant, some method of sampling must be developed. The most acceptable one is random sampling. However the area to be sampled is initially defined, the actual plots or locations to be sampled should be randomly located.

In many cases, however, the exigencies of cost and available time and manpower may make systematic sampling more cost effective. For example, the starting point and direction of transects may be randomly located but the individual samples along the transect laid out systematically. The main statistical effect of this is to inflate the estimate of the sample variance slightly, which is erring on the side of conservatism.

The most common random sampling method is stratified random sampling. Stratification means subdivision of the total region to be sampled into subregions. This stratification may be arbitrary or subjective. Arbitrary stratification results from an a priori subdivision of the total region into strata to be sampled. For example, samples could be arbitrarily placed at certain increments of altitude in a mountainous area. Or they could be arbitrarily placed on hilltops, slopes, and basins between hills, irrespective of any known or suspected variation of the vegetation in relation to topography.

Subjective stratified sampling, on the other hand, involves sample placement based on some apparent or suspected variation in the vegetation that would make completely random sampling of the region studied nonsensical. Suppose, for example, the region being monitored consisted of a mixture of forest and open grassland. A completely random sampling scheme would place study plots randomly over the whole region irrespective of the relative area occupied by each. A stratified random sampling scheme, in contrast, would place plots randomly within forest and within grassland, but in numbers that would provide a satisfactory sample of each. Subjective stratification is a perfectly reasonable method of sampling vegetation that is obviously heterogeneous, provided the means of stratification is explicitly reported so that the method can be duplicated in subsequent monitoring. In fact, almost all stratification will have an element of subjectivity, even when sample placement is arbitrarily defined. Since it is well known, for example, that vegetation varies with altitude or topographic position, even arbitrary sample placement of these criteria involves an element of subjectivity in defining the intervals of stratification.

Final sample placement must be completely random, however the region within which samples are to be placed has been defined. A random-number table is essential for anyone doing vegetation monitoring. It can be used to locate individual samples on a gridded area, if there is sufficient time and manpower to do so, or it may be used in other ways. One of the most rapid methods is to use the table to determine the number of paces to take between samples. Suppose you are placing quadrats (described below) in a grassland area and then are counting all the plants that fall within quadrats to determine species composition of the vegetation. Random samples might be obtained by the following procedure:

1. Set up a baseline along one edge of the area to be sampled and pace it off, starting at one end.

2. Select random numbers in pairs, one to represent the number of paces along the baseline, the other to represent the number of paces into the area from the baseline.

3. The plot to be sampled is then randomly located within the stand. This is a quite straightforward and appropriate method of assuring random stand placement and its only drawback is that you must return to the baseline between each sample.

An alternative method that does not have this requirement is as follows:

1. Set a reasonable range of distances between samples – at least 5 m but no more than 25 m.

2. Use a compass to determine the direction to walk from one sample to the next.

3. Start by using three digits of the random-number table to obtain the first angle from north to proceed from the starting point, and two digits to determine the distance to move between the limits of 5 m and 25 m (paces). Suppose the first number obtained was 93 and the second number was 09: using the compass, face the 93° mark (approximately east) and then march 9 paces. The first sample would be placed at this location.

4. After sampling the first quadrat, the procedure is repeated until an appropriate number of samples has been obtained.

Of course, a random-number table need not be carried around in the field. The sequence of random numbers is usually obtained before setting off for the field. For other methods of employing random numbers, see Awbrey 1977.

How many samples are enough? This question affects both the economy and usefulness of a monitoring programme. Often an arbitrary number of samples is decided upon as sufficient, and this number continues to be sampled time after time, in location after location, without asking whether it is too small, too big, or just right. But there is an objective method of determining how many samples are sufficient to meet the goals of the project (Poole 1974).

The sample size required depends on the variance of the data (s^2) and the range of resolution (L) required. The required number of samples, n, is related to these two terms by the equation:

$$n = 4s^2/L^2.$$

Suppose that the programme had established initial densities of a desirable forage grass as 500 shoots/m^2, with a variance of 125. If the project was willing to accept a 5 per cent range of resolution by deciding that a density change of less than 5 per cent $(500 \times 0.05 = 25$ shoots/m$^2)$ would be unimportant, then

$$n = 4 \times 125/5^2 = 500/25 = 20,$$

so 20 samples would have to be taken to detect the specified change of 25 shoots/m^2. As the variance increased or the range of resolution required by project goals decreased, the number of samples required would become larger.

2.6.3. Vegetation sampling methods

There are three basic methods of sampling vegetation: plot methods, intercept methods, and plotless methods. Plot, or quadrat-transect, methods involve establishing a border round a plot of vegetation, and counting and measuring the size of plants inside that border. Intercept methods involve measuring the intersection of a sampling line by plants. Plotless methods involve sampling plants round a randomly placed sampling point. Quadrat methods are very straightforward and involve few assumptions, but are more laborious and restricted in space. Plotless methods are quick, comparatively easy and commonly range over a wide area, but a number of assumptions about plant distribution is involved.

2.6.3.1. Plot sampling Counting and measuring the size of plants within areas of standard size is straightforward, easy to interpret, and very reproducible from area to area and investigator to investigator. Edges of plots may be marked with portable wood or metal frames of standard size when quadrat size is small and a permanent frame is light enough to carry easily. This is common for herbaceous vegetation. Sampling areas can be marked with heavy twine or small rope for larger quadrats. This would be common in woody vegetation. Circular or square plots are commonly called quadrats while ecologists commonly refer to rectangular plots as transects.

Quadrat and transect size and shape have been carefully investigated and it seems that circular quadrats of 0.2 or 0.5 m^2 or transects of 0.5 m^2 or 1.0 m^2 (with sides in a ratio of 1:2) are preferable for herbaceous vegetation. For shrublands, 1:5 or 1:10 plots of 50 m^2 or 100 m^2 are sufficient. Plots of 200 to 1000 m^2 with 1:5 or 1:10 ratios are used when trees are sampled. Some experience and preliminary sampling will be necessary since the size of quadrat finally used will depend on the density of vegetation. Sparser vegetation will commonly require larger sampling areas than denser vegetation. A wide range of sampling areas of comparable size but different shape is included in Table 2.4.

Table 2.4. Dimensions for sampling plots

Area	Circular (radius)	Square (side)	Rectangular (1:2)	Rectangular (1:5)	Rectangular (1:10)
1	0.56	1.00	0.71×1.41	0.44×2.20	0.32×3.16
2	0.80	1.41	1.00×2.00	0.63×3.16	0.45×4.47
3	0.98	1.73	1.22×2.44	0.78×3.86	0.55×5.48
4	1.13	2.00	1.41×2.82	0.89×4.45	0.63×6.32
5	1.26	2.24	1.58×3.16	1.00×5.00	0.71×7.07
10	1.78	3.16	2.24×4.47	1.41×7.07	1.00×10.0
20	2.52	4.47	3.16×6.32	2.00×10.0	1.41×14.1
30	3.09	5.48	3.94×7.88	2.45×12.2	1.73×17.3
40	3.57	6.32	4.47×8.94	2.83×14.1	2.00×20.0
50	3.99	7.07	5.00×10.0	3.16×15.8	2.24×22.4
100	5.64	10.0	7.07×14.1	4.47×22.4	3.16×31.6
200	7.98	14.1	10.0×20.0	6.32×31.6	4.47×44.7
300	9.77	17.3	12.3×24.5	7.74×38.7	5.48×54.8
400	11.3	20.3	14.1×28.3	8.94×44.7	6.32×63.2
500	12.6	22.4	15.8×31.6	10.0×50.0	7.07×70.7
1000	17.8	31.6	22.4×44.7	14.1×70.7	10.0×100.0

Once a plot has been laid out in the field, make a list of all species present. Then count the number of individuals of each species and take a size measurement of each individual of each species.

Although counting the number of individuals present seems obvious, it is not always so in the field. Some trees, for example, may have multiple trunks. And shrubs and herbs often produce many stems from a single root. This is not normally a problem except for densely-growing and sod-forming grasses, where individuals are so intermingled that it is impossible to delimit separate plants. In this case, the total number of separate shoots is commonly counted.

There are several methods of measuring plant size. The three most common are area at chest height, basal area, and foliage crown area. A tape measure can be used to measure the diameter of smaller, herbaceous plants, and stem circumference can be measured in larger, woody plants. These can be converted to area back in the office. Stem area at chest height is used when measuring trees, and either basal or foliage crown area is used when measuring shrubs or herbs.

When the vegetation includes trees, shrubs, and herbs use nested quadrats of different size for each stratum. A 1000 m^2 quadrat could be used for the trees, 200 m^2 quadrats inside this could be used for shrubs, and several 0.5 to 2 m^2 quadrats within this larger area could be used for herbs. Remember, however, that sample placement must be random for each stratum of vegetation sampled.

The following data are calculated from the field measurements:

1. Density=number of individuals per unit area.
2. Frequency=proportion of samples within which a species was recorded=number of samples where species was present divided by total number of samples taken.
3. Size=sum of individual size measurements for each species.
4. Relative density of a species=number of individuals of a species divided by the total number of individuals of all species.
5. Relative frequency of a species=frequency of a species divided by the sum of frequencies of all species.
6. Relative size=sum of individual sizes for a species, divided by the sum of sizes for all individuals.

Measure 3 is often referred to as dominance and measure 6 is often referred to as relative dominance. An importance value is calculated as:

7. Importance value of a species=(relative density+relative dominance+relative frequency) divided by 3.

It is common to express measures 4, 5, 6, and 7 as a percentage by multiplying each by 100. Notice that each of the relative measures will sum to 1 if expressed as a proportion, or to 100 if expressed as a percentage. Notice also that these different measurements convey different types of information about a species. The density measurements tell how many individuals were present, the dominance measurements tell which species were largest overall, and the frequency measurements tell how widely distributed a species was among sample plots. The density measurements can overemphasize the importance of species that consist of many small individuals; the dominance measurement can overemphasize the importance of a species that consists of a few, very large individuals; and the frequency measurements will overemphasize the importance of species whose individuals are widely distributed in the vegetation sampled, regardless of the size or numbers of those individuals. Therefore, importance value is a reasonable measure of the overall significance of a species since it takes into account several properties of the species in the vegetation.

2.6.3.2 Intercept methods There are three commonly used intercept methods of sampling vegetation: the step-count method counts the number of plants contacted by the point of the foot when walking through vegetation; line intercepts measure the intersection of a tape-measure; and point intercepts measure contacts on a pin passed through the vegetation. Line and point intercept methods are intermediate between plot and plotless methods in ease of application and assumptions about plant distribution patterns.

The step-count method is very quick. The observer simply walks through the vegetation and records the plant at the toe of each step or certain number of steps. If bare soil is under the toe, this is recorded. The technique is generally applicable only to low-growing herbaceous vegetation. It is best used as a preliminary survey method prior to applying more rigorous methods, but it can also be used for rapid rangeland monitoring where data precision is not essential.

The line-intercept method is applied by laying out a measuring tape in a randomly determined direction from a randomly placed point. Segments of the transect line interrupted by individuals (L), their width perpendicular to the transect line (W), and the species identification of the plant, are recorded by proceeding from one end of the tape to the other. The sum of the reciprocal widths, S, is used to calculate density (Strong 1966). Data are summarized as follows:

1. Density of a species $= (S)$ times (unit area in which density is to be expressed) divided by (total transect length in the same linear unit).

2. Frequency = number of transects in which a species was encountered divided by the total number of transects sampled.

3. Dominance, or proportional cover $= L$ for a species, divided by total transect length.

Relative density, relative frequency, relative dominance, and importance value are calculated exactly as described for plot sampling by dividing the values for each species by the sum for all species. The length of the transect interrupted by individuals can be either the basal length or the crown foliage length. Dominance will be expressed as basal cover in the former case and foliage cover (sometimes called crown cover) in the latter case.

The point-intercept method employs a frame containing pins that are passed through the vegetaion (Warren–Wilson 1963). The number of contacts per pin is counted. This method is most applicable to herbaceous vegetation because the size of the frame is prohibitive for larger plants. It is usually best to use an angle of less than 90° from the perpendicular. This method may provide more precision than the line intercept method since the number of contacts on a pin will reflect multiple levels of foliage in the vegetation canopy. These contacts are often proportional to the total weight of vegetation present (McNaughton 1979), referred to as biomass and described in more detail below. The method does not, however, provide a measure of density.

2.6.3.3 Plotless sampling Plotless sampling methods are based on the assumption that individuals are randomly distributed. Both the plot methods and the intercept methods can be used to determine how individuals are distributed and make no assumptions about those distributions. Plotless methods, therefore, should not be applied uncritically, but are best used in combination with plot or intercept sampling so that their assumption of randomness can be tested, and its importance evaluated in the context of monitoring goals. The principal virtue of plotless methods is the ease and rapidity with which they can be used. Nevertheless, ease and rapidity must always be weighed against sampling bias due to non-random distribution patterns of the plants being monitored.

The major plotless methods are nearest neighbour and point-quarter (or point-centred quarter). They are commonly used when sampling trees or shrubs, but they can easily be applied to herbs also. Both involve walking a transect by sighting along a compass direction or towards a distant landmark. Sampling points are randomly established by consulting a random-number table before going to the field. A sample is taken at each random point.

In the nearest-neighbour method, the plant nearest to the sampling point and its nearest neighbour are recorded, the size of each is measured, and the distance between them is recorded.

Provided that the plants are randomly distributed, density of nearest neighbours is:

$$d = (\tfrac{1}{2}r)^2,$$

where r is the mean distance between nearest neighbours.

In the point-quarter method, a sampling frame with two arms at 90° angles, forming a cross, is placed at each randomly determined point so that one arm is parallel to the transect being traversed. The closest tree to the centre point in each of the four quarters is sampled. The distance from the centre point to each is recorded, as is the appropriate size measure being employed. The data are initially summarized by dividing the total individual to point measurements by the number of measurements taken to obtain the mean distance from point to plant. The square of this distance gives the mean area per plant. Then, total density of all species = unit area/mean area per plant, where unit area is the area within which density is to be expressed, in the same units as mean area per plant.

As an example, suppose you have sampled 25 points; with 4 plants at each point, 100 plants have been sampled. The sum of all point-to-plant distances was 800 m; therefore, the mean point-to-plant distance was 8 m. The mean area per plant is then $(8)^2 = 64$ m^2. The density of plants per hectare, since 1 ha $= 10\,000$ m^2, is

$$d = 10\,000/64 = 156.$$

The calculations for nearest-neighbour and point-quarter data are identical once density has been calculated. To summarize the data further:

relative density of s species = number of individuals of a species divided by the total number of individuals;

density of a species = relative density × total density;

dominance of a species = average size × density of the species, divided by the total number of points.

Relative dominance, relative frequency, and importance value are calculated as indicated previously.

2.6.4. Summarizing and analysing community composition data

The initial stage of summarizing community composition data is to calculate mean densities, frequencies, and size dominances for each species. These are then converted into relative density, frequency, and size dominance, and, finally, an importance value for each species is calculated. If expressed as a proportion, each relative measure, including importance value, must sum to one, including all species present in the sample. If expressed as a percentage, of course, each relative measure must sum to 100. In many analyses, the frequency measure is not included, and only density and dominance are used to evaluate a species' importance in the community. This is a matter of judgement that should be decided early in a monitoring programme. Many ecologists feel that frequency places undue emphasis upon a distribution property that is not particularly important in community composition.

Beyond this, there are two basic approaches to further community composition analysis. Classification uses numerical methods of comparing species compositions in order to group individual samples into collections that are more similar within themselves than they are to other collections of other samples. Ordination is a numerical method of ordering samples on a quantitative gradient according to their similarities of species composition. These methods of data analysis involve numerous calculations requiring computers. See Whittaker (1978) for further details.

2.6.5. *Biomass and productivity measurements*

Biomass and standing crop are, respectively, the dry weight of living and total plant material per unit area. Above-ground biomass and standing crop occur from the soil surface upwards and are easily measured compared with below-ground weights, though the measurements are still laborious compared with those used in sampling species composition. Measures of plant size (basal area, area at chest height, and foliage area) are rough estimates of biomass and standing crop. But there are methods that can simplify monitoring considerably if they are first calibrated on real-weight measurements and are then used with care and judgement.

The initial step is to locate random quadrats or transects in the area to be sampled, harvest the above-ground vegetation by cutting it off at the soil surface, and take it to the laboratory for further processing. At the same time, litter should be collected. Soil cores should be taken to a depth sufficient to encompass the major rooting depth and in sufficient numbers to provide an adequate sample. The above-ground tissues are sorted by species, then in live and dead categories, put in separate containers, dried and weighed. Oven-drying at 80–100°C for 24 to 48 h is usually sufficient. Dried material must be weighted immediately upon removal from the oven so that it does not take up moisture from the atmosphere.

The total dry weight of living material is biomass, the total weight of dead material is called standing dead, and the sum of the two is standing crop. Soil cores are washed repeatedly in a sieve with rapidly running water, until all soil fragments are removed, sorted into living and dead tissues, oven-dried, and weighed to give below-ground biomass. Separating the root systems of different plants is usually impossible.

Sampling biomass and standing dead is both laborious and destructive, but it is essential if functional properties of the vegetation are of interest. There are no short cuts and no substitutions for this initial step. When, however, the initial step is combined with other measurements, it may be possible to develop indirect measurements that can subsequently be applied more rapidly and less destructively. Two such methods are canopy interception and plant spectroreflectance (McNaughton 1979).

To calibrate canopy interception for subsequent weight estimation, set up a point frame over each plot to be harvested. Pass a series of pins through the vegetation at an angle (about 45° is usually sufficient) and count the number of contacts on living and dead tissue of each species. The pins, of course, must be long enough to pass from above the canopy to ground level. Anywhere from 10 to 100 points may be used, depending upon the density and heterogeneity of the vegetation and the size of plots being sampled. Then, after the weights have been measured on oven-dried material, do a regression of number of pin contacts for each class of dead and live tissue on the weights determined from the dried material. If the regression is sufficiently significant, indicating that the number of contacts is an accurate measure of dry weight, canopy interception can be substituted for harvest in subsequent monitoring. As in any direct assay, however, periodic combinations of contacts and harvesting should be used to be certain that the accuracy of the method is being maintained.

Another indirect method depends upon the reflectance of different wavelengths of light by green vegetation (Pearson, Miller, and Tucker 1976). A photometer with photodiodes equipped with interference filters allowing passage of light at 675 nm and 800 nm is suspended above the plots to be harvested. Photometer readings are taken at each wavelength, and the plot is harvested and treated as before, sorting out the green tissue and weighing it. Since green tissue absorbs light at 675 nm and reflects light at 800 nm, the green biomass is positively correlated with the ratio R_{800}/R_{675} (Pearson, Miller, and Tucker 1976; McNaughton 1979).

This is a particularly useful method since it measures green tissue, often of particular importance to herbivores, and because it may be used to survey large areas from light aircraft, once properly calibrated. It also, of course, should be calibrated periodically on clip plots to ensure accuracy. But it does have some serious restrictions: first, it measures only green vegetation; second, it lumps all species together; and third, it cannot be used on vegetation that is a mixture of radically different forms, such as mixed woodland and grassland, because calibrations will be different for different types of plants.

Since productivity is a change in biomass with time, it seems a straightforward procedure in a monitoring programme to measure standing crop at two time-periods, subtract the first value from the second, and divide by the time-period to obtain a measure of productivity. In certain cases this may be sufficient, particularly if the time-period is sufficiently short and there is no significant movement of dead tissues into litter or significant consumption by animals. If animal consumption is believed to be important, of course, the plant tissue must be protected from this over the period of measurements, by fencing for larger animals and by the use of pesticidal poisons for smaller animals that cannot be excluded by fencing.

Biomass death and the movement of tissues from standing dead to litter are often significant and must be accounted for over any monitoring period to obtain an accurate estimate of net primary productivity (Wiegert and Evans 1964). One approach is to use three matched plots to be harvested in different ways over the period that productivity is to be calculated:

Plot 1: At the beginning of the period, harvest the standing crop and sort into biomass and standing dead.

Plot 2: At the beginning of the period, harvest biomass but leave standing dead in place; at the end of the period, harvest remaining standing dead.

Plot 3: Harvest standing crop and sort into biomass and standing dead.

All material, or course, should be dried and then weighed after collection. With the following measurement:

$$D_1 = \text{dead shoot material from Plot 1},$$
$$D_2 = \text{dead shoot material from Plot 2},$$

calculate the instantaneous rate of disappearance of standing dead as:

$$L = \ln(D_1/D_2)/t \text{ (in g/g . day)},$$

where t is the period in days between harvests. The quantity of dead disappearing over the period between harvests can now be calculated as:

$$Q = t(D_1 + D_2)/2 \text{ (in g/plot)},$$

where D_3 is the weight of standing dead from Plot 3. Death-rate of live shoot tissues over the period of measurement (R) can be determined as:

$$R = Q + (W_2 - W_1) \text{ (in g/plot)}.$$

Finally, productivity can be calculated as:

$$\text{NPP} = (B_3 - B_1 + R)/t \text{ (in g/plot}.t),$$

where NPP is net primary productivity and B_1 and B_3 are biomass on Plots 1 and 3 respectively. In many monitoring programmes, a knowledge of the rate of flow of plant biomass into litter will be necessary to make estimates of mineralization rates. This approach to harvesting provides a means of obtaining those estimates as well as accurate estimates of production.

The harvest methods described here are limited to plants small enough to be handled and so are restricted to herbaceous vegetation and small shrubs. Larger woody plants, particularly trees, require much more difficult methods. The most satisfactory of these is called dimension analysis (Whittaker and Woodwell 1968). This depends upon intensive harvesting of trees and determining regressions relating linear estimates of size to weights.

2.6.6. Permanent study plots

Many monitoring programmes need to evaluate trends in vegetation species composition and production, often in relation to climate or environmental changes. To monitor long-term trends, it is necessary to establish permanent study plots which can be returned to time and time again for monitoring. To monitor trends in species composition, it is best first to perform basic vegetation surveys using plots or plotless methods to determine average vegetation composition. Then choose several sites that appear to be representative of the overall species composition and sample them. Select those that are, in fact, representative – as revealed by classification or ordination – then mark them with conspicuous corner markers so that they can be located repeatedly for subsequent monitoring.

In some programmes, it may also be necessary to determine what the role of animals is in maintaining species composition of the vegetation. This involves establishing permanently fenced areas, called exclosures, from which animals are excluded by fencing. It may often be desirable to establish adjacent permanent study areas, one marked but unfenced, and one fenced. These can then be used to provide paired comparisons of the role of animals and other environmental factors in changing vegetation.

2.6.7. *Standardizing data collection*

Every vegetation monitoring programme should have a library of standard forms that are used at different stages of data collection and analysis:

1. *Methods forms* outline, in a step by step fashion, how each procedure is used to collect data in the field. Every person newly incorporated into the programme should make initial field trips with an experienced person and should carry out these methods until the methods are thoroughly understood.

2. *Data collection* forms should be standardized for each monitoring technique so that the data are always collected in the same format. These forms should contain unique information about each sample such as date, time, and location of sampling, and should provide a space for general observations about the area sampled. They should be set up in tabular form so that each data entry of a given type goes into exactly the same space for every sample.

3. *Data reduction* forms are used back in the office, after data have been collected, to perform initial analyses of the data such as calculating means, variances, and other properties of the samples. They should be a means of initially consolidating data from several samples into a common summary format.

4. *Final summary* forms should be designed to condense the data from

several data reduction forms into summary statistics that reveal the overall patterns being monitored. These forms will provide the information used in interim and final reports.

When a vegetation monitoring programme is planned and implemented, it is essential that each participant understand at the outset exactly how the data are to be used and what their final form is to be. The project managers, in particular, should have a very clear understanding of how each type of data is going to be summarized and analysed, and what its function is within overall monitoring goals. It is not sufficient to collect data and hope that its analysis will reveal something of interest. By its very nature, a monitoring programme takes a long view and this perspective should be maintained throughout all stages of data collection and analysis.

This does not mean that a project should be irrevocably committed to a certain plan right at the outset. Rather, the plan should evolve and develop as monitoring proceeds. This requires that data analysis be an ongoing part of the project so that there can be frequent interim evaluations of whether the monitoring plan is meeting programme goals. If it is not, it should be redesigned so that it does. Moreoever, goals should be re-examined regularly to see whether they are consistent with the developing data base. As more information becomes available, it may be desirable to reduce or even eliminate certain portions of the programme while others are expanded and new initiatives are implemented.

2.7. Large mammal herbivores

Introduction. Large mammal herbivores (LMH) are important components of terrestrial ecosystems, and land managers often need to monitor a number of different aspects of their ecology. The number of parameters finally chosen is usually determined by three main considerations: the aims of management, the costs of monitoring and the resources available.

A monitoring programme should be based on a good knowlege of the ecology of the species present. Usually this information is not available and the manager will have to base his programme on comparative and theoretical ecology, refining the programme as more knowledge becomes available.

To understand the use LMH make of the herb layer, it is necessary to review the major elements of their digestive physiology and of plant defences against the LMH. Most emphasis will be put on herbaceous plants, since these support most wild and domestic herbivores, but the same general principles apply to woody plants. A detailed treatment of this subject can be found in Van Soest (1982).

The plants. Plant material is so widespread and abundant that it might seem that the food of herbivores must always be in excess and that herbivore populations are only rarely limited by food availability. We now realize that this is not the case, because much plant tissue is of poor nutritional quality. It is important to distinguish between the three classes of plant material – cell contents, cell walls, and secondary compounds – which determine its utility to herbivores (Van Soest 1982).

Cell contents are easily digested by all mammals but the cell walls, composed of strengthening fibres, are partially digestible only to microorganisms capable of digesting cellulose. Secondary compounds are chemicals such as tannins and phenols which inhibit the digestive processes, and poisons such as alkaloids which may be lethal (Rozenthal and Janzen 1979).

When plants are growing, the photosynthetic parts contain large proportions of cell contents, but as they mature and become senescent, so the concentration of fibre increases, especially in the dead leaves and stems. Furthermore, many plants actively move cell contents into the root systems at the end of the growing seasons.

The herbivores. Some LMHs are 'monogastric' – they have simple stomachs with one compartment only. They include the subungulate (elephants), Perissodactyla (horses, rhinoceroses, and tapirs) and Suidae (pigs) of the order Artiodactyla. These animals grind their food into small particles when they first ingest it, liberating the cell contents of the walls which surround them. The cell contents are digested as the food passes through the stomach and small intestine, and the nutrients derived from the call contents are assimilated immediately.

The fibrous cell walls then reach the large intestine, where the cellulose and any cell contents which have so far been shielded from digestion are attacked by micro-organisms. Part of the cellulose is degraded into volatile fatty acids which are absorbed through the gut wall and are used to provide energy.

The digestibility of plants depends largely on the amount of cell contents relative to cell walls. Large amounts of fibre present a problem to herbivores not only because fibres are difficult or impossible to digest but also because they are so tough that they may protect a considerable amount of cell contents from the animals' enzymes and micro-organisms, with the result that the cell contents are excreted undigested. When there is a high proportion of these fibres in forage, its digestibility may be as low as 35 per cent (Robinson and Slade 1974). In such circumstances, monogastric animals could in theory assimilate more nutrients by eating as much food as the diameter of the alimentary canal will allow. Daily dry matter intake can be as high as 4 per cent of body weight per day in elephants.

Most LMHs are not, however, monogastric but have stomachs with more than one compartment. These animals ruminate, and they maintain populations of symbiotic micro-organisms in the stomach. This group includes the hippopotami, the Ruminantia, the Camelidae (camels, lamas, and vicunas) and, of course, the Pecora (such as bovines and antelopes) in which the multi-compartmented stomach reaches its most complex development (Janis 1976).

The ruminants have an elaborate, four-compartment stomach, the largest section of which, the rumen, contains similar populations of micro-organisms to those found in the large intestines of the monogastric herbivores. The digestive processes in the rumen are basically similar to those in the monogastric animals' large intestine, in that cellulose is fermented to produce volatile fatty acids, but the fact that the site of fermentation is at the beginning of the alimentary canal has two important consequences.

The first is that large fragments can be regurgitated and re-chewed (ruminated) to expose a greater surface area to the micro-organisms and to release any cell contents protected by fibre in the larger fragments. Food particles are not able to leave the rumen until they are smaller than a certain size; this means that the rumination/fermentation cycle exposes much of the plant tissue (cell contents and fibre) to digestion by enzymes and micro-organisms, and ruminants get more out of the coarse plant matter they eat.

The second consequence is that the cell contents are subject to microbial activity before they can be digested and assimilated in the alimentary canal. This is particularly important for dietary protein, most of which is in fact denitrified by rumen micro-organisms (Hungate 1966); the animal therefore depends for its protein largely on microbial protein, which is digested in the small intestine as micro-organisms leave the rumen. Fibrous plant matter takes longer to be broken up and thus has a longer retention time in the rumen; for this reason ruminants actually eat less when diet quality is low.

Seasonal requirements of LMH. Animals require nutrients for many purposes, the most costly being maintenance and reproduction. The cost of maintenance depends primarily on body size, climate, and season; in tropical areas, seasonal variations are slight compared with those found in temperate areas where maintenance costs are at a maximum in winter, when rates of nutrient assimilation are at their lowest (Moen 1973). The costs of activity have been estimated by Osuji (1974) and are often about 70 per cent of maintenance.

Reproductive costs are very high. At the peak of lactation, females require more than twice the cost of body maintenance; and, during the rut, male deer lose 35 per cent of their body weight (Nordan, Cowan, and Wood 1968). The peak of lactation is short-lived (1–4 months); typically it occurs in the season when the rate of nutrient assimilation is maximal, the wet season in the tropics and spring in temperate climates. In species where the gestation period is not close to 12 months (such as the red deer), it is impossible for both the peak of lactation and the rut to occur at the time of peak nutrient assimilation. In such cases, it is the rut that occurs at a nutritionally less favourable time (Moen 1973).

The time of reproduction in females is therefore a good indicator of seasonality in rates of nutrient assimilation, and examination of the state of protein and energy reserves at the time when female reproduction is at its least costly (dry period or early pregnancy) will give useful information as to the extent to which the population is resource limited.

Resource partitioning. There are some important differences in the morphology of the stomach within the suborder Ruminantia. Hofmann (1973) has shown that there are considerable differences in the size and degree of papillation of the rumens of two broad classes of species, the 'concentrate' feeders and the 'roughage' feeders. Concentrate feeders (such as dik-dik and goats) are generally small, have highly papillated rumens and feed selectively on plant parts and species which have high concentrations of cell contents (green leaves, forbs, and browse) while roughage feeders (such as wildebeest, buffalo, and cattle) tend to be larger, to have less papillated rumens and feed on a broad range of plant material, including the more fibrous fractions. The latter benefit from the greater quantity of food available although it is less digestible. A further group (the 'intermediate' feeders such as impala) have diets which are similar to those of roughage feeders in the growing seasons but they switch to browsing when good-quality graze is sparse. These animals show adaptations like those of the roughage feeders for reducing the rate of passage of fibrous particles, but the structure of their ruminal mucosa shows marked seasonal changes which correspond to the changes in diet quality.

Quality and quantity. Herbivores rarely eat all the food available to them. More often, they feed selectively, preferring certain usually high-quality foods and avoiding others. As preferred foods become rarer, the herbivores switch from preferred foods to ones of lower quality. Low quality usually means low digestibility and throughput rate, thus a lower intake rate. For these reasons, not only are the nutrients less digestible but less is eaten.

In these circumstances, nutrient deficiencies occur. Though intakes of calcium, magnesium, and some vitamins can be inadequate (Underwood 1977), the commonest deficiencies are in energy and protein. There has been some discussion as to which is the more important but the levels of digestible energy and protein in forages are so closely correlated (Van

Soest 1982), and the metabolism of nitrogen and energy in the ruminant so intertwined, that they can be separated only with difficulty. This has been demonstrated in experimental work on growth rates of cattle which were fed diets with varying amounts of protein and energy (Blaxter 1975). For these reasons, diet quality should be measured both in terms of protein and energy, and careful attention must be paid to the state of body reserves of both of these nutrients – body fat and labile body protein.

What happens when vegetation is of such poor quality that ruminants cannot digest it fast enough to maintain weight? There are two broad options for survival (Bell 1969; Jarman 1972).

The first option is to continue to feed largely on what remains of the high-quality plant matter such as the leaves of deciduous shrubs and trees, and the green leaves of grasses and forbs which often comprise as little as 10 per cent of the sward (Duncan 1975). Such a strategy assumes a small mouth size, and sharply limits body size.

The second option is to *increase* body size. A large animal can maintain weight on a diet of large amounts of nutrients which are of low digestibility and which can be digested only slowly. A small animal cannot.

These considerations, which are discussed in detail in Van Soest (1982), are important in understanding the use that herbivores make of plants. They imply that each species has specializations (body size, rumen morphology) which allow it to exploit efficiently only a part of the spectrum of plant matter. In any ecological system which contains both graze and browse, there will therefore be a number of niches available to mammalian herbivores which, together, will exploit the primary production more fully than can any one species alone.

The range and population densities of herbivores in an ecosystem depend on the amount and nature of the available food at critical times of the year. Studies of herbivore/plant interactions are needed to identify these critical times, either to obtain information on the functioning of natural ecosystems or to improve the economic exploitation of the systems. The following sections outline some of the methods available for determining how LMHs use primary production, and for identifying the critical times of the year.

2.7.1. Use of primary production by wild and domestic herbivores

The food available to LMH is always a mixture of variable quality. Not surprisingly, the animals' ranging behaviour is rarely random – they use their resources selectively.

Selectivity in the use of primary production is expressed at several levels. An animal first selects its home range, and the sum of the individual ranges is the population's range. Secondly, the animal selects certain vegetation types in which to spend most of its time; many factors, such as distance from water, affect this choice. Finally, the animal selects some plant species and parts from those that are available in the vegetation type. Because the main determinant of diet quality is the nature of the forage available (Dudzinski and Arnold 1973), the use an animal makes of the primary production will depend on decisions made at all levels. It follows that measurements of primary production will reveal little about LMH unless their eating habits are very well known.

2.7.2. Population ranges and the use of vegetation types

Aerial counts can often provide the data necessary on animal abundance but ground counts are needed when:

- an independent check on bias in aerial census is required;
- aircraft are not available;
- the terrain is too hilly or woody for accurate aerial counts;
- the animals are small, nocturnal or cryptic;
- it is necessary to obtain separate information for habitats, age/sex classes of animals, or activities which cannot be identified from the aircraft;
- simultaneous data on densities and habitat parameters (such as chemical composition of the herbage) are required.

The first step is to decide what precision and what accuracy are required. In particular, must absolute density be measured or is relative density sufficient?

It is often unnecessary to measure absolute densities – for example, when determining migration routes or the choice of a road system for game viewing. Many indices of relative abundance have been used but their value depends on standardizing the conditions in which the observations are made. Most workers have found it is more effective to use an accurate method of measuring absolute density than to spend a great deal of effort in standardizing a measure of abundance.

There are basically two methods of estimating abundance:

- counting occurrences of animals or their sign;
- measuring changes in the composition of a population caused by removing or adding known numbers of one type (such as males or marked animals).

The second technique always gives a measure of absolute density but counts of animals or their sign can provide either relative or absolute density. Thus, counts of faecal pellet groups (FPG per ha) provide a measure of relative density; if the rate of appearance of FPG per deer per day is known, then absolute density can be calculated.

Many questions can be solved with data on relative density: for example, are there more deer in the forest this year than last? Is the density of deer higher in regenerating than in mature forest? Yet data on relative abundance are not often used. Caughley (1977) has argued that because estimates of absolute density are usually more costly, more effort should be put into defining questions in terms which allow indices of relative density to be used. However, methods for measuring relative density are often superficially simple. When using them conscientiously, the investigator will often find that to standardize his work he is led naturally to use methods which provide data on absolute density.

The aim of this section is to give an overview of the range of methods available and the kinds of assumption they involve. It draws heavily on three recent reviews (Norton-Griffiths 1978; Caughley 1977; Davis and Winstead 1980).

2.7.2.1 Counting the occurrence of animals Animal counts always measure the ratio of numbers of animals or sign to a standard. The standard may be a unit of area, distance (impala seen per km of road), time (bongo drinking at a water-hole per day) or effort (roan antelope shot per man-day). The principal assumption is that each animal has the same constant probability of being counted (or shot).

Per unit area. The principals of ground counts are exactly the same as for aerial counts. Special problems include:

1. They take longer than aerial counts.
2. The observer is more likely to disturb animals; this can lead to undercounting.
3. Visibility is poor when vegetation is tall; this causes either an increase in time spent per unit area, or undercounting.

However, a properly conducted ground count in good conditions (habituated animals and good visibility) can be accurate enough to estimate bias in aerial counts. The two main problems are first to choose and locate the sample areas and, second, to minimize counting biases.

The fraction of the area sampled depends principally on the time and resources available, the size of the area, the degree to which the animals are clumped and the precision required. High precision, large resources, a small area, and a clumped distribution of animals means a high sample fraction, and vice versa. The methods of choosing sample areas are the same as for aerial counts.

Quadrat (block) counts may be preferred in areas with gulleys and rivers where block limits can be identified accurately and access is easy within but not between areas. An example is the work of Field and Laws (1970) in the Ruwenzori National Park, Uganda. A total count is a special case of quadrat sampling, and is preferred when the area is relatively small and well mapped; when visibility and access are good; and when the density of animals is low and/or clumped (Foster and Kearney 1967). The ideal conditions for a total count are found in a crater or valley where the whole area can be searched and the animals mapped with a telescope from a single vantage point (Sinclair 1977).

Transect counting provides narrower confidence limits than quadrat counts when the animals are clumped. When access allows, the transects are chosen as for aerial counts, either mutually parallel or in random directions through random points (Western 1973). The transects are drawn on a base map and the observer locates them in the field with reference to topographical features. The exact length of the transect is measured on the map, and with the kilometre gauge or pedometer on the ground.

In some studies, transects have been counted along a road system, but this is far from ideal: animals may not be randomly located with respect to roads (Rost and Bailey 1979) and roads are built along contour lines, so road transects are never representative of the areas they cover (Norton-Griffiths 1978).

The crucial task is the choice and measurement of transect width. Any mistake will lead to bias errors of unknown direction and magnitude. There are two basic approaches: the observer can count animals in a band of fixed width or he can count all animals and measure the distance from the animals to the transect. This information will allow him to calculate the transect width after the event.

Fixed-width transects are preferred. Clearly the wider the transect, the smaller the variance; the maximum width which all animals can be seen will depend on visibility. In grassland, 400 m on either side of the vehicle has been used (Western 1973) but in bushland or woodland careful trials are necessary to determine the safe upper limit (Jarman 1972). The observer then measures the actual width in the field with a calibrated rangefinder. He may use different widths in different habitats. A variant of the fixed-width transect which is particularly useful when simultaneous data on habitat conditions are required involves counting animals within circles of fixed radius centred on the transect, systematically or randomly (see Norton-Griffiths 1973). Habitat data can be obtained after the count at the centre of the circle, or throughout it.

When animal densities and visibility are low, the number of (narrow-width) transects necessary to obtain reasonable confidence limits becomes impossibly high. Many workers have preferred to use a transect method with a variable strip width which is calculated *a posteriori* from the actual distances at which animals were seen. The main problem is that there is no theoretical basis on which to choose a method for estimating strip width and so no consensus as to how a field worker should proceed (Eberhardt 1978; Davis and Winstead 1980).

Many methods use the mean 'flushing distance' (Davis and Winstead 1980) as the mean transect width. This always leads to an underestimate of strip width and thus an overestimate of the population because the mean flushing distance cannot include the area effectively searched *beyond* the animals counted. Kelker's transect method is unsatisfactory because it is arbitrary and the only approach which seems to hold some promise is that of Anderson (see Robinette, Loveless, and Jones 1974). But investigators determined upon this approach should read Burnham, Anderson, and Laake (1980) and Eberhardt (1978), and obtain professional advice.

Counting biases occur in both quadrat and transect counts; they are caused by double or undercounting. Double counting happens when animals move from a part of the sample area which has been counted to a part that has not. Undercounting can result from animals leaving a part of the study area before they have been counted or from a failure to sight groups. Both types of error occur only in counts of large quadrats and both are minimized by:

1. Dividing the block into natural subunits which are searched systematically along the long axis of the block. An overlap zone should be counted on adjacent subunits.
2. Marking the location and composition of each group on the map as well as the path of the observer, and noting the time taken to count.
3. Keeping careful note of the movements of animals which have been counted.
4. Making use of helpers to drive and/or spot.
5. Knowing the area and animals well.
6. Restricting this kind of count to animals which are not too mobile and which have a short flight-distance.
7. Conducting the count reasonably quickly.

These biases will not necessarily be self-compensating and are not easy to measure. When large blocks are counted by several observers, then the record of the location of groups in the overlap zones between subunits can be used to estimate the degree of undercounting. The mapped path of the observer will indicate any areas missed, and the relationship between density and the time spent searching per unit area will indicate the optimal searching speed. This kind of analysis is essential if large blocks are to be counted accurately.

One source of undercounting is common to all counts: undercounting the number of animals in a group. This is minimized when the animals' flight-distance is short and when the observer has a roof hatch, a pair of binoculars, and a tally counter or tape recorder.

From what has been said, it is clear that fixed-width transect counting usually gives the most reliable results.

Distance Methods. The distance from a set of randomly chosen points or individuals to the nearest individual can provide a linear measure of density. When the animals are randomly distributed then

$$D = (n-l)/x^2 \cdot n,$$

where D = density of animals per km^2, n = sample size, and x^2 = mean of the squared distances.

The assumption that the animals are distributed randomly is weak; when their distribution is only moderately contagious, then the method of Batchelor and Bell (1970) will still give an accurate estimate of absolute density. If the animals' distribution is highly contagious, then the distribution of the *groups* may be sufficiently random to allow the investigator to estimate the density of groups in this way. The density of individuals can then be estimated from a knowledge of mean group size, a parameter which can usually be estimated with great precision and accuracy.

In many species, group size itself increases with, and provides a useful index of, density (Christie and Andrews 1964). However, if, as so often happens, group size varies as a function of other variables such as season and habitat, it is necessary to restrict comparisons to the same time of year and habitat. This method is particularly well suited to species with groups of fixed membership such as zebra, feral horses, and vicuna. Smuts (1976) has shown that the smallest groups of zebra in the Kruger National Park occurred in the area with the lowest densities.

Group size should be used as a density index with great care because:

1. It may be difficult to define groups objectively.
2. Size varies with other factors (such as season).
3. The relationship is often non-linear.
4. The mechanisms involved are not well understood (Caughley 1964).

It is often obvious where one group ends and the next begins because the distances between groups are much greater than those between members of the same group. Where this is not so, statistical methods of analysing the frequency distributions of the distance between one animal and its next forward neighbour are available for determining objectively exactly how far apart animals should be to belong to different groups (Clutton-Brock, Guinness, and Albon 1982, Appendix 12).

Catch per unit effort. Catch per unit effort (CPUE) is never used to estimate the density of LMH but it does allow the density of a managed population to be monitored at little extra cost. The method was developed, and is used, extensively, in fisheries (Beverton and Holt 1957). An index of hunting success, the number of deer reported killed per year divided by the number of hunting licences bought per year, has been used to show how the Californian deer population changed between 1927 and 1960 (Dasmann and Dasmann 1963). A similar index has been used in Africa to examine the response of LMH to an attempt to reduce their numbers for tsetse control (Child, Smith, and von Richter 1970).

The CPUE is linearly related to density if:

1. The catch is made in standard conditions (climate and season, for example);
2. The equipment, and number and skill of the personnel is standardized;
3. The catching of one animal does not affect the probability of catching another. This assumption is clearly violated when single-catch traps are used.
4. The behaviour of the animals towards the catching technique does not change – a problem which bedevils applications of the method to large and small mammals alike.

The method has been used only rarely for LMH because these assumptions are rarely fulfilled in harvesting schemes. However, if it is possible to obtain accurate information on the changes in catch per unit effort as a population declines due to harvesting, then the size of the original population can be estimated by Leslie's or DeLury's methods (Caughley 1977).

2.7.2.2. Removing or adding known numbers of animals If the exact number of LMHs which have been removed or added to a population over a period is known, then absolute numbers can be estimated from any index of relative density (index calibration method).

If the animals can be classified into two types (such as male and female) and the numbers of each type removed or added are known, then the change in the ratio of the two types which is caused by a *selective* removal or addition can be used to estimate the absolute numbers of the two types (Kelker's method).

Index calibration. If a population's density is monitored by any linear index of abundance and a known number of animals is removed, then the index can be calibrated and the absolute densities before and after removal calculated.

The calibration can be done equally well by *adding* a known number of individuals. In this case, the increase in the index is measured. The main problem here is that the animals must increase the index as a function of their numbers only. If their behaviour differs from that of the residents the method may not be valid. This would occur if the index was a road count, and newcomer deer from a deer farm hung around the roads waiting for feed, or if the index was catch per unit effort and the newcomers were easier to shoot.

The usual assumptions (no births, deaths, immigration, or emigration) apply, which limits applications but the method is useful for estimating isolated populations of seasonal breeders.

Natural mortality will cause a downward bias in the density estimates from removals and an upward bias in estimates from additions. If natural mortality is negligible compared to the number added or removed, then the estimates will be accurate. Removals should therefore be done over a short period. Precision, on the other hand, is always a problem because the correction factor depends on the difference between two estimates, each of which has a variance. Both accuracy and precision are improved when the number of animals removed or added is large, and when the operation is done over a short space of time.

A final method, the *comparative index* (Caughley 1977) is simple but ingenious. It is useful on the sadly rare occasions when the target population lives in the same area as another population of known density. The investigator needs to calculate only the ratio of the numbers of the two populations to calculate the density of the other.

In the Camargue, France, it was known that there were 3510 cattle in an area of 420 km^2. The ratio of horses to cattle on a representative area was 0.875. The density of horses was thus $3510 \times 0.875/420 = 7.312$ horses/km^2.

The reference population need not be a mammal – it could be a heron, a tree, or any object whose abundance relative to the target species can be estimated accurately and precisely in the study area.

Kelker's method. When more than one class of individual can be recognized in a population and the ratio of the classes is changed by selective removals and/or additions, then the absolute size of the population can be estimated.

For example, suppose an original population of unknown size (N) is known to consist of equal numbers of males and females, and 30 females and 20 males are added to it. A survey then reveals that 48 per cent of the new population is male. The number of males in the new population is $0.5N + 20$ which must equal $0.48(N + 50)$. Hence N is 200.

This method was originally developed for sex ratios and male-biased harvests (Kelker 1940) but has since been generalized to cover additions as well as removals, and can be used for classes such as different colours, ages and even species (Caughley 1977). Appropriate formulae can allow for natural mortality and for extended periods of addition or removal.

The method is therefore extremely flexible but can be used only on populations where all removals and additions are known, where births and deaths, immigration, and emigration do not occur or are known, and where the class ratios can be estimated accurately and precisely before and after the addition or removal.

Capture–recapture. This method has been used widely in studies of the ecology of large and small mammals in temperate areas, but rarely in Africa. It is appropriate for relatively small populations where individuals can be caught easily. It can provide data on many population statistics other than size, including movement, fecundity, mortality, and the rate of change of population size.

For example, suppose 10 animals out of a population of N are caught, marked, and released. Some time later, a further 10 animals are caught, of which 2 are found to be already marked. The proportion of marked, recaptured animals is $2/10$ and this must equal the proportion of marked animals in the original population which is $10/N$. Hence $N = 50$.

The simplicity of the calculation contrasts with the complexities raised by the assumptions behind it. This depends on the model used, and therefore on the use to which the results will be put. For calculations of population size, the following must all apply:

1. Marked and unmarked animals must be equally catchable.

2. Animals' marks must not be lost.

3. Mortality rates of marked and unmarked individuals must be identical.

4. There must be no births or immigrations.

However, another technique may be more appropriate to the questions asked or to particular field conditions. The investigator should choose his technique only after a careful study of the literature – Seber (1981) and Caughley (1977) are two good starting points – and preferably after a pilot study to test the assumptions of the chosen technique. Small departures from the assumptions can cause serious errors.

2.7.2.3. Methods involving animal sign In theory, a wide range of animal signs can be used to estimate relative or absolute densities of LMH, such as plants bitten, defaecations, or cast antlers. In fact, only one has been used to any extent: the density of defaecations (Neff 1968; Cairns and Telfer 1980). Most work has been done on deer, which produce many pellets in a single defaecation; counts are made of these groups of faecal pellets (FPG). This method provides mean density over a period of time and has the important advantage of integrating information from day and night and over different meteorological conditions.

If more than one LMH is present, the observers will need to be able to distinguish the FPGs of the target species from others. Even for such dissimilar animals as roe and red deer, this is not always possible. The method is clearly inaccurate for animals which form dung piles. Unfortunately, these include all Perissodactyls and most of the abundant African ruminants such as wildebeest, topi, and the gazelles.

In some studies, the density of FPGs has been measured (Batcheler 1975), while in others it is the accumulation rate (FPG/ha/day, Bailey and Putman 1982). Density depends on the rate at which FPGs are deposited *and* the rate at which they disappear. FPGs disappear when scattered or broken up by rain or animals, and the disappearance rate may vary considerably. It is therefore preferable to estimate the rate of accumulation. This necessitates more than one visit to each plot. On the first visit FPGs in the plots are cleared or marked with paint or lime. The plots are later searched for new FPGs.

The estimate of accumulation rate will be accurate if:

1. The sampling design is unbiased.

2. No FPG disappears before it can be sighted.

3. All FPGs present are identified and recorded.

The time lapse between the first visit, for clearance or marking of FPGs, and the count depends on many factors including access and accumulation rate. It must not be so long that some FPGs disappear. Disappearance rates are so variable that they should be studied directly by visiting a number of plots regularly (say twice weekly) and marking each new FPG with a numbered stake. A record of the state of each FPG at each visit will allow the sensible choice of a maximum time lapse for the study of plots. Periods of heavy rain must be avoided.

The accumulation rate is an accurate index of animal density if the defaecation rate is constant. This assumption must be tested; in some species, defaecation rate varies between the sexes and between age classes (and even with seasonal changes in diet – see Neff 1968). Finally, defaecation rates vary with animal activity – horses defaecate more often when feeding than when resting.

2.7.2.4. Use of vegetation types Data on the use of different types of vegetation for feeding can be obtained only when the animals are observed in undisturbed conditions. Occasionally, such data are best obtained by radio-telemetry (Cheeseman and Mitson 1982). Aerial counts are unsuitable, as are catch per unit effort and the methods involving sign. All the other methods can be adapted by simply recording the activity of each animal and the vegetation type in which it is when first seen.

Petrides (1975) has introduced the terms 'principal' and 'preferred' resources. The principal feeding habitats of a population are those which are most used, and they can be ranked in terms of the percentage of feeding time spent in them or the number or percentage of feeding animals seen in them. The preference shown for a habitat can be measured by Hunter's index (Hunter 1962) which is the percentage of time spent in a certain crop divided by its percentage area of the habitat.

This could be the first step in an investigation of preferences. For example, why are there twice as many animals as one would expect in one kind of vegetation, and why only one-fifth in another? Approaches to these questions can be found in Belovsky (1981) and Duncan (1983). See also Johnson (1980) and Cock (1978) for a more detailed account of the drawbacks of Hunter's index and the alternatives available.

2.7.3. Herbivore diets

Animals are confronted with a wide range of possible foods, eating some and rejecting others. This section is concerned with methods of studying the composition of the diet (Holechek, Vavra, and Pieper 1982).

2.7.3.1. Diet components Fragments of individual plants can be identified either by eye or microscopically. The structure of the epidermal hairs is rather constant within species but varies enormously between species and this method has been used in many studies (Hercus 1960; Stewart 1967; Olsen and Hansen 1977). First, a reference collection of slides is made of all the plant species occurring in the study area (Stewart 1965). The characters of each species are then described, with variations, and a set of microphotographs is made as a supplement to the description.

Categorization by taxonomic group (species or higher) has several advantages. First, it is hierarchical, so that the investigator can choose from a broad range of levels of precision. In some studies, the species level has been used (Cederlund, Ljungqvist, Markgren, and Stalfelt (1980), identified 44 taxa in the diet of moose) while in others broader categories have been preferred. In a study of red deer, Van de Veen (1978) separated eight categories.

The second advantage is that knowledge of species helps in the interpretation of results. For instance, the species can be grouped according to their habitat, their size, their growth form, or their concentration of secondary metabolites. This may help the investigator understand the causes and functions of a particular diet.

A knowledge of the species composition of the diet is essential to the study of the impact of LMH on vegetation: data on the specific composition of the diet can be confronted with data on availability, and

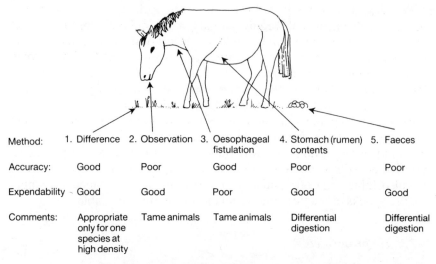

Method:	1. Difference	2. Observation	3. Oesophageal fistulation	4. Stomach (rumen) contents	5. Faeces
Accuracy:	Good	Poor	Good	Poor	Poor
Expendability	Good	Good	Poor	Good	Good
Comments:	Appropriate only for one species at high density	Tame animals	Tame animals	Differential digestion	Differential digestion

Fig. 2.13. Summary of the methods available for the study of diets of large mammal herbivores. The methods are evaluated according to their accuracy, and the degree to which their results can be expanded to a free-ranging population.

preference or avoidance determined for each species. This knowledge can then be used to interpret changes in the flora.

The major disadvantage of this system is that plants include many different types of food: leaves are generally far better than stems or twigs, for example. The method is also lengthy, particularly if it is decided to identify fragments at the species level. In a recent study Tieszen, Hein, Ovortrup, Troughton, and Imbaba (1979) distinguished monocotyledons from dicotyledons chemically.

It is generally possible to separate the larger plant parts (root, stem, leaf sheath, leaf, flower, seed) by eye. The smaller fragments must be separated microscopically (Gwynne and Bell 1968). Such data permit comparisons between the diets of different sexes and species, and also a rough evaluation of seasonality in diet quality.

2.7.3.2. Units of measurement The use made of dietary components has been measured in a variety of units including weight, volume, bites, and feeding minutes. Clearly, the last two are less accurate than the first two since both intake per bite and intake per minute can vary (Allden and Whittaker 1970).

2.7.3.3. Methods of obtaining samples The five principal methods are:

- the difference method (measurement of the sward before and after grazing)
- direct observation (bite counts or feeding minutes)

- oesophageal fistulation
- rumen or stomach-content analysis
- faecal analysis.

In each, the data are collected at a different stage of the process of feeding – a fact which has consequences which will be discussed below. The utility of each method depends on two criteria: the accuracy of the description of the diet it produces; and the validity with which the results can be expanded from the sample to the whole population.

The difference method. When a single species of herbivore uses a sward, it may be possible to obtain data on its diet by measuring the amounts of each component in the herb layer before and after grazing. The assumptions of this method are that there is no growth or loss between measurements and that only one species is removing significant herbage. The first assumption is met only when the grazing occurs in the space of a few days. This does happen in some domestic grazing systems but only occasionally in the wild. Though neither assumption is met very often, if the method can be used it is undoubtedly the best available.

The amount of each component can be measured by clipping a sample of the sward. When only a few easily recognized components are being studied such as leaf, sheath, and stem, these can be sorted by hand, dried, and weighed. When a larger number of components is studied, an indirect method is preferred.

Direct observation. This method has been used frequently on wild (Lamprey 1963; Leuthold 1970; Croze 1974), tame (Field 1968; Le Resche and Davis 1972), and domestic animals (Allden and Whittaker 1970). For wild animals, it has proved successful only when the object was to estimate roughly the proportions of obviously different components of the diet, such as graze and browse: as Talbot and Talbot (1962) note, it is almost impossible to identify with certainty the grass species bitten by an animal, since the observer will normally be at least 20 m away. With tame grazers, however, the difficulty is not so acute. Counts of the numbers of bites on each grass species can be made if the individual plants are easily recognizable and well separated.

The proportion of bites on a given species, together with mean bite size, will give the proportion of the diet composed of that species, which can then be compared with the available proportion in order to assess selectivity. A variant of this method is to count the number of plants of different species which have been bitten in an area recently grazed by a herd (Du Plessis 1972).

In some studies it has been assumed that bite size is constant (Field 1968; but see Le Resche and Davis 1972). However, Allden and Whittaker (1970) show that, in sheep, bite size can change by a factor of ten. Methods of estimating bite size are either very crude, or involve oesophageal fistulation. Other drawbacks include the fact that it is not possible to estimate the proportions of different plant parts in the diet and that the method often involves the use of captive animals.

Both the bite count and oesophageal fistulation methods differ from stomach content or faecal analysis in that they usually provide information on the diet of an animal over a short period only. It is important that observations are designed to represent accurately all the habitats used by the animals during a 24-h period. It is also important that the animals are exposed to the grazing conditions well before measurements are made: Allden and Whittaker (1970) found that sheep placed in sparse pastures refrained from grazing if they had been in abundant pastures before the experiments.

Oesophageal fistulation. Oesophageal fistulation is a surgical operation which leaves a hole from the oesophagus to the outside through the neck. Normally, the hole is closed by a plug (van Dyne and Torrell 1964; Taylor and Bryant 1977) designed to maintain the size of the hole and to prevent loss of saliva and food. During a grazing experiment, the plug is removed and ingested food is collected in a bag placed around the animal's neck (Marshall, Torrell, and Bredon 1967; McKay, Frandsen, Odero, Sondergaard, and Nganga 1969; Langlands 1966; Arnold, McManus, Bush, and Ball 1964).

If all the food passes out, this provides accurate information on the diet of the animal: however, there are difficulties in extrapolating from the fistulated animals to the wild population, since the operation may affect grazing behaviour, and since it is normally possible to work with only a small number of captive animals. Grazing may be affected by discomfort at the fistula, causing the animal to select a softer diet than normal; this has been observed in cattle where the fistula has failed to heal (M. D. Gwynne, personal communication). In some cases, failure to heal may result in enlargement of the fistula and a leakage of saliva. Since nitrogen is passed into the rumen as urea in the saliva (Munro 1964), salivary loss leads to nitrogen loss which may result in deficiency for which the animal may attempt to compensate by altering its feeding behaviour. However, when the operation is done correctly the presence of a fistula need not affect feeding. Powell, Clanton and Nichols (1982) have shown that there are no significant differences between fistulated and non-fistulated steers in either daily intake or in weight gains.

The need to handle the animals dictates that tame, captive individuals are used and, when they are caught very young, isolation from their normal environment can lead to differences in feeding (Leuthold 1971). This is less important when older animals are caught (Usenik, Krelen, and Duncan 1977). Further, the few captive animals that are used may not represent the different age and sex classes in the population and their number may be insufficient to study individual differences in diet.

The method has been used mainly on domestic animals, where only the difficulties relating to surgery are relevant (Van Dyne and Torrell 1964; Arnold *et al.* 1964; Bath, Weir, and Torren 1956; Hamilton, Hutchinson, Annis, and Donnelly 1973). There have been studies of wild animals involving fistulation (deer, Veteto, Davis, Hart, and Robinson 1972; topi and wildebeest, Usenik *et al.* 1977). As Talbot and Talbot (1962) remark, oesophageal fistulation is 'the most potentially accurate and satisfactory means' of studying the diet of wild herbivores.

Stomach analysis. The proportions of different dietary components in the rumen or stomach have been used as measures of the proportions of these components in the diet, and this is probably the most widely used technique in studies of the diets of LMH (Medin 1970).

However, different components may have different fibre contents, digestibilities (Terry and Tilley 1964), and rumen retention times (Laredo and Minson 1973). Clearly, if some components pass through the rumen more slowly than others, then a measure of these components in the rumen will over-represent their proportion in the diet (Campling, Freer, and Balch 1961). In caribou, for instance, the effects of differential digestion were so great as to invalidate the method (Bergerud and Russell 1964).

The biases thus introduced tend to underestimate the proportion of the less fibrous components in the diet; and they will be greatest at the end of the growing season since the differences in retention times between leaf and stem are then most marked (Laredo and Minson 1973). No satisfactory way of making the necessary corrections has yet been devised.

Recently, Tieszen *et al.* (1979) have used the fact that in lowland East Africa the photosynthetic pathways of most browse plants and grasses are different, the former proceeding via three-carbon molecules and the latter via four-carbon molecules. The plants are therefore referred to as C_3 and C_4 respectively. The proportions of C_3 and C_4 tissues (and thus the browse/graze ratio) in a rumen sample can be determined rapidly but the problem of differential digestion remains.

Stomach analysis provides data which can easily be expanded to the wild population, provided that the shot animals are taken at random (Du Plessis 1972). Bias error is much less of a problem in monogastric species such as zebra than in ruminants and can probably be safely ignored.

The distribution of particles in the rumen is not random: coarse fragments tend to occupy the dorsal and fine ones the ventral sac (Evans, Burnett, and Bines 1974); it is therefore important to sample the rumen contents so as to represent all the layers.

Faecal analysis. This technique (Stewart 1967) is similar to rumen-content analysis and has been widely used (Stewart and Stewart 1970; Hansen and Clark 1977). But the problem of differential digestion is more acute even than for the analysis of stomach contents.

Careful experiments with captive animals (Stewart 1967) have shown that the method depends on being able to take into account not only the differential digestibilities of the diet components but also differences between animal species in their digestive abilities. The problems are much less acute with monogastric species: faecal analysis is an accurate method with zebra, for instance (Stewart 1967; Owaga 1977).

A large number of faecal samples can be easily collected from the wild population and the method allows evaluation of seasonal, sexual, and individual differences in diet, as well as the possibility of investigating dietary changes with age and social status of a particular animal.

Faecal analysis is therefore a useful method in studies with such aims as: description of developmental and seasonal changes in diet; comparisons between individuals of different sex; social status of herd; and obtaining approximate information on the diets of species with unknown food habits.

2.7.3.4. Analysis The samples will be of two types – whole plants clipped for the difference method and samples of chewed plant matter from the others.

The clipped samples and parts of oesophageal samples can be sorted manually when wet or dry, but should be dried again before weighing because dry plant matter is hydroscopic. This method is commonly used when only a few easily recognizable components are studied (Chacon, Stubbs, and Haydock 1977).

Where data on more than about six components are required, it may be more efficient to use an indirect technique (Heady and Van Dyne 1965). These techniques depend on the fact that the area percentage of a plant component is often a good measure of its percentage by weight (Holechek and Goss 1982). This is not the case with components with very different densities, such as leaves and woody twigs, in which case correction factors must be developed (Heady and Van Dyne 1965). If the components are easily distinguished, a technique such as the point frame of Chamrad and Box (1964) or the point quadrats of Gwynne and Bell (1968) is appropriate.

Identification is more rapid and accurate on large fragments. In many studies, the investigators have therefore sieved out the smaller and studied only the larger particles. In such cases, tests should be done to compare the values for the components' proportions obtained from analyses of large and small particles. If these values are not different (Dirschl 1962), then only the large particles need be studied, but where there are differences (Bergerud and Russell 1964) both fractions should be analysed, separately or together. Chacon *et al.* (1977) were able to sort oesophageal samples into leaf and stem manually, except for a residue of small fragments. This was examined microscopically and then assigned a score of 0–10 for its leaf proportion. This procedure allowed accurate determination (error of less than 5 per cent) for grass samples but led to an error of 10 per cent for legume leaf.

When the microscope is used, slides are prepared and a number of fragments (say 50–100) chosen for identification. A common method of choosing fragments is to use a microscope with a 10×10 grid on one of the lenses, and to consider the 100 fragments under the intersections. The fragments can be recognized by a variety of characters, mainly in the plant epidermis, by reference to previously prepared photomicrographs. The identification of the specimens for the reference collection should be confirmed by a specialist.

A different analysis will be needed to answer each of the questions addressed. Typically, these include:

1. What is the diet of a herd of animals?
2. How does this vary seasonally?
3. Are the animals feeding selectively? If so, what are their preferred plants?

The data used in the following example are from a study of the diets of Camargue horses (Skelton 1978), based on the analysis of plant species proportions in the horses' faeces. At monthly or bi-monthly intervals, the research worker followed the herd and over two days collected one sample of about 100 g (dry) of faeces from each horse. The samples were stored after drying but could equally well have been preserved chemically (Stewart 1967) if they were not destined for chemical analysis. The material used for studying the overlap of horses and other herbivores comes from Hansen and Clark (1977) and was obtained using similar methods.

In the Camargue study, the accuracy of calculating dietary plant proportions from faecal material was tested by feeding known natural diets to stalled animals. The only species underrepresented in the faeces were Leguminosae. These formed less than 5 per cent of the annual diet, so the faecal proportions were taken as diet proportions.

Where little is known about the population being studied, a useful first step is to use a variant of factor analysis to expose the main sources of variance in large multivariate data sets. Correspondence analysis has been used extensively to display the main sources of variation. This technique has the advantage that both the individuals and their attributes can be plotted on the same ordination. The mathematical basis for the method can be found in Fisher (1940) and an evaluation of its utility for biological data in Hill (1974).

The analysis provides:

1. A measure of the importance of each axis – the percentage of the total variation in the data set it accounted for;

2. A measure of the importance of each individual and attributed in the construction of each axis: this information gives a basis for the interpretation of the biological 'meaning' of the axes; and

3. A coordinate for each individual on each axis: this allows the ordination of each individual and attribute on any two axes to be drawn, which display their relationship visually.

The technique has been used extensively in vegetation science and for the study of animals' time-budgets (Duncan 1980).

The matrix used in this analysis of the diets of Camargue horses is shown in Table 2.5. The proportion of the variance accounted for by the first axis of the correspondence analysis (44 per cent) is much greater than the other two. The importance of each attribute in the construction of the three axes is given in Table 2.6.

Two grasses characteristic of the edges of marshes, AE (*Aeluropus littoralis*) and PA (*Paspalum distichum*) are overridingly important in axis 1, while for axis 2 these and HO (*Hordeum* spp.) are important. In a case such as this, where one axis is overridingly important, it often happens that the second axis is largely a reflection of the first. For the third axis, a perennial grass DA (*Dactylis glomerata*) and an annual genus HO (*Hordeum* spp.) were important.

The ordination based on axes 1 and 2 is shown in Fig. 2.14. It is clear that the horses fall into two groups, composed of members of two different social units. The bachelor herd had a diet characterized by a higher proportion of AE and the breeding herd had a diet with more PA. The significance of such differences is measured with an appropriate test (Sokal and Rohlf 1969). The second and third axes were not interpretable in terms of any variables such as age, sex, reproductive state, or rank.

The conclusion of this analysis was that for these horses the most important factor determining the diet of any one of them in that season was the type of herd it belonged to.

This procedure can then be repeated in each herd separately to identify other important sources of variance which might have been masked by the strong first effect. Once the main sources of variation in diet have been isolated, the diet of the population can be calculated by weighting the categories in proportion to their abundance or biomass. The latter is generally more accurate because, as a first approximation, body weight gives a rough estimate of daily dry matter intake.

Table 2.5. Percentages of 11 plant taxa in the diets of Camargue horses

	Plant taxa										
Individual	AE	AG	BRA	DA	HO	HA	PA	PH	SC	IR	BRO
9	3	5	3	9	3	2	31	28	12	7	0
5	1	7	3	9	3	2	20	38	11	6	2
7	3	6	2	12	5	0	19	35	12	8	0
C1	2	6	0	13	5	1	14	39	10	10	2
1	3	10	2	16	5	2	14	33	9	6	2
D2	0	9	0	17	5	3	10	40	9	9	1
E1	0	11	4	19	0	3	8	43	9	6	0
G3	4	7	0	12	3	2	15	36	15	8	0
H2	0	10	0	10	0	3	16	36	16	12	0
G2	17	12	0	20	5	0	0	31	12	5	0
G4	16	11	0	16	0	2	0	34	15	5	3
H1	11	20	3	12	1	0	7	31	12	4	2
H4	13	13	0	8	4	3	2	39	12	5	3
I3	8	23	1	10	4	2	7	30	13	6	0
I4	8	18	3	8	2	1	0	40	19	2	0
I5	13	15	0	12	1	2	2	38	18	2	0
I6	19	18	0	11	0	1	2	32	17	2	0
J1	14	7	0	9	0	3	7	36	20	5	0
I1	2	11	0	21	0	0	10	38	12	7	0
I2	0	8	0	18	2	3	13	42	14	2	0
I7	3	9	0	17	0	0	19	38	11	5	0
I8	4	6	0	4	0	2	16	45	13	12	0
J2	0	8	2	11	2	2	16	39	10	13	0
J3	4	17	1	16	3	0	9	32	14	4	2
J4	2	14	2	17	2	1	16	26	10	10	2
J5	2	8	3	13	0	6	16	39	9	5	2
J6	3	17	2	20	0	0	4	39	12	6	0
J7	1	12	2	9	0	1	9	45	17	5	0
K1	2	13	2	11	0	2	9	42	13	7	0
K2	2	8	0	13	2	3	7	43	17	6	0
K3	0	17	0	10	2	0	5	45	18	4	2
K4	2	15	0	8	2	2	9	43	16	4	0
K5	3	9	2	5	0	2	3	51	17	9	1
K6	2	13	0	16	0	3	11	23	21	11	0
K7	0	9	1	7	0	0	17	43	20	5	0

Seasonal variations in diet can also be tested using correspondence analysis with the population diet on a given sampling date replacing the individual animals in the analysis. Alternatively a cluster analysis such as single or average linkage (Morgan, Simpson, Hanby, and Hall-Craggs 1976) can be used. An example is shown in Fig. 2.15.

The only distinct cluster is composed of the four samples from the spring (30.4–16.6). Within the rest, there is another relatively well

Table 2.6. Importance of plants in construction of three axes

Plant	Importance on axes axis 1	axis 2	axis 3
AE	5.2	0.7	0.3
AG	0.6	0.2	0.3
BRA	0.1	0.0	0.1
DA	0.0	0.0	0.6
HO	0.0	0.7	0.4
HA	0.0	0.0	0.1
PA	3.3	0.7	0.2
PH	0.0	0.4	0.0
SC	0.1	0.2	0.2
TR	0.4	0.0	0.0
BRO	0.0	0.1	0.1

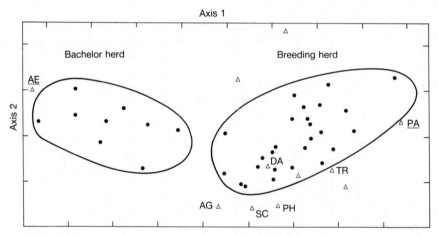

Fig. 2.14. Ordination of the summer diets of all the horses in the two herds.

defined cluster comprising the samples from mid-winter (18.12–2.3), which was flanked by two pairs of samples before (19.11–2.12) and after (23.2–9.4).

The samples from the summer and autumn are more heterogeneous; none the less, the July samples are distinct from an autumn cluster (21.8–7.11). However, two autumn samples are only weakly linked with the others of that season, 17.8 and 10.9. In general, therefore, the samples do cluster according to season. This analysis is a representative, and not a statistical technique, and the significance of differences between the seasons must be tested. The values in the cells are the percentage of each plant in the population's diet transformed by arcsine. Inclusion of a separate matrix for each herd allows the significance of differences

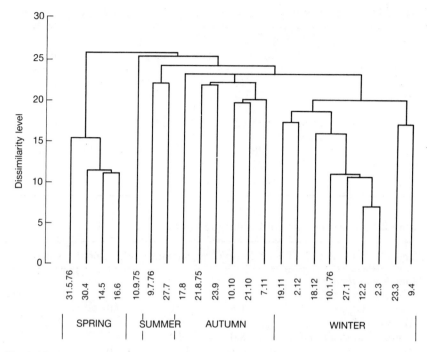

Fig. 2.15. Classification of the sample weeks by single-link cluster analysis.

between dietary composition in different herds and seasons to be tested at the same time, using a three-way arova (Sokal and Rohlf 1969). In this case, the main effects – Season and Herd – are of no interest, since the same number of plant fragments was always identified, and the totals did not vary. The interactions interest us particularly, because these test the significance of differences between seasons and herds in the species composition of the diets.

The result is shown in Table 2.7. The main effect, Plant is, not surprisingly, highly significant. Over the year, there were principal plant species and minor species. The interaction Plant/Season was highly significant, confirming the statistical validity of the classification. Herd/Season, however, was not significant, showing that the classification, based only on the data from the breeding herd, was valid for the bachelor herd, too. Herd/Plant, as expected, was highly significant, confirming that the diets of animals in the two herds did differ. The diets for the four seasons are given in Table 2.8.

Selectivity in foraging is tested by comparing the composition of the diet with the composition of the herbage on offer. The composition of the herbage should be determined using the same method of analysis as for the diet, and samples of the herbage should be cut to ground level in

Table 2.7. Variance analysis for two herds of Camargue horses

Source	Sum of squares	D.F.	Mean square	F	P
Plant	8114.1	14	579.6	44.8	0.001
Season	117.0	4	29.2	2.26	n.s.
Herd	14.9	1	14.9	1.54	n.s.
Interaction Plant/Season	8339.2	56	148.9	11.5	0.001
Interaction Herd/Season	2.3	4	0.57	0.05	n.s.
Interaction Herd/Plant	786.0	14	56.1	4.34	0.001
Interaction H/S/P	723.8	56	12.9		
Total	18097.3	149			

Table 2.8. Seasonal diets of Camargue horses

Plants	Spring	Summer	Autumn	Winter
Annuals and geophyte monocotyledons				
Juncus (JU)	11.8	0.0	0.0	2.7
Bromus (BRO)	9.8	0.7	0.0	0.0
Carex + Hordeum (HO)	8.0	3.1	0.3	1.7
Scirpus (SC)	16.1	11.3	0.0	0.0
Phragmites (PH)	17.8	36.1	23.8	3.8
Marsh Grasses				
Paspalum (PA)	0.0	16.0	15.0	8.9
Aeluropus (AE)	0.8	1.6	3.5	2.0
Perennial grasses				
Dactylis (DA)	16.8	12.7	1.3	0.0
Agropyron (AG)	14.9	7.7	30.1	40.0
Brachypodium (BRA)	0.8	1.4	16.9	10.8
Perennial halophytes				
Halimione (HA)	0.2	1.8	7.2	20.2
Arthrocnemum (AR)	0.0	0.0	0.0	2.0
Others	3.0	7.7	1.9	6.3

an appropriate sampling design. A typical result from such an analysis is shown in Table 2.9.

A problem with this kind of analysis is to decide what to include in the available food. In this case, we have not included woody vegetation. Had we done so we would have obtained rather different results, for the woody vegetation was abundant but was not used by the horses.

2.7.3.5. Impact of herbivores on the vegetation With a knowledge of the principal and preferred plant species of the LMH in an area, be it a

Table 2.9 Selection of herb layer components in the spring.

Plants	Herbage (%)	Diet (%)	Selection (diet/herbage)
Annuals and geophyte monocotyledons			
Juncus	0.8	11.8	14.8
Bromus	4.8	9.8	2.0
Carex + Hordeum	2.2	8.0	3.6
Scirpus	5.7	16.1	2.8
Phragmites	5.6	17.8	3.2
Marsh grasses			
Paspalum	0.6	0.0	0.0
Aeluropus	2.4	0.8	0.3
Perrenial grasses			
Dactylis	7.5	16.8	2.2
Agropyron	9.0	14.9	1.7
Brachypodium	2.3	0.8	0.3
Perennial halophytes			
Halimione	45.3	0.2	0.0
Others	14.6	3.0	0.2

National Park or a ranch, the manager may wish to evaluate the impact of the animals on the vegetation. Because LMH generally feed selectively, they inevitably reduce the biomass and vigour of preferred species compared to ones they avoid.

The detailed consequences depend on the site but in general grazing and browsing lead to an increase in structural and species diversity. Heavy grazing can so depress the preferred plants that the secondary productivity is diminished. Heavy browsing can so reduce the annual growth of trees that recruitment to the fire-resistant age classes is virtually nil (Pellew 1983).

The most satisfactory approach is to study the population dynamics of individual plant species which are of particular interest to management (Harper 1977; Pellew 1983). In many exploratory studies, cages of varying sizes (0.0001–1 ha) have been constructed so as to exclude the larger herbivore from sample plots ('exclosures') and the performance of the plant communities monitored when released from pressure by these herbivores.

In heavily grazed areas, the exclosures will rapidly develop a plant cover which is so much taller and denser than the surroundings that the exclosures begin to act as islands for small mammals and invertebrates which are rare or absent elsewhere. At this stage, interpretation of the meaning of changes in the plant communities becomes difficult and the exclosures may have outlived their usefulness.

2.8. Nutrition and population dynamics

There is little information on the dynamics of large mammal populations other than man. This is particularly true of wild LMH. The long lifespan and large size of these animals mean that the time and effort required to obtain adequate data to study the dynamics of these populations are much greater than for small mammals or invertebrates.

However, this kind of study may be needed to manage an LMH population effectively. Generally, management aims to keep the population between desired limits in the most economic way possible. The most common problem is that a population of a rare species, such as mountain zebra, declines dangerously fast. Alternatively, a population of, say, buffalo may become large enough to cause agricultural damage, or the manager of a deer population may wish to know how many animals hunters should kill to maximize the useable yield.

An analysis of population dynamics may help to avoid the costly mistakes which sometimes result from management by trial and error. Before undertaking such an analysis, the researcher should read Caughley (1977) and Fowler and Smith (1981).

The essential data for an analysis of population dynamics are

- the size of the population
- the composition of the population by age and sex
- the rates of age-specific fertility and fecundity (conceptions and births per female and per year)
- the rates of mortality between conception and birth, and between birth and recruitment to the breeding population
- the rate of adult mortality, ideally for each year class separately.

The size of the population can be estimated from aerial or ground counts, and the proportion of males and females from representative ground samples. The age structure can be determined by ageing a random sample of the population, or by constructing a life table from a collection of skulls of animals that have died naturally.

2.8.1. Body condition

The most common problem in the nutrition of free-living LMH is a protein–energy deficiency. In seasons of reduced plant growth, the animals often survive by drawing on body reserves of energy and protein.

Knowledge of the degree and timing of this use of body reserves is an important aid to understanding the performance of a population – some populations of LMH are regulated by mortality due to starvation at times when body reserves are inadequate to see the animals through a period of dietary deficiency (Sinclair 1977).

To assess an individual's condition, it is necessary to know the amount of protein and fat in its body, and the minimum amounts necessary to support life. The minimum values are not generally known (but see Wallace 1948 for cattle), so we are generally restricted to describing the differences between individuals in total fat and protein.

2.8.1.1. General body condition A generalized measure of condition, which varies with changes in either fat or protein, is live weight (Dudzinski, Schuth, Wilcox, Gardiner, and Morrisey 1978; for a portable balance, see Low and Hodder 1976). However, the measure becomes much more sensitive if corrections can be made for variations in gut fill, individual differences in skeletal size and variation in conceptus weight in females. Variations in conceptus weight can be corrected for if the age and growth rate of conceptus is known (see Hugget and Hammond 1952 for sheep).

Differences in gut fill can be minimized by taking the measurements at the same time of day; or, if the animals are dead, by measuring the field-dressed weight (live weight, less blood, and the internal organs from oesophagus to rectum, including the alimentary canal, heart, respiratory organs, pancreas, liver, and reproductive organs). The alimentary canal may be emptied and this and the other tissues weighed separately. The mesentary is usually left with the alimentary canal, but care should be taken when removing it to leave the kidneys and their associated fat with the carcass.

Field-dressed weight is not a particularly sensitive index of condition because variations of 10 per cent or more, due simply to differences in skeletal size, are common (Lowe 1972). Several different approaches have been used to remove this effect. In most cases the weight is divided by a length (such as body length or mandible length) though Laws, Parker and Johnstone (1975) divided the cube root of body weight by the shoulder height. The weight of a cleaned bone (tibia) has also been used (Duncan 1975).

A satisfactory index of skeletal size must be easy to measure accurately in the field and should be appropriate for both live and dead animals. Body length measured along the curves is perhaps the best (Caughley 1971).

Unfortunately, conditions can vary considerably between individuals at any one time, and changes may be rapid at some times of the year (Caughley 1970). Large and frequent samples are then necessary to obtain accurate and precise information. Often this is neither feasible nor desirable, so several workers have developed visual and/or tactile classifications of condition (Riney 1960; Lowman, Scott, and Somerville 1976).

These are all based on the fact that as subcutaneous fat and muscle protein are used up, the bones protrude markedly – particularly the ribs, the lumbar vertebrae, and the pelvic girdle. On this basis, Pullan (1978) has developed a classification for tropical cattle, and Pollock (1980) one for horses.

In using such indices it is as well to standardize the light conditions and distances at which observations are made: the elevation of the sun, in particular, can effect visual impressions of bone protrusion.

If it is possible to use both visual and measured indices of condition, then opportunities should be taken to calibrate the visual method against measurements of condition.

2.8.1.2. Fat reserves Two measures of fat reserves have been used widely in studies of LMH: the kidney fat index (KFI), and the marrow fat index (MFI). The KFI is a good index of total body fat and the MFI is a good indicator of prolonged malnutrition, since the marrow fat is the last body fat to be used up (Ransom 1965; Sinclair and Duncan 1972).

The KFI is measured by loosening a kidney, together with the fat surrounding it, from the liver and back muscle. In very fat antelopes, the fat deposit continues in an extension of the kidney mesentery for as much as 30–40 cm posteriorly. Traditionally, the fat has been trimmed, but a more sensitive index is obtained by weighing all the fat (Mitchell, McCowan and Nicholson 1976).

Other workers have preferred not to use the weight of the kidney, because it can vary seasonally by more than 30 per cent (Dauphine 1975; Mitchell *et al.* 1976) and because it increases if the animal is stressed (by wounding) before death.

A less widely used index of body fat is the depth of the subcutaneous fat on the rump. This method has little application for tropical ungulates which deposit little subcutaneous fat but has been used for horses. It has the great advantage that subcutaneous fat can be measured indirectly by the use of ultrasound (Westerfelt, Stouffer, Hintz, and Schryver 1976); it is also a better index of fatness in the upper part of the condition range than the KFI (Finger, Brisbin, and Smith 1981).

2.8.1.3. Protein reserves Animals with diets deficient in protein can draw on some of the protein in their skeletal muscles (Wallace 1948). The weights of such muscles can therefore be used as indices of the animal's protein status.

A satisfactory muscle for this index is the semitendinosus, a small well-defined muscle block in the posterior hindquarter. The weight of this muscle, corrected for body size, has been used as an index of body-protein levels (Duncan 1975). Another suitable muscle block is the extensor muscles of the tarsus. These are attached to the tibiofibula and are very well-defined.

2.8.2. *Nutritional value of the diet*

The capacity of an animal to grow and reproduce is primarily determined by its genotype and by the nutritional value of its diet. In most free-ranging LMH, the limiting factor is generally diet, hence the importance of understanding the nutritional value of the diet and its seasonal variations. This is determined by the rates of assimilation of nutrients such as protein and energy, minerals, and trace elements. In addition, some fibre is necessary for the proper functioning of the ruminant alimentary canal (van de Veen 1978). There are no essential amino acids for ruminants, but young equids require thymine (Robinson and Slade 1974); other non-ruminants probably do, too.

Nutritional value is measured by estimating the daily intake and digestibility of dry matter, or of each nutrient separately. When daily assimilation rates are known, these can be compared with known or estimated requirements for maintenance, and for reproduction and growth, to assess the nutritional status of the animals, seasonality in nutritional status, and long-term trends in nutritional status. This has been attempted only rarely for free-living LMH (Rees 1978; Stanley Price 1978). Such investgations require specialized knowledge and equipment (Moen 1973; Robbins 1983) beyond the capacity of most ecological monitoring programmes.

However, several indices of nutritional status are easily measured and can be of considerable value in identifying seasonal and long-term nutrient deficiencies.

A deficiency of any of the essential minerals or trace elements can limit secondary production, and excesses of some, such as selenium, can have the same effect. However, for free-ranging LMH trace element deficiencies are unusual though mineral deficiencies are more common (Underwood 1977). Mineral and trace element deficiencies can generally be detected by measuring nutrient concentrations in the blood (Payne, Drew, Manston, and Faulks 1970). Although these concentrations are buffered by body nutrient reserves, prolonged dietary deficiencies cause the levels to drop. Sampling during the major dietary seasons will generally expose any important deficiencies.

The interpretation of values obtained from a sampling programme requires a knowledge of the 'normal' values of these parameters. Detailed information is available in the literature for cattle in temperate conditions but data on other regions and species are sparse. Fortunately, there are broad similarities between species which mean that the cattle data can be used to identify gross abnormalities until better data are available (Rees 1978).

2.8.2.1. Protein–energy nutrition Measurement of protein concentration is costly, so in most studies nitrogen concentrations are measured and multiplied by a constant (6.25), as the average percentage of nitrogen in protein is 16 per cent.

Stomach content samples have been used for nitrogen determination (elephant, Malpas 1977; deer, Klein and Schonheyder 1970) but the only really satisfactory material for the direct determination of nutritional value is oesophageal fistula samples. Acosta and Kothmann (1978) have shown that the chemical composition of such samples is not significantly different from the composition of the diet. Where dietary energy is to be measured, the samples should be freeze-dried to minimize the enzymic degradation of soluble carbohydrates.

It is well known that faecal and dietary nitrogen values are closely correlated, provided that the animal is in positive nitrogen balance (Jarrige 1965; Bredon, Harkes, and Marshall 1963) and that it is not eating plants with high levels of phenolics (Mould and Robbins 1981). Faecal nitrogen determinations can therefore be used as an index of seasonal differences in dietary nitrogen.

The concentration of urea nitrogen in the blood (BUN) has also been used as an index of dietary nitrogen (Torrell, Hume, and Weir 1974). This index can give useful information on seasonal changes in dietary nitrogen but comparisons should be restricted to a single class of animal. Growth and production, in particular lactation, may cause variations in BUN but dietary differences cause much greater variations (Payne, Drew, Manston, and Faulks 1970).

Faecal nitrogen and BUN are useful indices of nutritional status of a population of animals. However, individual variations in digestive physiology are such that comparisons between individuals are unlikely to provide accurate information on differences in nutrition (Torrell *et al.* 1974).

2.8.3. Analysis of population dynamics

The aim of such an analysis is to identify the factors controlling population density. This means measuring inputs to the population (births) and losses (deaths). The results can be summarized in a life table.

2.8.3.1. Ageing animals Two kinds of method have been used to age animals: one applies to subadult animals and relies on developmental characters such as colour, horn size and shape, and the dental formula; the other applies to mature animals and relies on changes in the structure of the permanent teeth. These characters must be calibrated on animals of known age. This has been done for many species but more data are still required.

In some species there are distinct changes in coat colour during the first year. Topi calves are born fawn coloured, develop black patches on their flanks at two months, and become reddish like the adults by three months (Duncan 1975).

Horn shape and length have been used as an index of age in buffalo (Sinclair 1977) and goats (Brandborg 1955). Changes in body size are particularly useful where aerial-photographic samples are used. This method is applicable to very large herbivores; for other species see Rogers (1979), and Larson and Taber (1980).

When it is possible to handle animals, and their teeth can be examined directly or by making casts, the developmental changes in the dental formula provide an indication of age. However, the age at which each tooth erupts varies considerably – in buffalo, for example, by as much as six months (Grimsdell 1973).

The age of an adult can be estimated by assessing its general appearance; this is particularly easy with horned animals because the horns become worn and/or broken with age. More precise age classes can be defined with reference to tooth wear. This method has been used widely in studies of wildlife (Larson and Taber 1980) but is not very accurate in older animals because there is considerable inter-individual variation. Another major problem is that absolute ages cannot be assigned to the age classes without a large number of animals in which the stage of tooth wear and age are both known.

The most popular method is to count the annuli in the cementum of teeth. In LMH which have seasonal variations in diet quality, the cementum laid down in periods of poor nutrition is denser than at other times, and thus appears as 'rest lines'. Where there is one period of poor nutrition per year, the number of rest lines is equal to the number of years since cementum was first deposited around that tooth (Keiss 1969).

In Ugandan buffalo, Grimsdell (1973) found that the first year was not represented and that subsequent years had two rings each, possibly corresponding with the two dry seasons in that area. The method is generally accepted as accurate to within one year for most individuals.

Many variants have been used (Fancy 1980). Incisiform teeth are easy to collect and store but they are often not available because they are quickly lost from skulls in the field, so molars have been used in many studies. The teeth should be preserved – see Grimsdell 1973. Several sections should be examined from each tooth and the number of rest lines counted.

Where a large number of animals is to be aged and accuracy is not at a premium, the relationship between age (from cementum lines) and the

mean height of enamel on the first molar (Grimsdell 1973) can be calculated. The height of the enamel from the base of the root to the top of the
cusps can be measured with calipers. Once the relationship between age
and enamel height is known, the ages of a large number of animals can be
estimated rapidly with reasonable accuracy (Grimsdell 1973).

2.8.3.2. Reproduction The rate and the timing of the reproduction in a
population are both sensitive to external factors, especially nutrition
(Lamond 1970). Careful description of reproduction can therefore
provide useful information.

Reproductive rate (fecundity, calves per female per year) is the difference between the rates of conception (fertility) and of foetal mortality
(abortion plus resorption). In most studies, it is not feasible to measure
these parameters separately, and the population fecundity rate is taken as
the pregnancy rate of a sample of females examined post-mortem.
Because the pregnancy rate can vary considerably between years, and is
always age dependent, reliable data can be obtained only if a large,
random sample of females is taken. In seasonal breeders, the sample
should be taken when the females are in late pregnancy.

In some circumstances, it is possible to estimate the rate of fecundity
from a series of estimates of the calf/female ratio. The method involves a
number of assumptions which are not always justifiable (such as
constancy of new-born mortality rate between seasons and years) and it
is important that the results obtained are checked against those obtained
independently (see Sinclair 1977).

The timing of births can be determined approximately by counting the
ratio of new-born calves to females. However, where new-born mortality
varies, the results will be biased, and the method is inapplicable to
species in which the new-born calves hide. A more accurate method consists of calculating the age of the foetuses collected from shot samples of
females. The age of a foetus can be determined from its weight (Huggett
and Widdas 1951).

2.8.3.3. Disease, parasitism, mortality, and life tables Disease and parasitism may often be proximate rather than ultimate causes of mortality
(Sinclair 1977). None the less, they can be important in the regulation of
population density. Parasitism can, for instance, profoundly affect the
ability of animals to digest their food (Reveron and Topps 1970). Diagnosis requires specialized knowledge, and most field ecologists confine
themselves to conducting a general examination and collecting samples
for further analysis. Correct diagnosis will largely depend on the
accuracy and completeness of the description of the animal and relevant
circumstances, and of the selection and preservation of samples.

Like fecundity, rates of mortality vary with animal age, and often vary
between seasons and years. To obtain accurate and precise values, data

must be collected over a number of years which depends on the variance between years. For most LMH, three years is a minimum.

Data on mortality rates in small closely watched populations can be collected directly by observation, but usually the investigator will have to do this indirectly by constructing a life table for each sex, based on a knowledge of the proportion of the dead population which is comprised of each age class. The dead population is usually sampled by collecting skulls found in the field, and it is clearly necessary that the sampling programme be designed so as to represent the whole population accurately. In many species, the skulls of males are more durable than those of females and mortality rates differ, so the sexes should be treated separately. The skulls of young animals are more fragile than those of adults, so an independent method must be found to estimate mortality in these age classes. In most LMH species this is possible by direct observation for the first two years. For more detail, the reader is referred to Quick (1963), Caughley and Birch (1971) and Caughley (1977).

2.9. Social and economic surveys

Awareness of the need for ecological monitoring has increased in recent years as industrialization, population growth, and increased mobility have radically altered the quality, quantity, and spatial distribution of natural phenomena such as forests, wildlife, and water-bodies. Whereas monitoring concentrated initially upon the description of the numbers and distribution of particular phenomena, it is now recognized that in order to understand, predict and plan for ecological change it is also important to study the interactions between social and economic processes and the environment.

The study of the relationship between people and the environment has been transformed from the limited concept of environmental determinism so popular earlier in the century into an interdisciplinary approach embodying concepts drawn from the natural, social, and behavioural sciences, and is perhaps best exemplified by the work of geographers and human ecologists. People are seen both to respond to and to alter the environment to attain specific social and economic objectives.

An important theme in these studies has been to demonstrate the relevance of an historical approach. Social, economic, and environmental processes tend to act on different time-scales. For example, economic plans are frequently drawn up on a five-year basis, social processes such as changes in landholding patterns or in food consumption may take generations and climate may fluctuate over decades or centuries. Consequently, the full repercussions on the man–environment system of the implementation of a policy designed to achieve specific economic objectives relatively quickly may not be apparent immediately and, in time, unintended feedbacks may appear.

It may be that the origins of contemporary ecological problems can be traced to decisions taken years ago, decisions which at that time might have appeared to have little impact on the environment as it was then understood. For example, in the semi-arid lands of both east and west Africa, population movements from adjacent more humid areas were initiated by social and economic changes brought about by the colonial economies in the 1920s and 1930s, and developed into major flows in the 1950s and 1960s. The increase of population and the changes in land use from pastoralism to crop agriculture which altered population densities and distribution, and also the area's vegetation, took place during the years of relatively regular rainfall of the 1950s and 1960s. Over the long-term, however, the climate of Africa's semi-arid region is more variable and traditional societies in the areas had adopted strategies for coping with fluctuations in rainfall. The changes which occurred during the years following World War II were made with little attention to longer-term climatic variability and with the onset of the droughts of the 1970s they were shown to be detrimental both to people and to the environment over the longer term. In this way, short-term objectives created long-term problems (Berry, Campbell, and Emker 1977).

Among the individual social and economic factors which relate specifically to the people–environment interaction are those of land ownership and tenure, population growth and distribution, and land-management practices. Understanding of these factors requires analysis at a number of scales. National policies towards settlement, land tenure, agriculture and livestock development, and wildlife management have to be understood and their impact on local production strategies and social systems identified. Once these variables have been determined, the dynamnics of people–environment systems can be studied and the process of ecological monitoring initiated. Thus, in order to understand the relationship between socio-economic processes and environmental quality, ecological monitoring which includes the study of social forces is essential. It should not only describe existing characteristics but should identify processes and place them in an historical context so that predictions about future conditions and their implications for the environment can be made.

This section deals with procedures for conducting social and economic surveys.[1] General principles of data collection and analysis will be presented. It is intended to serve as a guideline for researchers and readers seeking more detailed information about the statistical concepts involved are referred to Blalock (1972), Hays (1973), and Yamane (1973).

2.9.1. Survey design

Though the understanding of contemporary ecological processes involves analysis of social and economic issues, not all the components of social and economic systems are relevant. Thus a first step in preparing this type of socio-economic study must be to identify relevant hypotheses and define appropriate questions. Once these have been identified, a strategy to provide the required information must be developed and implemented.

Definition of the appropriate hypotheses requires a theoretical understanding of the man–environment interaction and experience of the specific area under study. Once a problem has been identified, the relevant questions must be posed. There is a tendency among social scientists in this situation to attempt a complete description of the socio-economic system by asking all questions that come to mind. Such an approach is not only unrealistic but indicates a lack of discipline in formulating the problem. A useful approach is to define a small number, perhaps ten, indispensable questions which will indicate which issues the researcher considers most important. To these questions may be added supplementary ones which will enable the major questions to be fully answered and which will define the data base required to answer them.

The information required by the questions must then be gathered. A number of possible sources should be identified before a costly and time-consuming social survey is embarked upon. It should not be assumed that no data base exists: national governments, universities, and international organizations often gather information which can be invaluable, though problems such as institutional bias, incomplete records, and secrecy may limit their utility (Prewitt 1975). The reports, and even the primary data, of other researchers may be available which may reduce the need for a new research programme. Historical records are particularly important in providing the appropriate context for the analysis of contemporary processes. A search of available information sources, even if it only shows that no appropriate data exists, provides an opportunity for the researcher to become more familiar with the problem and region under investigation and to define more precisely the objectives of his/her own study. At this point, the list of questions can be organized into a logical format so that the type of information still required, the appropriate informants and the alternative data collection methods can be identified.

Having decided upon the nature of the additional information that is needed, the researcher then has to choose informants who will provide it. Not all informants will be in a position to answer all questions and different approaches will therefore be necessary to obtain the information. Government officials may be able to explain government policies but unable to detail their local impact, while local people may not be able to relate local conditions to national policies. Even at a local level not all members of a community may be appropriate respondents; it might be necessary to question only adults, or only adult women or only land-owners. The type of information required will also limit the procedures used to obtain it. General trends or records of events affecting a community may be obtained from group interviews but accurate information on more personal issues such as quantities of crops harvested, livestock ownership, income, and food consumption habits can be obtained only by interviews with individuals, if they are willing to respond. They are less likely to respond to such questions as a group than in a one-to-one interview.

Having defined the most appropriate respondent (sampling unit), a sample must be chosen which permits generalizations about the whole population to be made.

2.9.2. Sampling methods

In most surveys, the object of the research is to generate information about the population[2] in the survey area. To interview the whole popula-tion is usually impractical, and thus a sample of respondents has to be selected which is representative of the total population. The representa-tiveness of the sample will depend upon the sampling methods used and upon the number of interviews conducted. All sampling procedures will provide estimates which are subject to some error and the choice of methods and sample size must be made in recognition of this. Con-straints of time and cost[3] are often major considerations, but it is a false economy to choose a method which results in the researcher being unable to make statistically valid statements.

A number of different sampling procedures can be used. In some surveys, it may be appropriate to sample according to the spatial distri-bution of sample units rather than among all sample units. In this case, rather than drawing the sample from the population it will be drawn by methods which emphasize its spatial distribution. Sampling methods of this type include point, quadrat, and traverse sampling (Yeates 1974; Norcliffe 1977). These methods have the advantage that the researcher need not have a complete list of the population in order to select the sample. However, he must be prepared to make assumptions regarding the distribution of the population and must be aware of potential biases. In many cases, information such as census lists, landholding lists, tax lists, and voter lists may be available, but they may not include the total popu-lation[4] and are frequently out of date. Should lists be unavailable or existing ones inappropriate, then the researcher may need to create his/her own list. This can be time-consuming, but is necessary if the sample is to be representative of the population and the researcher does not wish to select a spatial sampling frame.

If a sample is to be representative of a population, the sampling procedure should reduce the opportunities for bias in sample selection. Random sampling provides the best estimate of population characteristics as each potential respondent has an equal choice of being selected.[5] The accuracy of the estimates provided by the sample depends not only upon the sampling procedures but also upon the sample size itself. In general, the sampling error 'decreases with sample size but at a decreasing rate, so that doubling the size of the sample does not imply that error will be halved' (Yeates 1974). Thus, for a simple random sample Prewitt (1975) presents the following table showing what sample size is needed to meet the degree of errors to be tolerated by the researcher:

Table 2.10. Sample size which produces different levels of precision and confidence: for random samples

Tolerable sampling error is plus or minus	Sample size necessary if you want to be	
	95 per cent certain of your sample estimate	99 per cent certain of your sample estimate
1%	9604	16,587
2%	2401	4147
3%	1067	1843
4%	600	1037
5%	384	663
6%	267	461
7%	196	339

There are a number of different random sampling methods. Simple random sampling consists of selecting a predetermined number of sample units from a population list. Each unit on the list is numbered 1 to N (where N is the number of units on the list) and units are selected using a random-number table. This is an easy procedure to conduct if an appropriate list is available. A similar procedure, but one which is much easier where the list is long or where a large sample is to be drawn, is that of systematic sampling. In this method, only the first unit is selected at random and the remainder are selected according to a regular pattern. For example, if the population consists of 3600 people and the desired sample size is 200 every 18th person on the list would be chosen. In order to select the first respondent, one among units numbered between 1 and 18 would be identified using random-number tables and every 18th after that would be incorporated in the sample. This method should not be used, however, if the population list is not in random order because biases may result.

In some cases, the researcher may want to bias the sample in a pre-determined manner; he may want to ensure that a certain number of units with specific characteristics are included. For example, a study of the effects of farming and herding upon soil erosion would necessitate interviewing both farmers and herders. A random sample of the total population of herdsmen and farmers might not generate sufficient respondents in each group to permit an adequate analysis and thus a sampling method which would provide both a representative sample and a sufficient number of respondents is required. Stratified random sampling and quota sampling are two such methods.

Stratified random sampling can be used when sufficient information is available about the population to stratify it into the appropriate groups for study. The first step is to separate the population into groups with the required characteristics, in this case farmers and herders, and then to select a random sample within each group. This method requires that a list of the population be available as well as the information needed to classify it into groups. If this is not the case, quota sampling can be used to overcome the problem. This method follows a similar procedure to random sampling for selecting respondents. Each respondent is then asked a series of questions to determine the group to which he/she belongs. The required number of respondents from each group is determined by the researcher and the respondents are interviewed until the quota for each group is filled. Should a respondent be selected and the preliminary questions demonstrate that he/she represents a category that has been filled then the researcher should not complete the interview but pass to the next respondent on the list.

These methods are particularly appropriate for ecological monitoring as they permit analysis and comparison of phenomena under different conditions. For example, in the Maasai areas of Kenya, ecological monitoring might require analysis of the environmental impact of agricultural encroachment on grazing land under different conditions of rangeland tenure. A researcher might need to stratify the population of herders and farmers to be interviewed according to their landholding characteristics – those owning individual rights to land, members of group ranches, and those on undemarcated lands.

In both quota and stratified random sampling, it is important to interview sufficient numbers within each group to ensure that generalizations regarding the group can be made. While comparison between groups is facilitated by these sampling procedures, caution is required in generalizing from the groups to the total population as the numbers interviewed in each group are determined by the researchers and may not reflect the relative proportions of each group in the total population.

Sometimes the sheer size of either the area or its population precludes the use of any of these methods. Under such conditions, multi-stage sampling is appropriate. For example, if a study of soil conservation practices in a province of a country were to be undertaken then the sample population might consist of 100 000 landowners spread over 8000 square kilometres. Clearly, it would not be feasible to mount a survey which required a list of the whole population, and even if such a list were available a sample of 500 to 1000 respondents drawn at random would be so widely distributed as to require a major investment in transportation to perform the survey.

A multi-stage sampling procedure would begin by listing all the administrative districts within the province and selecting a simple random sample of them in which to conduct the survey. These would be the first-stage sample units. The problems of logistics and listing would not yet be manageable, however, and further sampling within the districts to select the sampling units would be needed. In each of the selected districts, all the villages are listed and these are subjected to a simple random sample to select a small number of villages in which to conduct the survey. These are the second-stage sampling units. Once the villages have been identified, the survey team will be able to draw a sample of respondents from village population lists which might be available or need to be drawn up.

This method can be adapted to incorporate elements of quota and stratified sampling if that is necessary. For example, the province might include a number of ecological zones and it might be hypothesized that soil conservation practices would differ from zone to zone. In this case it might be appropriate, either at the stage of choosing districts or that of choosing villages, to do so within a context of grouping according to ecological zone.

While multi-stage sampling does reduce problems of survey implementation, the procedure is complex and it is often difficult to generalize to the total population from the selected local study areas.

The different methods outlined above each have specific advantages and disadvantages and they imply varying costs and logistical problems. The choice of the appropriate method depends upon the nature of the problem, the resources of the researcher, the quality of information existing in the survey area, and the analytical procedures available to the researcher. Having decided upon the nature of the sample to be drawn, the researcher has to select an appropriate data collection methodology.

2.9.3. Data-gathering techniques

Much social and economic information is available from such sources as census lists, government reports, research institutes and international agencies. However, this information may not be in a form that can be easily used in ecological monitoring. It may be too general, incomplete, out of date, or biased to reflect the viewpoint of the reporting institution.

In most cases, secondary sources will provide good contextual information which can be of assistance in clarifying hypotheses and data needs but new information will be required for the specific monitoring activity. There is a number of different data-gathering techniques and the choice will depend on the type of information required, and the time and the resources available. All primary data-gathering techniques require contact with the appropriate sampling unit, either directly in the form of a face-to-face interview or indirectly as in the case of a self-administered questionnaire. In preparing for a data-gathering exercise, the first task of the researcher is to outline the objectives of the survey and to formulate the fundamental hypotheses which are to be tested. The degree to which these can be specified depends upon the researcher's existing knowledge, but the exercise is necessary to avoid a situation in which research is conducted without direction.

The choice of survey technique will depend upon the knowledge of the researcher. For example, it would be unwise to mount an extensive questionnaire survey without a great deal of knowledge of the situation under study; a more appropriate procedure in such circumstances would be to conduct a limited exploratory survey to obtain information upon which to base a more detailed one.

The choice of technique will also depend upon the nature of the sampling unit. It would clearly be foolish to attempt a self-administered questionnaire survey, in which questionnaires are mailed to respondents who are requested to complete and return them, in an area with a high level of illiteracy. Similarly, attempts to gather representative general information from large meetings of people in the survey area would be inappropriate in societies which are highly socially stratified and in which only the leader would normally provide information.

Primary information-gathering techniques are frequently classified in two groups, structured and unstructured. The structured approach consists of asking each respondent the same questions in the same order so that the responses will be comparable. Unstructured procedures permit information to be gathered in much less formal situations in which a conversation takes place between interviewers and respondent with the interviewer guiding the discussion to cover the topics under investigation. While this method is applicable only to an interview situation, a structured approach can be applied in both interview and self-administered questionnaire situations.

Unstructured interviews are particularly useful in situations where the researcher has little knowledge of the topic under study. It often provides a basis for a more rigorous structured survey at a later time. The unstructured approach is flexible in that it permits the researcher to follow any interesting topic that may arise and thus allows access to a wide variety of information. The principal problem, however, is the difficulty of comparing responses and developing generalizations.

In a structured survey a set of questions must be prepared, all of which will be posed in the same order to the selected respondents. The method is inflexible in terms of the questioning process, but is flexible in terms of the interview situation and the latitude permitted in acceptable responses. Structured surveys can be conducted in the form of question-naires submitted to individuals (either self-administered or in the inter-view format), discussions with individuals, or group interviews. Whether the questions are open-ended or closed can influence the quantity and comparability of information received.

Open questions are phrased in such a way that the respondent is free to reply as he/she chooses, while in closed questions the choice of responses is limited to those selected by the researcher and the respon-dent is forced to choose among them. Each has its advantages and dis-advantages: closed questions limit the range of possible responses and may not elicit what a respondent really thinks. They do, however, permit much easier and less costly data analysis than open questions. The major difficulty with open questions is in the coding process in which the responses must be summarized into a manageable number of response categories. This can be costly and time-consuming.

Open questions are appropriate where the researcher has little infor-mation on the range of likely responses while closed questions can be formulated only if the researcher is already knowledgeable about the situation. One way of reducing the problems associated with summariz-ing open questions is to precode a series of likely responses to each ques-tion and to add to each question an open response category 'other responses'. A range of likely response categories to each question can often be provided from the background research for the survey.

The primary data required from a survey can be gathered from a number of primary sources such as individual members of a community, community leaders, government officers and groups of people made up from the population being studied. The quality and representativeness of the information will vary from source to source and thus the choice of response situation will greatly influence the nature of the analysis. When the survey seeks to identify general information about an area it would be costly and time-wasting to ask a large number of people to give responses. For example, if an inventory of local services such as schools, dispensaries, markets, and principal crops produced was required, then an interview with several hundred individuals would not yield substan-tially greater information than an interview with an individual or small group of local leaders. Such people can also describe contemporary and past developments in an area which might be relevant to the survey in providing a historical context for studying ecological related phenomena.

Village leader interviews have the advantage of providing general information quickly and are a good basis for preparing a more detailed survey. The researcher needs to be aware, however, of the possibilities for the information to be biased to portray good leadership by the élite.

A more representative forum is that of the group interview in which a general meeting is called in a survey location and a series of questions posed. In many societies, group discussions form the basis of local decision-making and if the researcher can gain the confidence of the people sufficiently to adapt his data-gathering technique to the traditional discussion format then a great deal of accurate and representative information may be obtained. There are, however, many potential drawbacks to this method and the researcher must be very deliberate in his interpretation of data gathered in the group interview context.

A major constraint is that of identifying how representative those present at the meeting are of the total population. A meeting called by a chief who may have been imposed upon the population may be boycotted by those resenting the chief, and thus the group might reflect the views of the local political hierarchy more than those of the local population. It is advisable when calling such a meeting to advertise it through a variety of channels such as the chief, the local school, and a local mission in order to attract as many people as possible.

Even if a representative group were present, the social circumstances might inhibit representative statements being made. For example, it is unusual for everyone to speak and the most vocal, often the leaders, can easily dominate the meeting; also it may be considered impolite to disagree, to argue, or to criticize other people in public. If a consensus is to be obtained from group meetings then they must be organized to facilitate participation of those present. One method of doing this is to break the meeting up into smaller groups to discuss specific questions and then report back to the whole group on their deliberations. This strategy has the clear advantage of promoting greater participation but to be successful the research team must be large enough and skilled enough to ensure that each subgroup addresses the same set of questions and that the results of discussion are accurately reported back to the group meeting.

Properly conducted group meetings can provide a large amount of highly representative information at low cost. Also the lack of mystery surrounding the data-gathering procedure can facilitate co-operation between the local people and the survey team which might be invaluable at the later stage of implementing activities devised on the basis of the survey (Campbell 1984).

The group meeting should not only be viewed as a means of gathering information but also as a forum for assessing information gathered by other methods such as a questionnaire survey, for evaluating the interpretation of that information and for discussing policies which might be proposed on the basis of the information. Such post-survey meetings can also be used to dispel the resentment generated by many researchers who are seen to gather data and then disappear with it, as if it were their property and of no interest to local people. A consequence of this attitude is that in some areas in which surveys are regularly conducted people are refusing to co-operate as they have had no feedback from previous ones.

The most widely practised technique for gathering primary data is that of the individual questionnaire interview. Such an exercise is time consuming and expensive, and it requires careful preparation and supervision, but properly managed it can produce statistically analysable information which can be generalized to a wide area or populations. The questionnaire interview technique involves interaction between a trained enumerator (interviewer) and a respondent selected from a population according to a specified sampling procedure. The advantage of this method is that it should enable the respondent to express opinions without interference from others, it allows for specific information on the individual's circumstances to be obtained and, as all respondents are asked the same questions in the same order, the variability within the population can be captured and analysed.

The interview is, however, an intense experience for both interviewer and respondent. It is an interaction in which a stranger is posing detailed questions regarding often very personal characteristics of the respondent.

The co-operation of the latter is essential to the success of the process and thus every effort should be made by the interviewer to encourage it. It is often difficult to isolate the respondent from relatives, friends or curious onlookers, yet this should be done to ensure privacy. Much depends on the skill of the interviewer who must initially create a working relationship with the respondent, ask all the questions on the questionnaire, follow up responses conscientiously while discouraging discursive diversions, and complete the interview in a reasonable time to prevent the respondent becoming bored, tired, or irritated and thus providing thoughtless or misleading information.

The enumerator can be assisted in this by careful training and by a carefully prepared questionnaire which includes only those questions that are relevant to the survey, is organized to facilitate a logical flow of questions and which effectively limits the interview to two hours.

The first step in constructing a questionnaire is to specify the information which is indispensable to testing the fundamental hypotheses of the research. This serves to focus attention on questions which will elucidate the necessary data and restrains the researcher from asking all the possible questions that might be asked. Having confined the research solely to the subject under investigation, the questions should be placed in a logical order so that the interview will flow easily from topic to topic. The initial questions should demonstrate an interest in the respondent as an individual and aim to set him/her at ease in the interview situation. Most surveys require some biographical information about the respondent which focuses attention upon the respondent and is not difficult for him/her to provide. To begin with, more sensitive information such as income, number of livestock owned, and access to credit could easily lead to a refusal to participate in the interview though the same questions might be answered without difficulty if asked later in an interview when the respondent and enumerator have developed more of a relationship.

In ordering questions it should also be recognized that some will be more easy to answer than others. To obtain accurate information, the respondent will need to have time to consider his/her responses. One means to facilitate the flow of information is to lead into discussion of a topic with a small number of relatively unimportant and easily answerable questions in order to set the respondent thinking along lines which will enable more difficult questions to be answered. For example, if a researcher in a semi-arid area were interested in peoples' reaction to drought it might be appropriate to begin the discussion with questions relating to behaviour during the annual dry season. Once the subject of reaction to dry conditions is raised, the examination of behaviour in past droughts is easier.

While careful ordering of the questions can facilitate the interview process, it is the wording of the questions which determines the quality of the information available for analysis. It is essential that each question be specific and unambiguous. Each question should contain only one question, technical terms which might be understood by some respondents and not by others should be avoided and if quantitative responses are required the measure should be specified in the question. For example, to ask 'How many livestock do you have?' might elicit responses concerning camels, cattle, donkeys, sheep, goats, chickens, ducks, dogs, and cats from some, while others might only provide cattle numbers. However, the research might only be concerned with cattle, sheep and goats and in such a situation three questions need to be asked:

> 'How many cattle do you have?'
> 'How many sheep do you have?'
> 'How many goats do you have?'

The researcher should avoid phrasing questions that encourage one response over others and also avoid asking questions which might cause offence. For example, it might be of interest to an ecologist to know how many people died as a result of a drought but in some societies, such as the Masai, to ask the question 'How many members of your family died in the most recent drought?' would cause great offence as such sad circumstances are not to be discussed.

In short, the questionnaire should be constructed in such a way as to enable the required information to be gathered in a manner which encourages the respondent to provide accurate data and without giving offence. As Prewitt (1975) puts it:

Perhaps the best advice on questionnaire construction is to examine every item in the final questionnaire against a check list such as the following one:

Is the question necessary?
Can you see how it will be used?
Does the respondent have the information necessary to provide the kind of data you are seeking?
Is the question respondent-centred?
Is the question neutral or does it favour a particular answer?
Does the question contain imprecise or unclear or difficult words?
Will the question be interpreted similarly by all respondents?
Will the question make the respondent uncomfortable or suspicious, or in any way lead him to resent the interview?

The procedure outlined above enables the researcher to prepare a questionnaire according to his objectives and within the bounds of his knowledge of the research situation. In order to succeed, not only must he find people capable of administrating the questionnaire but the instrument itself needs to be thoroughly tested to ensure that it will fulfil its objectives.

2.9.4. Organization of the survey

The choice of enumerators, their behaviour, and the nature of the interactions between the survey team and local residents and government officials are vital factors in ensuring that the objectives of the survey are not jeopardized by poor co-operation of those from whom information is sought.

The enumerators are the most important actors in the survey process. Their skill in posing questions and recording responses determines the quality of the data obtained by the survey. The best-prepared questionnaire and the most sophisticated analytical procedures may be available but it is the accuracy of the data-gathering process which determines the ultimate utility of the survey. The choice, training, and supervision of the enumerators are thus of vital importance.

A number of criteria has to be met in choosing interviewers. They have to be literate and numerate, and they must be able to communicate easily both with the population of the survey area and with those organizing the survey. People who are residents of the survey area are often the most appropriate as they are most likely to be trusted, they speak the local language and they understand the nature of the society under investigation and are therefore more likely to identify misinformation.

Some members of the community may not, however, be appropriate choices. The son of a local chief might be well-educated, personable, and an excellent interpreter, and his status in the society might be thought to be an asset in providing the survey with the stamp of authority; the fact that such an individual does represent authority may, however, result in inaccurate information being obtained as people conceal the truth for fear of repercussions. Distrust of this type might also be generated if representatives of the administration hierarchy such as extension agents are employed.

A number of surveys have employed university students during their vacations. While this choice has proved successful in some circumstances, where the survey involves spending time in villages and walking long distances, university students have been found to be unwilling to adjust to rural conditions and difficulties in maintaining a well-disciplined team with a positive work attitude result. The best all-round choice can often be that of local secondary-school leavers, many of whom may be unemployed, though where small numbers of interviewers are required the employment of schoolteachers during their vacation has proved successful.

The type of information being gathered and the nature of the society under investigation are important factors to be considered in choosing enumerators. In many societies, there is a strong age and/or sex differentiation in activities and responsibilities and the survey process should be responsive to such circumstances. To employ male interviewers to discuss food consumption and preparation, or women to ask questions about livestock management practices would, in many societies, cause embarrassment and/or inhibit the generation of accurate information.

The training of enumerators is a crucial and often poorly implemented phase of the survey process. The objective of the training is to ensure that all members of the team will implement the survey in a comparable manner so that there will be a minimal variability in responses resulting from biases introduced by the interviewers themselves. Differences in attitude, style, and perseverance between enumerators are inevitable but the impact of these characteristics upon the comparability of information from different interviewers should be kept to a minimum. Any interviewer who tends to distort the information and who resists correction should be dropped from the survey team.

The first step in training enumerators is to establish their responsibilities and the conditions of work. Questions relating to the location of the work, rates of pay, allowances for travel time, overnight expenses, medical benefits, and the type of work and work hours, should be resolved as early as possible. Failure to do so may lead to frequent bickering and uncertainty which might prevent the generation of a positive attitude to the work; such an attitude is essential if the hard, tiring work of interviewing is to be completed successfully.

It is also necessary to promote an attitude on the part of the enumerators which will enable them to interact effectively with the population. There is a tendency for people associated with a survey to develop an attitude of superiority regarding other members of the community and to expect them to show respect or even to provide them with food, lodging, and gifts. Such attitudes and expectations may lead to resentment on the part of the population and reduce their level of co-operation with the survey. Enumerators should view themselves as representatives of the population under study as well as of the organization implementing the survey.

Actual training should include familiarizing the team with the objectives of the survey and with the questionnaire, and demonstrating how to ask questions and record answers. During the course of the survey, most respondents will ask the enumerators to explain the goals of the survey and its relevance to them. If the enumerator can explain this clearly, a positive response from those being interviewed is more likely. If the interviewer does not clearly understand what he/she is doing, however, he/she may be tempted to give misinformation or make unrealistic promises regarding the outcome of the survey. Misrepresentation of the purpose of the survey may lead to future problems of disenchantment or lack of co-operation on the part of the population.

The tool which the interviewers will use is usually a questionnaire. Issues concerning the design of questionnaires have already been discussed, but the preparation of the final format should be made during the training period. It is essential that the enumerators understand the precise meaning of each question and the type of information it is expected to generate. The draft questionnaire prepared by the research team should therefore be examined carefully by the survey team and the wording of the questions should be discussed and any changes which would clarify them made.

The process of familiarization with the questionnaire can be carried out concurrently with the initial training in the skills of posing questions and recording responses. The review of the draft questionnaire can be organized in a mock interview format in which the whole group discusses the questionnaire question by question, with members of the team taking turns as interviewers and respondents.

Once the group as a whole has worked through the complete questionnaire a number of times, the revisions can be incorporated into a final draft and the training can concentrate on improving the skills of enumeration. This stage is best organized on the basis of small groups in which one person acts as enumerator, another as respondent and the remainder observe as a complete interview is conducted. At the end of the interview the group discusses what it has seen and notes any inaccuracies in questioning or recording, and any inconsistencies in response which the interviewer failed to recognize. During the training period each member of the survey team should have acted as both interviewer and respondent at least once.

An important aspect of the training concerns the translation of the questionnaire into the local language. In some cases this is done by printing the questionnaire forms in the local language, but this may prove impracticable if a number of local languages is to be used. The questionnaire is often printed in a language with which both the survey enumerators and organizers are fluent but the respondents not; the interviewer is then responsible for translation during the interview. This requires a great deal of skill and concentration and can be done successfully only if the interviewer is familiar with the meaning and purpose of every question. Hence, the process of discussing the questionnaire cannot be a cursory one. During training, the interviewers should also, therefore, practise translation of the questionnaire into a local language and back into the 'survey language'; other members of the group should check on the accuracy of this procedure.

In some cases the interviewers may find themselves in an area where they will need an interpreter. Use of an interpreter, usually a person in a village who speaks the survey language and that of the village but has no training as an interpreter, entails risks of inaccuracy in posing of questions and reporting of answers. The enumerators should be made aware of the difficulties and told to be careful to avoid inconsistencies in response due to these circumstances.

When this aspect of training is completed, the final activity of field testing can take place. This is a dress rehearsal for the actual survey and all the necessary procedures such as informing officials, holding meetings to explain the survey, choosing the sample, and conducting interviews should be included. Both the mechanics of interviewing and the logistics involved in implementing the survey need to be examined so that any problems that arise can be discussed and resolved.

The length of time required to complete the training process will depend upon the quality of the enumerators and the complexity of the questionnaire. While surveys have been conducted with only a few days training, two to three weeks are required to complete a training programme such as that outlined above: the first week, examining the questionnaire and preparing the final draft; the second, working in small groups to learn interviewing techniques and deal with the problems of translation and the use of interpreters; and the third week, carrying out a practice survey in the field.

The implementation of the survey requires careful organization. Survey sites have to be selected in advance, the authorities have to be notified as to the date and time of the survey, transport for the team has to be available, sufficient questionnaires printed, and essential supplies such as pencils, erasers, clipboards, carrying cases, and waterproof protection made ready. Arrangements also have to be made for overnight accommodation of the team members, and some method devised to ensure the security of the completed questionnaires.

Success depends not only upon the skill of the team and logistical organization but also upon the responsiveness of the population of the survey area. As has been emphasized, care must be taken not to antagonize local people through a lack of courtesy or through generating a sense of inferiority or fear. Clear explanation of the goals and purpose of the survey, its likely outcomes, and of the procedures to be used is an essential part of the implementation process.

While each respondent will have his/her own concerns, the community as a whole will also want to know what is occurring. Thus, in each area it is appropriate to organize a meeting for the population before the survey team begins its work to explain what the team is doing. Such meetings should be organized with village leaders and other local authorities and all aspects of the survey discussed. One process which often gives rise to misunderstanding is the choice of the sample, and of the respondents. People do not comprehend why some members of the society should be selected as respondents and others not. To avoid complications arising from this process, the sampling procedures must be carefully explained and where a sample is to be drawn at random it has been found to be more beneficial for the sample to be drawn at the explanatory meeting, by members of the community. Haugerud (1979) had local people select names during a meeting or baraza, and the names of those chosen were read out so that everyone knew who was participating and how they were selected:

After the purposes of the research were explained to the people, the two assistant chiefs and many individuals attending the baraza took turns drawing names of individuals until we had the requisite number for the sample. As each name was drawn, it was read aloud to the crowd, often evoking cheers, laughter and jokes. There are several advantages to this kind of public sampling technique. By using barazas, a researcher in Kenya can make use of one of the most effective established local mechanisms for communicating with a largely illiterate rural population. Publicly drawing a sample is an effective way of demonstrating the impartiality of the selection procedure and helps to reduce suspicion and ill feelings which otherwise tend to be aroused when an outsider moves in to do research on certain members of a community. The reasons for selecting certain individuals and not others otherwise may be interpreted by local people as favouritism or as covert government investigation.

Not all sampling procedures are amenable to such an approach but participation of the local community does enhance the possibility of co-operation.

A second factor that requires attention is the timing of the survey. In semi-arid areas there are major seasonal differences in peoples' work loads and in ease of movement. During the rainy season, farmers work full-time on the land, and their ability and willingness to spend a few hours responding to the survey is likely to be less than during the dry season when their work-load is less. During the rainy season the enumeration team is also less likely to be able to move easily in the survey area as roads and paths become impassible due to flooding, erosion, or the presence of mud. While logistically it might be preferable to conduct the survey during the dry season, the nature of the survey, and the types of questions to be asked, may relate to wet season activities, and a survey conducted during the dry season would rely on peoples' recall of information from previous years rather than upon their current behaviour. On some issues recall can be accurate but on others, such as time spent on different activities, it is very inaccurate. Such problems must be borne in mind in planning surveys.

During the survey the dominant activity is the interview between enumerator and respondent. Success is largely dependent upon that of the training programme, but it is essential that careful supervision of the enumerators takes place. Differences between interviewers will emerge and if they are not controlled there is a possibility that analysis of the data will show greater differences between enumerators than between respondents. A clear procedure of supervision must therefore be implemented.

Supervision must include monitoring of the interviews, of the recording process, and of differences between enumerators. To be effective a survey team must include sufficient supervisors to ensure adequate monitoring. A ratio of five interviewers to one supervisor should not be exceeded. Supervisors need to sit with the enumerators during interviews to ensure that questions are being posed correctly, answers recorded, and inconsistencies resolved. The supervisor should also be responsible for checking each completed questionnaire soon after the interview, and if errors are found the enumerator should return to the respondent to correct them.

Maintaining consistency in asking questions and recording answers between enumerators is difficult. Once an interviewer has completed a number of interviews there is a tendency to expect certain responses and neglect others. He/she may begin to rephrase the question with an expected answer in mind. Should this occur then repetition will be evident within the work of particular enumerators. One method of maintaining an open attitude to questions is to organize regular team meetings during the survey at which completed questionnaires are exchanged between enumerators and discussed. In this way, enumerators can be made aware of the range of responses being given and will be drawn away from any tendency to restrict the number of acceptable responses. Supervision is also required to ensure that the enumerators are, in fact, conducting interviews and are not sitting in a bar or under a tree completing questionnaires with 'appropriate' responses.

2.9.5. Data analysis

Questionnaire surveys produce a vast amount of information. If the questionnaire has been carefully designed and the survey implemented rigorously all the information should contribute to the understanding of the topic under investigation. The complexity of the analysis of the data depends upon the analytical procedures available to the research team. In many circumstances computers are used, either micro-computers in the field or larger ones in research or government institutions. Although in some cases manual data tabulation is necessary, the advent of small, cheap, light, semi-portable micro-computers in the past few years has changed the situation radically. A small investment in these machines is now normally well worthwhile.

Manual data analysis, usually with the aid of electronic calculators, has the advantage that little time is needed to prepare the data for analysis but the range of computational techniques is severely limited. Manual analysis entails high risk of errors being made in entering data, as the information has to be entered anew for each calculation. Under these circumstances, a complete analysis would require each piece of data to be entered many times, permitting multiple opportunities for error. In most circumstances, manual analysis yields only descriptive data such as means and standard deviations, and simple correlations and regressions. If more complex analysis is required it is essential that computer facilities be available to the researchers. Analytical packages such as SPSS[6] and specially written programs permit a wide range of descriptive and analytical procedures[7] to be applied to the data.

In order to conduct computerized data analysis, the data must be carefully prepared for entry into a data file and the data file checked before analysis proceeds. This is a time-consuming process but has the advantage that once the data file has been created it is immediately and repeatedly available for analysis and the possibility of entering incorrect information, so great in manual analysis, is eliminated. Computer analysis greatly improves the capacity of the researcher to test the hypotheses set out at the outset of the research and new ones generated by analysis of the data. There is a temptation when using computer analysis to 'fish' for interesting relationships in the data. This can produce misleading interpretations of the data if the researcher relies on statistical relationships and does not test them further in the field.

Analysis of the data produces many interesting insights into relationships between different variables. Interpretation of the meaning of these relationships, and of their practical significance, depends upon the skill and knowledge of the researcher. The information produced by analysis has to be placed within the context of the area and problem being studied. Usually this is done by the researcher relying upon his understanding of the situation and in consultation with others familiar with the problem, and verification of survey results, through comparison with those of other research, provides an estimate of the reliability of the data and can suggest possible biases.

Frequently, the analysis of survey data is translated into policy recommendations. The relevance and appropriateness of the recommendations depends on the ability of the researcher to interpret the results of the data analysis accurately within the framework of the region under investigation. Unfortunately, the process of interpretation and recommendation often takes place far from the survey area and there is little communication between the researcher and the survey population regarding the results. As stated earlier, this situation has caused many people to be disillusioned with the survey process as it appears to be of little value to those providing the information. In order to allay such attitudes and to promote the quality and relevance of the recommendations, the researcher should attempt to communicate the results of the work to the survey population. Ideally, this should be done directly, for example in the form of a group meeting (Campbell 1984) but, failing that, the minimum that should be done is to ensure that all reports are made available to the leaders of the community so that they may be in a position to disseminate the information.

It is at the analysis stage that all the efforts made to design and implement the survey come to fruition. Accurate, representative information which is skilfully interpreted provides an invaluable basis for policy making and all survey work should aim to attain the highest possible standards within the constraints imposed by the specific field conditions.

2.9.6. Conclusion

The survey process is demanding in terms of the preparation of the survey instrument, training of the survey team and implementation of the research. In most situations, problems will be encountered such as difficulties in sampling, lazy enumerators, uncooperative officials, distrustful respondents, inclement weather conditions, the loss of completed questionnaires, and vehicle breakdowns. Such problems have to be resolved on the spot and may lead to deviations from the optimum research strategy. If the researcher has to alter his strategy, the information gathered may be biased. This should not be a reason to regard the information as useless but the researcher should be explicitly aware of any biases when analysis and interpretation of the data are made.

Despite the potential shortcomings of social survey research, it is an invaluable tool in understanding social and economic processes. In the context of ecological monitoring, the role of man in altering the environment must be understood and by specifying socio-economic processes and articulating attitudes the researcher can contribute greatly to this end (Brokensha, Warrne, and Werner 1980).

The goal of ecological monitoring is not to provide a basis for implementing policies to protect the environment *qua* environment but rather to promote policies which will create a man–environment system which allows for long term productivity, for a system of land use which allows a sustained yield. Both the ecological and socio-economic processes have to be described and their interactions analysed so that the future implications of contemporary trends can be forecast. It is in the light of such carefully prepared forecasts that society will be able to choose its ecological destiny.

Notes

[1] Few guidelines for conducting socio-economic surveys exist. In preparing this section valuable information was obtained from the agricultural economics literature (Bernsten 1979; CIMMYT 1979) and from Prewitt (1975).
[2] The population need not necessarily be the total number of people in the survey area but is the total number of sampling units – be they chiefs, farm households, head of families, or mothers, for example.
[3] Costs include not only salaries, transportation, and accommodation but also those of sorting, verifying, and analysing the data after it has been collected, and of writing and disseminating the survey reports.
[4] For example, tax lists are frequently available, but incomplete because people avoid being listed to escape having to pay taxes. Also. if the tax is a land tax those people not owning land, such as tenant farmers and squatters, will not be included. If the sampling unit is the farmer such lists may be inappropriate.
[5] Non-random sampling procedures are also available but it is not possible to generalize from the sample to the population as a whole. For example, one might arrive at a village of herders and interview all those present. Since the majority of herders may spend the day away from the village grazing and watering their livestock, the sample taken from those who remain may represent the old, the infirm, and/or the wealthy who have herdsmen. It would not therefore be representative of the herders from that village.
[6] Statistical Package for the Social Sciences, see Nie, Hall, Jenkins, Steinbrenner, and Bent (1975).
[7] Methods appropriate for analysing the data are not discussed at this point. Methods are discussed in statistics texts, such as Blalock (1972).

References

Acosta, R. A. and Kothmann, M. M. (1978). Chemical composition of oesophageal fistula forage samples as influenced by the drying method and salivary leaching. *J. Anim. Sci.* **47**(3), 691–8.

Allden, W. G. and Whittaker, I. A. McD. (1970). The determinants of herbage intake in grazing sheep: the interrelationships of factors influencing herbage intake and availability. *Aust. J. Agric. Res.* **21**, 755.

Arnold, G. W., McManus, W. R., Bush, I. G., and Ball, J. (1964). The use of sheep fitted with oesophageal fistulas to measure diet quality. *Aust. J. exp. Agric. Anim. Husb.* **4**, 71.

Awbrey, F. T. (1977). Locating random points in the field. *J. Range Mgmt* **30**, 157–8.

Axelsson, B., Gardenfors, D., Lohm, U., Persson, T., Tenow, O., and Wallin, L. (1970). Components of variance and the cost of sampling programmes concerning biomass of hazel *Corylus avellana* L. available to insects. *Oikos* **21**, 203–7.

Bailey, R. E. and Putman, R. J. (1982). Estimation of fallow deer populations from faecal accumulation. *J. Appl. Ecol.* **18**(3), 697–702.

Batcheler, C. L. (1975). Development of a distance method for deer census from pellet groups. *J. Wildl. Mgmt* **39**(4), 641–52.

—— and Bell, D. J. (1970). Experiments in estimating density from joint point – and nearest – neighbour distance samples. *Proc. N.Z. Ecol. Soc.* **17**, 111–17.

Bath, D. L., Weir, W. C., Torrell, D. T. (1956). The use of the oesophageal fistula for the determination of consumption and digestibility of pasture forage by sheep. *J. Anim. Sci.* **15**, 1166.

Bell, R. H. V. (1969). The use of the herb layer by grazing ungulates in the Serengeti National Park, Tanzania. Ph.D. Thesis, Manchester University.

Belovsky, G. E. (1981). Optimal activity times and habitat choice of moose. *Oecologia* **48**, 22–30.

Bergerud, A. T. and Russell, L. (1964). Evaluation of rumen food analysis for Newfoundland caribou. *J. Wildl. Mgmt* **32**, 809.

Bernsten, R. (1979). Design and management of agricultural research: a guide for agricultural researchers. IRRI, mimeo.

Berry, L., Campbell, D. J., and Emker, I. (1977). Trends in man–land interaction in the West African Sahel. In *Drought in Africa* (ed. David Dalby, R. J. Harrison-Church, and Fatima Bezzaz) pp. 83–91. International African Institute, London.

Beverton, R. J. H. and Holt, S. J. (1957). On the dynamics of exploited fish populations. *Fishery Invest. Ser.* **2**(19), 1.

Blalock, H. M. (1971). *Social statistics,* 2nd edn. McGraw-Hill, New York.

Blaxter, K. L. (1975). Energy-protein relationships in ruminants. In *Proc. 9th int. Congr. Nutrition, Mexico 1972.* pp. 122–7. Karger, Basel.

Brandborg, S. M. (1955). Life history and management of the mountain goat in Idaho. Idaho Dept. Fish & Game, *Wildl. Bull.* **2**, 142.

Braun-Blanquet, J. *Pflanzensoziologie, Grundzuge der Vegetationskunde,* 3rd edn. Springer-Verlag, New York.

Bredon, R. M., Harker, K. W., and Marshall, B. (1963). The nutritive value of grasses grown in Uganda when fed to zebu cattle. *J. Agric. Sci. (Cambridge)* **62**, 101–4.

Brokensha, D., Warrne, D. M., and Werner, O. (eds) (1980). *Indigenous knowledge systems and development.* University Press of America, Washington, D.C.

Brown, G. W. and Krygier, J. E. (1971). Clear-cut logging and sediment production in the Oregon Coast Range. *Water Resources Res.* **7**, 5, 1189–98.

Burnham, K. P., Anderson, D. R., and Laake, J. J. (1980). Estimation of density from Line transect sampling of biological populations. In *Wildl. Monogr.* 72.

Cairns, A. L. and Telfer, E. S. (1980). Habitat use by four sympatric ungulates in boreal mixed wood forest. *J. Wildl. Mgmt* **44**(4), 849–57.

Campbell, D. J. (1984). *Community participation in field research: an example from Kenya Masailand.* Occasional Paper No. 4, CASID, Michigan State University.

Campling, R. C., Freer, M., and Balch, C. C. (1961). Factors affecting the voluntary intake of food by cows. *Br. J. Nutr.* **15**, 531–40.

Caughley, G. (1964). Social organization and daily activity of red kangaroos and grey kangaroos. *J. Mammal.* **45**, 429–36.

—— (1970). Fat reserves of Himalayan Thar in New Zealand by season, sex, area and age. *N.Z. Jl Sci.* **13**(2), 209.

—— (1971). Demography, fat reserves and body size of a population of red deer in New Zealand. *Mammalia* **35**, 369–83.

—— (1977). *Analysis of vertebrate populations.* J. Wiley, London.

—— and Birch, L. C. (1971). Rate of increase. *J. Wildl. Mgmt* **35**(4), 658–63.

Cederlund, G., Ljungqvist, H., Markgren, G., and Stalfelt, F. (1980). Food of Moose and Roe Deer at Grimso in Central Sweden: results of rumen content analyses. *Swedish Wildl. Res.* **11**(4), 1–224.

Chacon, E., Stobbs, T. H., and Haydock, K. P. (1977). Estimation of leaf and stem contents of oesophageal extrusa samples from cattle. *J. Aust. Inst. Agric. Sci.* **43**(1 & 2), 73–5.

Chamrad, A. D. and Box, T. W. (1969). A point frame for sampling rumen contents. *J. Wildl. Mgmt* **28**, 473–7.

Cheeseman, C. L. and Mitson, R. B. (eds) (1982). Telemetric studies of vertebrates. *Symp. Zool. Soc. Lond.,* Vol. 49. Academic Press, London & New York.

Child, G., Smith, M. B. E., and von Richter, W. (1970). Tsetse control hunting as a measure of large mammal population trends in the Okavango Delta, Botswana. *Mammalia* **34**, 34–75.

Christie, A. H. C. and Andrews, J. R. H. (1964). Introducing ungulates in New Zealand. (a) Himalayan thar. *Tuatara* **12**, 69–77.

CIMMYT (1979). *Planning technologies appropriate to farmers: concepts and procedures.* Centro Internacional de Mejoramiento de Maiz y Trigo, Mexico, mimeo.

Clutton-Brock, T. H. Guinness, F. E., and Albon, S. D. (1982). *Red Deer: behaviour and ecology of two sexes.* Chicago University Press, Chicago.

Cock, M. J. W. (1978). The assessment of preference. *J. Anim. Ecol.* **47**, 805–16.

Croze, H. (1974). The seronera bull problem (I and II). *E. Afr. Wildl. J.* **12**(1), 1–48.

Dasmann, W. P. and Dasmann, R. F. (1963). Abundance and scarcity of California deer. *Calif. Fish Game* **49**, 4–15.

Dauphine, T. C. (1975). Kidney weight fluctuations affecting the kidney fat index in caribou. *J. Wildl. Mgmt* **39**, 379–86.

Davis, D. E. and Winstead, R. L. (1980). Estimating the numbers of wildlife populations. In *Wildlife management techniques manual* (ed. S. D. Schemnitz). Blacksburg Wildlife Society.

Denny, C. S. and Goodlett, J. C. (1956). Micro-relief resulting from fallen trees. In *Surficial geology of Potter County, Pennsylvania.* US Geological Survey Professional Paper 288, pp. 59–66.

Dietrich, W. E. and Dunne, T. (1978). Sediment budget for a small catchment in mountainous terrain. *Z. Geomorph.* Suppl. Bd. **29**, 191–206.

——, Dunne, T., Humphrey, N. F., and Reid, L. M. (1981). The construction of sediment budgets for drainage basins. *Proc. Symp. on Sediment Budgets and Sediment Routing in Forested Drainage Basins.* US Forest Service, Corvallis, Oregon.

Dirschl, H. J. (1962). Sieve mesh size related to analysis of antelope rumen contents. *J. Wildl. Mgmt.* **26**, 327–8.

Dudzinski, M. L. and Arnold, G. W. (1973). Comparisons of diets of sheep and cattle grazing together on sown pastures on the southern tablelands of New South Wales by principal components analysis. *Aust. J. Agric. Res.* **24**, 899–912.

——, Schuth, H. J., Wilcox, D. G., Gardiner, H. G., and Morrissey, J. G. (1978). Statistical and probabilistic estimators of forage conditions from grazing behaviour of merino sheep in a semi-arid environment. In *Appl. Anim. Ethics* **4**, 357–68.

Duncan, P. (1975). Topi and their food supply. Ph.D. Thesis, University of Nairobi, Kenya.

—— (1980). Time-budgets of Camargue horses. II. Time-budgets of adult horses and weaned sub-adults. *Behaviour* **72**(1–2), 26–49.

—— (1983). Determinants of the use of habitat by horses in a Mediterranean wetland. *J. Anim. Ecol.* **52**, 93–109.

Dunne, T. (1979). Sediment yield and land use in tropical catchments. *J. Hydrol.* **42**, 281–300.

—— and Leopold, L. B. (1978). *Water in environmental planning.* 818 pp. Freeman, San Francisco.

——, Dietrich, W. E., and Brunengo, M. J. (1978*a*). Recent and past rates of erosion in semi-arid Kenya. *Z. Geomorph.* Suppl. Bd. **29**, 130–40.

——, Dietrich, W. E., and Brunengo, M. J. (1979). Rapid evaluation of soil erosion and soil lifespan in the grazing lands of Kenya. In *Int. Assoc. Hydrolog. Sci. Publ.* **128**, 421–428.

Du Plessis, S. S. (1972). The ecology of blesbok with special reference to productivity. *Wildl. Monogr.* 30.

Eberhardt, L. L. (1978). Transect methods for population studies. *J. Wildl. Mgmt* **42**, 1–31.

Evans, E. W., Burnett, J., and Bines, J. A. (1974). A study of the effect of exposure in the reticulo-rumen of the cow on the strength of cotton, grass, hay and straw. *Br. J. Nutr.* **31**, 273.

Fancy, S. G. (1980). Preparation of mammalian teeth for age determination by cementum layers – a review. *Wildl. Soc. Bull.* **8**(3), 242–8.

Field, C. R. (1968). The food habits of some wild ungulates in Uganda. Ph.D. Thesis, University of Cambridge.

—— and Laws, R. M. (1970). The distribution of the larger herbivores in the Queen Elizabeth National Park, Uganda. *J. Appl. Ecol.* **7**, 273–94.

Finger, S. E., Brisbin, I. L., and Smith, M. H. (1981). Kidney fat as a predictor of body condition in white-tailed deer. *J. Wildl. Mgmt* **45**, 964–8.

Fisher, R. A. The precision of discriminant functions. *Ann. Eugen. Lond.* **10**, 422–9.

Foster, J. B. and Kearney, D. (1967). Nairobi National Park game census, 1966. *E. Afri. Wildl. J.* **5**, 112–20.

Fowler, C. W. and Smith, T. D. (eds) (1981). *Dynamics of large mammal populations.* Wiley, New York.

Fairbridge, R. W. (1968). *Encyclopedia of geomorphology.* Reinhold, New York.

Geiger, A. F. (1965). Developing sediment storage requirements for upstream retarding reservoirs. In *Proc. Fed. Interagency Sedimentation Conf. US Dept. of Agriculture Misc. Publ.* 970, 1965.

Guy, H. P. (1969). Laboratory theory and methods for sediment analysis. In *Water resources inventory,* Book 5, Chapter C-1. US Geological Survey.

—— and Norman, V. W. (1970). Field methods for the measurement of fluvial sediment. In *Techniques for water resources investigations,* Book 3, Chapter C-2, US Geological Survey.

Grimsdell, J. J. (1973). Age determination of the African buffalo, *Syncerus caffer,* Sparrman. *E. Afr. Wildl. J.* **11**, 31–54.

Gwynne, M. D. and Bell, R. H. V. (1968). Selection of vegetation components by grazing ungulates in the Serengeti National Park. *Nature, Lond.* **220**(5165), 390.

Hamilton, B. A., Hutchinson, K. J., Annis, P. C., and Donnelly, J. B. (1973). Relationships between the diet selected by grazing sheep and the herbage on offer. *Aust. J. Agric. Res.* **24**(2), 271.

Hansen, R. M., and Clark, R. C. (1977). Foods of elk and other ungulates at low elevations in northwestern Colorado. *J. Wildl. Mgmt* **41**(1), 76–80.

Harper, J. L. (1977). *Population biology of plants.* Academic Press, New York.

Haugerud, A. (1979). *Methodological issues in a study of resource allocation decisions among Embu farmers.* Working Paper No. 357, Institute of Development Studies, University of Nairobi.

Hays, W. L. (1973). *Statistics for the social sciences,* 2nd edn. Holt Rinehart & Winston, New York.

Heady, H. F. and Van Dyne, G. M. (1965). Prediction of weight composition from point samples on clipped herbage. *J. Range Mgmt* **18**, 144–8.

Helley, E. J. and Smith, W. (1971). *Development and calibration of a pressure-difference bedload sampler.* US Geological Survey, *Open File Report,* Menlo Park, California.

Hercus, B. H. (1960). Plant cuticle as an aid to determining the diet of grazing animals. In *Proc. 8th int. Grassld. Congr.,* pp. 443–7.

Hill, M. O. (1974). Correspondence analysis: a neglected multivariate method. *Appl. Statist.* **23**, 340–54.

Hofmann, R. R. (1973). The ruminant stomach. In *E. Afr. Monogr. in biology,* 2. East African Literature Bureau, Nairobi.

Holechek, J. L. and Goss, B. D. (1982). Evaluation of different calculation procedures for microhistological analysis. *J. Range Mgmt* **35**(6), 721–3.

——, Vavra, M., and Pieper, R. D. (1982). Botanical composition of range herbivores' diets: a review. *J. Range Mgmt* **35**(1), 309–17.

Huggett, A. St. G. and Hammond, J. (1952). Physiology of the placenta. In *Marshall's physiology of reproduction.* II (ed. A. S. Parkes) pp. 312–97. Longmans, London.

—— and Widdas, W. F. (1951). The relationship between mammalian foetal weight and conception age. *J. Physiol., Lond.* **114**, 306.

Hungate, R. E. (1966). *The rumen and its microbes.* Academic Press, New York.

Hunter, R. F. (1962). Hill sheep and their pasture: a study of sheep grazing in south-east Scotland. *J. Ecol.* **50**, 651–80.

Hynes, H. B. N. (1963). *The biology of polluted waters.* 202 pp. Liverpool University Press, Liverpool, UK.

Janis, C. (1976). The evolutionary strategy of the Equidae and the origins of rumen and caecal digestion. *Evolution* **30**, 757–74.

Jarman, P. J. (1972). Seasonal distribution of large mammal populations in the unflooded middle Zambesi valley. *J. Appl. Ecol.* **9**, 283–99.

Jarrige, R. (1965). The composition of sheep faeces and its relation to forage digestibilities. In *Proc. 9th int. Grassl. Congr.* 1, 809–14.

Johnson, D. H. (1980). The comparison of usage and availability measurements for evaluating resource preference. *Ecology* **61**(1), 65–71.

Keiss, R. E. (1964). Comparison of eruption-wear patterns and cementum annuli as age criteria in elk. *J. Wildl. Mgmt* **33**(1), 175–80.

Kelker, G. H. (1940). Estimating deer populations by a differential hunting loss in the sexes. *Proc. Utah Acad. Sci. Arts &Lett.* **17**, 65–9.

Kilford, W. K. (1966). *Elementary air survey*. Pitman, London.

Klein, D. R. and Schonheyder, F. (1970). Variation in ruminal nitrogen levels among some cervidae. *Canad. J. Zool.* **48**, 1437–42.

Kunkle, S. H. and Comer, G. H. (1971). Estimating suspended sediment concentrations in streams by turbidity measurements. In *J. Soil Wat. Conserv.* **26**, 18–20.

Lamarche, V. C. (1968). *Rates of slope degradation as determined from botanical evidence*. US Geological Survey Professional paper 352–I, White Mountains, Calif.

Lamond, D. R. (1970). The influence of undernutrition on reproduction in the cow. *Anim. Breed. Abstr.* **38**, 359–72.

Lamprey, H. F. (1963). Ecological separation of large mammal species in Tarangire Game Reserve, Tanganyika. *E. Afr. Wildl. J.* **1**, 1.

Langlands, J. P. (1966). Studies in the nutritive value of the diet selected by grazing sheep. 1. Differences in composition between herbage consumed and material collected from oesophageal fistulae. *Anim. Prod.* **8**, 253.

Laredo, M. A. and Minson, D. J. (1973). The voluntary intake, digestibility, and retention time by sheep of leaf and stem fractions of five grasses. *Aust. J. Agric. Res.* **24**, 875.

Larson, J. S. and Taber, R. D. (1980). Criteria of sex and age. In *Wildlife management techniques manual* (ed. S. D. Schemnitz). The Wildlife Society.

Laws, R. M., Parker, I. S. C., and Johnstone, R. C. B. (1975). *Elephants and their habitats. The ecology of elephants in North Bunyoro, Uganda*. Clarendon Press, Oxford.

Leopold, L. B. and Dunne, T. (1972). *Field method for hillslope description*. British Geomorphological Research Group Tech. Publ. No. 7.

——, Emmett, W. W., and Myrick, R. M. (1966). *Channel and hillslope processes in a semiarid area*. US Geological Survey Professional Paper 352–6, pp. 193–253. New Mexico.

Le Resche, R. E. and Davis, J. L. (1972). Importance of non-browse food to moose on Kenai Peninsula, Alaska. *J. Wildl. Mgmt* **37**(3), 279.

Leuthold, W. (1970). Preliminary observations on the food habits of Gerenuk in the Tsavo National Park, Kenya. *E. Afr. Wildl. J.* **8**, 73.

Leuthold, W. (1971). A note on the formation of food habits in young antelopes. *E. Afr. Wildl. J.* **9**, 154.

Low, W. A. and Hodder, R. M. (1976). A facility for weighing free-ranging cattle. *J. Aust. Inst. Agric. Sci.* **42**, 68–70.

Lowe, V. P. W. (1972). Variation in mandible length and body weight of red deer (*Cervus elaphus*). *J. Zool., Lond.* **166**, 303–11.

Lowman, B. G., Scott, N. A., and Somerville, S. H. (1976). Condition scoring of cattle. In *East of Scotland College of Agriculture Bull.* **6**, 1–31.

McKay, A. D., Frandsen, P. B., Odero, J. C., Sondergaard, M., and Nganga, S. P. (1969). Chemical composition of herbage from *Themeda* grassland in Kenya, before and after collection from oesophageal fistulated steers. *E. Afr. Agric. Forest. J.* **35**, 190.

McNaughton, S. J. (1979). Grassland-herbivore dynamics. *Serengeti, dynamics of an ecosystem* (eds. A. R. E. Sinclaire, and M. Norton-Griffiths). University of Chicago Press, Chicago.

Malpas, R. C. (1977). Diet, condition and growth of elephants in Uganda. *J. Appl. Ecol.* **14**(2), 487–504.

Marshall, B., Torrell, D. T., and Bredon, R. M. (1967). Comparison of tropical forages of known composition with sample of these forages collected by oeso-phageal fistulated animals. *J. Range Mgmt* **20**, 310.

Medin, D. E. (1970). Stomach content analyses: collections from wild herbivores and birds. In *US Dept. Agric. Misc. Publ.* 1147, pp. 135–45.

Miller, V. C., *Photogeology* (1961). McGraw-Hill, New York.

Murray-Rust, D. H. (1972). Soil erosion and reservoir sedimentation in a grazing area west of Arusha, Tanzania. *Geografiska Ann.* A. **54**, 325–44.

Mitchell, B., McCowan, D., and Nicholson, I. A. (1976). Annual cycles of body weight and condition in Scottish Red Deer, *Cervus elaphus. J. Zool., Lond.* **180**, 107–27.

Moen, A. N. (1973). *Wildlife ecology.* Freeman, San Francisco.

Morgan, B. J. T., Simpson, M. J. A., Hanby, J. P., and Hall-Craggs, J. (1976). Theory and application of cluster analysis. *Behaviour* **56**, 1–43.

Mould, E. D. and Robbins, C. T. (1981). Nitrogen metabolism in elk. *J. Wildl. Mgmt* **45**, 323–34.

Munro, H. N. (ed.) (1964). *The role of the gastro-intestinal tract in protein meta-bolism.* Blackwell, Oxford.

Neff, D. J. (1968). The pellet-group count technique for big game trend, census and distribution: a review. *J. Wildl. Mgmt* **32**(3), 597–614.

Nie, H. H., Hall, C. H., Jenkins, J. G., Steinbrenner, K., and Bent, D. H. (1975). *SPSS: Statistical package for the social sciences,* 2nd edn. McGraw-Hill, New York.

Nordan, H. C., Cowan, I. McT., and Wood, A. J. (1968). Nutritional requirements and growth of black-tailed deer (*Odocoileus hemionus columbianus*) in cap-tivity. In *Comparative nutrition of wild animals* (ed. M. A. Crawford). *Symp. Zool. Soc. Lond.* **21**, 89–96.

Norcliffe, G. (1977). *Inferential statistics for geographers.* Halsted Press, New York.

Norton-Griffiths, M. (1973). Counting the Serengeti migratory wildebesst using two-stage sampling. *E. Afr. Wildl. J.* **11**(2), 135–49.

—— (1978). *Counting animals.* 2nd edn. East African Wildlife Foundation, Nairobi.

Olsen, F. W. and Hansen, R. M. (1977). Food relations of wild free-roaming horses to livestock and big game, Red Desert, Wyoming. *J. Range Mgmt* **30**, 17–20.

Ollier, C. D. (1974). Terrain classification: methods, applications, and principles. In *Appl. Geomorph.* (ed. J. R. Hails) pp. 277–316. Riley, Chichester, UK.

Ongweny, G. S. (1978). Erosion and sediment transport in the Upper Tana

Catchment with special reference to the Thiba Basin. Ph.D. thesis, 310 pp. University of Nairobi, 1978.

Osuji, P. O. (1974). The physiology of eating and the energy expenditure of the ruminant at pasture. *J. Range Mgmt* **27**(6), 437–43.

Owaga, M. L. A. (1977). Comparison of analysis of stomach contents and faecal samples from zebra. *E. Afr. Wildl. J.* **15**, 217–22.

Payne, J. M., Drew, S. M., Manston, R., and Faulks, M. (1970). The use of a metabolic profile test in dairy herds. *Vet. Rec.* **87**, 150–58.

Pearson, R. L., Miller, L. D., and Tucker, C. J. (1976). Hand-held spectral radiometer to estimate graminaceous biomass. *Appl. Optics* **15**, 416–18.

Poole, R. W. (1974). *Quantitative ecology.* McGraw-Hill, New York.

Pellew, R. A. P. (1983). The impacts of elephant, giraffe and fire upon the *Acacia tortilis* woodlands of the Serengeti. *Afr. J. Ecol.* **21**, 41–74.

Petrides, G. A. (1975). Principal foods versus preferred foods and their relations to stocking rate and range conditions. *Biol. Conserv.* **7**(3), 161–70.

Pollock, J. I. (1980). *Behavioural ecology and body condition changes in New Forest ponies.* Scientific publication 6. Royal Society for the Prevention of Cruelty to Animals, Horsham.

Powell, D. J., Clanton, D. C., and Nichols, J. C. (1982). Effect of range condition on the diet and performance of steers grazing native Sandhills range in Nebraska. *J. Range Mgmt* **35**(1), 96–9.

Prewitt, K. (1975). *Introductory research methodology: East African applications.* Occasional Paper No. 10, Institute for Development Studies, University of Nairobi.

Pullan, N. B. (1978). Condition scoring of White Fulani cattle. *Trop. Anim. Hlth Prod.* **10**(2), 118–20.

Quick, H. F. (1963). Animal population analysis. In *Wildlife investigational techniques* (ed. H. S. Mosby) 2nd edn., pp. 190–228. The Wildlife Society, Blacksburg.

Ransom, A. B. (1965). Kidney and marrow fat as indicators of white-tailed deer condition. *J. Wildl. Mgmt* **29**, 397–8.

Rausch, D. L. and Heinemann, H. G. (1977). *Reservoir sedimentation survey methods in hydrological techniques for upstream conservation.* FAO Conservation Guide 2. FAO, Rome.

Rees, W. A. (1978). The ecology of the Kafue lechwe: its nutritional status and herbage intake. *J. Appl. Ecol.* **15**(1), 193–203.

Reeves, R. G. (ed.) (1975). *Manual of remote sensing,* Vols. 1 and 2. American Society of Photogrammetry, Falls Church, Virginia.

Reid, L. M. (1981). *Sediment production from gravel-surfaced forest roads.* University of Washington Fisheries Research Institute Report FRI-UW-8108. Clearwater Basin, Washington.

Reveron, A. E., and Topps, J. H. (1970). Nutrition and gastrointestinal parasitism in ruminants. *Outl. Agric.* **6**, 131–6.

Riney, T. (1960). A field technique for assessing physical condition of some ungulates. *J. Wildl. Mgmt* **24**(1), 92.

Robbins, C. T. (1983). *Wildlife feeding and nutrition.* Academic Press, New York.

Robinette, W. L., Loveless, C. M., Jones, D. A. (1974). Field tests of strip census methods. *J. Wildl. Mgmt* **38**(1), 81–96.

Robinson, D. W., and Slade, L. M. (1974). The current status of knowledge on the nutrition of equines. *J. Anim. Sci.* **39**(6), 1045–66.

Rogers, D. J. (1979). *A bibliography of African ecology: a geogaphically and topically classified list of books and articles.* Greenwood Press.

Rost, G. R. and Bailey, J. A. (1979). Distribution of mule deer and elk in relation to roads. *J. Wildl. Mgmt* **43**(3), 634–41.

Rozenthal, G. A. and Janzen, D. H. (1979). *Herbivores: their interaction with secondary plant metabolites.* Academic Press, New York.

Seber, G. A. F. (1981). *Estimation of animal abundance and related parameters,* 2nd edn. Charles Griffin, London.

Sinclair, A. R. E. (1977). The African buffalo. Chicago University Press, Chicago.

—— and Duncan, P. (1972). Indices of condition in tropical ruminants. *E. Afr. Wildl. J.* **10**, 143–9.

Skelton, S. T. (1978). Seasonal variations and feeding selectivity in the diets of the horses (*Equus caballus*) of the Carmargue. Unpublished M.Sc. thesis, Texas A. & M. University.

Smuts, G. L. (1976). Population characteristics of Burchell's zebra (*Equus burchelli antiquorum,* H. Smith, 1841) in the Kruger National Park. *S. Afr. J. Wildl. Res.* **6**(2), 99–112.

Sokal, R. R. and Rohlf, F. J. (1969). *Biometry.* Freeman, New York.

Stanley Price, M. R. (1978). The nutritional ecology of Coke's hartebeest (*Alcelaphus buselaphus cokei*) in Kenya. *J. Appl. Ecol.* **15**, 33–49.

Stewart, D. R. M. (1965). The epidermal characters of grasses with special reference to East African plains species. *Bot. Jb.* **84**(1), 63–116.

—— (1967). Analyis of plant epidermis in faeces: a technique for studying food preferences of grazing herbivores. *J. Appl. Ecol.* **4**, 83.

—— and Stewart, J. (1970). Food preference data by faecal analysis for African plains ungulates. *Zool. Africana* **15**(1), 115.

Strahler, A. N. (1964). Quantitative geomorphology. In: *Handbook of applied hydrology* (ed. Ven T. Chow). McGraw-Hill, New York.

Strong, C. W. (1966). An improved method of obtaining density from linetransect data. *Ecology* **47**, 311–13.

Swanson, F. J. and Dyrness, C. T. (1975). Impact of clearcutting and road construction on soil erosion by landslides in the western Cascade range, Oregon. *Geology* **3**, 392–6.

Talbot, L. M. and Talbot, M. H. (1962). Food preferences of some East African wild ungulates. *E. Afr. Agric. Forest. J.* **27**, 131.

Taylor, C. A. and Bryant, F. C. (1977). A durable oesophageal cannula for sheep and goats. *J. Range Mgmt* **30**, 397–8.

Terry, R. A., and Tilley, J. M. A. (1964). The digestibility of the leaves and stems of perennial ryegrass, cocksfoot, timothy, tall fescue, lucerne and sainfoin as measured by an *in vitro* procedure. *J. Br. Grassl. Soc.* **19**, 363–72.

Tieszen, L. L., Hein, D., Ovortrup, S. A., Troughton, J. H., and Imbamba, S. K. (1979). Use of ^{13}C values to determine vegetation selectivity in East African herbivores. *Oecologia* **37**(3), 351–9.

Thomas, M. M. (ed.) (1966). *Manual of photogrammetry,* Vols 1 and 2. American Society of Photogrammetry, Falls Church, Va.

Torrell, D. T., Hume, I. D., and Weir, W. C. (1974). Factors affecting blood urea nitrogen and its use as an index of the nutritional status of sheep. *J. Anim. Sci.* **39**(2), 435–40.

Underwood, E. J. (1977). *Trace elements in human and animal nutrition.* Academic Press, New York.

Usenik, E. A., Krelen, D. A., and Duncan, P. (1977). Oesophageal fistulation of topi and wildebeest. *E. Afr. Wildl. J.* **15**, 207–12.

Van de Veen, H. E. (1978). Food selection and habitat use in the red deer (*Cervus elaphus* L.). Thesis, University of Groningen.

Van Dyne, G. M. and Torrell, D. F. (1964). Development and use of oesophageal fistula: a review. *J. Range Mgmt* **17**, 7–19.

Van Soest, P. J. (1982). *Nutritional ecology of the ruminant.* O. and B. Books, Corvallis, Oregon.

Veteto, G., Davis, C. E., Hart, R., and Robinson, R. M. (1972) An oesophageal cannula for white-tailed deer. *J. Wildl. Mgmt* **36**(3), 906.

Wallace, L. R. (1948). The growth of lambs before and after birth in relation to the level of nutrition. *J. Agric. Sci. (Cambridge)* **38**, 243–367.

Wallis, J. R. and Anderson, H. W. (1965). *An application of multivariate analysis to sediment network design.* International Association of Scientific Hydrologists, Publ. No. 67.

Warren-Wilson, J. (1963). Estimation of foliage denseness and foliage angle by inclined point quadrats. *Aust. J. Biol.* **11**, 95–105.

Wentworth, C. K. (1930). A simplified method of determining the average slope of land surfaces. *Am. J. Sci.* **20**, 184–94.

Western, D. (1973). The structure, dynamics and changes of the Amboseli ecology system. Ph.D. Thesis, University of Nairobi.

Western, D. and Dunne, T. (1979). Environmental aspects of settlement site decisions among pastoral Maasai. *Human Ecol.* **7**(1), 75–98.

Westervelt, R. G., Stouffer, J. R., Hintz, H. F., and Schryver, H. F. (1976). Estimation of fitness in horses and ponies. *J. Anim. Sci.* **43**(4), 781–5.

Whittaker, R. H. (ed.) (1978). *Classification of plant communities.* Junk, The Hague.

—— and Woodwell, G. M. (1968). Dimension and production relations of trees and shrubs in the Brookhaven Forest, New York. *J. Ecol.* **56**, 1–25.

Wiegert, R. G. and Evans, F. C. (1964). Primary production and the disappearance of dead vegetation in an old-field in southeastern Michigan. *Ecology* **45**, 49–63.

Yamane, T. (1973). *Statistics: an introductory analysis,* 3rd edn. Harper & Row, New York.

Yeates, M. (1974). *An introduction to quantitative analysis in human geography.* McGraw-Hill, New York.

3. Aerial monitoring

3.1 The use of light aircraft

3.1.1. Introduction

This chapter deals with the uses of light aircraft for inventory and monitoring activities. The term 'light aircraft' refers here to small, 2–6 seater, single-engined aircraft and to small, light, twin-engined machines. Larger and heavier aircraft are used for high-altitude, small-scale photography, and for airborne surveys using side-looking radar, multispectral radiometers, and other devices.

In the early 1960s, light aircraft began to be used extensively by wildlife biologists, in Africa and North America, who were faced with the task of studying large populations of animals in huge and undeveloped areas. In many of the African National Parks, roads were poor, cross-country travel was difficult, especially during the rainy season, and maps were almost non-existent. Animals moved over vast distances, as did the poachers who invariably followed them and preyed upon them. Light aircraft provided both game wardens and scientists with a highly mobile observation platform. This rudimentary beginning led to a number of observation and survey methods that are now widely used throughout the world.

For broad-scale regional surveys, and monitoring of a wide range of attributes, the Systematic Reconaissance Flight (SRF) allows large areas of country to be covered on a routine basis. This method has been applied for both inventory and monitoring purposes in areas ranging from 50 to 500 000 km². Where there is a need for intensive studies of a restricted range of attributes, the method of stratified random sampling (STRS) should be used. Finally, conditions are sometimes met where block counting is the only appropriate method.

All these methods share a number of common characteristics. First, they are sampling methods, which means that only a sample, or portion, of the total study area is in fact examined. Secondly, the aircraft used are always high-wing monoplanes or high-wing light twins, so that the observers on board have an unobstructed view of the ground. Thirdly, data are collected both by direct observations and by photography. And, finally, the aircraft are flown at a slow speed (typically 160 km/h) and close to the ground (typically about 100 m above ground level).

To apply these methods successfully calls for a high degree of skill, training, and dedication from all those involved at all stages of the data collection and analysis. Although the methods appear seductively easy to carry out, highly erroneous data will be collected if the methods are misapplied, leading to a waste of financial and human resources, and the risk that inappropriate management and development decisions will be taken.

This chapter is divided into two main sections. The first gives an overview of the major applications of aerial surveys, and of the most widely used methods. The second discusses a number of operational procedures that must be followed in order to apply the recommended methods successfully. It is not possible to specify these procedures in great detail. Instead, the broad outlines only are given, with references for further reading. This information should be adequate to allow those interested in the methods to decide whether they have the required expertise and resources to implement them without recourse to outside help.

3.1.2. Major applications

3.1.2.1. Long-term monitoring of animal populations

Aerial surveys and monitoring from light aircraft have been used most often in rangeland and wildlife areas, where development and management programmes have always required information on animal numbers, distribution, movements, and population structure. Specifically:

(i) *Total numbers:* estimates of the total numbers of animals form part of the basic inventory of any area selected for development. Total numbers are needed to calculate grazing pressure, carrying capacity, and off-take rates, while series of counts spread over a number of years yield important information on trends in population size.

(ii) *Distribution and movements:* data on the seasonal patterns of movement and rangeland utilization are necessary to identify key grazing and watering areas, and basic migratory routes.

(iii) *Population structure:* data on population dynamics are required to calculate off-take rates, and the possible causes underlying any observed population trends.

Monitoring animal numbers. Two examples of successful long-term monitoring programmes of large mammal populations, using aerial sampling methods, come from East Africa. In the Serengeti National Park, Tanzania, the populations of migratory wildebeest, zebra, and gazelle have been monitored since the early 1960s. The wildebeest population, which currently number some 1.5 million individuals (Sinclair and Norton-Griffiths 1979), has been studied the most intensively, and there is now a time series of census data from 1960 to 1984.

Initially, the population was counted using the total count method, but since 1970 a combination of Systematic Sampling (to quantify distribution patterns at the time of the census) and Stratified Random Sampling (to estimate numbers) has been applied. The zebra have been censused less frequently, but are now counted biannually, using the same SRF as that used to describe the wildebeeste's distribution. The gazelle data are relatively poor, but they are now censused at the same time as the wildebeest.

These three populations make up a unique assemblage of migratory animals, which together number more than two million individuals. All three populations are now censused during a single operation which requires a light aircraft, pilot, and three observers for about ten days, including some 40 h in the air.

The results of this on-going programme have been summarized by Sinclair and Norton-Griffiths (1979). The spectacular eruption of the wildebeest population from some 200 000 animals in 1960–62 to its present size of 1.5 million is clearly documented. In contrast, the zebra population has remained relatively constant at around 200 000 individuals, while the gazelle have begun an apparent decline, possibly through competition with the wildebeest. This monitoring effort has provided consistently useful information to the Serengeti Park management on their most important populations of animals; in addition, it has produced hard data which can be used to investigate the interactions between these grazing species.

The second example comes from Kenya, where the Kenya Rangeland Ecological Monitoring Unit (KREMU) carries out routine monitoring of wildlife and livestock populations over some 500 000 km² of rangeland. Started in 1976 with support from the Canadian International Development Agency, and supported since by the World Bank among others, the KREMU provides important information to national and regional planners on range conditions and trends, and on the numbers, distribution and seasonal movements of wildlife and livestock. The KREMU aims to cover the whole rangeland areas of Kenya at least once every three years, while more important areas, and areas undergoing rapid development, are monitored much more frequently. The KREMU has also been able to carry out a number of detailed studies into threatened species, such as the Grevy's zebra, the elephant, and the rhinoceros. In addition to its aerial survey aircraft and aircrew, the KREMU maintains a number of ground control plots for monitoring vegetation.

Monitoring seasonal movements. In 1969, a series of SRFs was started in the Serengeti National Park, Tanzania. The objectives were to describe and map:

the seasonal movements of the migratory wildebeest, zebra, and gazelle;

the seasonal patterns of environmental changes (such as quality and quantity of forage, availability of water, and extent of fires);

the distribution, abundance and diversity of the resident wildlife; and

the patterns of land-use around the boundaries of the National Park.

Twenty-eight monitoring flights were undertaken in a 36-month period, each flight covering the 30 000 km² of the Serengeti ecosystem. The results of these studies have been summarized by Sinclair and Norton-Griffiths (1979), especially in the chapter by Maddock. A wide range of extremely useful and important information was acquired during these flights, which gave for the first time insights into the dynamics of this unique ecosystem.

The Amboseli Ecological Monitoring Programme, Kenya, also uses SRF sampling three or four times a year to monitor long-term seasonal movements of stock and wildlife. Although this data set is yet to be worked up in full, it will provide a fascinating picture of how movement patterns change in response to both environmental fluctuations and to changes and developments in land-use patterns.

In Turkanaland, Kenya, two SRF surveys across the 64 000 km² District have mapped and quantified the wet and dry season distributions of domestic stock and the pastoral people associated with them. These data are being used to define the important wet and dry season ranges for each type of stock; to design and implement veterinary services; to locate new access tracks so that the veterinary services can operate effectively; to select the position of new boreholes and dams; and to design health, education, and food relief operations for the population.

Monitoring population structure. In both the Serengeti and the Amboseli monitoring programmes, special flights were made to monitor the structure of wildlife and livestock populations throughout the year. Low-level, oblique 35-mm photography provided important data on calf production, ratios of different age groups, mortality, and survival. Careful co-ordination with ground studies was required initially to ensure correct identification of sex and age classes from the aerial photographs. But once this was done, the light aircraft provided an efficient tool to sample the wide ranging and very numerous populations on a routine basis.

3.1.2.2 Regional resource inventories Low level aerial surveys from light aircraft have now been widely applied for regional resource inventories, usually as part of donor-assisted development programmes. These resource inventories aim to quantify both the abundance and the distribution of resources within a development area, in terms of:

settlements: numbers of houses of different kinds
numbers of other structures

population: distribution and structure of nomadic and resident populations

agriculture: area under active cultivation
area of major crops and crop combinations
area of fallow land
methods of field management
field sizes

livestock: numbers of each type of livestock

wildlife: numbers of each type of wildlife

vegetation: canopy cover of woody vegetation
canopy cover of herbaceous vegetation
area of bare ground

Both SRF and stratified random sampling have been used with equal effectiveness, though the SRF sampling design has usually proved to offer greater flexibility in the range of analyses that can be carried out from the data. In each case, however, it was the addition of vertical 35-mm colour photography to the conventional observations that created the new application.

Descriptions of such resource inventories are given by Norton-Griffiths, Hart, and Parton (1982), and ILCA (1981).

3.1.2.3. Environmental impact assessment Aerial survey methods have proved particularly useful for identifying, predicting and monitoring the environmental impacts of major development projects. One example involved the Jonglei Canal in Southern Sudan, a 350-km canal running from Bor to Malakal on the Nile river and thus short-cutting the river flow into the massive Sud swamp.

Three SRF surveys were made to study the seasonal patterns of flooding, range production, and the associated seasonal movements of livestock and wildlife. Both cattle and wildlife moved towards the Nile during the dry season from the north and from the west. However, the most significant movement was across the line of the canal itself, some 275 000 cattle and 300 000 head of wildlife migrating from east to west across the intended line.

The surveys also yielded important information on the patterns of agricultural activities, on the movements of people associated with the domestic stock, and on the seasonal availability and utilization of grazing resources. These data were later integrated with data from comprehensive ground surveys of production, population dynamics, and disease, to plan agricultural and livestock development projects along the Jonglei Canal, and to lessen the environmental impacts of the canal.

A second example comes from the Selous Game Reserve, Tanzania, where a major hydroelectric dam was planned for Stiegler's Gorge. Three SRF surveys were used to study the seasonal movements of wildlife within the immediate impact area. The analysis indicated that the reservoir upstream of the dam would have relatively little impact on the wildlife. However, downstream of the dam site, the Rufiji flows into an inland delta which supports a very high density and diversity of wildlife. The impact on this delta from the changed flooding regime was likely to be much greater, and it proved possible to identify the populations most at risk and estimate the probable magnitude of the impact on them.

3.1.2.4. Vegetation monitoring Light aircraft have been used very effectively for monitoring vegetation changes, and have provided a cost-effective alternative to large-format aerial photography. In these applications, as with regional resource inventories, the aircraft is fitted with a 35-mm camera system.

In Kenya, a number of long-term vegetation studies has been implemented in the arid rangelands of Turkanaland. On the Upper Turkwell River, 35-mm sample photography from light aircraft was obtained along an 80-km stretch from Amolem to Katilu, where ten irrigation schemes have been built over the past 20 years. These schemes have attracted a large number of destitute Turkana over and above those settled formally on them. Satellite settlements have sprung up around the schemes with informal agricultural activities, and both people and their agriculture are competing directly with tenant farmers for their schemes' infrastructure and services. Furthermore, the same stretch of river still provides important dry-season grazing and watering resources for nomadic Turkana, and conflicts are rapidly developing between the nomadic and settled portion of the Turkana population.

The 35-mm sample photography had a number of objectives, including mapping all settlements and counting all structures in them; measuring the areas of informal and irrigated cultivation; and measuring the impact of these settlements on resources, such as woody canopy, in their immediate vicinity. Data were also obtained from existing large-format photography dating back over 30 years, and from the analysis of 10 years of Landsat imagery.

Elsewhere in Turkanaland, routine sample 35-mm photography is being used to monitor the environmental impacts of famine relief camps and of development schemes, specifically on the important riverine resources. Long-term vegetation dynamics are also being studied, specifically to study the process of desertification.

The Office of Arid Lands Studies at the University of Arizona has also been extremely active in developing the applications of 35-mm sample photography for the long-term monitoring of arid rangelands. It has concentrated primarily on photographing control plots which are also visited on the ground. The ground-truth data are then used to interpret more extensive photographic sampling.

3.1.2.5. Monitoring land-use changes Of particular importance to development planners over the past decades has been the rapid expansion of people, stock, and agriculture into marginal rangeland areas. Often these areas support at best very sporadic agricultural production, and significant environmental degradation can occur without careful land-use planning and effective extension services. Too often, such services are simply not available in these marginal areas. Of additional concern is the impact of such land-use changes on nomadic or semi-nomadic livestock systems, for these marginal lands usually represent important dry-season grazing reserves.

Light aircraft, equipped with 35-mm camera systems, can again provide a cost-effective tool for quantifying and monitoring such changes. Although such programmes are at present few in number, study areas have been established along the agricultural/rangeland interface in Kenya, while a more ambitious programme is to start soon in Peru to monitor agricultural incursions into previously forested areas.

3.1.3. The systematic reconnaissance flight

3.1.3.1. General concepts The SRF was developed initially to study the seasonal movements of domestic stock and wildlife, and the seasonal patterns of associated environmental factors such as grazing resources, water, and fire. More recently, the SRF has evolved into a cost-effective method for rapid survey, inventory and monitoring of renewable natural resources over very large areas. Typically, SRFs are now used to quantify the abundance and seasonal distribution of surface-water, domestic stock, and wildlife; and to quantify patterns of settlement, land-use, and agricultural activities.

The SRF is a sampling technique for quantifying the spatial distribution of land-use parameters through a combination of visual observations and vertical photography from low-flying, high-wing light aircraft. The aircraft flies parallel transects (flight lines) across the study area at a ground speed of about 160 km/h and at a height of about 120 m. Visual observations are recorded continuously along the length of each transect, but are divided into successive 'sub-units' on the basis of elapsed time (such as one minute) or elapsed distance (such as 5 km). One or more vertical, sample photographs are taken within each subunit, and all data recorded during the survey are cross-referenced to an individual transect/subunit.

Although the spacing of the parallel flight lines can be varied depending on the size of the area and on the objectives of the survey, it is the navigation of the aircraft along the transects which is of fundamental importance. Typically, an OMEGA/VLF navigation system is used for accurate navigation and for the accurate demarcation of each subunit. The key characteristic of the SRF method is that it delivers a set of data points each of which is geo-referenced with a high degree of accuracy.

The width of the observers' sampling strip and the scale of the vertical photographs both depend upon the height of the aircraft above the ground. This is controlled by reference to a radar altimeter which is recorded at least once every subunit.

The SRF is typically carried out within the framework of a sampling grid. The UTM grid system is widely used for such sampling frames, for it is a world-wide standard grid system which is projected onto many maps, and which can be projected easily onto aerial photographs or other cartographic/thematic data sources. Each subunit is assigned to an individual grid cell, and each grid cell contains a unique set of subunits.

The grid cells within an SRF survey area have three important uses. First, they provide standard locational information. Secondly, they provide very convenient thematic mapping units. Thirdly, they can be used to standardize map and thematic information, and for data input to the SRF data set.

3.1.3.2. Visual observations Visual observations of livestock and of wild-life are made by observers sitting in the rear two seats of the aircraft. They continuously scan a 150-metre-wide sampling strip demarcated by rods attached to the wing struts of the aircraft. The observers record all their data onto tape for later transcription, along with time pulses to distinguish between successive subunits. Domestic stock and wildlife are thus tallied within each subunit, and all large herds of animals are photographed for accurate counting at a later date.

3.1.3.3. Vertical 35-mm photography The vertical 35-mm colour diapositives taken along the length of each transect, provide the bulk of the data on vegetation and on land-use characteristics. A vertically mounted 35-mm camera, fitted with an 18-mm lens, photographs an area of approximately four hectares at a flying height of 120 m, at an image scale of approximately 1/6700. The actual height of the aircraft above ground level is recorded each time a photograph is taken so that the photo-scale can be controlled for each frame individually.

The photographs provide two types of data: count and area. Count data are simple enumerations of objects on the colour slides such as buildings of different types, water tanks, cattle dips, individual trees, woodlots, or erosion gullies. Area data are measurements of the proportional area on the diapositives of different land-cover classes. Area data can be obtained for land under active cultivation; land under different crops and intercrops; fields of different sizes; land taken up by roads, tracks and house compounds; fallow land; land under different kinds of forest cover or other vegetation classifications; canopy cover of the tree, bush, and herbaceous components of the natural vegetation; area of bare ground; and area affected by gully or sheet erosion.

3.1.3.4. Ancillary data One of the most useful characteristics of the SRF is the ease with which ancillary data can be integrated into the SFR data set. Data derived from maps can include administrative boundaries; local slope angles, elevation and land-form; rainfall and other climatic data; soil boundaries; transport and service networks; and service centres. Data derived from ground surveys – such as information on population structure and mortality, erosion rates, crop yields, and farming systems – can also be incorporated. Finally, data are often derived from conventional aerial photography (such as previous land-use patterns), from satellite images, and from the digital analysis of satellite data (such as green biomass ratios from Landsat or from NOAA-7).

3.1.3.5. Data integration All data collected in the course of an SRF survey, including the ancillary data, are in one of three forms: point, grid, or polygon. Point data are individual samples or observations collected at a precisely determined point in space represented by the physical position of an individual subunit. Point data include the observers' livestock and wildlife observations within a subunit, and all the count and area data obtained from a 35-mm sample photograph.

Grid data are more coarse, and involve classifying an individual UTM grid cell on some particular attribute such as rainfall, mean slope angle, elevation, drainage density, or percentage cultivation measured off historical air photos. All of the subunits assigned to an individual cell are thus assigned the same classification.

Polygons represent contiguous areas demarcated by boundaries. They may represent soil types, administrative divisions, national parks, rainfall isohyetes, or special development areas. As with grid cells, each subunit is assigned to an individual polygon and each polygon contains a unique set of subunits. Once assigned, the subunits are classified from the polygon's data.

Polygons are also used to integrate data which do not fall easily into point or grid form. For example, once the subunits are classifed by soil type polygons they may also be classified by the characteristics of those soil types. Similarly, once the subunits are classified by administrative area polygons, they may be reclassified by any characteristic of that area such as population density and structure, disease incidence, or ethnic diversity.

Polygons are, in fact, extremely flexible, and can represent curious but useful boundaries such as increasing radii from service centres, towns, or boreholes; distance bands from road or river networks; or areas within which certain data variables combine in some important manner (such as given soil type(s) within a given altitude range). They can also represent important socio-economic factors such as the wet- and dry-season grazing areas of tribal groups in pastoral land.

3.1.3.6. Data recombinations Once the SRF and ancillary data are integrated into a common data set, new variables can be created from combinations of the original ones. For example:

total livestock numbers, or livestock units, from the individual livestock counts;

total wildlife numbers, or wildlife biomass, from the individual species counts;

estimates of pastoral populations by multiplying hut numbers by people/hut derived from ground census;

land suitability, from a combination of elevation, slope, soil characteristics, and climatic factors;

potential crop production, from a combination of climate, soil, land husbandry, and infrastructure factors;

fertilizer requirements, from soil and crop factors;

rangeland potential, from the characteristics of the vegetation and climate, modified perhaps by satellite data;

constraints to development, in terms of population, water availability, access, soils, disease, and infrastructure; and

sediment budgets, from field measurements of erosion rates on rangeland, on cultivated land under different crop types and husbandry, and on bare areas such as tracks and unmetalled roads.

3.1.3.7. Data analysis The fully integrated SRF data set can be analysed in many ways to give information of immediate use and relevance to development planners.

Thematic maps provide the development planner with a description of the spatial distribution and abundance of resources throughout the survey area. Although in principle any SRF-generated variable can be mapped in a variety of formats and scales, in practice careful thought is required to produce useful results.

Both the thematic mapping units and the variable ranges within them must be selected carefully so that both regional trends and local variations can be portrayed. Very small thematic mapping units and a multiplicity of narrow variable ranges produce too much noise for useful results, while large mapping units and wide variable ranges will degrade the information.

Thematic maps are typically produced in one of two formats: as grid

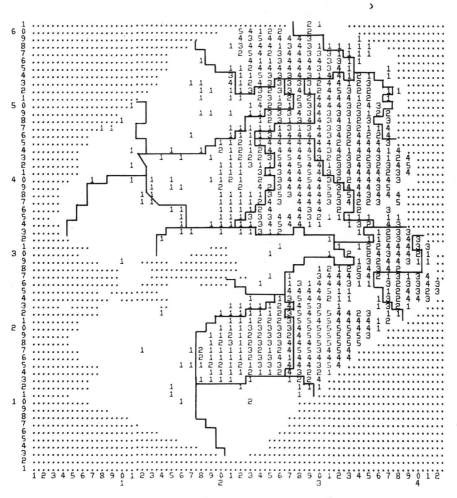

Fig. 3.1.

CODE	RANGE No/Km2	MEAN No/Km2	AREA Km2	% AREA	OBSERVED No.	% OBSERVED
			19825	51		
1	< 10.00	3.66	6525	17	23,860	4
2	< 20.00	14.86	2750	7	40,860	6
3	< 40.00	29.23	3625	9	105,970	16
4	< 100.00	65.94	4850	13	319,810	49
5	>= 100.00	127.27	1225	3	155,900	24
	TOTAL	16.66	38800	100	646,399	100

cell maps or as polygon maps. In grid cell maps, each cell receives the average value, or median value, of the subunits assigned to it, thus removing very local variation. Figure 3.1 is a typical grid cell map showing the density of grade cattle within 1566 UTM grid cells of 5 × 5 km in western Kenya. The data are presented both as class values (Fig. 3.1) and as calculated densities (Fig. 3.2), and both local and regional patterns are clearly seen.

Polygon maps represent thematic information within boundaries such as administrative areas, vegetation zones, altitude zones, soil types, drainage basins, or whatever thematic unit is most appropriate for a given set of development objectives. In general, however, polygon maps have less local detail then do grid square maps, and are used primarily for portraying regional trends, and trends within selected spatial units. Figure 3.3 presents the same information on grade cattle within 222

INTEGRATED LAND USE SURVEY
GRADE CATTLE (Density/Km↑2)

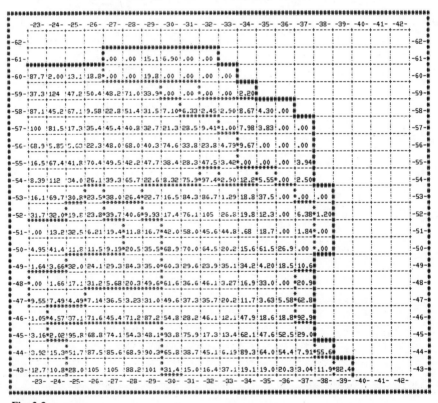

Fig. 3.2.

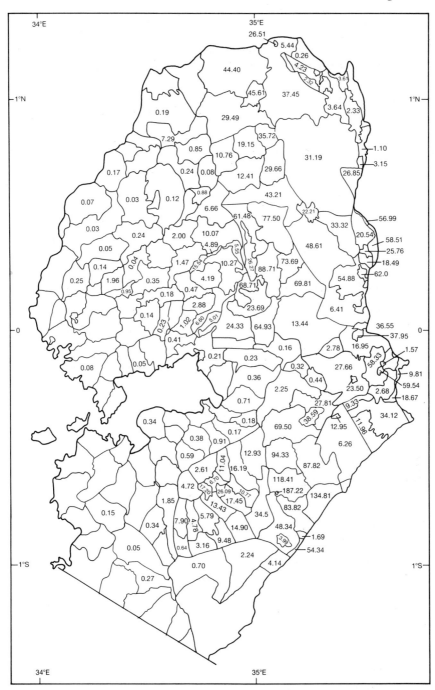

Fig. 3.3.

administrative locations in western Kenya. The regional patterns are still clearly seen, but the local variation has been suppressed and smoothed.

Resource inventories are tabular listings of resources within a specified geographical area or within a set of contiguous strata. These inventories are typically produced in one of two formats: the sector summary and the stratus profile.

The sector summary quantifies an individual resource within a set of strata, and the tabulations allow the development planner to compare the abundance of the resource within each stratum. Table 3.1 presents a sector summary of grade cattle within twelve Districts of western Kenya, the same survey area as shown in Figs 3.1 to 3.3.

In contrast, the stratum profile tabulates all resources within a selected

Table 3.1. Livestock densities in western Kenya

District		Local cattle	Grade cattle	Sheep and goats
Kisii	density*	56.1	12.4	12.0
	number	124 000	28 000	27 000
Kisumu	density	66.4	0.2	28.1
	number	149 000	—	63 000
Siaya	density	66.6	0.2	17.1
	number	175 000	—	45 000
South Nyanza	density	64.5	0.1	15.7
	number	407 000	1000	99 000
Bungoma	density	53.5	2.1	6.2
	number	176 000	7000	20 000
Busia	density	49.7	0.1	7.5
	number	88 000	—	13 000
Kakamega	density	54.6	6.3	9.3
	number	201 000	23 000	34 000
Kericho	density	33.3	44.8	15.9
	number	148 000	100 000	71 000
Nandi	densisty	24.9	42.6	9.1
	number	68 000	116 000	25 000
Narok	density	130.4	0.8	21.4
	number	263 000	2000	43 000
Trans Nzoia	density	15.5	30.0	14.0
	number	34 000	66 000	31 000
Uasin Gishu	density	22.3	31.3	19.6
	number	86 000	121 000	76 000

*density: individuals per km^2

Source: SRF survey of 40 000 km^2 of western Kenya using visual observations and vertical 35-mm photography for crop cover, on behalf of the Lake Basin Development Authority, Kisumu, and funded by Netherlands Technical Aid.

stratum to as much detail as a planner requires. Table 3.2 presents a simplified stratum profile for Kakamega District in western Kenya.

Resource inventories can be produced for any geographical unit within a survey area, and one of the strengths of the SRF method is the ease

Table 3.2. Simplified stratum profile for Kakamega District in western Kenya.

Area: 3678 km²			
	Density	Number	
Population			
1962	161.6	595 000	
1969	208.6	767 000	
1979	283.7	1 043 000	
Dependency	59%		
Increase 1962–69	3.7% pa		
Increase 1969–79	3.1% pa		
Livestock			
Local cattle	54.6	201 000	
Grade cattle	6.3	23 000	
Sheep and goats	9.3	34 000	
	ha/km²	Hectares	
Land-budget			
Agriculture	51.2	188 000	
Natural vegetation	43.9	161 000	
Infrastructure	4.3	16 000	
Miscellaneous	0.6	2000	
Crops			
Bananas	2.0	7300	
Cassava	1.1	4000	
Finger millet	0.1	200	
Maize	15.1	55 500	
Sweet Potatoes	1.0	3900	
Coffee	0.3	1100	
Tea	0.4	1300	
Sugar cane	8.5	31 200	
Natural vegetation			
Tree cover	16.0	59 000	
Bush cover	5.0	18 300	
Herbaceous cover	21.1	77 600	
	Density	Number	%
Individual trees			
In natural vegetation	69.1	254 000	19%
In cropland	165.5	609 000	45%
Around homesteads	111.4	410 000	30%
On roads and tracks	25.2	93 000	6%

Source: As for Table 3.1

with which this can be done. Depending upon the detailed requirements of the development planner, resource inventories can be made for administrative areas, conservation areas, drainage basins, soil types, climatic zones, special development areas, or catchments of proposed hydroelectric schemes.

Finally, the SRF method generates data in a format that allows for a wide range of analyses. Some of the analyses that development planners have found of particular relevance are listed below.

Environmental influences (Table 3.3): relationships between elevation, slopes, land systems, climate, and soil characteristics on land-use patterns or individual crops, and the extent to which they provide constraints to development or opportunities for development.

Table 3.3. Influence of elevation on crop distributions

Elevation (m)	% crop in each elevation range							
	EXP	CO	CV	SC	CF	TE	WH	MZ
— 1200	10	38	21	4				5
— 1400	22	55	61	55	1			15
— 1600	15	7	14	34	19	5		15
— 1800	12		3	5	44	20	1	17
— 2000	19		1	2	33	52	15	27
— 2200	10				2	21	46	10
— 2400	6				1	2	30	7
— 2600	4						4	3
> 2600							4	

EXP: Expected % if each crop were randomly distributed with respect to elevation.

Crops: CO – Cotton; CV – Cassava; SC – Sugar cane; CF – Coffee; TE – Tea; WH – Wheat; MZ – Maize.

Most crops show strong relationship to elevation. Maize is more ubiquitous due to breeding programmes that have created numerous varieties for local conditions.

Source: As for Table 3.1.

Service networks and centres (Table 3.4): distribution of crops and land-use patterns with respect to service networks (such as transport) and centres (such as markets, farm supplies, and collection points); seasonal distribution of pastoral livestock with respect to veterinary centres and water points.

Land-budgets (Table 3.5): of most application in agricultural surveys, a land-budget quantifies all land in use, and characterizes the land still available for development. Of immediate application in areas where

Table 3.4. Distributon of people and livestock around permanent settlement sites in Turkana District, Kenya.

Distances from sites (km)	0–5	<10	<15	<20	<25	>25
% District	5%	14%	16%	15%	15%	35%
Settled population						
Density/km^2	27.1					
% of total	100%					
Pastoral population						
Density/km^2	—	2.7	3.5	1.8	0.9	0.4
% of total	—	24%	39%	18%	9%	10%
Cattle						
Density	2.1	7.6	3.3	1.8	1.8	0.6
% of total	4%	41%	21%	17%	10%	7%
Camels						
Density	0.7	3.7	1.2	2.4	2.0	0.5
% of total	2%	31%	13%	23%	19%	12%
Sheep and goats						
Density	16.6	37.7	26.6	26.3	13.3	5.7
% of total	4%	28%	24%	22%	11%	11%

Source: SRF survey of 64 000 km^2 of Turkana District, Kenya, on behalf of the Turkana Rehabilitation Programme, and funded by the European Economic Communities.

Table 3.5. Land-budget for western Kenya

(100% of Land = Agriculture + Infrastructure + Natural vegetation + Miscellaneous)

Agriculture	38%	Staple crops	15%
		Cash crops	7%
		Vegetables and fruit	<1%
		Other crops and bare ground	4%
		Fallow fields	7%
		Managed pastures	4%
		Unused bits and pieces	<1%
Infrastructure	6%	Transport	2%
		Hedges	2%
		Homesteads	2%
Natural vegetation	55%	Tree cover	16%
		Bush cover	8%
		Herbaceous cover	31%
Miscellaneous	1%	Marsh and papyrus	<1%
		Open water	<1%
		Barren scars and rocks	<1%
		Streambeds	<1%

Source: As for Table 3.1.

rural population densities are placing intense pressure on land resources.

Intensity gradients (Table 3.6): the analysis of land-use changes along gradients of increasing population density or agricultural intensity reveals insights into the dynamics of land-use, and into the possible boundary conditions that will limit further development. In pastoral areas, the ratios of livestock species along gradients of increasing aridity or vegetation cover reveal local adaptations to environmental stress.

Table 3.6. Land-use along the gradient of increasing population density in western Kenya

1979 Population density/km^2	AR %	LV d	AG %	IN %	NV %	TR %	BS %	HB %
0	6	23	10	1	80	47	13	19
0–50	11	75	12	2	82	39	10	32
50–100	23	86	34	4	60	16	7	37
100–150	23	87	41	5	53	10	7	35
150–200	17	85	46	7	46	8	7	30
200–250	9	94	48	10	41	7	7	26
250–300	3	81	50	10	39	6	6	27
300–350	3	69	54	10	34	7	6	20
350–400	2	76	55	11	33	6	6	20
400–500	2	82	59	11	29	9	4	15
>500	1	56	51	13	34	9	5	20

AR – % of study area; LV – density of livestock/km^2; AG – % agriculture ha/km^2; IN – % infrastructure ha/km^2; NV – % natural vegetation ha/km^2; TR – % tree canopy cover ha/km^2; BS – % bush canopy cover ha/km^2; HB – % herbaceous cover ha/km^2

Livestock densities peak in the mid-population density range and then decrease; % agriculture increases until the highest population densities; natural vegetation cover decreases, but stabilizes at population densities above 250/km^2; tree and bush cover stabilize at around 15% cover at population densities above 150/km^2.

Source: As for Table 3.1.

Land suitability (Table 3.7): one of the most useful applications of SRF-generated data. Land suitability can be assessed for individual crops or crop combinations, for farming systems, and for different kinds of development projects, and can also give advanced warning of development conflicts. This is of particular relevance in semi-arid and arid lands where agricultural developments often conflict with pastoral livestock husbandary.

Table 3.7. Constraints to livestock development in Turkana District, Kenya

Variable	Levels	Constraint Score
1. Index of water accessibility		
	Within 10 km	1
	Within 20 km	4
	>20 km	12
2. Local raiding problems		
	Rare	1
	Occasional	6
	Persistent	12
3. Tsetse fly challenge		
	Unlikely	1
	Likely	6
	Probable	10
4. Accessibility index for vehicles		
	Existing access	1
	<2 h off road	1
	<4 h off road	4
	>4 h off road	6
	Foot access only	8

A combined score on all four variables was calculated in turn for each 10×10 km UTM grid in the District. These combined scores were then ranged as follows:

Constraint	Score	km^2	% District
Light	<=7	8100	13%
Medium	>7 and <15	27 500	44%
Heavy	>=15	26 900	43%

Areas of low constraints are thus characterized by:

Water access:	within 20 km		within 10 km
Raiding problems;	rare	OR	rare
Tsetse challenge:	unlikely		unlikely
Vehicle access:	<2 h off road		<4 h off road

Source: as for Table 3.4.

3.1.4. *Stratified random sampling*

3.1.4.1. The concept of stratification No survey area is completely homogeneous in terms of land-form, soils, vegetation, land-use patterns, settlements, domestic stock, and wildlife. All these attributes will vary across a survey area, often in a very marked way. For example, agricultural land-use may be restricted to areas of certain types of soils within a certain range of slopes, and to areas with certain rainfall reliabilities; domestic stock may be found concentrated only in areas with grazing or water resources; certain types of vegetation may be very restricted in distribution; and some types of land-use (such as tea or coffee plantations) may be strictly limited by altitude.

The process of stratification consists of dividing up a survey area into sub-areas of strata which are more homogeneous within themselves with respect to one or a number of attributes than is the survey area as a whole. For example, a survey area might consist of flood-plains, some gently sloping foothills, and some steep scarps leading to a highland plateau. An obvious stratification of such an area would be on the basis of these landforms, namely 'flood-plain', 'foothills', 'escarpments', and 'highland plateau'.

This stratification would undoubtedly also reflect basic land-use patterns. Agricultural land use would be concentrated on the foothills and the highland plateau; maize-type crops would be common on the foothills, and perhaps tea and coffee on the plateau; and there might be small pockets of rain-fed or irrigated rice in the flood-plain – which could always be demarcated as another stratum. Domestic stock might show seasonal movements between lowland and highland areas.

A stratification of a survey area can be made on any combination of environmental or land-use characteristics, and it can be as detailed or as broad as is required by the objectives of the survey. In the above example, the simple land-form stratification would suffice for a generalized land-use survey. However, if the objectives of the survey were to classify the details of cropping types, land-use criteria would be much more important and many smaller strata would be demarcated to reflect the spatial variation in cropping intensities and crop combinations.

In contrast, if the objectives of the survey were to enumerate domestic stock, the stratification would reflect vegetation zones and perhaps areas of water availability, factors known to influence stock distributions.

Two important principles must be borne in mind in order to stratify an area successfully.

First, there is nothing to be gained by stratifying just for the sake of it. The stratification must be guided in the sense that it must reflect the major objectives of the survey. A stratification for describing woodland vegetation types will be different to one for describing agricultural land-use patterns; and different again to one for describing the distributions and numbers of livestock. No single stratification can meet all possible survey objectives, and any given stratification will be effective only for the criteria on which it was drawn up. Thus, a stratification for describing livestock will give poor results on agricultural land-use patterns, and vice versa.

Secondly, as wide a range of information as possible must be used in the stratification process. This may involve satellite imagery, maps and small-scale aerial photographs, and previously published material on the study area. All this must be used and integrated into a stratification. Furthermore, the area should be flown over once the boundaries of the strata are drawn up to ensure that they are distinct and meaningful.

Once the strata have been demarcated, the sampling effort is concentrated in those strata of particular interest. In a stratification of agricultural land-use patterns; for example, more sampling effort would be directed towards the strata containing crops than to those not containing crops. Similarly, in a stratification designed for a census of domestic stock, more effort is spent sampling strata with known high stock densities than those with low densities.

Finally, once decisions have been made on the stratum boundaries, and on the proportional allocation of sampling effort within each stratum, the flight-line transects are distributed randomly within each.

3.1.4.2. Data collection The procedures for collecting data, making visual observations of livestock and wildlife, and taking 35-mm sample photographs along the length of each transect are the same as those described in Sections 3.1.3.2 and 3.1.3.3. Given that all data are collected within successive subunits along the transects, and that these subunits can be geo-referenced, ancillary data can be incorporated into the stratified random-sample data set in the same ways as described in 3.1.3.4. However, grid data are more difficult to incorporate.

3.1.4.3. Data integration and analysis Although in principle the same range of analyses can be made from survey data generated with stratified random sampling as from SRF sampling, in practice the situation is slightly different. The first major difference is that the samples (transects) are selected at random within each stratum. Therefore, distribution data, population estimates, and resource inventories are largely restricted to the stratum boundaries themselves. Statements about the whole survey area – for example the distribution of domestic stock or of maize fields – can be made only with respect to the stratum boundaries, and it is effectively impossible to obtain data in more detail than that of the individual stratum. None the less, thoroughly valid, precise, and useful distribution data and resource inventories are obtained by stratified random-sampling, but always within the framework of the stratum boundaries.

3.1.4.4. Comparison between the SRF and the STRS methods Systematic sampling (the SRF method) and stratified random sampling (STRS) produce apparently similar results but in quite different ways. There is, however, a fundamental difference in the two approaches.

The SRF method gathers information evenly over a survey area (although sampling can be more intensive in areas of particular interest), and therefore all variation within an attribute and all variations between attributes are sampled proportionally to their occurrences. Thus, if a given land-form (such as a flood-plain) covers 23 per cent of a survey area, then 23 per cent of the systematic sample will fall on it. Similarly, if a certain soil–altitude association covers only 1 per cent of a survey area then 1 per cent of the sytematic sample will fall on it – unless, of course, the association was previously identified as being of particular interest and was therefore sampled more intensively.

Stratified sampling takes a very different approach. The survey area is first stratified on a variety of attributes into homogeneous strata which reflect the main objectives of the survey. The random sampling is then more intensive in those strata of particular interest, and it may be extremely low (effectively nil) in areas of no interest whatsoever.

These two approaches have a number of consequences:

Precision: for a given amount of sampling effort (such as aircraft hours), stratified random sampling will give more precise estimates than will systematic sampling, but only for those attributes that harmonize with the stratification.

Distribution maps: thematic maps of the distribution and abundance of resources within a survey area are particularly useful to development planners. Data derived from SRF can be mapped within any thematic unit of relevance to the development objectives, such as administrative areas, altitude zones, soil types, land-forms, or UTM grid cells. In contrast, the STRS data can be mapped only with reference to the stratum boundaries.

Resource inventories: as with thematic mapping, resource inventories can be produced from SRF-generated data for any required subdivision of the survey area. In effect, this is achieved by stratifying the data after the event, rather than before the event as with STRS. Data derived from SRF can thus be 'stratified' to provide resource inventories within adminstrative areas, altitude zones, climatic zones, land-forms, soil types, vegetation zones, development areas, distance radii from service centres, or any combination of these. The SRF creates a true data base for the development planner. In contrast, useful flexibility is largely lost with stratified random sampling, because the samples are valid only for the stratum within which they were drawn.

Influence of the environment, and infrastructure: perhaps the most significant difference between the two methods lies in the possibilities for analysing the influence of environmental variation on land use, livestock, wildlife, and natural resources. The SRF collects information on all variation and combinations of variations between resources and the environment within the study area. Simple statistical methods, primarily the analysis of variance, are then used to determine which factor, or combination of factors, explains (in the statistical sense) the observed variations in distribution and abundance. This flexibility is largely lost with a stratified random sample, for the stratification imposes a rigid framework on the data set which is extremely difficult to break.

This lack of flexibility in the stratified random sample becomes even more marked when the influence of infrastructure is to be assessed. It is straightforward, for example, to analyse from an SRF data set the seasonal movements of livestock with respect to water holes, and the potential influence on these movements of providing more waterholes. Similarly, it is straightforward to analyse the seasonal proportion of livestock within easy reach of veterinary services, and the influence of building new access tracks on the provision of veterinary services. Neither of these analyses would be possible with data derived from stratified random sampling.

These two methods for aerial inventory and monitoring are, however, truly complementary and are used to provide very different kinds of information under quite different sets of circumstances.

The Systematic Reconnaisance Flight (SRF) method is most appropriate under the following conditions:

(a) For multidisciplinary development programmes in large study areas, where each facet of the programme is involved with different aspects of the environment, resources and development potential.

(b) When it is important to quantify the seasonal distributions and abundance of resources, and the seasonal distributions of land-use patterns.

(c) When a wide range of ancillary data is to be incorporated into the data set.

(d) When it is important to analyse the influence of environmental variation, as well as infrastructure and service networks, on the distribution, abundance and utilisation of resources, and to land-use patterns.

Stratified random sampling is most appropriate under the following conditions.

(a) When the survey design calls for the maximum precision of a small range of attributes.

(b) When the strata with low sampling intensity are indeed of little interest to a development project.

In practice, therefore, stratified random sampling is most usually used in monitoring situations where small deviations from trends need to be quantified with a high degree of precision. The SRF method, in contrast, is most often used to acquire the initial inventory and baseline data on which the monitoring phase is designed.

Two examples demonstrate the complementarity of the two methods. In the Serengeti National Park, Tanzania, the SRF method was used to quantify the seasonal distributions of migratory wildlife with respect to seasonal environmental variations. Stratified random sampling was used to estimate as precisely as possible the total numbers of animals in these migratory populations.

The second example comes from northern Kenya, where two SRFs of Turkana District have yielded a wide range of information on the movements and distribution patterns of livestock and pastoralists, and on the seasonal dynamics of rangeland productivity and utilization. In the monitoring phase, stratified random sampling is being used to estimate annually the sizes of the most important livestock populations. Stratified random sampling is also being used within vegetation strata to monitor in detail the impacts of developmental activities and any trends towards desertification.

3.1.5. Block and total counting

Although block and total counting are now rarely used, conditions are still encountered where they are the most appropriate method.

3.1.5.1. Block counting Transect counting, as described above, is difficult and quite dangerous to use in hilly and mountainous country. Apart from the risks involved in attempting to contour-fly over very rough terrain, the control of height above ground becomes highly problematical.

Block counting should be used under these conditions. The first stage is to divide the area into blocks on the basis of obvious physical features in the landscape such as rivers, ridges, valley bottoms, and roads. A sample of blocks is then chosen at random, and each selected block is covered intensively from the air and all animals and other needed attributes in it are counted.

Perfectly valid and accurate data can thus be obtained and the results can be integrated easily into both SRF and STRS data sets. However, block counting absorbs a great deal of flying time and should therefore be used only when absolutely necessary. Furthermore, it is difficult to count a wide variety of attributes when using block-counting methods.

3.1.5.2. Total counting Total counting is only feasible in smaller survey areas where a very restricted set of attributes is to be enumerated. Total counting works well for large and very visible objects such as herds of buffalo, elephant, and livestock. The approach is the same for block counts, and in practice a total count is a block count in which all the blocks are counted.

Total counting has been used to good effect on livestock in small study areas of up to 5000 km². The first step is often to map all the pastoral settlements in use, and then visit each in turn from the air and photograph all animals as they emerge from the stockades at the beginning of the day.

3.1.6. Important publications

There is a wealth of publications on aerial inventory and monitoring methods which will be referred to in this text. There are, however, three important publications which are worth describing individually, and which would form a useful basis for designing and implementing field programmes.

1. *East African Agricultural and Forestry Journal,* Vol 34 (1969)
   This special issue presents the proceedings of a seminar on aerial survey methods. It is very wildlife-orientated but has a number of important publications on the basic methodologies. Two important papers by G. M. Jolly (1969*a*, *b*) are titled 'Sampling methods for aerial censuses of wildlife populations' (pp. 46–49), and 'The treatment of errors in aerial counts of wildlife populations', pp 50–5. These are both seminal papers.

2. *Low-level aerial survey techniques* ILCA Monograph No. 4, 1981.
   Published by the International Livestock Centre for Africa, P.O. Box 5689, Addis Ababa, Ethiopia; also available through the United Nations Environment Programme, Global Environmental Monitoring System, P.O. Box 30552, Nairobi, Kenya.
   This publication presents the proceedings of a seminar on aerial survey methods held in 1979. The monograph has an excellent series of papers on all aspects of survey methods, including new ideas on controlling error and biases. There is a spirited discussion on the relative advantages of systematic versus stratified sampling, and it is particularly interesting to see how the emphasis of the applications has shifted away from wildlife and rangeland to agricultural and land-use.

3. *Counting animals,* 2nd edn.
   Published by, and available through, the African Wildlife Foundation, P.O. Box 48177, Nairobi, Kenya.
   This is a new edition of the first in a series of handbooks on wildlife management techniques. *Counting animals* (Norton-Griffiths 1978) is a primer on aerial survey methods, and sets out in exhaustive details the steps required in the design, implementation, and analysis of aerial surveys. It is an extremely useful and practical guide to aerial survey methods, and many of the practical details that are well explained in the handbook are omitted from this text.

3.2. Operational procedures for aerial surveys and monitoring

3.2.1.   Aircraft and equipment

3.2.1.1. Basic considerations Aerial surveys are most effective when carried out by a four-man crew, with each member having specific duties. The pilot is responsible for aircraft safety and operation; the front-seat observer monitors flight parameters, operates the cameras, and records some environmental information; the two rear-seat observers collect visual and photographic data from defined sampling strips. The aircraft must therefore be capable of carrying a crew of four with their equipment over significant distances, in addition to sensible safety equipment.

Two-man crews of pilot and observer are rarely used today except when purely photographic data are being collected.

3.2.1.2. Aircraft Of the light aircraft available, the high-wing, six-seater Cessna 185 and 206 models are widely used. These are extremely robust and very powerful; they can carry a four-man crew, their equipment, and safety equipment with ease; and when fitted with long-range tanks can cover huge areas very effectively. Operators sometimes specify STOL conversions and turbocharged engines: STOL equipment is always useful, but turbocharging is necessary only when the aircraft is operating at high altitudes, or in mountainous country.

The four-seater Cessna 180, 182, and 'Reims Rocket' are also popular as survey aircraft, but they can carry smaller loads and have a more restricted range. Some operators have also used the high-wing, twin-engined Paternavia. This aircraft has the disadvantages of not having wing struts and of not flying as slowly as the Cessna models, while the potential advantages of twin engines have yet to be demonstrated.

3.2.1.3. Avionics In addition to the usual NAV/COM and ADF normally found in light aircraft, the first and most essential additional piece of equipment is a radar altimeter to show the actual height of the aircraft above ground level. The radar altimeter is essential for aerial surveys and cannot be dispensed with, and the King Gold Crown (Model KRA 40) has proved reliable.

Another important item is an OMEGA/VLF navigation system which tunes into the world-wide network of very low frequency (*c.* 18 km) radio beacons. They allow for accurate aircraft positioning and navigation, and although expensive are essential for precise operations in areas where maps are poor. They also provide extremely useful information such as ground speed and the precise location of each subunit. A highly recommended system is the Global Navigation System GNS500A Series 2, fitted with course deviation indicator (CDI) and pilot numerical display (PND).

The cost of such navigation systems is decreasing each year, and it will not be long before satellite-based navigation systems become standard equipment in light aircraft.

3.2.1.4. 35-mm cameras The vertical, 35-mm sample photographs taken within each subunit provide a significant range of information. The cameras must therefore be robust and of high quality.

The Cannon F1 and the Nikon F3, fitted with motor drives and 250-exposure backs, are both robust and reliable. Nikon also supplies a 500-exposure back, but there are few details on its reliability. The Olympus OM2 is not recommended for this purpose.

The choice of lens will depend upon the required scale of photography and the flying height. For photography during animal counts at 400 ft above ground level, an 18-mm lens is recommended. This gives excellent results and from 400 ft images an area of approximately four hectares, with very little (2 per cent) distortion, at an image scale of 1:6700. So long as diapositive film, such as high-speed Ektachrome, is used these photographs can be projected at a ten-times enlargement for interpretation at a scale of 1:670.

It is quite straightforward to cut the necessary holes in the skin of the aircraft to mount a 35-mm camera, and no special mounts are needed since a high shutter speed can be used. In a Cessna 206, for example, the floor and skin panels beneath one of the rear seats can be cut away and the camera mounted on simple metal braces. A baffle is required on the outer skin of the aircraft so that air is sucked out of the hole rather into it. It is also important that the camera can be reached in flight by one of the rear-seat observers, not only to check on the film remaining but also to change film. However, this last procedure is surprisingly difficult and a dual camera system is preferable.

The control leads from the camera(s) are run to the front of the aircraft where the front seat observer can operate them. Intervalometers are not recommended because they frequently break down. A stop-watch and a manual firing button are much more reliable.

A recommended system consists of two Nikon F3 cameras with 250-exposure backs and 18-mm lenses, each with a daylight filter. The control cords run to a simple junction box in the front of the aircraft, and the cameras are fired by a push-button. The dual camera system has many advantages. First, a second camera is available for backup if one fails. Secondly, the 440 useable frames permit significant country to be covered before reloading. Thirdly, for certain types of photographic mission, the cameras can be fitted with lenses of differing focal lengths which, when the cameras are fired simultaneously, provide a large-scale photograph 'boreholed' within a small-scale photograph.

3.2.1.5. Ancillary equipment A number of smaller items of equipment is also required for the aircraft and crew. These include glass fibre rods attached to the wing struts for demarcating the observer's sampling strips; 35-mm motor drive cameras with 50-mm lenses for all three observers, plus one spare, for photographing herds of animals (the Olympus OM2 is recommended here); tape recorders for each rear-seat observer, and one spare; full intercom between all crew members (this greatly cuts down on noise and fatigue); stop-watch (and spare) for both pilot and front-seat observer; full range of safety equipment including water and food, simple shelter, drugs (morphine), flares, signalling mirror, emergency locator beacon, and hand-held VHF transmitter.

3.2.2 Crew duties

3.2.2.1. Pilot The pilot is responsible for the safety of the aircraft, for navigation, and for the control of height above ground and ground speed. Whenever possible, the pilot records onto his flight map the exact starting and finishing points of each transect, as well as *en route* landmarks. Before the start of a transect, he calls out over the intercom the transect number and the direction of flight. He also calls out the start of each successive subunit along the length of each transect, either on the basis of elapsed time (1 min or $\frac{1}{2}$ min on the stop watch) or elapsed distance (from the PND on the navigation system).

3.2.2.2. The front-seat observer (FSO) The duties of the front-seat observer include recording flight information, camera operation, and recording data.

Flight information. For each flight, the FSO records the date, aircraft registration, the names and seating positions of all crew, and the take-off and landing times. For each transect, the FSO records the transect number, the direction of flight, the start time and the end time. For each subunit, the FSO records the subunit number, and once during each subunit the height of the aircraft above the ground.

If sample photographs are taken in each subunit, the radar altimeter is read at the time of photography. If GNS navigation is used, the FSO records the 'distance FROM' at the start of each subunit.

Camera operation. The FSO is responsible for all aspects of camera operation including checking the camera before flight, mounting the camera in the aircraft, testing before take-off, and operating the camera in the air. Before take-off, the FSO records the film number(s) onto his data sheet and takes some blank frames while the aircraft is still on the ground.

In the air, he fires the camera once in every subunit. It is most convenient to fire the camera at the very start of a subunit, recording at the same time the frame number, the height of the aircraft above ground level, and the 'distance FROM' on the GNS/PND. This helps in locating the exact position of each photograph.

A 'blank frame' must be taken at the end of each transect. This is most easily done by holding a piece of white card under the lens before firing the camera. One of the rear-seat observers can do this, while at the same time checking that the camera is working, and the number of frames remaining.

The FSO must also keep check of the total number of frames taken, and must reload the film or change cameras when appropriate.

Data recording. An experienced FSO will still have some time available to record data within each subunit, writing his observations onto a data sheet. However, the FSO should not record more than three or four data variables unless vertical photography is not being used.

3.2.2.3. The rear-seat observers (RSO) The two rear-seat observers record quantitative information from their defined sampling strips, speaking into tape recorders. For each flight, they record the date, aircraft registration, crew members, and their position in the aircraft. For each transect, they record the transect number, the direction of flight, and the subunit numbers when called out by the pilot.

The RSO continuously scan the defined sampling strips, keeping their heads in the correct 'counting position' by lining up window marks with the counting rods. Any animals within the strip are counted, and any outside the strip are ignored, whatever the height or attitude of the aircraft. For example, when a herd of animals is cut by the counting strip, only those animals within the strip are tallied.

The RSO photograph any herd of animals larger than 5–10 for accurate counting after the survey. They record onto their tapes the film and frame number of every photograph, as well as a visual estimate of the number of animals photographed. The main job of the RSO is thus to spot herds of animals within their strip and photograph them.

3.2.3. Selection of data variables

3.2.3.1. Introduction A wide range of information can be incorporated into an aerial survey data base, both from the survey itself and from ancillary data sources. Accordingly, there is alway the danger of collecting too much information. The mindless accumulation of data 'just for its own sake' must be avoided, and this is particularly important with respect to the aerial survey itself. The wider the range of variables to be collected on a survey, the less time the crew has to spend on each. Furthermore, a data base that is cluttered up with odd bits and pieces of information becomes quite unwieldy.

There are two important principles to follow then defining the range of data to be collected in the course of an aerial survey:

1. A clear statement must be made on the objectives of the survey, with a careful evaluation of the data requirements and the uses to which the data will be put.

2. The sources of all data must be evaluated carefully, and the most appropriate one(s) chosen.

Data derived from the aerial survey itself can come from the front-seat observer (FSO), the rear-seat observers (RSO) or from the vertical 35-mm sample photography. While the FSO data are usually collected as class variables, (for example, the percentage of the landscape that has been burnt), the RSO data almost always consist of numeric counts from within defined sampling strips. In contrast, the 35-mm sample photography yields both numeric data (for example, on land cover – as a percentage or as ha/km^2 – or on the numbers of houses), and class data, (for example, the quality of crop cover).

There are four main sources of ancillary data. First, there are thematic or other types of maps, from which many kinds of important information can be collated. Secondly, there are the orbiting satellite systems that provide data in both numeric (digital) and processed image form. Thirdly, there is conventional, small-scale aerial photography. And, finally, there is the mass of published material and reports on a study area.

All these data sources can be of use, and all can be misused. Data collected from an inappropriate source may well be of little use and may mislead development planners. Table 3.8 sets out the range of data variables that have been found useful when incorporated into an aerial survey data base, along with their most appropriate sources.

3.2.3.2. Land-form The elevation, slope, and aspect of the land, the land systems, and the underlying geology and soils are all of great importance when creating an aerial survey data base. The most useful sources of information are maps, reports, satellite images, and conventional aerial photographs. Aerial surveys have little to offer except that the front seat observer can collect corroborative information if required, perhaps from areas where the map or image base is poor. In general, however, the low-level aerial survey should not be looked on as a method for obtaining data on land-form. This is particularly so with soils information, for it has proved extremely difficult to make any useful observations on the nature of soils, or even on their colour, from a low-flying light aircraft.

3.2.3.3. Climate Data on climatic parameters are again to be found from maps and published reports. Satellite imagery, both digital and processed, is also becoming more widely used, especially the low-resolution

Table 3.8. Data sources for an aerial survey data base

	Ancillary sources				Aerial survey		
	Maps	Sats	AirP	Rpts	FSO	RSO	35-mm
Land-form							
Elevation, slope, and aspect	3	1	3	—	1	—	—
Land systems	3	2	2	—	2	—	—
Geology	3	2	2	—	—	—	—
Soils	3	2	2	—	—	—	—
Climate							
Rainfall	3	2	—	3	—	—	—
Temperature	3			3	—	—	—
Evapotrans.	3	—	—	3	1	—	—
Climatic zones	3	2	—	3	1	—	—
Hydrology							
Catchments	3	2	—	—	—	—	—
Drainage density	3	1	3	—	—	—	—
Ground water	3	—	3	3	—	—	—
Natural sources	3	2	2	—	2	2	—
Artificial sources	3	—	—	3	1	1	—
Ephemeral sources	—	1	—	—	2	3	—
Flooding	—	2	1	—	3	—	2
Erosion							
Nature	—	2	3	—	3	—	2
Extent	—	2	3	—	3	—	2
Sources	—	—	2	—	3	—	2
Rates	—	—	—	3	—	—	—
Vegetation							
Botanical classes	3	2	3	3	2	—	—
Physionomic classif.	3	2	3	3	2	—	3
Cover	—	1	2	—	1	—	3
Phenology	—	3	1	—	3	—	1
Fire	—	3	1	—	3	—	—
Agriculture							
Crop types and cover	—	1	2	2	1	—	3
Fallow land	—	—	2	2	1	—	3
Land-management	—	1	2	1	2	—	3
Land-overhead	—	—	2	1	—	—	3
Animals							
Livestock	—	—	—	1	—	3	—
Wildlife	—	—	—	1	—	3	—
Dynamics	—	—	—	3	1	1	—
Settlements							
Towns/villages	3	1	2	3	1	—	1
Rural households	—	—	1	1	1	1	3
Pastoral households	—	—	1	1	2	3	—

Table 3.8.—*continued*

	Ancillary sources				Aerial survey		
	Maps	Sats	AirP	Rpts	FSO	RSO	35-mm
Population							
Urban	2	—	—	3	—	—	2
Rural	1	—	1	3	1	1	2
Pastoral	—	—	—	2	—	3	—
Dynamics	—	—	—	3	—	—	—
Administration, infrastructure, and services							
Boundaries	3	—	—	3	—	—	—
National Parks, etc.	3	—	—	3	—	—	—
Roads and Rail	3	1	2	—	1	—	—
Tracks	2	—	2	—	2	2	—
Health and Educ.	2	—	—	3	—	—	—
Veterinary and mkts.	2	—	—	3	—	1	—

(1) Data sources
   Maps = Published maps
   Sats = Satellite data (imagery or digital)
   AirP = Conventional aerial photographs
   Rpts = Published reports, statistical abstracts, etc.

   FSO = Front-seat observer
   RSO = Rear-seat observer
   35-mm = 35-mm colour sample photography

(2) Usefulness of data source
   3 = Primary data source
   2 = Secondary data source
   1 = Corroborative information only
   — = No useful information or data

satellites operated by the National Oceanic and Atmospheric Administration (NOAA). The FSO can again provide some corroborative information; for example, on the transitions between arid and mesic climatic zones from observations on the vegetation.

3.2.3.4. Hydrology Most information on hydrology is to be found in ancillary data sources, including data on boreholes (and their yields), shallow wells, dams, and ground-water. However, more ephemeral water sources are described effectively by aerial surveys. These include surface pools, river pools, flowing streams, wells dug in sand rivers, and even springs.

   These data are usually collected by the rear-seat observers counting the different kinds of water sources seen within their sampling strips, from which estimates of the total numbers of water sources are calculated. This information is of immediate use especially in rangeland areas where water sources are often limiting factors during dry seasons.

Low-level aerial surveys are also effective in detecting and mapping the extent of flooding. These data are best collected by the FSO, although useful information has been obtained from the 35-mm sample aerial photographs.

3.2.3.5. Erosion The front-seat observer can collect extremely useful data on the nature, extent, and sources of erosion. Typically, the observations will characterize the nature of erosion in terms of gullies, rills, and sheetwash; the extent of erosion in terms of how widespread or advanced it is; and the sources of erosion in terms of cropland (under different management regimes), rangeland, and natural vegetation.

These observations are supported by the 35-mm sample photography from which a number of useful measurements can be made. For example, the sizes of gullies can be measured, as can ground cover of eroded areas.

The FSO integrates his observations within each subunit, and can thus provided regional descriptions of erosion phenomena. These, in turn, can be used to design field programmes for measuring the contemporary rates of erosion and their immediate causes and impacts.

3.2.3.6. Vegetation Low-level aerial surveys are useful as a source of primary data on vegetation, as a means of corroborating or amplifying existing information, and as a means of describing the growth stages of vegetation.

Primary data. A low-level survey is particularly efficient when vegetative resources have not been described. The FSO plays the most important role here, and can describe the vegetation in botanical or physionomic terms, integrating observations within each sub-unit. Botanical descriptions have, in general, proved not very useful, for there is no simple way of generating production figures from them. For example, an observation 'Miombo woodland' gives little information about the different productive components of the vegetation type.

Typically, therefore, the FSO will collect data on the relative abundance of the tree, bush, dwarf shrub and grass components of the vegetation, using a scale of '0' (absent) to '5' (nearly continous cover). The FSO might also describe more subtle characteristics, such as the proportion of all woody cover associated with riverine strips. This is extremely important in arid rangelands where the production of browse varies significantly in the riparian strips compared to the interfluves.

The 35-mm sample photographs yield point-sample measurements of the cover values of the vegetation components described by the FSO. From such combined data, it is possible to generate first order approximations of primary production which are both robust and precise.

Ground studies are then required to calibrate these first-order approximations to local conditions.

Corroboration. Survey observations can provide important corroboration in cases where the vegetation patterns have already been described for a study area. Furthermore, specific components of the vegetation, known to be important, can be described in more detail. For example, in an area classified as 'Miombo woodland', the survey can quantify the extent and distribution of patches of open grassland where livestock congregate.

Phenology. Data on the phenology (growth stage) of the different components of the vegetation can be easily collected by the FSO during a survey. This gives a regional description of the phases of vegetation production and senescence which often correspond to observed patterns of livestock distributions. The extent and impact of fires are also easily quantified.

3.2.3.7. Agricultural land-use The low-level aerial survey provides excellent data on agricultural land-use, specifically in areas of smallholder cultivation. Large commercial agriculture is equally well quantified by conventional-scale aerial photography and even, in some cases, by the new generation of satellites. Smallholder cultivation is quite a different matter, and the very large scale required for successful photo-interpretation (around 1:600) calls for a sampling approach.

In studies of agricultural land-use, the 35-mm photography provides virtually all the required information. Of particular interest are the woody resources for fuel and building, and the grazing resources for livestock.

Table 3.9 shows a set of agricultural land-use data derived from 35-mm sample photographs. This level of interpretation simply cannot be carried out from conventional photography, either black-and-white or colour.

The aerial observers have little to offer in describing agricultural land-use, except perhaps at the very broad level of class 2 land-cover (e.g. cultivated land, rangeland, and forest). Some corroborative information can of course be collected, while observations on land management (where the integrated subunit data are more appropriate) have proved useful.

3.2.3.8. Livestock and wildlife The low-level, aerial survey is very efficient at livestock and wildlife census, especially in remoter areas and where ground travel is difficult. Indeed, in many parts of the world an aerial census is the only practical method. Aerial livestock surveys, even in well settled and developed areas, consistently provide higher estimates of numbers than do ground surveys. This is basically because the livestock cannot be easily hidden from the aircraft.

Table 3.9. Photo-scales for combinations of lens and height

Lens (mm)	Height (ft)	Scale (1:)	Sample in hectares (full frame)
18	400	6773	4.0
18	500	8467	6.2
18	600	10 160	8.9
28	400	4354	1.6
28	500	5433	2.6
28	600	6531	3.7
28	700	7620	5.0
28	800	8709	6.6
35	400	3483	1.0
35	500	4354	1.6
35	600	5225	2.4
35	700	6096	3.2
35	800	6967	4.2
35	900	7838	5.3
35	1000	8709	6.6
50	400	2438	0.5
50	600	3658	1.2
50	800	4877	2.1
50	1000	6096	3.2
50	1100	6706	3.9
50	1200	7315	4.6

The low-level survey provides data primarily on the numbers of different livestock. Little useful data about age structures can be obtained when the survey is designed primarily for numbers. Instead, further surveys must be carried out based on the observed distribution patterns to obtain age structure information from large-scale oblique photographs. However, these data are quite crude and are rarely cost-effective. It is better to use the observed distribution of the livestock to mount immediate ground surveys.

3.2.3.9. Settlements and population Aerial surveys can provide very useful data on settlements and population, especially in areas where conventional population census is difficult.

In agricultural areas, ancillary data sources will usually provide perfectly adequate information on towns, villages, and population. However, rural homesteads can be easily interpreted on the vertical 35-mm sample photographs, from which contemporary distributions of population can be obtained.

The situation is quite different in rangeland and pastoral areas where ground census teams have difficulty in operating. Here, aerial survey can provide settlement and population data so long as some ground control is possible. First, all settlements can be photographed by overlapping obliques and the numbers of dwelling compounds can be counted. Population within each settlement is then found by multiplying the numbers of house compounds by a multiplier representing the numbers of people per dwelling compound. This second multiplier is naturally also obtained from ground sample surveys.

The size and distribution of pastoral populations can be tackled in a similar manner. First, the RSO count in their sampling strips all dwelling units that are 'in use'. Very strict criteria must be set up to distinguish between those in use and those recently abandoned, and usually every pastoral settlement will be photographed for checking later. Population density is then estimated by multiplying the in-use dwellings by a factor representing the numbers of people per dwelling. This factor must again be obtained by ground work, and usually different factors will be needed in different parts of a study area.

3.2.3.10. Administration, infrastructure, and services These are best described from ancillary data sources, and the aerial survey has little to offer. Qualitative data on animal tracks can help demarcate areas that are particularly heavily or lightly used, while casual observations can always be made if a school, clinic, or veterinary centre is flown over.

3.2.4. Survey planning

3.2.4.1 Maps Low-level survey flying requires maps at a number of scales for flight planning and for navigation. The 1:1 000 000-scale ONC series of maps is particularly suitable for general flight planning, locating airfields and navigation aids, for demarcating danger or prohibited areas, and for an initial appreciation of the landscape and of any problem areas. These are all aided by a 1:1 000 000 or 1:500 000 false-colour satellite image of the survey area.

Maps of 1:250 000 scale are the most suitable for detailed flight planning and for navigation. The flight lines are marked directly on to these maps so that navigation features and specific problem areas can be thought about in advance. Larger-scale maps of 1:500 000-scale are not usually required, except when the study area is very small or when very precise OMEGA/VLF navigation is to be attempted.

In all cases it is best to have three complete sets of maps. One is for reference only and is never marked up. The second set is for planning purposes, while the third set is carried in the aircraft.

3.2.4.2. Survey-timing The timing of a survey is an inevitable compromise between many conflicting factors. The first is the weather, for in many parts of the world flying is almost impossible at certain times of the year due to rain, low clouds, or dust storms.

If a single survey is to be carried out, the timing must be chosen to reflect the most important characteristics of the survey area for development planning. Wet-season surveys characterize an area when resources are most abundant, while dry-season surveys characterize an area when resource levels are critical.

The background vegetation can also be important because it influences visibility, and in general livestock are most easily seen on fresh regrowth at the start of a rainy season. Movements must also be taken into account, especially of wildlife. An example here is afforded by the movements of a million or so migratory wildebeeste in the Serengeti/Mara ecosystem in Kenya/Tanzania which at times can make it practically impossible to see, let alone count, the livestock.

A minimum of two surveys is required to describe the seasonal patterns of distribution and movements, timed to represent the extreme dry-season and wet-season distributions. A third, intermediate season survey is always to be recommended, however. It is also important to carry out the seasonal surveys within the same climatological cycle, for too often the results from seasonal surveys are weakened by a wet-season being followed by a dry-season survey in the 'next-but-one' cycle.

Where a survey is aimed primarily at describing vegetative resources, it should be timed for the phase of maximum vegetation response to recent rainfalls. Photo-interpretation will be easier, and the results will be more effective.

Agricultural surveys pose endless problems, usually because the cropping patterns vary over the survey area. In general, however, results are best when the crops are at a middle stage of growth, at which time they are most easily recognized on the aerial photographs. There is also a better chance of getting results out before the actual harvest. Crops are difficult to interpret and recognize at very early stages of growth, while at the later more mature stages the survey results may be confounded by premature harvesting, disease outbreaks, or even fires.

Surveys for linking erosion events to land-use patterns should be carried out when ground cover is minimal; namely, just before the new rains. Gullies, rills, and sheetwash are all easily visible to observers and on photographs, while the land-use patterns can be deduced from the sizes and shapes of the fields. Erosion events are almost impossible to see at the mid-stage of crop growth.

3.2.4.3. Designing a systematic sample The first factor to consider when designing a systematic sample is whether or not all parts of the survey area are equally important. Quite often they will be, and it is then as

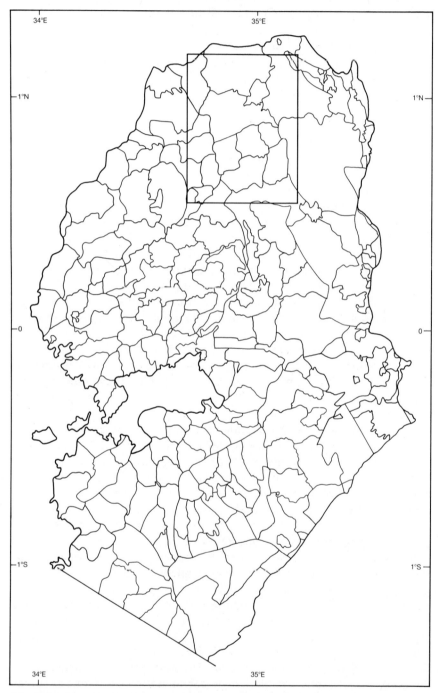

Fig. 3.4(a). Integrated land-use survey area, showing District and Location boundaries.

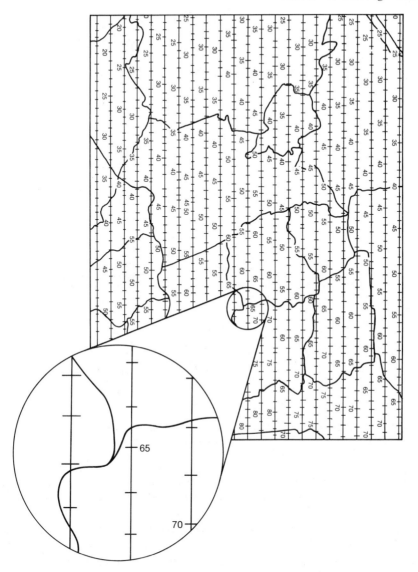

Fig. 3.4(b). Flight lines and subunits. Photo locations along systematically spaced flight lines. Flight lines are spaced 2.5 km apart, photographs are 1.33 km apart. Photo locations are accurate to within 300 m.

important to fly over the areas where livestock are as it is to fly over the areas where they are known not to be. Similarly, in a land-use survey, all parts of a study area are usually of equal importance.

Under these conditions, the sampling transects (flight lines) are spaced systematically and evenly across the study area. They should be oriented

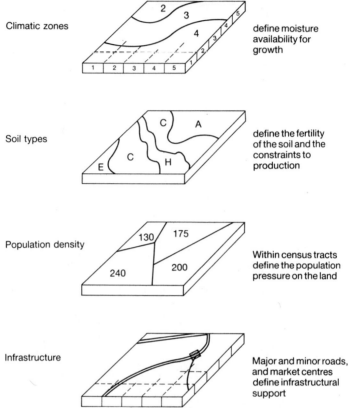

Climatic zones — define moisture availability for growth

Soil types — define the fertility of the soil and the constraints to production

Population density — Within census tracts define the population pressure on the land

Infrastructure — Major and minor roads, and market centres define infrastructural support

Fig. 3.5. Collation of ancillary data sources. Ancillary data are mapped at a common scale, and are justified to a standardized UTM grid system.

to cut across important environmental gradients such as climatic gradients, drainage gradients, or elevation gradients. Thus, if there is a strong climatic gradient from north to south then the flight lines should also run north to south. In contrast, if the major gradient is a north–south drainage pattern then the flight lines would be oriented east–west. The objective is always to maximize the variations within each flight line and minimize the variations between them.

The actual sample intensity is yet another compromise between the funds available for the survey, the size of the study area, and the desired resolution of the survey. The resolution of the survey is really the most important, and is set by the average size of the area about which statements must be made. For example, a very high intensity of sampling is required to make population estimates in sublocations averaging 25 km². In contrast, a much lower intensity of sampling is required if population estimates are needed only for rangeland units of 2000 km² in extent.

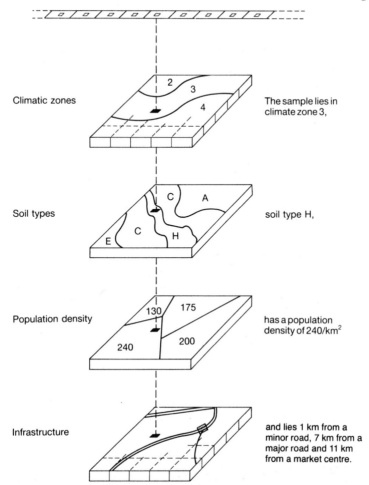

Fig. 3.6. Integration of aerial survey and ancillary data. Vertical colour photographs are taken at known intervals. Observer and photographic data are geo-referenced to a common grid system. The sample points have known densities of domestic stock (observer data) and, from photo-analysis, a measured set of land-use attributes.

Generally, the resolution of a systematic survey will be 40 times the flight-line spacing, expressed in square kilometres. Thus, a survey in a large ($>50\ 000$ km²) survey area with flight lines spaced at 10-km intervals will have a resolution in the order of 400 km², equivalent perhaps to a major vegetation zone. Similarly, a survey with a 2.5-km spacing between flight lines will have a resolution of around 100 km², equivalent to an administrative location.

However, different parts of a survey area will often be more important than others; for example, the part containing livestock at the time of the survey. Under these conditions, more sampling effort should be directed towards the areas of more importance compared to those of lesser importance, and this is most easily achieved by multi-level sampling.

An example is afforded by a recent series of surveys in the 64 000 km² Turkana District in northern Kenya. The initial SRF survey covered the entire District with flight lines spaced at 10-km intervals. All livestock seen were mapped after each flight, and on each survey the 35 per cent of the District containing the most livestock were resurveyed with flight lines at 5-km intervals. This was achieved by simply 'infilling' between the original flight lines spaced at 10-km intervals. The entire District was thus sampled at 3 per cent intensity, and 35 per cent of the District was sampled at 6 per cent intensity.

A third level of sampling was restricted to the areas around major town and settlements, and along important riverine strips. This covered 10 per cent of the District and was sampled at 12 per cent. Finally, every settlement was photographed in its entirety, effectively a 100 per cent sample in more than 1 per cent of the District.

Multi-level samples of this nature are extremely effective, and they make use of one of the most important characteristics of the SRF method which is its ability to describe distribution patterns. An initial low-intensity sample is used to map precisely where the next higher level of sampling should be, and so on.

3.2.4.4. Stratification The objective of stratification is to divide the study area into smaller parts that are homogeneous for a particular attribute or combination of attributes. The most frequently used attributes for stratification are topography, vegetation, livestock densities, and land-use patterns.

Topography is important because it may demarcate areas where different sampling methods should be used: for example, highland areas with steeply dissected valleys, compared to flat, lowland plains. Vegetation is important, not only through its influence on livestock distributions (e.g. within rangeland types), but also because it influences visibility, and therefore counting bias. Different correction factors are used in areas of different vegetation. Livestock densities are an obvious basis for stratification in a livestock census, while land-use patterns are an obvious basis for stratifying a land-use survey.

Stratifications can be superimposed one on top of another to reflect important combinations of attributes. Thus, an initial topographic stratification could have superimposed onto it a land-use stratification. The end-result in this case would be a set of land-use strata within topographic zones, and the sampling methods would reflect their spatial combinations. However, this process must not be taken too far or it may result in a confusing set of strata.

Once the strata are established, samples are drawn independently within each on either a random or systematic basis. Flight lines are again oriented to cut across important gradients, and absorb as much variation as possible within them rather than between them. Systematic flight lines are set up as described above. Random flight lines are set up slightly differently. A baseline is constructed across the axis of the stratum and random points are selected along it. The lines are then drawn in so that they pass through these random points.

Once an area has been stratified, the sampling can be more intensive in the important strata compared to the unimportant ones. For example, 50 per cent of a study area might be known to contain so few stock that it is scarcely worth visiting. This could be demarcated as a stratum for sampling at a very low intensity, say only six lines. In general, sampling effort should be proportional to the density of the most important attribute. Thus, in a livestock survey, the sampling would be proportional to the livestock densities in each stratum. In an agricultural survey, the sampling would be made proportional to the most important of the crops that were being studied.

Stratification therefore tends to be very efficient in terms of sampling intensity and thus lends itself to situations in which a precise estimate is required on a limited number of attributes for a minimum cost. For example, in Turkana District, Kenya, initial surveys of a wide range of attributes were made using the SRF method, all parts of the District being initially of equal importance. In the follow-on monitoring phases, stratified random sampling is being used to obtain annual estimates of just the pastoral populations and of their livestock.

The second major application for stratification is in very large survey areas of hundreds of thousands of square kilometres. If drawn up properly, large strata can be sampled with just a few flight lines (never less than six) to obtain a perfectly valid population estimate. Indeed, the variance of the population estimates can be calculated as the survey proceeds, and sampling can be terminated once a desired variance is achieved.

None the less, the drawbacks to stratification are also important, and must be carefully considered. First, it is difficult to stratify so that a range of variables is taken into account. A stratification for one will not necessarily suit another. Therefore, stratification should be avoided in multiattribute sampling. Secondly, distribution within a stratum is often difficult to obtain, for if the sampling is at a high enough intensity to show within stratum variation then the whole point of the stratification is lost. Thirdly, data from a stratified census are more difficult to manipulate and recombine, and it is considerably more difficult to integrate data from ancillary sources into the survey data set.

3.2.4.5. Subunits With both systematic and random sampling, data are collected in successive subunits along the sampling flight lines. In general, the smaller the subunits the greater is the spatial resolution of the data and the easier it is to integrate ancillary data into the survey database.

Subunits are often demarcated on elapsed distances of 5 km. This places a significant load on the pilot, who has to identify the start of each subunit from the map. This is not easy to do, especially in featureless country, although GNS navigation makes it more straightforward. However, a 5-km subunit has proved to be too large for the effective integration of ancillary data and therefore the most usual way to demarcate them is by elapsed time.

A one-minute interval has proved to be very effective for most survey applications in large areas. This gives a ground distance of about 2.7 km at the typical survey ground speed of 160 km/h. Subunits of 30 s duration have also been used in cases where higher resolution is required. This is equivalent to a ground distance of some 1.35 km. Smaller subunits, say of 20 s or 15 s, should be avoided. They place a heavy load on the observers and often create an unnecessary plethora of data records.

Typically, a single vertical 35-mm sample photograph is taken in each subunit. It has proved best to take the photograph at the beginning of the subunit, for this makes geo-referencing and photo-location much easier. Naturally, in surveys using only 35-mm photography and no visual observations, the aircraft can fly significantly faster, thus reducing costs, and the subunits (which are now equivalent to the photo-intervals) can be shortened.

3.2.4.6. Pre-survey flights The success of an aerial survey depends on the crew acting together as a team and carrying out their respective jobs professionally and competently. This is greatly assisted by at least two pre-survey flights over the study area.

The first flight is a general reconnaissance flight to observe the nature of the study area, the terrain and land-form, the boundaries of any strata, and the attributes which the observers are to count. Livestock vary considerably in their herd sizes and appearance, and the observers must get used to this before the survey. Special attention must also be paid to pastoral dwellings if these are to be counted as part of a population census. The pilot can also check out any problem areas, and can get the feel of the country and of the local flying conditions.

Pre-survey flights are of special importance in agricultural surveys, for they give the photo-interpretation team a chance to observe the cropping patterns at first hand. In these conditions, it is best to carry on board a person who is familiar with the local crops.

The second flight should be a full dress rehearsal along practice transects. This allows the crew to become familiar again with all the operational procedures for navigation, data recording, and data transcribing. It also offers an opportunity to test all survey equipment thoroughly.

3.2.5. Piloting and navigation

Survey piloting and navigation require a high degree of skill; no pilot will be able to carry out effective survey work without some preliminary training. Particular emphasis must be placed on contour flying and on low-level navigation, and on slow flying close to the ground and around hills.

3.2.5.1. Control of height above ground level Height control is maintained by reference to the radar altimeter which gives a continuous indication of height above ground-level. Aerial surveys are typically carried out at 400 ft although height might be reduced to 300 ft if small wildlife were being counted.

The radar altimeter must be calibrated before any operations are carried out by flying over a selected point, such as an aircraft parking area, at gradually increasing and decreasing altitudes as shown by the pressure altimeter. The pressure altimeter must be given time to settle down after each change in height, otherwise errors will accumulate.

The pilot switches the radar altimeter off as he crosses the selected point, thus freezing the needle on the dial and giving him time to record the pressure altimeter. In this way several pressure altitude readings are obtained, each with an equivalent radar altimeter height, including the pressure altitude when the aircraft is stationary on the selected point.

The points are plotted against each other on graph paper and should theoretically fall on a straight line passing through the origin. They rarely do, and a simple regression analysis provides a correction factor for the radar altimeter.

It is quite impossible to contour-fly with complete accuracy. The radar altimeter is there to guide the pilot so that he maintains a relatively consistent variation from an average. The FSO records height throughout the survey from which the 'actual' as opposed to the 'nominal' height is calculated, so the pilot need not worry about short-term deviations.

Contour-flying is an art that must be learned and practised. It is not particularly easy to start with. The ground speed and attitude of the aircraft must be controlled otherwise the observers' task becomes extremely difficult. This is basically achieved by the use of power settings. Particular problems are met when flying into rising ground, and when flying along falling ground, especially with strong winds.

However, safety is always the first priority, and should override any considerations of census design. Under very turbulent conditions, especially in hilly areas, it becomes dangerous to fly close to the ground and flying heights must be increased.

3.2.5.2. Control of ground speed Most survey work is carried out at ground speeds of about 160 km/h. This requires modest power settings on most light aircraft, and pilots must practise until they are used to flying at these speeds and power settings.

Counting bias is influenced by ground speed, and bias increases with speed. The faster the aircraft is moving, the more animals are missed. The pilot must therefore learn to recognize and control excessive speeds. Low ground speeds are less important.

Unless the aircraft is fitted with a GNS navigation system which gives ground speed as a read-out, the pilot must judge speed by reference to the ground and by comparing planned durations along flight lines, or flight line segments, against actual durations. Excessive speeds are likely to be met when flying downwind along falling ground. Power settings must sometimes be drastically reduced and flaps may need to be deployed. The aircraft will be flying at air speeds approaching the stall, so considerable care must be exercised.

Although ground speed must be controlled because of counting bias, this does not mean that it need be maintained in areas where there is nothing to see or count. It is perfectly acceptable to speed up in areas where animals are known to be scarce. Under these conditions, an increase in bias will not greatly influence the final result. The aircraft can always be slowed down again when areas containing animals are approached.

For example, in a recent survey in Turkana District, Kenya, the open Lotikipi plains were completely dry, burned over, and devoid of any livestock. The aircraft crossed these plains at very high speeds and was then slowed down once the livestock areas were reached.

3.2.5.3. Navigation without the GNS The pilot must navigate the aircraft to the starting point of each transect, navigate along the transect, and identify the finishing point. With practice, all this can be done with great accuracy. Low-level navigation is not particularly easy to start with, and requires quite some practice before effective survey flights can be attempted.

The actual flight path of the survey aircraft must be re-created once the survey is over in order to geo-reference the subunits along the flight lines. It is therefore most important that the pilot notes on his map any serious deviations from the planned flight lines, and the subunit number when passing over prominent landmarks such as rivers, woodland edges, isolated hills, or ridges. The pilot should also mark on his map the starting point of any subunit whenever it can be exactly determined.

3.2.5.4. Navigation with OMEGA/VLF The OMEGA/VLF systems, such as the Global Navigation System (GNS), tune into a world-wide network of 16 OMEGA/VLF radio beacons which transmit at a wavelength approaching 18 km. When the aircraft is in motion, the system detects

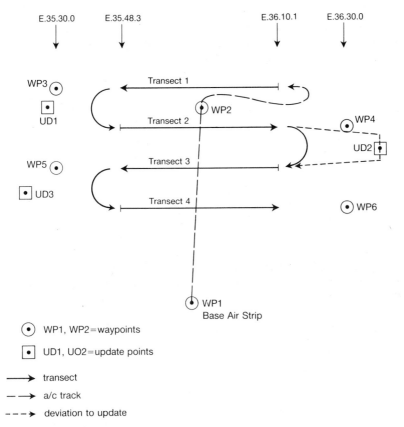

E.35.30.0   E.35.48.3   E.36.10.1   E.36.30.0

WP3

UD1

Transect 1

WP2

Transect 2

WP4

UD2

WP5

Transect 3

UD3

Transect 4

WP6

WP1
Base Air Strip

WP1, WP2 = waypoints

UD1, UO2 = update points

transect

a/c track

deviation to update

Fig. 3.7. Navigation with OMEGA/VLF.

phase shifts between the low-frequency signals and uses them to provide navigation data.

On initialization, the system must 'know' its starting position, the date, and the time (GMT). Waypoints (WP) can then be stored in the computer memory, and the system will provide navigation instructions to the pilot so that he can travel from waypoint to waypoint. The system also gives continuous position information, and read-outs of ground speed, distance to go, and time to go.

The OMEGA/VLF systems are expensive but have added a new dimension to survey flying. First, they make it possible to achieve accurate navigation even in remote areas where maps are poor and out of date. Secondly, accurate navigation makes it possible to integrate a wide range of ancillary data into the survey data base. Serious survey flying can no longer be carried out without such a system.

At heart, however, OMEGA/VLF systems are simply computers programmed to carry out certain calculations. Usually, these systems are found in commercial or corporate jet aircraft, and they are programmed on the assumption that most of the time the aircraft is travelling in a straight line and at a constant speed. The system may therefore become confused when used for survey flying in light aircraft, which travel slowly and erratically. This explains some of the curious navigation read-outs from these systems when used on surveys, especially around waypoints.

Set out below are guidelines for using an OMEGA/VLF system for survey flying. The system as configured consists of the GNS500A Series 1, with Course Deviation Indicator (CDI) and Pilot Numerical Display (PND). All COMMANDS refer to GNS500A operation modes, but are easily applied to other systems. Navigation will be achieved with an operational accuracy of 280 metres.

1. BASE AIR STRIP

   The latitude/longitude of the base airstrip must be known very accurately. Indeed, all latitudes and longitudes must be determined to the nearest 0.1 nautical mile. Let the GNS warm up for 20 min before programming (e.g. during ground checks). After programming, wait until SIGNAL STRENGTH 6 or better. On take-off, head for WP2 which is an *en route* update.

2. UPDATING

   Update the GNS *en route*, at least 20 min flying time after take-off. This update should set up the system for the next 4/5 h, but have other update points located (UD1, UD2 ... etc.) for use. Do not update along a flight line. Only update between flight lines.

   When updating, hold a CONSTANT course over the point, select POSITION HOLD, update if displayed lat./long. is off by more than 0.2 nautical miles, maintain course for at least three minutes after updating.

3. FLIGHT LINE NAVIGATION

   Each flight line (transect) requires a single WP (waypoint) set at least 15 min past the end of the flight line. Do not let the WP correspond to the end of the flight line.

   Operate in MANUAL and not AUTOMATIC mode. Select PSEUDO VORTAC MODE, display POS, CDI to EN ROUTE, PND TO DST. GNS now displays position, course deviations to 0.1 nautical miles, and distance TO WP in decimal nautical miles.

   Slowly come round onto course, using CDI and POS. Let system settle for at least 1 min before start of flight line. Use POS read-out to determine start and end of flight line. Maintain CDI needle in centre, ignore minor 'jumps'.

4. BETWEEN FLIGHT LINES

Select next WP as PSEUDO VORTAC, slowly come round onto course, let system settle down at least 1 min before start of flight line. Deviate to previously determined UPDATE POINT (UD1, etc.) if necessary. Maintain constant course over update point, and for 3 min after updating.

5. FLIGHT PLANNING

Latitude/longitude of base field, update points and waypoints must be determined to the nearest 0.1 nautical mile from maps. A scale of 1:50 000 should be used if possible.

East–west flight lines

Determine the northing along which the aircraft will fly, position the WP at least 15 min east (or west) of the end of the flight line. Determine the easting of the start and finish points.

North–south flight lines

Determine the easting along which the aircraft will fly, position the WP at least 15 min north (or south) of the end of the flight line. Determine the northing of the start and end points of the flight line.

Pilot map

Has each flight line marked in, Start and End points, and position of update points.

Pilot data sheet

For each flight line, shows WP number as programmed into GNS; the northing along which the aircraft will navigate; the easting of the waypoint; the eastings of the Start and End points of the flight line; the direction of flight; the length of the line in kilometres; and the expected duration in minutes.

Some OMEGA/VLF systems can hold only nine waypoints in memory and must be reprogrammed during flight. This is perfectly straightforward to do, and indeed offers a welcome break for all crew members.

Even when navigating by OMEGA/VLF, the pilot must still refer to his map to monitor navigation accuracy. Deviations from planned flight lines, perhaps because of bad weather, must be noted as already described. The pilot should also mark his map when he crosses prominent landmarks, writing down the subunit number and the DISTANCE to the WP shown on the PND.

Ground speed is monitored by briefly switching PND function from DST to GND.

3.2.5.5 Other operational procedures The pilot must call out to the crew over the intercom the transect numbers, the direction of flight, the subunit number, and the end of transect. Procedures are as follows.

Approaching transect start:	Transect number zero – one – two; repeat zero – one –two.
	Direction west, repeat west.
At start of transect:	Start transect; subunit one, repeat subunit one. GNS distance three four decimal nine, repeat three four decimal nine.
Next subunit:	Subunit two, repeat subunit two. GNS distance three three decimal two, repeat three three decimal two.
Repeat for all subunits.	
End of transect.	End of transect, end of transect. GNS distance one five decimal eight, repeat one five decimal eight.

Note: (i) The GNS distances are called out only if a GNS is fitted.

(ii) The GNS distances are recorded by the FSO for the start of every line, the start of every subunit, and for the end of every transect. The positions of each subunit can then be accurately marked in on the maps.

Transects often have to be broken along their length, perhaps for observers to change films. The pilot simply calls out 'break – break' over a convenient landmark and circles until the observers are ready to resume. Sometimes weather prevents transects from being completed, and the aircraft may have to stop 20 or 30 km from the end of a transect, and start the next one 20 or 30 km on from the start. All that is required here is to mark on the map exactly where the transects were stopped and started, and the remaining portions can be completed another time. When a GNS if fitted, the eastings of the stop and start points need to be recorded.

Often a survey area will have a number of hazards which requires transects to be flown in separate segments. Each segment is simply given a different transect number. For example, transect segment 0121 might be flown west towards the base of a high and steep escarpment, while segment 0122 is flow east from the top of the escarpment to the bottom, both segments ending at the same place.

3.2.5.6. Geo-referencing the subunits Since the pilot flies and navigates the aircraft, it is primarily his responsibility to recreate as accurately as possible the actual flight path followed. His annotations onto his flight maps are used for this, both for the flight lines and for the subunits.

Where there is no GNS information, these annotations are the only source of data. Subunits are marked in from the known position fixes along the transects on the assumption that ground speed was constant between position marks. Observer information can also be used to calibrate the flight lines, by noting the subunits in which major landmarks such as rivers or main roads were seen. Geo-referencing is much more straightforward with GNS data, for the start of each subunit can be measured exactly from the recorded distances to the waypoints. In both cases, the subunit numbers are written in on the maps.

Geo-referencing is extremly important, for once the map positions of each subunit are known, ancillary data can be integrated into the database. For example, the distance of each subunit to the nearest town, borehole or veterinary centre can be measured. Alternatively, the subunit positions can be transferred onto a soils map and each can be given a soil type. Furthermore, each subunit can be assigned to a grid cell for making thematic maps, or to a polygon such as a location boundary for making statistical analyses.

This is particularly important when photographs have been taken. So long as the photographs are taken at the start of each subunit, the geo-referencing fixes their location in space to within some 300 m. This in turn allows the photographs to be related to many other spatial data sets, such as elevation, local slope angle, and soil type.

3.2.6. The front-seat observer records

The front seat observer (FSO) has a number of tasks to carry out, including monitoring flight parameters, operating the vertical camera system, and making environmental observations from the aircraft.

3.2.6.1. Flight parameters The FSO records a number of important flight parameters which are essential for recreating the flight path of the aircraft and for analysing the survey results. First, the FSO records for each flight the date, the aircraft registration, the crew members and their seating positions, and the take-off and landing times. Next, for each flight line he records the start and stop times, and the direction of flight. The FSO records these parameters even though they are also recorded by the pilot and by the rear-seat observers.

For each subunit, the FSO also records the distance from waypoint (when an OMEGA/VLF system is being used), and the height above ground-level. Distance to waypoint is used to geo-reference each subunit, and each photograph, along the flight lines. Height above ground level is required to calculate the width of the observer sampling strip and the scale of each photograph. Height above ground is always recorded at the same time as the camera is fired. If vertical cameras are not being used, height can be recorded at any time during the subunit.

3.2.6.2. Camera operation It is the responsibility of the FSO to fire the vertical 35-mm camera once in every subunit. In general, it is best to fire the camera as soon as the pilot calls out the subunit number, at the start of the subunit. Simultaneous records are then made of the height above ground and the distance to waypoint.

The FSO must record onto his data sheet the identity of the camera in use (right or left camera if there are two of them) and the number of the loaded film. He must also keep track of the exposures made, changing cameras (or films) when necessary. Furthermore, he must make sure that a blank frame is exposed at the end of each transect. This is most conveniently done by getting one of the observers to hold a piece of card in front of the camera lens while a frame is fired. This also offers an opportunity to check that the camera is functioning correctly.

3.2.6.3. Qualitative observations The FSO has limited time available for making observations on the environment. With 30-s subunits, flight monitoring and camera operation take up a significant portion of his time and his abilities to collect environmental data are limited. With longer subunits, of 1 min duration, he has much more time for observing.

The FSO records qualitative data from the aircraft, and does not restrict his observations to a defined sampling strip as do the two rear-seat observers. Typically, the data are recorded in the form of a two-character code written directly onto a data sheet along with all the other subunit information.

It is best to collect data on a range or scale, rather than in classes, using the double blank as the lowest value in the range. Three examples are given below:

Tree cover	*% Burnt*	*Gully erosion*
.. absent	.. no burning	.. none seen
01 scattered	01 <25% burnt	01 minimal/slight
02 open	02 <50% burnt	02 moderate
03 medium	03 <75% burnt	03 extensive
04 thicket	04 >75% burnt	04 severe
05 nearly continuous		

Note: .. denotes 'double blank'

Table 3.8 (p. 000) describes the range of data that can be efficiently collected by the FSO. In general, the FSO should not collect data that can be obtained from other sources for his main job is to monitor flight parameters and operate the camera system. However, when carefully thought out, the FSO data records can make valuable contributions to aerial survey data sets.

3.2.7. The rear-seat observations

The two rear-seat observers collect quantitative information by counting the numbers of objects seen within defined sampling strips, photographing groups too large to count on a single pass, and recording all data and information onto tape for later transcription.

3.2.7.1. Defining the counting strip Each observer has a defined sampling strip within which he counts animals and other objects. The sampling strip (or counting strip) is demarcated by fibreglass rods attached to the wing struts of the aircraft. The inner rod is positioned so that it is clear of the undercarriage, and the outer rod is positioned so that the strip is about 150 m in width.

The outer rod is roughly positioned, when the aircraft is on the ground, by simple geometry. The observer is seated in the aircraft and the inner rod is positioned so that it is clear of the wheel. The width w of the counting strip on the hanger floor is given by $(H \times W)/h$, where H is the selected flying height (say 400 ft above ground-level), h is the height of the observer's eye above the hanger floor, and W is the desired strip width (say 150 m). The distance w is marked out on the floor from the line of sight of the inner rod, and the outer rod is simply positioned to the correct place.

This gives only an approximate position for the outer rod, and it must be calibrated. Once airborne, the observer first marks two grease-pencil lines on his window to line up with the two fibreglass rods. This ensures that his head is always in the same position when making observations.

For calibration, markers are laid out on the ground 20 m apart, every fifth marker being twice or three times the size of the others. About 300 m of markers are required, and it is best to lay them out at right angles from a runway so that the pilot can easily line up on them.

The aircraft flies across the line of markers a number of times at different heights, for example four passes for each observer at 500 ft, 400 ft, 300 ft, and 200 ft above the markers. Each time the aircraft crosses the line, the observer counts the numbers falling in his strip. He also calls out when he crosses the line so that the pilot knows when to record the height from the radar altimeter.

The actual width of the strip W at the selected flying height H is found by averaging all the observations and multiplying up, and down, to the selected height. The outer rod is then repositioned if necessary.

Typically, a strip width of 150 m is used with a flying height of 400 ft above ground level. Observers find it easy to scan a strip of this width, and 150 m at that height subtends the angle of the eye. Narrower strips, and lower flying heights, are used in thickly-covered country, or when small and cryptic animals are to be counted.

3.2.7.2. The observations Typically, the rear-seat observers will count all livestock and wildlife seen in their counting strips, distinguishing the different species from one another. It is usually possible to differentiate between local (indigenous) cattle and exotic 'improved' breeds. However, sheep and goats are more difficult to differentiate, and often recorded as a single species ('shoats') unless there are clear reasons for not doing so. Wildlife are easily identified, although some of the smaller gazelle can present problems.

The RSO can also count pastoral settlements, noting the different kinds of encampment and whether or not they are in use. The pre-survey flights are important here for familiarization, and for selecting the key attributes by which in-use and out-of-use settlements are distinguished.

In all cases, the observers' main task is to spot the herds of animals, or the settlements, and then photograph them. The photographs are later analysed in the laboratory, and the animals on them counted. Hand-held 35-mm cameras are used for this, fitted with 50-mm lenses and loaded with diapositive colour film such as high-speed Ektachrome. The motor-driven Olympus OM2 has proved reliable for this work.

Although photography sounds easy, it requires much practice before really useful results are obtained. Fully automatic cameras need getting used to, and it takes practice to reload quickly in a bouncing light aircraft. Furthermore, the camera must be held vertically so that the lens is at the same height as the observers' eye when the photograph is taken. This also needs getting used to.

The fibreglass rods show up clearly in the photographs so long as the camera is held in the vertical position, and back in the laboratory all animals between the rods are counted and all those outside are ignored. This follows the same rule as for all visual observations. Any object within the strip is counted, and all objects outside the strip are ignored, whatever the attitude of the aircraft when the observation is made.

Certain other precautions must be taken. The camera lens should be taped with the lens focused at infinity. Each film should be numbered before the census starts, both on the cassette and on the film leader. This number on the leader must be scratched into the emulsion otherwise it vanishes during developing, and it must also be underlined to distinguish a 6 from a 9. When reloading, the used film should be rewound completely back into its cassette so there is no chance of using it again.

The rear-seat observers must not be overloaded, for the time they spend counting one set of objects detracts from the time available for counting others. Good observers can handle livestock and wildlife easily, along with pastoral settlements. Observers should never be asked to count rural (agricultural) settlements, or to make observations on crops or land-use, for their observations will not be worth the effort. The 35-mm vertical sample photography is best used for this.

3.2.7.3. Recording and transcribing The rear-seat observers record all their observations onto tape and in this way do not have to take their eyes away from the sampling strips. At the start of the flight they must record the date, registration of the aircraft, identities of the crew members, their position in the aircraft, and the number or other identification mark of both their tape recorder and camera. This allows faulty equipment to be identified.

During the census, they record the transect number at the start and end of each transect, and each subunit as it is called out by the pilot. Finally, they record the film number in use, and the new film number when they reload.

The observers often use a microphone with an in-built on/off switch. While convenient, this can cause problems because the tape takes a second or so to come up to full speed. It is therefore safest to repeat the first phrase twice; for example 'subunit three, subunit three'.

The recordings must be quite unambiguous so that no mistakes are made during transcription, and a widely used convention which is known to work well is to record first the species, then the visual estimate, and finally the number of photographs taken. For example, 'cattle, cattle, fifty, one frame'; note that the species 'cattle' is repeated twice in case the tape has not come up to speed.

The visual observations are important. It takes time and practice before an observer can produce consistent visual estimates. The photography, however, is even more important, for most of the census information comes from these photographs. While some aspects of photography have been mentioned already, it is most important that the tape record is quite clear. The following convention should be used, the example being for a visual estimate of 50 grade cattle.

Grade cattle, grade cattle, fifty, . . .

ONE FRAME	One single frame holds all the cattle.
TWO FRAMES	Two overlapping frames, the area of overlap must be demarcated to avoid counting any animals twice.
THREE FRAMES, etc	As above, only there are three (or more) overlapping frames.
TWO FRAMES, ONE FRAME	Two overlapping frames, and a single frame of a subgroup; the animals in the subgroup should be added to those counted on the two overlapping frames.
ONE FRAME, ONE FRAME	There are a number of quite independent frames with no overlap, and the estimate refers to all animals counted on all the photographs together.

ONE PLUS ONE   Here, two independent shots have been
                                  taken of the same group (perhaps the
                                  animals were more clearly seen in the
                                  second) and the best of the two
                                  photographs should be used.

A large herd of livestock may require quite a few frames and the observer may loose count. In this case he records 'cattle, cattle, three hundred
and fifty, many frames, one blank' and then takes a frame when holding
the camera against his knee.

Care must be also be taken with overlapping frames. The photographs
are trapezoid in shape on the ground, with the side nearest the aircraft
smaller than the one further away. The overlap must therefore by based
on the nearside of the viewfinder.

The observers must transcribe their data onto data sheets while they
are still fresh in their minds after a flight. Normally, an 80-column data
sheet is used, with the left-hand columns reserved for the transect and
subunit numbers. Flight information as to who the observer is, on which
side he was sitting, his camera number, and tape recorder, all go on the
top of the form, and a new form is started for each transect.

The data are usually transcribed in the form of two character codes
followed by the visual estimate, the frame numbers (and number of
frames) being placed in a right-hand remarks column. However, a separate sheet, one for each film, is also used for the photo-data. Initially this
shows the camera and film number, and against each frame the animals
recorded and the visual estimates. Back in the laboratory the numbers
counted off the photographs are entered in against the appropriate
frames, and it is from these data that each observer's correction factors
are derived.

3.2.8. 35-mm vertical sample photography

The recent devlopment of 35-mm sample photography for measuring
land-cover and the characteristics of vegetation has added a new dimension to low-level, aerial surveys. 35-mm photography is cheap; it can be
used to quantify exactly those variables which are difficult to quantify on
conventional format photography, or by using observers; and its very
limitations impose a sampling approach which immediately lends great
flexibility to the method.

Set out below are a number of guidelines for using 35-mm photography on low-level aerial surveys. The guidelines are based on hard,
practical experience and have little formal research and development
behind them.

3.2.8.1. Cameras and mounts The Nikon F3 has proved to be extremely reliable. The electronics, 250-exposure camera backs, and motor drives can be relied on for many tens of thousands of exposures. The Cannon is also very reliable.

The 35-mm cameras require very basic mounts which need not even be vibration free, because very high shutter speeds can be used. The cameras can have simple floor mounts with the lens pointing out through a hole cut in the outer skin. An ideal system is two 35-mm cameras mounted side by side. This gives 500 exposures if the same lenses are fitted, or 250 exposures using lenses of different focal lengths. However, the camera can be slung over a window-ledge, or poked out of a door.

Intervalometers should never be used for they impose restrictions on what should be a very flexible operation. It is much better to fire the cameras using a stop-watch and thumb-button. It is also much cheaper, very much less prone to breakdowns, and much more accurate, for intervalometers tend to drift. A simple junction box with leads going to the two cameras suffices for all occasions.

3.2.8.2. Film High speed Ektachrome (HSE) should be used whenever possible, for it has many advantages over other film. First it is cheap, widely available, and can be developed almost anywhere in the world in 24 hours. Secondly, the first generation diapositive photo-product has a much higher resolution than does a print, which is a second generation product. Thirdly, it can be rated at ASA 400 or even higher, which means that useable photographs can be obtained under almost any light conditions.

HSE can only be purchased in bulk rolls from specialized dealers, so a good supply must be ordered well in advance of requirements. Also needed is a film loader, so that the 250-exposure cassettes can be filled.

Few, if any, commercial laboratories can handle a roll of 250 exposures and must instead cut them up into 36-exposure lengths for machine processing. This does not matter at all, and the cut frames can still be analysed with no loss of data.

However, explicit instructions must be given to the photo-laboratory not to throw away the cut ends, and on no account should the frames be mounted. Furthermore, each roll of 250 exposures must be submitted as a separate 'job' to the photographic laboratory. This ensures that the cut lengths from an individual roll will not get muddled up with others. The cut lengths of film are easily put back into sequence prior to mounting into negative holders.

It is best to discuss the entire matter in detail with the chief technician of the photo-laboratory where the developing is to be done. A single roll should be submitted first so that everybody can learn by their mistakes.

3.2.8.3. Photo-scales Although in theory the photo-scale can be adapted to specific requirements, the whole point of using 35-mm photography on low-level aerial surveys is to obtain large-scale, small-format sample photography. Choice of scale is therefore quite limited within the constraints of the method.

The two image-scales which have proved to be very effective for land-use and vegetation work are 1/7000 and 1/19 000. These scales are somewhat arbitrary and reflect a number of constraints: flying at low level in order to count livestock; sampling as large an area as possible on each photograph at a usable scale; and always needing to fly under the clouds in effectively any weather conditions.

About 400 ft above ground level is the normal height for a low-level survey, and from this height an 18-mm super-wide angle lens photographs an area of approximately four hectares at an image-scale of approximately 1/7000 (Table 3.9, p. 000). This gives a very adequate ground sample at an excellent scale for photo-interpretation. A longer lens would photograph a smaller area at a larger scale than necessary, and the slight (<2 per cent) scale distortion across the field of view is easily compensated for. The diapositives are interpreted at a ten-times enlargement, which enables Level 3 and 4 land-cover classes to be identified and measured.

A flying height of 400 ft is required only when livestock are to be counted. If this constraint is released, the aircraft can fly higher and use longer lenses to obtain the same image scale. Table 3.9 sets out a range of height/lens combinations. Important criteria, however, include the response of the radar altimeter, the abilities of the pilot, and the weather conditions. At around 1000 ft, pilots often find it hard to contour-fly and most radar altimeters (except the extremely expensive ones) have a sluggish response time. Accurate measurement of height above ground is needed for scaling each sample photograph. At heights much above 1000 ft, the aircraft will often fly into and out of cloud, which is less than convenient, and many radar altimeters run out of scale.

In general, therefore, heights of around 600 ft are recommended for surveys in which livestock are not being counted. At this height, pilots can still feel their way across the landscape, the radar altimeter should be giving a good response, and the aircraft will be below the cloud.

The second, very useful image-scale is around 1/19 000. This is excellent for broader-scale land-use classification (Levels 1 and 2), for assessing land husbandry, and especially for certain kinds of vegetation work such as stem counts.

Sometimes, two cameras will be used, each photographing at different scales. A typical combination will be simultaneous photography at 1/19 000 scale and 1/7000 scale, the larger scale being 'boreholed' into the smaller scale. The 1/19 000-scale photography is very easy to georeference, especially onto existing photography, while the 1/7000 scale is readily located on the smaller-scale photograph.

Sometimes the smaller-scale photography can be taken as a continous strip with subsamples along it at larger scale. This is particularly effective for photography of riverine strips, general vegetation, and special test areas such as SPOT satellite simulations.

3.2.8.4. Set-up for photo-interpretation For interpretation, each dia-positive is projected down onto a desk-top dot-grid at a ten-times enlargement. A projector, which can take film strips rather than individually mounted slides, is mounted on a vertical wall bracket which can be adjusted to obtain the exact enlargement. A good system is a vertical pole some 4 ft long, mounted on 18-in brackets away from the wall. The lower bracket should be no more than 2 ft above the desk. The projector housing is attached to the vertical pole by a strong clamp and can be moved up and down it. It is most important that the projector can be swivelled in and out as well as up and down, so that it can be exactly aligned with the desk top.

The semi-random dot-grid consists of an array of 18×12 cells of 2×2 cm in size, in each of which are two randomly-located dots of 2-mm diameter. The dot-grid should be first drawn on stable-base acetate and then photographed. It is then printed on the highest quality, matt, laminated paper at exactly the required size.

Photo-interpretation is carried out within an inner interpretation area of $16 \times 10 = 160$ cells containing 320 dots. This overcomes any interpretation problems associated with the edges of the field of view, and also restricts the interpretation to the most distortion-free part of the image.

Once the projectors and the dot-grids are set up, an exact ten-times enlargement is obtained by carefully fixing the height of the projector above the desk top. Interpretation can then proceed, and count and area data are obtained from the colour diapositives.

This dot-grid system may appear to be archaic. However, it works effectively, is cost-effective, and provides data that are both unbiased and accurate. It is immensely more effective and efficient than any high-technology approach using image analysers or digitizers. Furthermore, relatively untrained people can use the method with little additional training, and an experienced interpreter can get through some 40 slides in a working day with little trouble.

3.2.8.5. Count and area data Count data are simple enumerations of objects within the inner interpretation area, such as house compounds, buildings with mabati roof, buildings with thatched roofs, other structures, cattle dips, stock compounds, or even the numbers of individual plants or trees. In general, the 50 per cent rule is followed, which specifies that 50 per cent or more of the object being counted must lie within the inner interpretation area for it to be included in the tally.

The only exceptions to this concerns fields, for it is usually impossible to see if more than half of a field falls in the image. All fields and parts of fields are therefore counted, and corrections must be made later to adjust for the numbers of partial fields. These corrections are cumbersome to calculate and must be worked out empirically from the observed distributions of field sizes and shapes.

Area data are measurements of the proportional area of different kinds of land-cover, the proportions being expressed in terms of the number of dots falling within each land-cover classification. Area data are obtained for individual crops and crop combinations; for the canopy cover of the natural vegetation; for the land taken up by roads, tracks, houses, and other kinds of overheads; and for fallow land. The 50 per cent rule is again used to decide if a dot should be included in a particular area measurement.

3.2.8.6. Interpretation procedures The procedures that must be followed during the interpretation of colour diapositives are designed to control the accuracy and consistency with which the interpretation is carried out. Although the procedures must be adapted to each particular survey task, they are iterative and should always include the following stages.

  (i) Pre-reconnaissance survey to qualify the range of crop types and crop combinations, natural vegetation classes, etc., that might be used as individual photo-interpretation classes. This is usually carried out in the survey aircraft, and some, if not all, of the interpretation team should be involved.

 (ii) Helicopter survey to obtain control photography as an aid to photo-interpretation and crop identification. Although helicopters appear expensive, they are the only cost-effective method for this important ground control work. The helicopter cruises at low level over the various crop types, low hovers are made to identify crops and intercrops, landings are made if necessary, and control photography at the same scale as the survey photography is obtained. Roughly an hour of helicopter time is needed per 2000 km^2 of survey area.

(iii) Initial selection of interpretation classes, examination of a range of colour diapositives to check feasibility. Classes are then added/deleted, merged/split, and an initial key is formulated which defines the important visual, textural and other characteristics of each interpretation class.

(iv) Testing the interpretation classes with a further selection of diapositives, cross-checks and discussions between entire photo-interpretation team.

 (v) Further field orientation for entire photo-interpretation team, including flights over the study area and discussions of the different classes.

(vi) Final selection of the interpretation classes.

There are two other important things to bear in mind. First, the interpreters must be continuously monitored and checked, otherwise their interpretation tends to 'drift'. Secondly, the interpretation classes must be non-overlapping so that a single dot is never assigned to more than one land-cover class.

Table 3.10 shows an interpretation key for land-use survey of Kiambu District, Kenya. The first point to note is that the land-cover is split into the main headings of agriculture, infrastructure, natural vegetation, and miscellaneous, so that:

100 per cent of land = agriculture + infrastructure + natural vegetation
+ miscellaneous

and it is clear why the interpretation classes must be non-overlapping.

The agricultural classes represent the important crops and crop combinations in the District. They can be recombined later to give selected totals, such as total area under cultivation, total cash-crop area, total food-crop area, or whatever else is deemed important.

The infrastructural classes represent the land that is set aside in order to work it. Here roofs are quite important for they are simple indicators of economic progress.

The natural vegetation classes are extremely important, and here reflect an interest in woody resources for local fuel and buildings purposes. In other applications — for example, rangeland – the natural vegetation classes might include stem-counts for canopies of different diameters, and cover-values for tree, bush, dwarf shrub, grass, and bare ground.

Finally, the miscellaneous class contains any dot that cannot be put anywhere else; for example, a dot falling in the middle of a flowing river, or a dam, or on top of a rock outcrop.

Table 3.10 gives a single example of a classification key. Many other variables can be collected; for example, on the methods of cultivation, on the numbers of plants per row and the row spacing, on the presence of terracing or contour ploughing, on the incidence and extensiveness of gullies, rills, and sheetwash, and on anything else considered important. However, it must be borne in mind that the time taken to interpret the photography, the amount of cross-checking, and the number of errors, are all dependent on the total number of classes to be interpreted.

3.2.9. The aerial survey data base

3.2.9.1. Data base structure To understand the basic structure of an aerial survey data base it is important to define carefully a number of terms.

Table 3.10.

Transect:	Subunit:		Interpreter:

AGRICULTURE

		No.	dots				No.	dots
Managed Pastures	MP				Maize	MS		
Fallow fields	FF				Coffee	CF		
Bare fields	BF				Tea	TE		
Field dividers	FD				Pyrethrum	PY		
					Irish potato	IP		
					Horticulture	HT		
Orchard/other crops	RU				Fodder grass	NG		
Maize/banana	MB				Pineapple	PA		
Maize/I. potato	MI				Sisal	SL		
Maize/other crops	MU				Orchard	RR		
Banana/horticulture	BH				Banana	BN		
Banana/other	BU				Unidentified crops	UC		
Horticulture/other	HU				Complex cropping	XX		
Irish potato/other	IU							

INFRASTRUCTURE

		No.				dots
Rural House compounds	HC		Total Compound Area	CA		
Other Building comp	BC		Total roof area	RA		
Mabati roofs	MA		Access (roads/ tracks/paths)	AC		
Other Modern roofs	MR					
Thatched roofs	TR		Hedges - clipped	IC		
			- others	II		

NATURAL VEGETATION

		dots	No.
Plantation	PL		
Woodlots	WL		
Planted windrow	WR		
Nat. Tree hedge	WT		
Indig. Forest	IF		
Bamboo	BM		
Bush	BS		
Herbaceous	HE		
Riparian Strips	RW		

Scat/Isolated Trees		dots
- fruit trees	TF	
- in crops	TC	
- around buildings	TN	
- in bush	TB	
- in open grassland	TG	
- in hedgerows	TH	

MISCELLANEOUS   KK

No.=number of items   Dots=number of dots

Subunit: A subunit is a short segment of a flight line defined usually by an elapsed time. Within each subunit is a single vertical sample photograph.

Sample point: The vertical photograph within a subunit defines its physical location by means of spatial coordinates recorded from the GNS navigation system, or from other flight records. These coordinates can then be considered as sample points distributed within the survey area.

Data record: Each subunit (and therefore each sample point) has a number of data variables associated with it. These include observer data from the sampling strips either side of the aircraft, data from the vertical sample photographs, and ancillary data from existing data sources. Each set of data from a subunit or sample point forms a data record in the aerial survey data base.

The terms subunit, sample point, and data record are thus synonymous and interchangeable. Subunits are referred to in the context of the survey operations; sample points are used to discuss the distribution of the samples across the survey area, and the relationships between their distribution and other spatial data; and data records are used to refer to the data as stored in the data base.

Each data record in the data base contains control and survey data. The control data include the flight-line number, the subunit number along the flight line, the spatial coordinates of the photograph within the subunit, the UTM grid cell within which the photograph falls, the height of the aircraft when the photograph was taken, the length of the subunit, the combined width of the observers' strips, and the spacing between the flight lines.

The survey data include ancillary data variables, the observer data variables, the air photo-data variables, and the recombinant data variables. Each of these data variables occupies a fixed position in the data record.

3.2.9.2 Collation and integration of ancillary data The ancillary data from existing documentation can include land-form, soils, climate, hydrology, physical infrastructure, population, administration, land tenure, crop infrastructures, crop potentials, and special development areas. Usually, these are transferred first onto 1/250 000-scale base maps of the study area before integration into the survey data base.

In contrast, 1/50 000-scale maps are more often used for defining boundaries of, for example, a study area or catchments; for making land-form measurements such as average slopes and elevations; and for fixing the precise positions of settlements. These data are compiled first at 1/50 000-scale before being transferred to 1/250 000-scale. Similarly, the boundaries of population census tract boundaries are often compiled only at 1/100 000- or even 1/500 000-scale.

The procedures for integrating these ancillary data with the aerial survey data are very straightforward once the spatial coordinates of each sample point are known.

Grid cell data (e.g. slope and elevation)
Mean slope angle and mean elevation can be calculated for each UTM grid cell from 1/50 000-scale map sheets. Once each sample point is assigned to an individual grid cell, it receives the slope angle and elevation for that cell.

Polygon data (e.g. locations, soils, agro-ecological units)
The polygons are first mapped on the 1/250 000-scale base map of the survey area. Then, each sample point is assigned to an individual polygon, either by hand or by computer.

Any data associated with a polygon can then be assigned to the relevant sample points. For example, once the sample points are assigned to a set of census tracts (polygons) they can receive the population density, age structure, and ethnic diversity for each. Similarly, once a sample point is assigned to a soil type it can be given all the characteristics of the soil type; and once a sample point is assigned to an agro-ecological unit it can be assigned the climatic and crop-potential characteristics of that unit.

Remoteness indices (e.g. to towns and roads)
Indices of remoteness are given by distances to defined points such as towns, power stations, railway stations, or any other kind of service centre, such as a hospital. Alignments of roads of different standards, railways, or even rivers are treated simply by considering them to be a series of points lying close together.

Each point, or series of points, is considered to be a 'node' whose coordinates are compared in turn with those of all the survey sample points. Three kinds of remoteness index can be calculated:

 (i) distance to nearest node, e.g. distance to nearest town or market centre;

 (ii) distance to nearest alignment, e.g. class A roads, rivers, or railway; and

 (iii) Catchment area, e.g. of a hospital, town, or even a meteorological station. This is in effect the same as (i) above, only the identity of the nearest node is found rather than the distance to the nearest node.

These indices of remoteness can themselves be treated as polygons, and other data may be associated with them. For example, distances to market centres can be associated with a transport cost; health statistics can be associated with the catchments of hospitals; and crop production figures can be associated with areas covered by meteorological stations.

3.2.9.3. Data transformations The observer and aerial photographic data, count, and area, are all transformed before being stored in the survey data base. Cross-referenced to each data record are:

l = length of a subunit (km),

h = aircraft-height above ground-level (ft) recorded from the radar altimeter,

w = combined width (m) of the two observer sampling strips
$= (W/H) \times h,$

where:

W = width of sampling strips at the calibration height H.

Then:

A2 = area of a subunit $\qquad = l \times w \times 10^{-1}$ ha,

A3 = inner interpretation area of a photograph

$= \dfrac{h^2 \cdot c^2}{f^2} \; 0.68817 \times 10^{-5}$ ha

where f = the focal length of the lens in mm and c = the area of the negative in mm^2. In the case of a 35mm camera c is $36 \times 24 = 864$ mm^2, and for a 70mm camera c is 4900.

Observer data: The number of, for example, grade cattle counted by both observers in a given sub-unit are first corrected for counting bias and are then summed and stored.

Count data (C): Count data from a sample photograph are stored as $(C/A3) \times A2$.

Area data (D): The number of dots (D) counted within a given interpretation class, for example maize monocrop, are stored as $(D/320) \times A2$ (where 320 is the number of dots on the dot-grid).

3.2.9.4. Data manipulation The most important feature of an aerial survey data base is the ability to integrate data in a spatial context. As described above, this depends on knowing the spatial coordinates of each sample point which are defined by the vertical aerial photographs. The GNS navigation system provides an accuracy of around 300 m which is adequate for the purposes of a regional data base. However, this accuracy can be improved upon at individual project sites if there is recent large-format aerial photography of not less than 1/20 000-scale. Each photograph, and therefore each sample point, may then be fixed exactly.

Once the coordinates of each sample point are known, they can be assigned to any spatial domain imposed upon the data base. Grid cells offer a simple example, and each sample point is assigned to an individual UTM grid cell. The sample points are also assigned to polygons, such as Location boundaries, soil types, rainfall isohyetes, and agro-ecological units. The distance between each sample point and any other defined point in the survey area, such as principal towns, railway stations, or major roads, can also be calculated.

The data base can be manipulated in a number of ways to meet user requirements for mapping, inventory, or analysis. Some of the more important routines are described below, along with their main applications.

Continuous strata. A continuous stratum is defined as a set of sample points which fall within a single, contiguous geographical area, for example a District, Location, drainage basin, development area, or catchment area of a hospital. Such continuous strata are used primarily to define areas within which a complete inventory and assessment of resources is required. Continuous strata are also used for mapping purposes, either within contiguous grid squares or within contiguous polygons such as Locations.

Discontinuous strata. A discontinuous stratum is, as its name implies, one which is scattered in discrete pieces within the study area; for example, soil types which may occur in many different patches many kilometres apart. Sample units are assigned to such discontinuous strata in the same fashion as before, but they lack spatial coherence.

Examples of discontinuous strata include slope and elevation classes, and slope classes at different elevations; distances from major/minor roads; and areas of selected population density. These strata are used primarily to analyse relationships between land-use patterns; or between land-use patterns and the environment; or between land-use patterns and infrastructure.

Recombinant data variables. Recombinant data variables can be created from any existing variable in the data base, either singly or in combination, and with or without ancillary data. A simple example is afforded by soil types, for once a sample point is assigned to a soil type it can be characterized on a wide range of soil attributes.
More complicated examples include:

— The forage available for livestock can be calculated from the managed pastures and homestead areas; the weed regrowth and crop residue value of different crop types; and from the naturally occurring herbaceous and woody vegetation.
— Livestock units can be calculated from the observed numbers of livestock types weighted by body mass.

— Sediment budgets can be calculated for a catchment from a combination of slope angles, soil characteristics, position in drainage basin, and measured erosion rates of land-cover/soil-type combinations.

— Cost functions for crop transport can be calculated from the measured distances between each sample point and road/rail networks.

— Health statistics can be applied to the population within the calculated catchment areas of hospitals.

— Crop suitabilities can be determined from slopes, elevation and climate, soils characteristics, population density and structure, land tenure, and infrastructural support.

— Fertilizer requirements can be calculated from combinations of soils, crops, and climate.

These applications for creating and modifying the survey data are extremely powerful, and allow the data base to be used both as a modelling tool and as an information retrieval system.

3.2.9.5. The survey estimates The survey estimates provide densities and total numbers within defined areas such as Districts, Locations, and drainage basins. Densities express the numbers per square kilometre of, for example, grade cattle, houses, or woodlots, but when applied to crops they express hectares per square kilometre, which is equivalent to percentage of cover. Total numbers (or hectares) express the totals within the defined area.

The survey estimates are calculated using a derivation of the ratio method, which is designed for unequal-sized sampling units and which eliminates the influence of sample unit-size on the sample estimate and the sample variance. It is known as the ratio method because the estimates are derived from the ratio between the amount of material sampled and the area sampled; in other words, the density.

In this application of the ratio method, the individual flight lines are treated as the primary sampling units. The subunits are not involved in the calculations, and serve only as convenient entities for data storage and retrieval.

The basic calculations are set out below. If we consider one animal, or crop, at a time, then:

z = the area of each primary sample unit (flight line)

y = the number of animals or crop hectares enumerated along the sample unit

$\hat{R}$ = total animals or hectares counted/total area counted
  = the average density
  = $\sum y / \sum z$.

The survey estimate is then found by:

$$\hat{Y} = \hat{R} . Z,$$

where Z is the total area under survey.

The z for each sample unit is found by summing the lengths of all the subunits and multiplying by the average strip width. The Z for the whole survey area is found by summing, over all subunits, the product of subunit length and subunit spacing.

3.2.9.6. Precision of the survey estimates The precision of a survey estimate is calculated as follows. Let

s_y^2 = the variance between the numbers or hectares in all sample units,

s_z^1 = the variance between the areas of all sample units,

s_{yz} = the covariance between numbers or hectares and the areas of the sample units,

Then:

Variance of a survey estimate

$$\text{Var}\,(\hat{Y}) = N(N-n)/n \times (s_y^2 - 2 \times R \times s_{yz} + R \times s_z^2)$$

(note the negative sign of the covariance term),

and standard error of the estimate

$$SE(\hat{Y}) = \text{square root of Var}\,(\hat{Y}).$$

Here, y, z, and R are as defined above; n is the number of sample units in the sample; and N is the total number of sample units from which the sample was drawn, which is found by summing over all sample units (flight lines) the spacing between flight lines divided by the mean strip width.

The 95 per cent confidence limits of a survey estimate can be calculated by multiplying the standard error by the t value for $n-1$ degrees of freedom. These confidence limits can then be expressed as a percentage of the estimate itself.

There is a second term to the variance of the survey estimate derived from the variance between photographs within sample units. This term is fortunately very small and contributes no more than 1.5 per cent of the total variance. It can therefore be safely ignored.

The precision of a survey estimate is influenced by three main factors:

The absolute size of the sample. A sample of 50 units will always be more precise than will be a sample of 25 units, whatever the sample fraction;

The size of the area. For a given sample fraction, an estimate from a large area will always be more precise than will be an estimate from a small area; and

The abundance of the attribute under survey. An estimate of a crop with 10 per cent cover will always be more precise than will be an estimate of a crop with only 5 per cent cover.

The influence of these two factors at a sampling intensity of 12 per cent is shown in Table 3.11.

— The colums of the table represent areas of different sizes (in square kilometres) such as Districts, Locations, or special development areas.

— The rows of the table represent mean densities of attributes such as livestock, houses, and crop areas. These densities range from 0.02 per cent to 80 per cent.

Table 3.11 Standard errors of survey estimates (expressed as % of the estimate)

ha/km²	\multicolumn{10}{c}{Area (km²)}	%
	50	100	200	400	600	800	1000	2500	5000	>5000	
0.02	95	68	50	36	30	27	24	17	13	11	8%
0.04	68	50	36	27	23	20	18	13	11	9	3%
0.06	57	41	30	23	19	17	16	11	9	8	3%
0.08	50	36	27	20	17	15	14	11	9	7	2%
0.10	45	33	24	18	16	14	13	10	8	7	6%
0.20	33	24	18	14	12	11	10	8	7	6	9%
0.40	24	18	14	11	10	9	9	7	6	6	7%
0.60	21	16	12	10	9	8	8	6	6	5	5%
0.80	18	14	11	9	8	8	7	6	6	5	5%
1.00	17	13	10	9	8	7	7	6	5	5	9%
2.00	13	10	9	7	7	6	6	5	5	5	10%
4.00	10	9	7	6	6	6	5	5	5	5	7%
6.00	9	8	7	6	6	5	5	5	5	4	3%
8.00	8	7	6	6	5	5	5	5	5	4	2%
10.0	8	7	6	5	5	5	5	5	4	4	5%
20.0	7	6	5	5	5	5	5	4	4	4	7%
40.0	6	5	5	5	5	4	4	4	4	4	4%
60.0	5	4	4	4	3	3	3	2	2	1	2%
80.0	5	4	3	3	3	2	2	2	2	1	3%
%	10%	19%	29%	14%	10%	5%	3%	6%	3%	1%	100%

Frequency analyis

s.e.%	% of all estimates
>20%	10%
15–20%	20%
10–15%	20%
5–10%	30%
<5%	20%

— Each cell in the table shows, for a given mean density and area, the standard error (expressed as a percentage of the mean) of 95 per cent of all survey estimates.

Table 3.11 thus provides a simple look-up table for assessing the precision of any survey estimate at this sampling intensity. For example:

crop cover   1.0 ha/km²   (equivalent to 1 per cent cover)
survey area   1000 km²   (e.g. a District)

standard error of 95 per cent of survey estimates is 7 per cent.

Thus, 95 per cent of all the estimates of 1.0 ha/km² in areas of 1000 km² have standard erros of 7 per cent or less, and only 5 per cent of these estimates have standard errors of more than 7 per cent. Although the standard errors of some of the estimates are quite large, this does not affect the data base as a whole for only 10 per cent of all estimates have standard errors greater than 20 per cent of the estimate.

3.2.9.7. Applications for thematic mapping Thematic maps provide the development planner with a description of the spatial distribution and abundance of resources. Both the thematic mapping units and the variable ranges must be chosen so that both regional trends and local variations are portrayed.

The maps can cover the broad subject headings of land-form, climate, population, land tenure, service networks, livestock, agriculture, natural vegetation, infrastructure, and land saturation. Each map must be described fully and be accompanied by an extensive key and where appropriate by a statistical analysis of the variable being mapped.

Typically, the UTM grid system is used for thematic units, for the grid cells clearly demonstrate both regional patterns and more local variations. The values in each grid cell are either mean densities (numbers/km² or ha/km²) or mean class values (for example, slope angles). Both are calculated from the sample points assigned to each grid cell.

3.2.9.8. Applications for resource inventories A resource inventory is a tubular listing of all resources within a specified geographical area, such as a District, a Location, or a drainage basin. These inventories can be produced either as sector summaries or as stratum profiles.

The sector summary quantifies a single resource such as grade cattle, or a restricted range of resources such as sugar-cane hectares, field sizes, and potential, within a number of selected strata; for example, Districts within the study area, or subcatchments within an individual catchment. The sector summary allows the development planner to compare the abundance of each resource among the various strata.

In contrast, the stratum profile quantifies all resources within a stratum to as much detail as the planner requires. These stratum profiles are exhaustive, and offer a cornucopia of data on a survey area. They also form a tangible physical data base.

3.2.9.9 Data base analyses The possible range of analyses from an aerial survey data base is very wide indeed. However, certain applications have proved consistently useful to development planners.

Population. In agricultural areas, simple demographic analyses can relate the rates of population increase to the population density. Evidence for density dependent population regulation will have significant implications for future planning. In rangeland areas, it is the seasonal shifts in population distribution, the relationship between pastoral population and livestock, and the influence of development centres on population movements that are important.

Land-budgets. A land-budget accounts for all the land in use, and quantifies the abundance and characteristics of the land still available for cultivation. Special variables can be created to express the difficulty of bringing uncultivated land into cultivation. Land-budgets have significant implications for assessing the degree of land-saturation.

Gradient analyses. The analysis of land-use changes along gradients of increasing population density and cultivation intensity affords insights into the dynamics of land-use development. Such analyses have important applications for the design of long-term land-use policies.

Environmental constraints to cultivation. The relationships between environmental factors such as elevation, temperature, and climate, and the abundance and distribution of crops can highlight important constraints, and opportunities, for development.

Crop potentials. The potential for introducing new crops, or encouraging the more widespread use of well-tried variables, is an important aspect of development planning. The suitability of the land for given crops may be assessed from soil characteristics, climatic parameters, population structure, present land-use patterns, and availability of required infrastructure and services.

Service networks. Analysis of the infrastructural support within the survey area, the relationship between this support and land-use patterns, and the implications for long-term development are an important part of the planning exercise. The costs of infrastructure development can be modelled and benefits assessed.

Crop production. Crop production can be assessed or forecast by integrating actual rainfalls, or water balances, against the known areas of crops and intercrops on different soil types. Assessments can also be made of areas most prone to crop failure.

Primary production and off-take in rangelands. The ecological balance between livestock and their range in pastoral areas constantly occupies the attention of development planners. A survey data base that contains data on seasonal livestock movements, vegetation components, and climatic parameters can produce robust estimates of grazing pressure and carrying capacity. Production and off-take can be modelled on the data base from existing research data to show areas of relative resource abundance, balance, or over-utilization.

3.2.10. The control of bias

3.2.10.1 General considerations Errors and bias in aerial surveys are two very difficult things. Errors, by definition, are random and their cumulative effects cancel out. Errors affect the precision of a survey estimate, and are quantified by the standard error or confidence limits of a survey estimate. In contrast, a bias is an error in a consistent direction whose cumulative effect does not cancel out. Biases affect the accuracy of a survey estimate, and must be controlled if accuracy as well as precision is sought.

Biases can arise through the design of an aerial survey, from inaccurate maps, from the way in which an aircraft is flown, from observer performance, and from the analysis of the vertical photography. There are three aspects to the control of biases. First, design the survey operation to minimize biases; secondly, hold biases constant throughout the survey; and thirdly, identify the major sources of bias and, where practicable, correct them.

The possibility of undetected sources of bias always remains. However, as a general rule, the effect of a bias on the accuracy of a survey estimate is negligible if the bias is less than one-tenth of the standard deviation.

3.2.10.2. Bias from survey design Systematic sampling is known to give unbiased estimates so long as simple precautions are taken when designing the orientation of the flight lines. It is, for example, conceivable that the flight-line spacing might harmonize exactly with some feature of the landscape. This possibility is minimized by orienting the flight lines so that they cut across the dominant relief and drainage features in a surveyed area.

However, the variances of the estimates from a systematic sample are always biased in an upward (positive) direction. Estimates from systematic samples are therefore always more precise than indicated by the calculated variances.

The selection of ground speed, height above ground level, and width of counting strip is an inevitable compromise between considerations of safety, bias, precision, and costs. Extensive work within East Africa and elsewhere has shown that the combination normally used on surveys (ground speed of 160 km/h, height above ground level of 400 ft, and observer strip width of 150 m either side of the aircraft) is well within the capabilities of experienced observers.

Observer counting bias is only marginally reduced by flying lower and slower, and the reduction is not offset by the loss of precision, by the increase in costs for the same sampling fraction nor by the decrease in safety margins. Similarly, the marginal reduction in counting bias by narrowing the width of the counting strip is not offset by the increased costs of the same sampling fraction nor by the decreased precision of the estimates.

3.2.10.3. Bias from aircraft operation Bias can arise from the way in which the aircraft is flown, from inaccurate navigation, poor speed control, and poor height control. However, the flight information collected during the survey is used to test whether such biases are present, to estimate their magnitude, and to correct them before the data are analysed.

Navigation. The GNS navigation system virtually eliminates bias from gross errors in navigation. The accuracy of the GNS system has been tested by comparing the GNS lat./long. read-out against map references. In a survey of land-use and agriculture in Machakos District, Kenya, lat./long. position fixes were obtained from the GNS system at approximately the same time as the vertically mounted 35-mm camera was fired. The 35-mm photographs were then located on 1:20 000-scale black-and-white photographs of the District and these locations were then transferred to 1:50 000-scale map sheets. The lat./long. of the photographs were then taken from the map sheets.

It is very possible that this method overestimates the true error in the GNS navigation system, for it is open to a number of sources of inaccuracies. For example, the GNS read-out may not have been obtained at exactly the same time as the photographs were taken; there are bound to be errors in locating the 35-mm photographs on the 1/20 000-scale black-and-white photographs and then in transferring these locations to 1/50 000-scale map sheets; and finally there will be both map errors and errors in reading off the lat./long. positions from the maps.

None the less, on a sample of 300 comparisons, the mean error in the GNS navigation system was found to be 380 m (Table 3.12). The GNS position fixes are therefore accurate to within 0.45 km^2, compared with the nominal accuracy of 0.11 km^2.

Control of ground speed. The GNS navigation system allows the pilot to monitor ground speed very accurately and to adjust the air speed of the aircraft accordingly. None the less, aircraft tend to travel faster across the

Table 3.12. Comparison between GNS position fixes and map references

	Absolute error	East–west error	North–south error
Number of comparisons	300	300	300
Mean (m)	380	250	240
Standard deviation	210	200	180
Standard error	12	12	10
Nominal accuracy (m)	261	185	185

ground when flying downwind as opposed to upwind, a potential source of bias since the observer counting bias increases with the ground speed of the aircraft. The magnitude of any bias from this source must be tested by comparing the observed densities along upwind and downwind flight lines.

Height above ground. Height above ground is continuously monitored by reference to the radar altimeter, and any bias from poor height control is corrected during data analysis from the heights recorded in each subunit.

3.2.10.4. Observer counting bias Observer counting bias is primarily controlled through the use of oblique photography. Having spotted a group of animals, the observer first makes a visual estimate of the number of animals in the counting strip and then photographs the group if there are more than about five individuals. The fibreglass rods show up clearly in the photographs, so that only those animals 'in' the strip are counted.

The ratio of the visual estimates to the photographic counts is then used as a correction factor for each individual observer's visual estimates. However, even the counts off the photographs are biased, in that animals are often hidden behind one another. A further correction factor is therefore applied to the counts off the photographs to take this into account. These correction factors have been derived from a large series of comparisons between oblique photographs and near-vertical photographs.

A further source of observer counting bias comes from domestic stock hidden inside buildings, especially small stock. It is possible to estimate the magnitude of this source of bias only by ground enumeration at the time the aerial survey is carried out.

Bias from crew fatigue can be very important, and studies have shown that counting efficiency falls off after 4 h of work. Survey flights should therefore be kept to 3.5 h to minimize this source of bias.

3.2.10.5. Bias from photo-scale The height above ground level of the aircraft is recorded every time a photograph is taken so that the scale and area imaged can be calculated exactly. This removes any bias from inaccurate flying on the part of the pilot.

However, if the aircraft is in a straight and level altitude but the ground beneath is sloping, the area photographed will be larger than that calculated from the height above ground level. The slope of the ground relative to the altitude of the aircraft is therefore another potential source of bias.

Table 3.13 shows the slope angle of the ground under the aircraft for each of 4200 photographs exposed over Machakos District, Kenya. Also shown is the 'correction factor'; namely, the amount by which the area of each photograph calculated from the height above ground level must be multiplied to take the slope into account. These calculations were based on the assumption that the aircraft was at the mean flying height of 400 ft above ground level and that the direction of any slope was parallel to the direction of flight. Over the whole set of photographs, the mean correction factor was only 1.0080, so the influence of this source of bias is negligible.

Theoretically, it would be possible to correct for this bias by locating every 35-mm photograph on a topographic map and using the height above ground level and the local slope angle to calculate the area photographed. However, in practice this is not possible, not the least because

Table 3.13. Correction factors for mean slope angles.

Slope angle (degrees)	Frequency	Percentage of photographs	Correction factor*
0	7	10	1.0000
1	21	22	1.0003
2	18	17	1.0011
3	14	14	1.0026
4	12	9	1.0046
5	7	7	1.0073
6	4	4	1.0105
7	3	3	1.0143
8	3	3	1.0188
9	2	2	1.0239
10	1	1	1.0297
11	1	1	1.0361
12	2	1	1.0433
13	1	1	1.0512
14	1	1	1.0599
15	1	1	1.0649
16	1	1	1.0798
17	1	1	1.0910

*at mean flying height of 418 ft above ground level.
Source: Machakos Integrated Development Programme, Survey of Agriculture and Land Use, February 1981, 4200 35-mm diapositives.

accurate topographic maps are often unavailable. Furthermore, this method would be possible only if the altitude of the aircraft were known, as well as its heading, at the time each photograph was taken.

3.2.10.6. Bias from photo-interpretation In general, bias from photo-interpretation is minimized by first training the photo-interpreters on the interpretation key being used, and second by carefully monitoring and checking their performance while the photographs are being analysed.

The presence of bias can be detected by carefully reanalysing a sub-sample of photographs, treating the recounts as giving the more accurate information. Table 3.14 shows the results of recounting the number of houses and other buildings on a subsample of 429 photographs from Machakos District. Over the whole subsample, the recount gave a figure of 1886 buildings compared to the original count of 1818 buildings, a difference of 3.7 per cent.

Over the whole set of recounts, the mean number of houses per frame was 4.24 on the original count, compared with 4.40 on the recount, the standard error of the recount being 0.11 (2.5 per cent of the estimate). These two estimates are not significantly different from one another. Furthermore, none of the subsets of recounts are significantly different from

Table 3.14. Recounts of houses and structures from 35-mm diapositives

No. of frames	Mean of first count	No. of houses on 1st count	No. of houses on 2nd count	Difference (%)	Mean of 2nd count	s.e. %
126	1	126	128	+1.6	1.02	9.6
63	2	126	136	+7.9	2.16	7.2
83	3	249	262	+5.2	3.16	6.3
32	4	128	135	+5.5	4.22	5.4
21	5	105	112	+6.7	5.33	6.8
26	6	156	163	+4.5	6.27	7.2
8	7	56	59	+5.4	7.38	6.4
18	8	144	151	+4.9	8.39	3.9
16	9	144	147	+2.1	9.19	3.4
8	10	80	80	0.0	10.00	3.2
8	11	88	90	+2.3	11.25	3.8
4	13	52	53	+1.9	13.25	3.5
4	14	56	56	0.0	14.00	3.6
4	15	60	62	+3.3	15.50	3.6
4	16	64	65	+1.6	16.25	3.2
4	19	76	76	0.0	19.00	3.8
4	27	108	111	+2.8	27.75	1.9
429	4.24	1818	1886	+3.7	4.40	2.5

Source: Machakos Integrated Development Programme, Survey of Agriculture and Land Use, February 1981.

one another. Count data from the 35-mm frames, when carefully controlled and monitored, are thus both unbiased and of acceptable precision.

The most important data derived from the 35-mm diapositives are the estimates of crop areas, cultivation and other aspects of land-use. Table 3.15 presents an analysis of a recount of 116 'areas' measured off a subsample of 35-mm diapositives. A total of 258 recounts was carried out, on areas ranging from less than 5 per cent of the field of view to more than 50 per cent of the field of view. In no case are any of the recounts significantly different from the original counts.

Table 3.15. Recounts of crop areas from 35-mm diapositives

Crop cover (ha/km^2)	Original counts			Recounts		
	n_1	Mean	s.e. %	n_2	Mean	s.e. %
0–5	16	3.2	6.6	37	3.2	4.5
5–10	23	7.3	3.9	51	7.3	2.7
10–15	12	12.6	3.7	29	12.7	2.2
15–20	8	16.3	1.7	19	16.3	1.4
20–30	26	22.9	2.3	57	23.3	2.5
30–40	14	37.2	2.2	30	36.9	1.5
40–50	7	46.7	2.4	13	46.1	2.0
> 50	10	63.9	5.3	22	63.1	3.5

n_1 is the number of occurrences.
n_2 is the number of counts.
Source: Machakos Integrated Development Programme, Survey of Land Use and Agriculture, February 1981.

Whereas the data in Tables 3.14 and 3.15 test the consistency of the photo-interpreters under operational conditions, a controlled experiment was set up on a survey data base, to test if there was any bias in the estimation of sizes and shapes arising from the design of the dot-grid itself. Seven areas were chosen (Table 3.16) ranging from 92 m^2 to 3670 m^2 at the average interpretation scale of the photography, the expected number of dots ranging from 1 to 40.

Each area was counted in seven different shapes in which the ratio of length to breadth varied from 1:1 (Shape A) to 1:25 (Shape F). Shapes A–E simulate fields, while Shape F simulates long thin linear features such as roads and hedges.

Table 3.16 shows the expected number of dots for each size and shape combination, their areas in hectares and square metres, and their approximate dimensions in metres. Also shown are the percentage of all observations in the survey data base arising from each of the size classes, and the percentage of all dots counted in the photo-interpretation exercise. Thus, the smallest area of one dot, equivalent to 92 m^2, contributed

Table 3.16. Shapes and sizes for testing dot-grid bias (nominal height of 400 ft above ground level)

Expected dots:	1.0	3.5	8	13	20	29	40
Hectares	0,01	0.03	0.07	0.12	0.18	0.27	0.37
Square metres	92	321	734	1193	1835	2661	3670
Dimensions of shapes (m)							
A 1:1	10*10	18*18	27*27	35*35	43*43	52*52	61*61
B 1:1.5	8*12	15*23	22*23	28*42	35*53	42*63	49*74
C 1:2	7*14	13*26	19*38	24*48	30*60	38*76	43*86
D 1:4	5*20	9*36	14*56	17*68	21*84	26*104	30*120
E 1:11	3*33	6*66	8*88	10*110	13*143	16*176	18*198
F 1:25	2*50	3*107					
% Observations	6	19	25	12	6	6	6
% All dots	0.2	2	5	6	6	5	2

Dimensions (m) of each shape A–F are approximate.
% Observations > 40 is 20%.
% Dots   > 40 is 74%.

6 per cent of all observations in the data base but accounted for only 0.2 per cent of the 3.4 milion dots that were counted.

Fifty dot-counts were carried out on each combination of size and shape (Table 3.17) and for each combination the mean, standard deviation, standard error, and standard error expressed as a percentage of the mean were calculated. The first important result is that none of the estimates shows any bias, and in no case is the mean estimate of a size/shape combination significantly different from the expected value.

The recommended design for the dot-grid is therefore providing completely unbiased estimates of areas of different shapes. Indeed, a two-way analysis of variance (Table 3.17) shows that the shape of the area has no influence at all on the number of dots being counted; the only influence comes from the size of the area.

The second important result is that the standard errors of the estimates are all acceptably small apart from the smallest shape (one dot expected). However, we have already seen that areas of this size contribute only 6 per cent of the observations and 0.2 per cent of the sampled material. The influence of the high standard errors of these very small areas is thus negligible on the data base as a whole.

3.2.11. Conclusion

This account of low-level aerial monitoring has covered the problems and prospects which practitioners are likely to encounter. Inevitably, the description given is insufficient for the design of individual monitoring

Table 3.17. Results of bias test on dot-grid

Expected dots		1.00	3.50	8.00	13.00	20.00	29.00	40.00
Shape								
A 1:1	x	1.06	3.72	8.00	13.14	19.68	28.14	39.20
	s.d.	0.76	1.01	1.26	18.6	3.64	4.72	3.19
	s.e.	0.11	0.14	0.18	0.26	0.51	0.67	0.45
	s.e.%	11%	4%	2%	2%	3%	2%	1%
B 1:1.5	x	1.02	3.52	7.84	13.28	20.47	29.26	40.16
	s.d.	0.84	1.20	1.62	1.80	2.10	2.66	3.09
	s.e.	0.12	0.17	0.23	0.25	0.30	0.38	0.44
	s.e.%	12%	5%	3%	2%	1%	1%	1%
C 1:2	x	1.18	3.54	7.60	13.34	20.33	29.24	39.80
	s.d.	0.94	1.22	1.56	1.42	2.46	2.95	3.39
	s.e.	0.13	0.17	0.22	0.20	0.35	0.42	0.48
	s.e.%	11%	5%	3%	1%	2%	1%	1%
D 1:4	x	1.18	3.60	7.62	13.00	20.52	29.50	39.98
	s.d.	0.94	1.34	1.61	1.84	3.05	2.96	3.10
	s.e.	0.13	0.19	0.23	0.26	0.43	0.42	0.44
	s.e.%	11%	5%	3%	2%	2%	1%	1%
E 1:11	x	0.96	3.50	7.56	12.78	19.58	27.84	39.82
	s.d.	0.86	1.49	2.17	2.89	3.61	5.29	5.63
	s.e.	0.12	0.21	0.31	0.41	0.51	0.75	0.80
	s.e.%	13%	6%	4%	3%	3%	3%	2%
F 1:25	x	0.98	3.62					
	s.d.	0.91	1.82					
	s.e.	0.13	0.26					
	s.e.%	13%	7%					

Two-Way ANOVAR, 7 sizes, 5 shapes (A–E only)

Source	s.s.	d.f.	m.s.	F
Size	6017.7	6	1003.0	100030
Shapes	1.5	5	0.3	3
Residual	2.6	30	0.1	
TOTAL	6021.8	34		

projects. Further more detailed information can be found in the references which follow.

Bibliography: Chapter 3

Bell, R. H. V., Grimsdell, J. J. R., Van Lavieren, L. P., and Sayer, J. A. (1973). Census of the Kafue lechwe by aerial stratified sampling. *E. Afr. Wildl. J.* **11**(1), 55–74.

Bergerud, A. T., and Mandel, F. (1969). Aerial census of moose in central Newfoundland. *J. Wildl. Mgmt* **33**(4), 910–16.

Buechner, H. K., Buss, I. O., Longhurst, W. M., and Brooks, A. C. (1963).

Numbers and migration of elephants in Murchison Falls National Park, Uganda. *J. Wildl. Mgmt* **27**(1), 36–53.

Caughley, G. (1974). Bias in aerial survey. *J. Wildl. Mgmt* **38**, 921–33.

—— and Goddard, J. (1972). Improving the estimates from inaccurate censuses. *J. Wildl. Mgmt* **36**, 135–40.

—— —, Sinclair, R. G., and Scott-Kermiss, D. (1976). Experiments in aerial survey. *J. Wildl. Mgmt* **40**(2), 290–300.

——, Sinclair, R. G., and Wilson, G. R. (1977). Numbers, distribution and harvesting rate of kangaroos on the Inland Plains of New South Wales. *Aust. Wildl. Res.* **4**, 99–108.

Cochran, W. G. (1954). The combination of estimates from different experiments. *Biometrics* **10**, 101–29.

Evans, C. D., Troyer, W. A., and Lensink, C. J. (1966). Aerial Census of moose by quadrat sampling. *J. Wildl. Mgmt* **30**(4), 767–76.

Goddard, J. (1967). The validity of censusing black rhinoceros populations from the air. *E. Afr. Wildl. J.* **5**, 112–20.

—— (1969). Aerial census of black rhinoceros using stratified random sampling. *E. Afr. Wildl. J.* **7**, 105–14.

Gwynne, M. D., and Croze, H. J. (1975*a*). East African habitat monitoring practice: a review of methods and application. *Proc. Symp. Evaluation and Mapping of Rangeland in Tropical Africa*, pp. 95–135. ICLA, Bamako, Mali.

—— —— (1975*b*). The concept and practice of ecological monitoring over large areas of land: the systematic reconnaissance flight (SRF). *Proc. Ibadan/ Garoua Int. Symp. on Wildlife Management in Savanna Woodland.* University of Ibadan, Nigeria.

ILCA (1981). *Low-level aerial survey techniques.* ILCA Monograph No. 4. International Livestock Centre for Africa, Addis Ababa.

Jolly, G. M. (1969*a*). Sampling methods for aerial census of wildlife populations. *E. Afr. Agric. Forest. J.* **34**, 46–9.

—— (1969*b*). The treatment of errors in aerial counts of wildlife populations. *E. Afr. Agric. Forest. J.* **34**, 50–5.

Milligan, K., and De Leeuw, P. (1983). Low altitude aerial surveys in pastoral systems research. *Proc. Pastoral Systems Research Workshop.* International Livestock Centre for Africa, Addis Ababa.

Norton-Griffiths, M. (1973). Counting the Serengeti migratory wildebeest using two-stage sampling. *E. Afr. Wildl. J.* **11**(2), 135–49.

—— (1974). Reducing counting bias in aerial census by using photography. *E. Afr. Wildl. J.* **12**, 245–8.

—— (1975). The numbers and distribution of large mammals in Ruaha National Park, Tanzania. *E. Afr. Wildl. J.* **13**, 121–40.

—— (1976). Further aspects of bias in aerial census of large mammals. *J. Wildl. Mgmt* **40**(2), 368–70.

—— (1978). *Counting animals* (2nd edn.). East African Wildlife Foundation, Nairobi, Kenya.

—— (1981). Applications of systematic reconnaissance flights for resource inventory and monitoring in arid and semi-arid lands. In: *Environment monitoring for the Arab world* (eds. Y. Elmehrik, F. A. Daghestani, H. J. Croze, and W. Al-Hashimi), pp. 192–248. Royal Scientific Society, Amman.

——, Hart, T., and Parton, M. (1982). Sample surveys from light aircraft combining visual observation and very large scale colour photography. In *Remote Sens. Newsl.* **2**, 1–4.

Pennycuick, C. J. (1973). The shadowmeter: a simple device for controlling an aircraft's height above the ground. *E. Afr. Wildl. J.* **11**(1), 109–12.

—— and Western, D. (1972). An investigation of some sources of bias in aerial transect sampling of large mammal populations. *E. Afr. Wildl. J.* **10**(3), 175–91.

——, Sale, J. B., Stanley Price, M., and Jolly, G. M. (1977). Aerial systematic sampling applied to censuses of large mammal populations in Kenya. *E. Afr. Wildl. J.* **15**, 139–46.

Pennycuick, L. (1975). Movements of the migratory wildebeest population in the Serengeti area between 1960 and 1973. *E. Afr. Wildl. J.* **13**, 65–87.

Piennar, U. de, Wyk, P., and Fairall, N. (1966). An aerial census of elephant and buffalo in the Kruger National Park and the implications thereof on intended management schemes. *Kudu* **9**, 40–107.

Sinclair, A. R. E. (1971). Long term monitoring of mammal populations in the Serengeti: census of non-migratory ungulates. *E. Afr. Wildl. J.* **10**, 287–98.

—— (1973). Population increases of the buffalo and wildebeest in the Serengeti. *E. Afr. Wildl. J.* **11**, 93–107.

—— (1974). The natural regulation of buffalo populations in East Africa 1: introduction and resource requirements. *E. Afr. Wildl. J.* **12**, 135–54.

—— and Norton-Griffiths, M. (eds.) (1979). *Serengeti: dynamics of an ecosystem.* University of Chicago Press, Chicago.

Siniff, D. B., and Skoog, R. O. (1964). Aerial censusing of caribou using stratified random sampling. *J. Wildl. Mgmt* **28**(2), 391–401.

Turner, M. I. M., and Watson, R. M. (1964). A census of game in Ngorongoro Crater. *E. Afr. Wildl. J.* **2**, 165–68.

Watson, R. M., and Turner, M. I. M. (1965). A count of the large mammals of the Lake Manyara National Park: results and discussion. *E. Afr. Wildl. J.* **3**, 95–8.

——, Graham, A. D., and Parker, I. S. C. (1969). A census of the large mammals of Loliondo Controlled Area, Northern Tanzania. *E. Afr. Wildl. J.* **7**, 43–59.

——, Parker, I. S. C., and Allan, T. (1969). A census of the elephant and other large mammals in the Mkomazi region of Northern Tanzania and Southern Kenya. *E. Afr. Wildl. J.* **7**, 11–26.

Western, D. (1976a). *An aerial method of monitoring large mammals and their environment, with a description of a computer program for survey analysis.* Project Working Document 9, UNDP/FAO Kenya Wildlife Management Project (KEN/71/526), Nairobi.

—— (1976b). *The distribution of animals in relation to resources.* Handbook No. 2, Techniques in African Wildlife Ecology, African Wildlife Leadership Foundation, Nairobi.

Yates, F. (1960). *Sampling methods for censuses and surveys.* Charles Griffin, London.

4. Remote sensing

Remote sensing is a means of acquiring information about the environment by devices not in direct physical contact with the objects or phenomena being studied. Although the human eye is actually one of the most sophisticated remote sensors known, the term is normally restricted to mean information acquired by man-made devices, usually carried on aircraft or satellites, which record information from some part of the electromagnetic spectrum.

In theory, imaging systems for environmental monitoring can utilize radiation from any part of the spectrum which passes through the Earth's atmosphere. In practice, the limitations of sensor sensitivity and background radiation (noise) have restricted the development of remote sensing systems to those which operate at wavelengths which are either strongly emitted or strongly reflected from environmental targets.

Remote sensing was first developed in airborne equipment, and is still much used in that mode today. However, the development of space technology has provided a new platform for remote sensing which has had dramatic results for ecological monitoring. Remote sensing data from space is now a key input to almost any survey of the terrestrial environment.

4.1. Principles of remote sensing

Three major sectors of the electromagnetic spectrum (see Fig. 4.1) are used for remote sensing:
- the ultraviolet to near infra-red (0.3 to 1.1 μm – μm is 10^{-6} m);
- the thermal infra-red (1.5 to 14 μm); and
- the microwave (1 mm to 30 cm or 1 to 300 GHz).

These regions of the spectrum can be used to image a terrain in one of a number of ways, the best known of which is photography. In fact, film is available which is sensitive to wavelengths other than in the visible region and in remote sensing the concept of photography is greatly extended from its traditional meaning. However, image data are not always recorded directly on film. Various kinds of television cameras and scanners are also used which produce an electronic output. The data generated by such systems can be transmitted quickly over large distances (even from space) and then reconstituted into images of one kind or another elsewhere and at leisure. A summary of the major techniques of remote sensing is presented in Fig. 4.2 which also demonstrates the techniques which are best suited to various different applications.

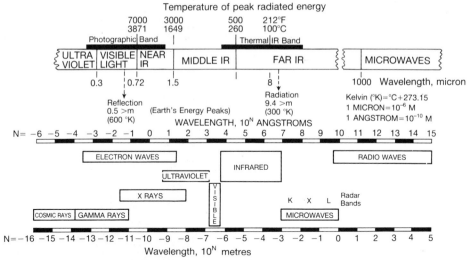

Fig. 4.1. Electromagnetic spectrum.

Sensors may be either active or passive. Passive systems, such as the camera, record radiation from targets which is either self-emitted or reflected from another source, usually the sun. Active systems, such as radar and flash photography, generate their own illumination, and form the image from signals reflected by objects on the ground. Generally, photographic systems provide views of the way targets reflect radiation while thermal sensors provide pictures of how they emit it. Often, it is desirable to obtain information about both the reflectance and emittance of environmental phenomena simultaneously. In this case, multispectral photography or scanners can be used.

Remote sensing, however, involves much more than data acquisition. Data analysis is equally important and includes a number of methods of interpretation and viewing, and computers to analyse the data themselves. Ground-truth and reference data are usually needed to assist in data analysis. The information which is finally extracted is usually presented in the form of maps, tables, and technical reports (see Fig. 4.3).

4.2. The history of remote sensing

Since the invention of the camera in the nineteenth century, remote sensing has evolved through four distinct stages:

(i) *Pre-1925.* An era of rather primitive experiments on balloon and low-altitude photography. One of the first experiments on aerial mapping was made in 1840 by Arago, Director of the Paris Observatory. In 1858,

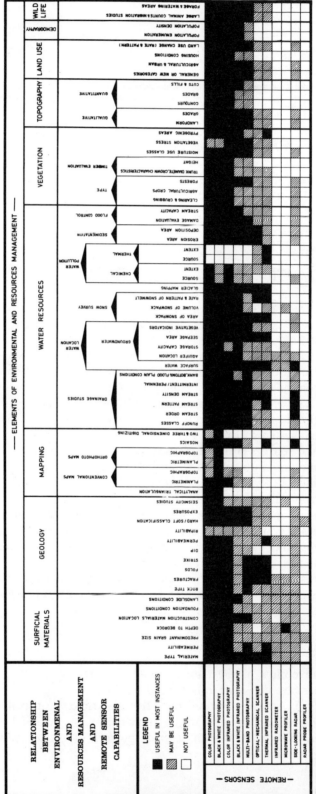

Fig. 4.2. General uses and limitations of remote sensing in selective spectral bands and modes in environmental monitoring. (Courtesy, Raytheon Company 1971.)

Colonel Aime Laussedat, of the French Army Corps of Engineers, developed a mathematical technique for converting overlapping glass-plate aerial photos taken by balloon over Paris into orthophotographic projections. For this reason, Laussedat is often considered the father of photogrammetry.

Between 1910 and 1923, stereographic equipment was developed by several mapping agencies around the world. Photographs taken from balloons and aircraft came to be recognized as an important source of information about geology and the environment. This led to the formation in 1980 of the Committee on Photographs of the Geological Society of America, which became the base for the science of photogeology. In about 1920, petroleum geologists began to use aerial photography to help in geological mapping for oil exploration.

(ii) *1925–45.* From about 1930, many US government agencies began to make extensive use of aerial photography in agriculture, forestry, and ranchland development. The US Geological Survey, the Tennessee Valley Authority and other agencies used the technique for geological mapping, mineral exploration and planning, and the official monthly journal of the American Society of Photogrammetry was first published in 1934. World War II stimulated the use of aerial photography even more, mainly for topographical mapping and for military interpretation. Several major advances took place, including the development of infra-red sensitive film which was used for haze penetration and camouflage detection. Knowledge of the spectral reflectance properties of natural terrain elements was greatly extended.

(iii) *1945–60.* Second World War knowledge and experience were developed for civilian applications in geology, agriculture, forestry, archaeology, and other environmental areas. Although colour aerial photography was discussed as early as 1941, its importance for geological and mineral exploration was not fully appreciated until 1952.

The concept of multispectral photography also advanced, with the British Army Air Photo Research Unit experimenting as early as 1945 with two-band aerial photography for assessing water depth. Significant research was done on thermal infra-red systems, most of the work being focused on the development of radiation models, keys and signatures to aid in the interpretation of infra-red data.

(iv) *1960 on.* A period of very active platform and sensor development, with the two technologies of remote sensing and space exploration beginning to merge. More sophisticated multispectral cameras and additive colour viewers were also developed. At the same time, the computer processing of images came into its own. Although this technique is not new – medical, agricultural and military experts have used digital image processing for a number of years – environmental scientists are now also becoming increasingly aware of the potential of the method.

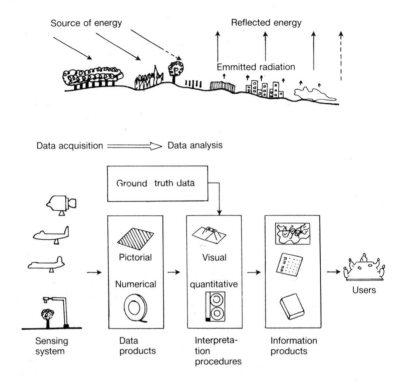

Fig. 4.3. Elements of the remote sensing of the environment.

4.2.1. *Remote sensing from space*

Rocket photographs stimulated interest in orbital and terrain reconnaissance as early as 1946 when small automatic cameras were carried aboard V-2 rockets fired from the White Sands Proving Ground in New Mexico. Although crude by today's standards, these experiments demonstrated the potential of remote sensing from space.

The Mercury programme produced the first orbital photography in 1961, in the form of several hundred 70-mm colour photographs taken by automatic camera in the unmanned MA-4 Mercury spacecraft. These demonstrated the value of orbital as opposed to hyperaltitude photography for regional, environmental and terrain reconnaissance.

On 5 May 1961, Alan Shepherd made a 15-min suborbital Mercury flight from which 150 excellent photographs were taken using an automatic 70-mm camera. Because of the flight trajectory, these photographs showed only sky, clouds, and oceans. On 20 February 1962, John Glenn made three historic orbits round the Earth and with a 35-mm camera took 48 colour photographs, of which several showed the deserts of north-west Africa. Later, L. G. Cooper obtained 29 usable terrain and ocean photographs on Mercury flight MA-9, which included outstanding views of Tibet that revealed many unmapped topographic and geological features.

The Gemini programme (1965–66) extended space photography much further. Although the first manned flight (GT-3) did not carry a formal photographic experiment, the crew used a 70-mm camera with an 80-mm lens to obtain photographs of southern Arizona and north-western Sonora which were of immense geological value. These results led the US Geological Survey to formulate a general plan for repetitive surveys of the earth's environment and resources. Most of the Gemini photography was restricted by tracking and re-entry requirements to areas between 35° N. and 35° S. and to altitudes of 160–320 km. The first formal photographic experiment was flown by McDivitt and White on the GT-4 mission. Coverage included nearly vertical and overlapping photographs of Mexico, north America, Africa, and Asia. These led to new and exciting discoveries in tectonics, volcanology, and geomorphology.

All the remaining Gemini missions were given specific photographic assignments. By the end of the programme, more than 1000 high-quality colour photographs had been obtained and the value of remote sensing from space was well established. However, several problems were encountered: the oblique angle at which many of the photographs were taken caused distortion; cloud cover over many areas obscured the targets; and debris from rocket exhaust and other sources caused distortion and degradation of the photographs.

The Apollo programme produced further advances in space photography. The unmanned Apollo-6 produced a remarkable series of overlapping vertical photographs across North America, the Atlantic and West Africa. In the manned Apollos-7 and -9, the crew hand-held cameras. In Apollo-9, the SO-65 experiment acquired the first orbital multispectral photographs in an attempt to evaluate the feasibility and value of this technique. The astronauts used a series of coaxially mounted 70-mm cameras which could be triggered simultaneously, and with different film/filter combinations. Three cameras produced black-and-white photographs in the green, red, and infra-red spectral regions. The fourth used infra-red colour film with a yellow filter. Some 140 sets of photographs were obtained, covering parts of Mexico, the United States, and the Caribbean. An aircraft was used to provide simultaneous imagery and data over test areas on the ground while the mission was in progress.

The Skylab programme, begun in 1973, put the first manned space station into orbit. Launched as an unmanned vehicle, it was subsequently occupied by three crews of three people who took more than 35 000 images of the earth with the Earth Resources Experiment Package (EREP). The 50° inclination of the orbital path allowed photographic coverage between 50° N. and 50° S. at an altitude of 435 km. EREP included a six-camera multispectral array, a long focal length 'earth terrain' camera, a 13-channel multispectral array and two microwave systems. The magnetic tape records and exposed films were returned to earth by the crews.

The Earth terrain camera had a 45.7-cm focal length, allowing ground coverage of a 109-km square. Normal colour, infra-red, and minus blue, black-and-white photographs were acquired at a scale of 1:950 000. Ground resolution for the second generation images was 15 m for the black-and-white photographs and 30 m for the normal colour and infra-red colour photographs.

The Apollo–Soyuz programme was a joint US/USSR project held in 1975 which included a remote sensing experiment. It was limited, however, to obtaining photographs using hand-held 35-mm and 70-mm cameras because Earth-resource imaging was not a primary goal of the programme.

The Landsat programme, began in the late 1960s when the Earth Resources Observation Satellite (EROS) office was established by the US. Geological Survey. The developmental work done by this office resulted in NASA's Earth Resources Technology Satellite (ERTS) programme, which launched its first satellite, *ERTS-1*, on 23 July 1972. This was an experimental programme to obtain a systematic remote sensing coverage of the earth's surface by unmanned satellites. The first satellite was renamed *Landsat-1* on the launch of the second satellite in January 1975 and all subsequent satellites in this series have been named Landsat, the most recent being *Landsat-5*. Together with the weather satellites, especially *NOAA-7*, the Landsat programme provides the most important source of space data for ecological monitoring purposes; it is described in detail below (see 5.4.2. and 7.1.1.).

4.3. Photographic sensors and applications

4.3.1. The metric camera

Metric cameras (often called mapping or cartographic cameras) are the most common cameras used today in remote sensing and photogrammetry. They all have the same basic configuration, with a single lens, a low-distortion lens system, a carefully calibrated focal length and a vacuum platen to provide a high-quality geometrical image. Film size is normally 23×23 cm with a magazine capacity of 120 m. Flight and camera data are usually recorded on the side of each frame. Lenses with $75-120°$ total field of view are usually used for mapping and are classified as normal angle (with an angular field of view up to $75°$); wide angle (with a field of view of $75-100°$); and super-wide angle (field of view of more than $100°$). Plate 1 shows an RC-8 metric camera used for aerial mapping in the Remote Sensing Centre in Egypt. The exposure interval is automatically controlled by an electronic device known as an intervalometer, and exposure intervals can be chosen so that a sequence of overlapping images can be obtained. This overlap is essential for stereoscopic viewing.

The scale of aerial photographs obtained by these cameras is determined by a simple relationship between the focal length and the height of the camera above ground:

$$\text{scale} = f \text{ (focal length)}/H \text{ (height of camera above ground)}.$$

For example, the scale of a photograph obtained at a camera height of 4560 m, with a 152-mm focal length, is:

$$0.152/4560 = 1/30\,000 = 1:30\,000$$

This means that 1 cm on the photograph represents 300 m on the ground.

4.3.2. Photographic resolution

The terms resolution and resolving power are often used interchangeably. It is important, however, to make a distinction between resolving power – which applies to an imaging system – and resolution, which applies to the image produced. They are related since, for example, the lens and the film in a camera each has its own characteristic resolving power and these together determine the resolution of the resulting photograph.

Other factors, such as atmospheric conditions, target illumination, and contrast, and conditions of film processing, have a marked influence on resolution. In remote sensing, resolution can be defined as the ability to distinguish between two closely spaced objects on a photograph or, more specifically, as the minimum separation between two objects at which the objects appear distinct and separate on an image. Therefore, objects spaced closer together than the resolution limit of an image appear as a single object. Resolution is thus not the size of the smallest object that can be seen. However, a knowledge of the resolution and scale of an image is all that is needed to estimate the size of the smallest detectable object on it.

Film resolving power is expressed in units of lines/mm at a specific contrast ratio between lines and background (because resolution is strongly influenced by contrast).

The effects of scale and resolution can be combined to express image quality in terms of ground resolution distance (GRD):

$$\text{GRD (m)} = \text{reciprocal of image scale/}$$
$$\text{(system resolution (lines/mm)} \times 1000).$$

For example, a 1:40 000-scale photograph taken with a system having a resolution of 50 lines/mm would have a GRD given by:

$$\text{GRD} = 40\ 000/(50 \times 1000) = 0.8 \text{ m.}$$

The GRD provides a convenient way of comparing the detail available on an image. However, care is still needed because of the many variables which affect the level of detection, recognition, and identification of an object in a photograph. Detectability is the ability to record the presence or absence of an object in a photograph, without necessarily being able to recognize or identify it. (It is often possible to detect objects which are smaller than the resolving power of a system.) Recognizability is the ability to recognize an object. Objects which can be detected and resolved may not necessarily be recognizable; for example, vegetation may be detected on an image but not recognized as trees or crops, and features such as roads may be detected as narrow lines on an image but these lines might also be railway lines or canals. Finally, identifiability is the step beyond detection and recognition in which objects such as types of trees or crops can actually be identified as such.

The image resolution required for each of these levels of interpretation would be different. Many other factors, however, must also be con-sidered in the process of interpretation, including tone, colour, texture, shape, and size. Sometimes a process of deductive and inductive analysis is used; for example, the association of different types of vegetation with certain land-forms can be used to identify different types of soil or rock, without detecting the soil or rock itself.

Because of its high spatial resolution and information content, aerial metric photography is an important means of remote sensing; it is also relatively simple and cheap. Its use, however, is limited by the need for good illumination and weather, and by atmospheric scattering and absorption which reduce contrast ratio and resolution in the shorter wavelengths.

4.3.3. Black-and-white panchromatic aerial photography

This is the classical form of aerial photography, using wavelengths ranging from 0.30 to 0.72 μm, a region which extends much further into the red range than the sensitivity of panchromatic films used in normal photography. A minus blue filter is normally used during aerial photography to cut off ultraviolet and blue light below 0.5 μm which are selectively scattered by the atmosphere.

4.3.4. Black-and-white infra-red film

Black-and-white infra-red films are available for both 35-mm and aerial metric cameras. Their sensitivity extends typically from 0.36 to 0.9 μm. They are less sensitive to green but more sensitive to the infra-red than is normal panchromatic film; however, this sensitivity extends only into the reflected portion of the infra-red spectrum and not into the emitted thermal energy range. If an infra-red film is used in combination with a red (Wratten 25A) or dark red (Wratten 89B) filter, broad-leaved vegetation appears lighter in tone, whereas water, streams, and moist soil appear darker. Broad-leaved plants that are diseased or losing vigour show up darker than their healthier neighbours.

There are several advantages in using infra-red film:

— because the blue and green regions of the spectrum are normally cut out by the use of appropriate filters, haze penetration is improved;
— the elimination of scattered radiation in the ultraviolet and visible regions of the spectrum produces higher contrast and hence higher spatial resolution. On the other hand, this also produces poor shadow penetration, making it difficult for cartographers to see the ground in areas covered with vegetation;
— boundaries between land and water are clearer and more distinct because water absorbs infra-red radiation strongly, and therefore appears as a dark tone on the image (see Plate 2).

4.3.5. Colour film

Photo-interpreters are used to identify objects not only by shape and form but also by colour. Because the human eye can distinguish many more shades of colour than it can tones of grey, a colour photograph has a higher information content than a black-and-white one. Colour photography is now only marginally more expensive than black-and-white photography, and the increased cost is now often offset by the improved results. Readers are referred to the *Manual of color aerial photography*, published by the American Society of Photogrammetry and Remote Sensing (1968), for a comprehensive treatment of colour photography in environmental and earth resource studies.

4.3.6. Colour infra-red film

Colour infra-red film was originally known as camouflage film because of its military applications, but it is now also widely used in Earth-resource

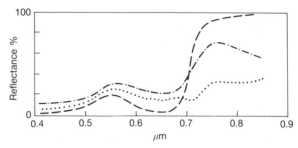

Fig. 4.4. Typical vegetation reflectance curves, showing great anomalies in reflected infra-red.

monitoring. It is also called false-colour film because objects do not appear in the final image with the same colours as they possess on the ground. This is due to the different spectral sensitivities of the three colour-sensitive layers used to produce the film. For example, healthy vegetation appears red in an infra-red colour film because of the high infra-red reflectance of plant material. However, if it is diseased or about to die, vegetation loses infra-red reflectance and is therefore more sharply contrasted with healthy vegetation than is the case with other types of film. Loss of plant vigour, through disease, soil salinity or moisture loss, causes vegetation to appear as a light-red or even white colour, in contrast to the bright red of healthy plants.

In some cases, plants under stress can be distinguished from healthy plants on this type of film even before symptoms appear on the ground. Different types of vegetation can often be better distinguished on colour infra-red film than on other film (see Fig. 4.4). The reason for this is as follows. Normal colour film shows vegetation as green because leaves reflect about 20 per cent of incident green light. Infra-red colour film, however, shows leaves a red because vegetation also reflects infra-red radiation, and colour infra-red film is red sensitive to these wavelengths. It is because vegetation has a wider range of reflectance in the infra-red than in the green, that different types of vegetation are more easily distinguished on infra-red colour film than on other films.

Because of its high absorption of infra-red radiation, clear water appears dark blue or black on colour infra-red film, in contrast to the red of vegetation. This ability to enhance the differences between water and vegetation is valuable in environmental monitoring, particularly in wetland studies and in mapping heavily vegetated terrain.

4.3.7. Multiband photography

Multiband photographs are taken simultaneously at different wavelengths using different combinations of films and filters. Scientists began to use the technique for aerial survey, especially for military purposes, in the early 1960s. At first, multiple camera systems equipped with various spectral filters were used, resulting in a rather lengthy and difficult process of data reduction and analysis. By 1962, Zaitov and Tsuprun of the Russian MIGAIK had constructed a nine-lens camera system, permitting photography of 6×6 cm size on three different films that rolled side by side simultaneously. At about the same time, the US Air Force Cambridge Research Laboratories developed a similar multi-spectral nine-lens camera. The camera used nine simultaneous exposures in the 0.37–0.9-μm range. Six of the exposures were made on 70-mm panchromatic-film and three exposures on 70-mm infra-red film. From 1963 to 1965, a number of experimental multispectral camera configurations were developed, mostly for military use.

In March 1969, a multispectral camera experiment was conducted on the Apollo-9 flight, which was the first satellite photography of the Earth's surface in three distinct spectral bands, covering the visible and near infra-red part of the spectrum. An array of four Hasselblad cameras equipped with green, red and near infra-red films were used. The cameras were synchronized, and three of them loaded with black-and-white film and one with colour infra-red film. At the same time, NASA used a four-lens multispectral camera from an aircraft to provide support photography in approximately the same spectral bands.

During the past decade, multiband photography, mostly using four-lens aerial cameras, became a widespread technique of environmental and resource monitoring. Plate 3 shows a multispectral four-band camera used aboard a Beech-King Air aircraft at the Remote Sensing Centre in Egypt. The four lenses have the same focal length of 150 mm and are aimed at the same point on the ground. Each lens has a filter allowing the transmittance of a different spectral band, typically blue, green, red, and near (photographic) infra-red. The camera uses a standard black-and-white infra-red film. An example of the photographs acquired with such a system is shown in Plate 4. These photographs show the identical scene imaged on the black-and-white infra-red film filtered for discrete wave-length bands in the blue, green, red, and reflected infra-red portions of the spectrum.

The best combination of images for studying environmental phenomena varies with the spectral reflectance of the phenomena being studied. Each of the four bands distinguish differently between certain features and the surrounding terrain because objects on the terrain usually reflect differently at different wavelengths.

Each photograph can be interpreted and examined separately. However, in some cases such an analysis is difficult. Colour additive viewers were therefore developed to assist in interpretation. Most types are of similar design, with four projectors aimed at a single viewing screen.

Each projector has a variable brightness and colour filter control. The technique results in the production of colour composite images on the screen. By varying the colour filters and light intensity on each projector, images can be produced on the screen to enhance discrimination of features of interest, such as soil or crop types.

4.3.8. The large-format camera

The significance of the large-format camera stems from NASA's use of it aboard a space shuttle flight, in October 1984. The results are very interesting, and stereo coverage is available for topographic mapping over some areas. The camera parameters are shown in Table 4.1. This camera is designed in such a way that at a nominal altitude of 300 km, high-resolution colour or black-and-white film provides ground resolution of bettern than 15 m, which is adequate for map production at a scale of 1:50 000 with 30 m contour intervals.

Table 4.1. Major parameters of the large-format camera

Lens:	
— focal length	305 mm
— f number	6.0
— distortion	15 µm max. over format
	10 µm over central 230×230 mm
Format:	230×460 mm
Magazine capacity:	1200 m of film for 2400 frames

4.3.9. Filters used in photography

Filters are used to select, amplify or eliminate portions of the spectrum. Haze-cutting filters and those used to reduce atmospheric scattering of blue light are commonly used in aerial photography. Absorption filters can be very useful in environmental monitoring because they allow the differentiation of objects with nearly identical spectral response patterns in major portions of the spectrum. For example, two different types of vegetation or soils may appear with similar colour or tonal contrasts when viewed in the visible part of the spectrum but may have different reflection characteristics in the ultraviolet or near infra-red. In such a case, the use of a special filter allowing maximum transmission in the ultraviolet or infra-red may enhance the differentiation between the two objects. A large selection of filters is commercially available.

4.4. Imaging with non-photographic sensors

Normal photographic cameras, although small, light, and relatively simple to use, have two basic limitations in remote sensing. First, the output is a photograph which is difficult to transmit or to manipulate in an automatic data-processing system. Secondly, photographic films are limited in their spectral response from the near ultraviolet to the near infra-red (0.3 to 0.9 µm). Moreover, adverse weather conditions, such as clouds, fog, and smog, can make observation impossible. However, very low-level, large-format 35-mm photography has been used recently to monitor details of land use in areas of small utilization units and rapid change.

Research on a variety of non-photographic imaging systems has been progressing since 1945. Non-photographic sensors operate in portions of the spectrum from the ultraviolet to the microwave region, can operate during the day or the night, and radar sensors are not seriously hindered by clouds or bad weather. Since the data produced are collected in electrical form, they can be transmitted to remote locations. In addition, they can be processed, analysed, and categorized by computer processing systems.

Non-photographic systems can be classified as scanning and non-scanning. The scanning systems have rotating mirrors that cause the sensor to view portions of the scene sequentially in some regular manner. Non-scanning devices generally view a larger field and convert the radiation from it into a visible image without the use of moving mechanical parts. Technological advance over the past decade has produced systems which are compact, reliable, practical, reasonably simple, and capable of producing imagery with photographic quality.

4.4.1. TV cameras or image tubes

Television cameras and image tubes scan the image with a focused beam of electrons at very high speed and without the need for moving mechanical parts. The technology is well developed, having been used in television since 1945; image tubes have high resolution, a wide field of view and high scan rates.

There are many different types of image tube but all use a focused electron beam to scan the image. This beam is generated in an electron gun, accelerated, focused in an electron lens, and deflected either electromagnetically or electrostatically into a scanning pattern.

Most tubes store the image information as a charge pattern on the electron-beam target. This target is capacitative in the sense that a charge deposited on it by the electron beam will remain in position until discharged by electrons produced by the optical image. All TV tubes work like this and they differ only in the way in which the charge pattern is developed and in the way output signals are created. The two best-known systems are known as orthicons and vidicons. The operating details need not concern us here, but the vidicon is smaller, cheaper, simpler to operate, more robust, has a longer lifetime, and does not require critical adjustment. A derivative of the vidicon, known as the return beam vidicon (RBV), has been developed specifically to provide high resolution in remote sensing.

The RBV has provided satellites with a means of obtaining high-resolution images in the 0.36–1.1-μm wavelength range without the need for film replacement or converting a film image into a video signal. Vidicon cameras have proved very valuable for producing real-time, or near real-time, imaging of the Earth's surface, especially from weather satellites. Experience with television cameras aboard the Tiros, Nimbus, the Ranger Moon-shots, Apollos, and Mariners has led to great improvements in vidicon systems.

Landsats-1 and -2 both carried three-channel RBV systems. The RBV can provide multispectral data either by using a series of filters on the optical system or by using a number of different vidicon sensors operating simultaneously and covering each wavelength band. The latter approach was used in Landsat-1 and -2 where the three vidicon cameras covered the ranges 0.475–0.575 μm (green), 0.580–0.680 μm (red) and 0.690–0.830 μm (reflected infra-red). These bands are designated as channels 1, 2, and 3. Unfortunately, the RBV cameras failed on Landsat-1, although some imagery was obtained.

This RBV system was shuttered, and the imagery was obtained a frame at a time, in contrast to the multispectral scanners which were also carried on Landsat (see below).

A different unfiltered RBV camera system was used on Landsat-3 which increased linear resolution two- to threefold. This was achieved by using lenses of twice the focal length, cycling the cameras at twice the rate, and arranging them so that they imaged slightly overlapping adjacent areas in the across-track direction. The characteristics of this system are summarized in Table 4.2.

Table 4.2. Characteristics of RBV camera used on Landsat-3

Configuration	2 cameras at 5.24° divergence
Spectral band	0.505–0.750 μm
Number of lines	4125 per frame
Number of samples	5375 per frame
Instantaneous field of view	24 m
Focal length	236 mm
Frame coverage	98
Reseau	81-point pattern
Geometrical fidelity	internal errors 2–40 m r.m.s.

4.4.2. Optical-mechanical scanners

Airborne line scanners developed rapidly after World War II, largely sponsored by the military. Details of their design and operation were therefore classified for some time. During the early 1950s, the Haller-Raymond & Brown company, under US Air Force sponsorship, developed the Reconofax system which operated in the visible region and used a photomultiplier detector. Its imagery lacked resolution compared to photography but line scanners have since been rapidly improved.

Compared to photographic cameras, line scanners are complex instruments. However, they can be used to obtain images outside the photographic region (at wavelengths longer than 1.2 μm) and the output signal, being in electrical form, can be transmitted, recorded, analysed or processed as needed. Line scanners also have a wider dynamic range than photographic film.

A scanner consists of a rotating mirror and a telescope that focuses the radiation from a small portion of the object. As the field of view moves across the terrain, a strip map of the ground image is produced (see Fig.

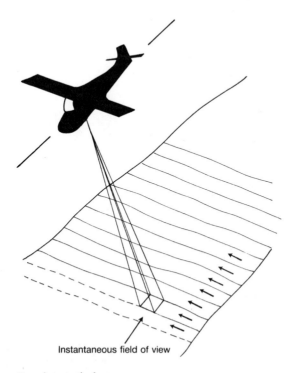

Instantaneous field of view

Fig. 4.5. Scan pattern for a typical scanner.

4.5). The principles of operation are shown in Fig. 4.6, in which a multi-faced prism is used for the rotating mirror.

Such a device has a very fine angular resolution (about 1 mrad^2) which provides an instantaneous ground resolution of 30 cm for an aircraft altitude of 300 m, or 180 m for a satellite at 150 km altitude. The motion of the vehicle carries the scanner forward so that successive scans cover different strips of the ground.

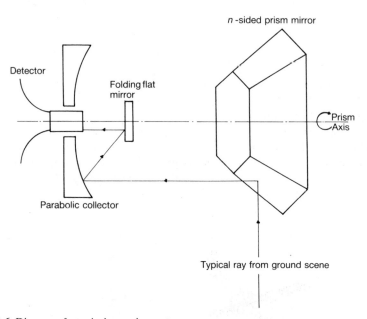

Fig. 4.6. Diagram of a typical scanning system.

4.4.3. *Thermal infra-red scanners*

Infra-red radiation can be detected either by photography or by imaging systems which are sensitive to infra-red radiation and which produce electrical signals, proportional to the strength of the incoming infra-red radiation, which are then used to produce imagery. Thermal infra-red scanners fall into the latter category. They normally operate in the atmospheric windows of 3.5–5.5 µm and 8–14 µm. Photography and infra-red imagery are compared below.

Infra-red photography	*Infra-red imagery*
Records reflected radiation.	Records emitted radiation.
Records directly on infra-red sensitive film.	Recording is an electrical signal converted to light which exposed the film and produces an infra-red radiation image.

Infra-red photography	*Infra-red imagery*
Only records up to about 0.9 µm unless shielded from the emission of the camera.	Can record all infra-red wavelengths except those restricted by the atmospheric absorption bands.
Usable in daytime or when a source of infra-red radiation is available other than the Sun.	Best used at night unless filtering devices are used to eliminate ambient reflected radiation.
Measures reflection qualities of objects.	Measures apparent temperature and emissivity of objects.

Because of their use for night-time military reconnaissance, thermal infra-red scanning systems remained classified until the mid-1960s. Today, several models are available for unrestricted use. When used for environmental investigations, they are normally operated in the 8–14 µm wavelength region because the average surface temperature of the Earth (300 K) causes the maximum intensity of radiation from most surface features to peak in this range.

Thermal images can be interpreted only from an understanding of the physical processes which govern the interactions between thermal energy and matter and of the thermal properties of objects appearing in the image. The mechanics of heat conduction, convection, and radiation, control the signatures of targets in a thermal infra-red image.

Thermal scanner images are generally crude forms of thermal maps, and depict emitted thermal radiation in qualitative form. The images produced have a low geometrical and radiometric integrity. However, valuable information can be obtained from them about relative temperature differences of objects on the ground; they can reveal sources of thermal pollution and expose the ways in which such pollution is dispersed. Nevertheless, interpreters of thermal images must bear in mind that thermal sensors detect radiation from the surface of objects which may not be indicative of an object's internal temperature.

The operating principles of a thermal infra-red scanner, and the method used to transform the collected signals into an optical image, are illustrated in Fig. 4.7. Signals from the detector can also be recorded on tape, which can then be used to generate imagery later on in the laboratory.

Thermal imagery has been successfully used in lithological mapping, differentiating between different rock and soil types, mapping geological structures and faults, detecting soil moisture variations, determining the thermal characteristics of volcanoes and active areas of geothermal energy, studying evapotranspiration from vegetation, locating freshwater springs under saline water, detecting and mapping sources of industrial thermal pollution, determining the extent of forest fires, and locating underground cavities. Preliminary work has shown that thermal scanners

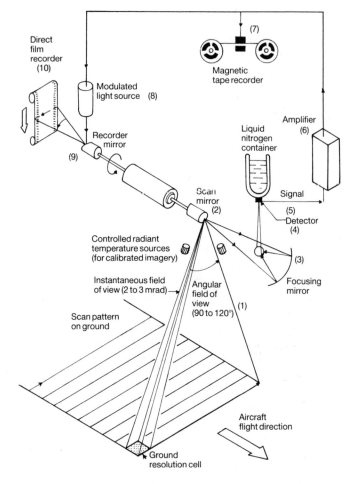

Fig. 4.7. Diagram of a thermal infra-red scanner system. (After Sabins 1969.)

mounted in aircraft are able to detect medium-sized animals, such as cows and deer, under a light, temperate canopy cover.

Thermal studies can be carried out during either the day or night, but most environmental surveys are made at night because the thermal effects of differential solar heating and shadowing are greatly reduced. Variations in surface lithology of terrain material and moisture content are also more apparent at night.

Maximum thermal contrasts occur near sunset, but the radiant temperature changes as the night progresses. The most stable radiant temperatures occur in the pre-dawn hours. Figure 4.8 shows the relative radiant temperatures of soil and rock versus water during a typical diurnal cycle. The differences are greatest at about 15.00 hours.

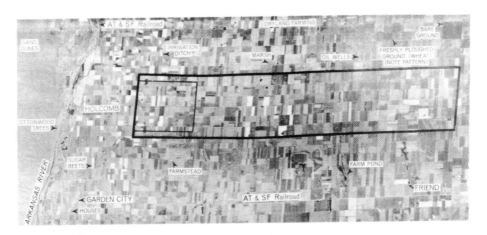

K-BAND RADAR IMAGE

COLOR-COMBINED HH-HV POLARIZATION IMAGE

LAND USE

ALFALFA
BARE
CROP RESIDUE
FARMSTEAD
MARSH
PASTURE
SORGHUM
SUDAN
SUGAR BEETS
WHEAT
IRRIGATION DITCH

◄N►

Plate I. Radar crop identification, Garden City, Kansas.

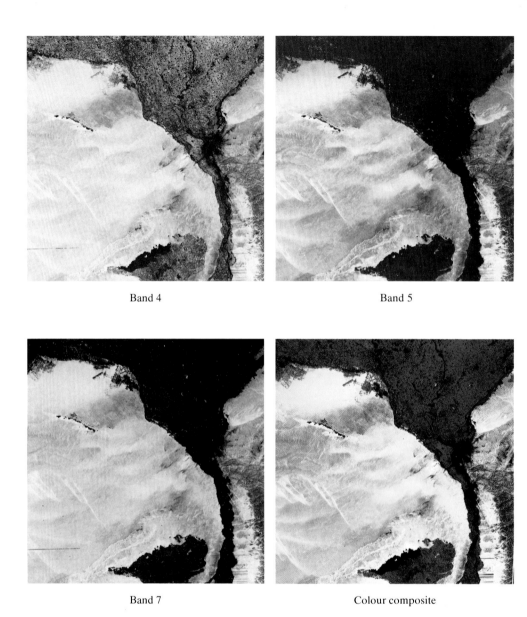

Band 4 Band 5

Band 7 Colour composite

Plate II. Three black-and-white bands of Landsat MSS data (4, 5, and 7) over the Nile Delta in Egypt, and colour composite of these three bands.

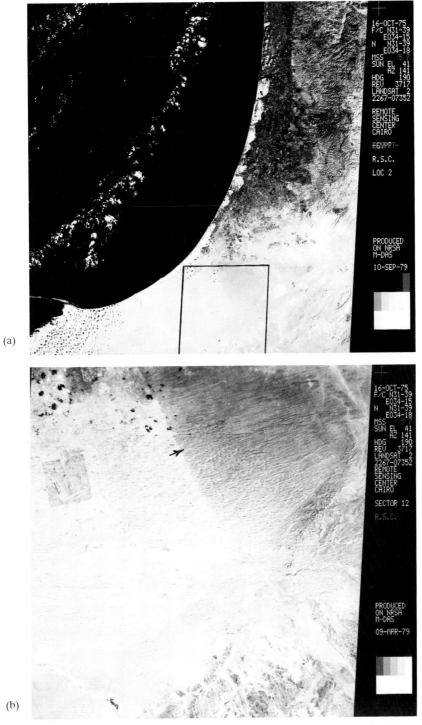

16-OCT-75
F/C N31-39
E034-15
N N31-39
E034-18
MSS 5 7
SUN EL 41
AZ 141
HDG 190
REV 3717
LANDSAT 2
2267-07352

REMOTE
SENSING
CENTER
CAIRO

EGYPT

R.S.C.

LOC 2

PRODUCED
ON NRSA
M-DAS

10-SEP-79

16-OCT-75
F/C N31-39
E034-15
N N31-39
E034-18
MSS 5 7
SUN EL 41
AZ 141
HDG 190
REV 3717
LANDSAT 2
2267-07352
REMOTE
SENSING
CENTER
CAIRO

SECTOR 12

R.S.C.

PRODUCED
ON NRSA
M-DAS

09-MAR-79

Plate III. (a) Landsat colour composite image, scale 1:1 000 000, of eastern Sinai Peninsula. (b) One sector of the image shown in (a) digitally processed with special enhancement and contrast stretching. Image shows interesting environmental details.

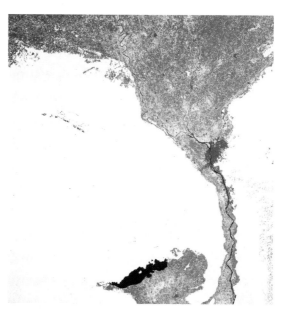

Plate IV. Computer supervised categorization of Landsat MSS image for the Nile Delta and Fayoum area in Egypt, showing land-use patterns. (Cultivated fields—green; fallow lands—yellow; and urban areas, villages, and other features—red.)

Plate V. Landsat computer categorized image for sedimentation levels in the section of Lake Nasser, behind the Aswan Dam in Egypt.

Plate VI. Computer supervised classification of Landsat data over the Qatar peninsula, showing various water depths off the shores of Qatar and Bahrain.

Plate 1. Metric camera (RC-8) used for aerial mapping in the RSC in Egypt.

Plate 3. Four-lens multispectral aerial camera.

(a) Panchromatic

(b) Infra-red (reflected)

Plate 2. Comparison between panchromatic and infra-red black-and-white aerial photographs, demonstrating how boundaries between water and land show clearly and more distinctly in infra-red photographs.

Plate 4. Example of an aerial photograph near the Suez Canal area in Egypt, taken with a four-lens multispectral camera (blue, green, red, and near infra-red).

(a)

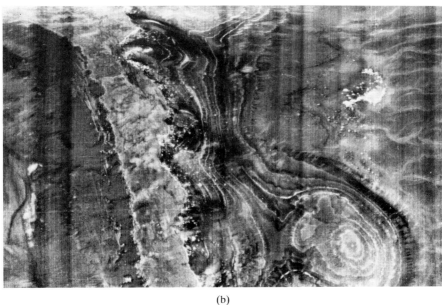

(b)

Plate 5. (a) Ground photograph of the thermal image shown in (b) below. (Interbedded sandstone and shale.)
(b) Thermal image of a plateau of sandstone (bright), alternating with clay shale (grey). The plateau is flanked with dry sand (dark grey). An irregular bright anomaly in the right upper corner of the image represents a forest of Tamarax shrubs growing in a shallow depression.

Plate 6. Daytime thermal infra-red image in the 8–14 μm wavelength band, for the Pyramids area in Egypt, showing thermal shadows on the sides of the Pyramids shaded from direct sunlight.

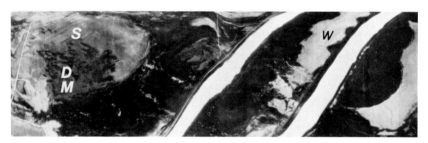

Night-time infra-red thermal image where rock-salt layer (*S*), wet salty mud (*M*), and water-body (*W*) are identifiable with sharp boundaries. Sand dunes (*D*) are clearly differentiated.

Daytime infra-red thermal image, where rock-salt layer (*S*) and wet salty mud (*M*) are noted, but not possessing sharp contrasts. The relatively deep part of the water-body (*W*) only is showing.

Plate 7. Daytime and night-time thermal infra-red images of an area west of El-Ballah Island, along the dual-channels section of the Suez Canal area in Egypt.

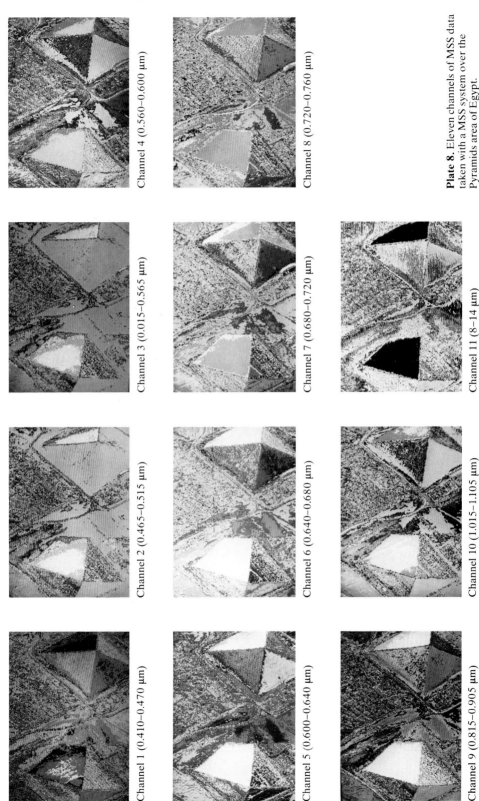

Channel 1 (0.410–0.470 μm)

Channel 2 (0.465–0.515 μm)

Channel 3 (0.015–0.565 μm)

Channel 4 (0.560–0.600 μm)

Channel 5 (0.600–0.640 μm)

Channel 6 (0.640–0.680 μm)

Channel 7 (0.680–0.720 μm)

Channel 8 (0.720–0.760 μm)

Channel 9 (0.815–0.905 μm)

Channel 10 (1.015–1.105 μm)

Channel 11 (8–14 μm)

Plate 8. Eleven channels of MSS data taken with a MSS system over the Pyramids area of Egypt.

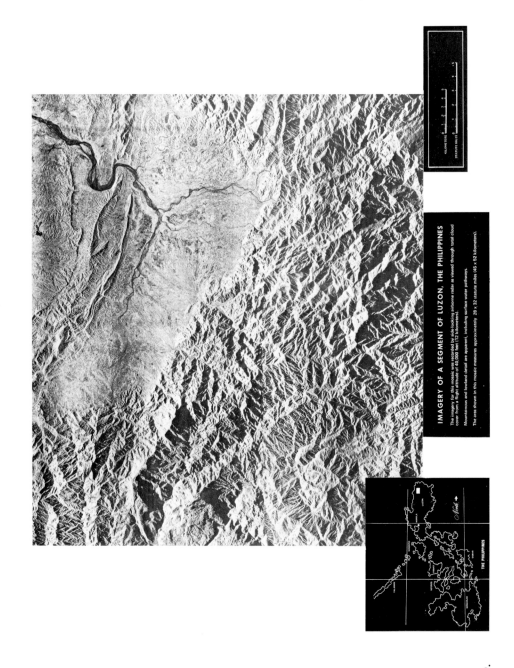

IMAGERY OF A SEGMENT OF LUZON, THE PHILIPPINES

The imagery for this mosaic was recorded by side-looking airborne radar as viewed through total cloud cover from a flight altitude of 40,000 feet (12 kilometers).

Mountainous and lowland detail are apparent, including surface water pathways.

The area shown in this mosaic measures approximately 28 x 32 statute miles (45 x 52 kilometers).

THE PHILIPPINES

Plate 9.

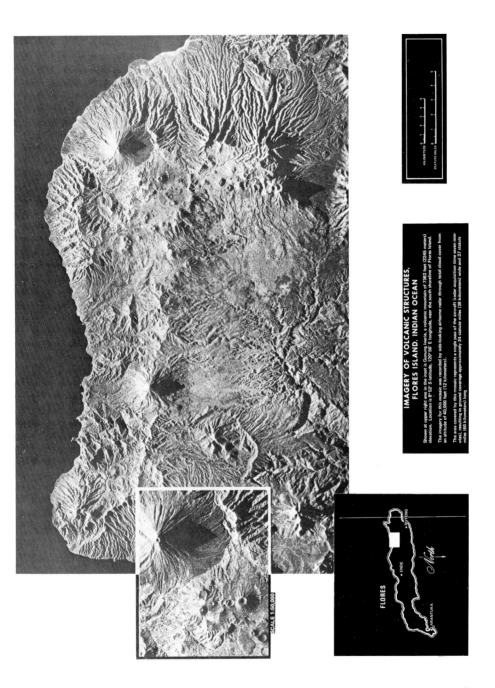

**IMAGERY OF VOLCANIC STRUCTURES,
FLORES ISLAND, INDIAN OCEAN**

Shown at upper right and in the inset is Gunung Inierie, a volcanic mountain of 7363 feet (2245 meters) elevation. Location is 8°52' S latitude, 120°56' E longitude, near the south shoreline of Flores Island.

The imagery for this mosaic was recorded by side-looking airborne radar through total cloud cover from an altitude of 40,000 feet (12 kilometers).

The area covered by this mosaic represents a single pass of the aircraft (radar acquisition time seven minutes), resulting in ground coverage approximately 24 statute miles (38 kilometers) wide and 37 statute miles (60 kilometers) long

SCALE 1:50,000

FLORES

Plate 10.

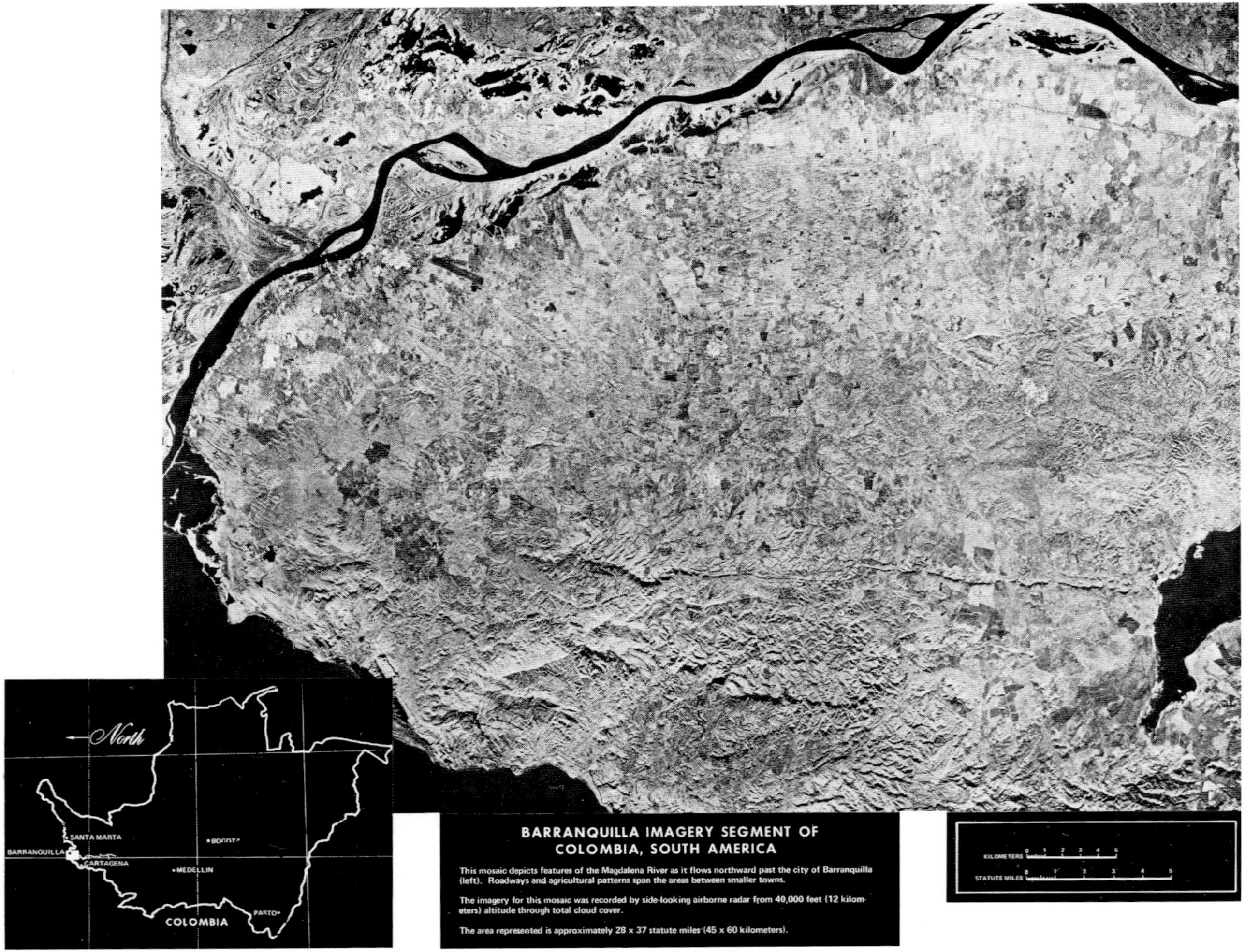
BARRANQUILLA IMAGERY SEGMENT OF COLOMBIA, SOUTH AMERICA
This mosaic depicts features of the Magdalena River as it flows northward past the city of Barranquilla (left). Roadways and agricultural patterns span the areas between smaller towns.
The imagery for this mosaic was recorded by side-looking airborne radar from 40,000 feet (12 kilometers) altitude through total cloud cover.
The area represented is approximately 28 x 37 statute miles (45 x 60 kilometers).
North
SANTA MARTA
BARRANQUILLA
CARTAGENA
MEDELLIN
PASTO
COLOMBIA
KILOMETERS
STATUTE MILES

Plate 11.

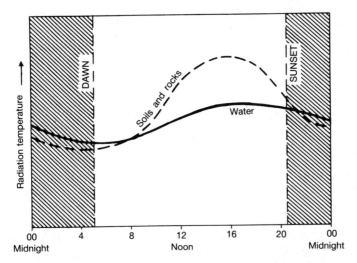

Fig. 4.8. Relative radiant temperature of soils and rocks versus water, during a typical day.

When planning infra-red thermal scanning missions, several factors other than image irregularity resulting from normal scanner distortion must be considered. For example, clouds can produce undesirable patchy warm and cool patterns on thermal images, and surface winds may cause patterns of smears and streaks. Aircraft radio transmissions can also cause strong interference patterns on thermal images. Electronic shielding of the scanner equipment may prevent this interference, but radio silence is usually observed during thermal infra-red image runs.

The interpretation of thermal imagery requires an understanding of the thermal properties of the elements found in the terrain under study. These properties include thermal conductivity, a measure of the rate at which heat is conducted through a material; thermal capacity, the ability of a material to store heat; thermal inertia, a measure of the response of a material to temperature changes; and thermal diffusivity, the ability of a material to transfer heat from the surface to the interior during solar heating.

Materials with low thermal inertia, such as shale and sandy soils, reach relatively high surface temperatures during the day, and low ones at night. Materials with high inertia, such as sandstone and basalt, are cooler during the day and warmer during the night. Generally, materials with high inertia have more uniform surface temperatures over the day/night cycle.

Plate 5 shows a daytime ground photograph of a shale and sandstone plateau in the Western Desert of Egypt. When the area is scanned by an infra-red airborne thermal scanner at about midnight, alternating bands of light and dark tones appear in the image indicating higher and lower thermal emissivity. At this time of night, sandstone is warmer than shale and therefore appears brighter on the thermal imagery. The figure also shows that green deciduous vegetation has a warm signature during the night. An irregular bright anomaly in the right upper corner of the image represents a small forest of *Tamarex* shrubs growing in a broad depression.

Damp ground is usually cooler than dry ground, especially during the day, and therefore appears darker on thermal infra-red images. It should be noted also that although daytime thermal images recorded in the 8–14 μm waveband has virtually no effect from reflected sunlight, such images do contain thermal shadows in cool shaded areas and in some topographic features. Also slopes receive differential heating according to their orientation. Plate 6 shows a daytime thermal image of the pyramids area in Egypt. The effect of differential heating on sides facing the sun and other shaded faces is clearly demonstrated. Some of the other differences between day and night thermal images are shown in Plate 7. For these reasons, many earth scientists prefer night-time or pre-dawn infra-red imagery. However, many other factors must be considered in the timing of thermal scanning missions. For example, in surveying effluents from power plants, scanning must be conducted at periods of peak power plant generation.

An alternative to aerial thermal scanning is the use of ground-based systems, which is designed to obtain images from a fixed position. These systems include two scanning components: one to scan vertically and the other to scan horizontally. In addition, special filters, coatings, and apertures can be employed to limit the amount and wavelengths of the energy received at the detector. The output, an electrical signal, can be used in many ways. The simplest is to display the resulting image in real-time on a small television-type screen that may be photographed to produce a permanent record. To obtain a quantitative image, colour or grey levels are used to show discrete levels of thermal energy. Other kinds of processing include analogue and digital recording, and data analysis techniques.

These systems operate in the 2–5-μm or 8–14-μm bands. The equipment has an operating range of $-20\,°C$ to $+2000\,°C$ and can resolve temperature differences of $0.1\,°C$ on surfaces with a temperature range of $30\,°C$.

Stationary scanners are useful for many environmental applications, including studying heat radiation patterns from human or animal bodies, watching animal migrations and movements at night from stationary platforms or helicopters, detecting forest fires, and measuring radiative thermal loss in selected residential and industrial structures to reduce wasteful energy-losses. They can also be used to monitor industrial facilities for 'hot spots' that may indicate potential problems.

4.5. Multispectral scanners (MSS)

In many environmental applications, it is desirable to acquire information concerning reflectance and emittance properties of various objects simultaneously. Multispectral scanners were therefore developed to observe scenes in a number of discrete bands allowing both reflected and thermal emitted energy to be recorded simultaneously. These bands may range from the ultraviolet through the visible, reflected infra-red, and thermal wavelength bands of the spectrum.

Multispectral scanners can, in certain situations, greatly improve our ability to identify and distinguish a number of features. They have several advantages over multispectral photography:

1. Photographic multispectral cameras are only capable of recording reflected wavelength bands in the visible and near (photographic) infra-red (0.3 to 0.9-µm spectral range). But multispectral scanners using electronic detectors can extend this sensitivity range to 14 µm, allowing both reflected and emitted spectral bands to be recorded simultaneously.

2. Multiband photographs are acquired in photographic form on sensitive films, and are difficult to calibrate radiometrically. Pictorial images are interpreted visually using additive colour viewers. On the other hand, multispectral scanner data are recorded electronically using an array of photon detectors, and are therefore more amenable to calibration, automatic processing, and categorization using computer systems.

3. In using multispectral photographic systems, films must be brought to the ground for processing. Multispectral scanner data may however, be recorded on-board aircraft using high-density digital tapes and/or simultaneously transmitted to ground receiving stations, allowing real-time data acquisition. This is important in satellite systems.

Figure 4.9 shows the typical components of an MSS system. The video signals from each of the channels are recorded in parallel on magnetic tapes, permitting data play back in an automatic data-processing system and visual observation on a monitor. The line-scanning collection geometry is identical to that of a thermal scanner. A rotating mirror moves the field of view of the scanner along a scan line perpendicular to the direction of flight. The forward motion of the aircraft advances the scanned stip to form a continuous record.

The incoming energy is separated into several discrete bands by a dichroid grating. The emitted components of the radiation are sufficiently resolved to go straight to the detectors but the reflected wavelengths are directed from the grating through a prism that splits the

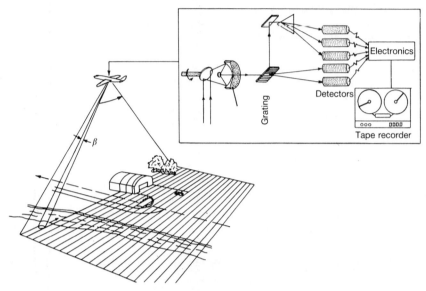

Fig. 4.9. Operating features of the multispectral scanner system.

energy into ultraviolet, visible, and reflected infra-red wavelengths. By placing an array of detectors at the proper geometric positions behind the grating and the prism, the incoming beam is essentially separated into a number of narrow bands, or channels, each of which is measured independently. Scanners with as many as 24 channels have been developed. Plate 8 shows 11 channels of MSS data collected over the pyramids area in Egypt.

Processing of MSS data often involves making both geometric and radiometric corrections. For radiometric correction, most MSS systems use an internal reference source to calibrate the data collected in each channel. Internal black-body sources are used to calibrate the thermal channels. Ambient skylight energy is used to calibrate the reflected energy channels.

As with multiband photography, MSS images may be colour coded and superimposed to form colour composite images. For example, an image with a colour combination similar to that of a colour film can be produced by combining data collection in blue, green, and red bands of the spectrum. Similarly, a simulated colour infra-red image can be produced by combining data from green, red, and reflected infra-red channels of the MSS.

The most important use of multispectral scanners so far has been in the Landsat satellites which are described in detail later in this section (see 7.1.1.).

4.6. Active microwave systems

The radar or microwave band of the electromagnetic spectrum is another potentially useful means of imaging the Earth. The radar band extends from wavelengths of about 30 cm down to about 1 mm. However, the range of 3–30 cm is most commonly used. These frequencies, unlike many others in the visible and infra-red regions, are able to penetrate cloud cover. This confers a considerable advantage on radar imaging systems, particularly for use over tropical areas which are frequently covered by cloud.

4.6.1. The history of microwave imaging

Basic radar was already generating operational information for military objectives early in the Second World War. By its end, airborne imaging radar was a major component of military reconnaissance and it remained classified for another decade.

The first large-scale, radar-imaging operation outside the military domain finally took place in 1967: the radar mapping of the region south of the Panama Canal. Thereafter, several declassified radar systems were left in the hands of major aerospace contractors who undertook to develop the technology at their own expense for resource analysis and monitoring. A well-concerted effort to keep airborne radar products profitable then led to restrictive policies in the field. Two groups of users appeared:

— The mineral and energy resources exploration industry, which was able to pay for airborne radar data, and which is now a firm believer in the cost-effectiveness of radar. It has full rights to the proprietary data and their interpretation.

— Government and academic research groups, mostly in North America and in Europe, which are now engaged in applied research to develop an 'optimal' spaceborne system for monitoring the environment and agricultural resources.

Radar-imaging data have been purchased for a number of programmes in Latin America, in south-east Asia and more recently in Africa during the past decade. Overall feasibility of the technique is no longer disputed in view of the successful Seasat and SIR-A/SIR-B experiments (see below).

4.6.2. Principles of active microwave imaging

Active microwave imaging systems that direct a narrow beam of energy at right angles to the flight path of the vehicle on which they are installed are said to be 'side-looking'–the source of the generic name of SLAR or side-looking radar. Side-looking radar imaging systems utilize a segment of the electromagnetic spectrum which differs from that used by other sensing devices and by the human eye. Because SLAR ground resolution depends primarily on the length of the radar pulse which is used (rather than upon distance from the source to the ground)–and also because SLAR can penetrate cloud and can be used during both the day and the night–it is a natural supplement to other sensing devices. SLAR systems tend to emphasize morphological and vegetation features of the ground differently from other imaging sensors, whether they are airborne or spaceborne.

When flown from space, radar systems are configured to image very large areas from a few orbital paths. The technique is so rapid that sub-continental areas could be completely monitored in a matter of days.

A short burst, or pulse, of microwave energy is directed from a high-powered transmitter in a fan-shaped beam (see Fig. 4.10). The resulting wave train impinges on the terrain and becomes scattered. A portion of the energy is reflected back to the vehicle, where it is intercepted, ampli-fied and time-correlated by a sensitive radio receiver. There, a signal is

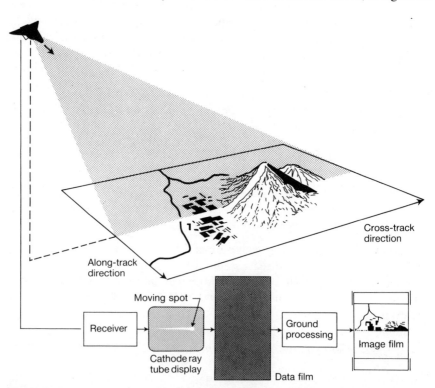

Fig. 4.10. The SAR image reconstruction process, through a data film.

created with an amplitude which depends on the magnitude of the micro-wave energy returned at any instant. This detected signal is used either to control the brightness of a moving spot of light which is then imaged on photographic film, or is stored digitally on a high-density recorder.

As the vehicle advances along its flight path, the beam is moved to new positions, so that succeeding pulses sense adjacent strips of terrain. When data are being recorded directly on film, the film advance is synchronized with the vehicle motion. The resulting record of terrain reflectivities is later used to produce a microwave image of the terrain.

4.6.3. Radar resolution

The level of detail which can be displayed by a sensor is a function of its ground resolution and of local contrasts. Radar resolution is determined by two main factors: range resolution (or linear distance between barely separable objects across the track of the vehicle in which the system is carried) depends on the duration of the microwave pulse used; and the along-track resolution, which depends on the width of the antenna beam. Range resolution is now sufficient for most applications in resource monitoring.

The along-track resolution of ordinary SLAR systems, however, limits the usefulness of the technique, unless special systems are developed. These take advantage of the fact that the angular extent of an antenna beam is inversely proportional to the physical antenna length, and directly proportional to the sensing wavelength. Because the along-track resolution is the product of this beamwidth and of the distance from the vehicle to the terrain, an imaging technique known as 'synthetic aperture radar' (SAR) was developed to increase resolution. A synthetic aperture is formed by storing several returns from each terrain feature as it passes through the antenna beam, and recombining them later to form one single image element. The returns are stored and processed, and used later to create an optical analogue, or a numerical playback, of the physical situation sampled by the SAR system. The optical analogue is created by illuminating the film on which the data are stored, this time with coherent light, to create a hologram (see Fig. 4.11).

4.6.4. Performance of SAR systems

The performance criteria for SAR data include image resolution, dynamic range, geometric accuracy, and image uniformity. These factors are affected by the flight path of the vehicle from which data are collected, and by the techniques used to receive and record the reflected signals.

The holographic storage method on an intermediate data film is the

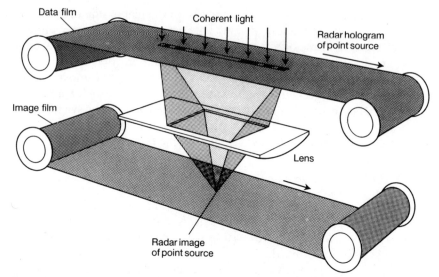

Fig. 4.11. Schema of SAR coherent light processor to reconstitute optically the SAR scene.

key to the production of special extended-range/false-colour SAR imagery, to the removal of scale and geometric distortions, and to producing SAR imagery of average quality.

The numerical approach follows the same process with the help of appropriate software. Numerical SAR images are generated on dimensionally stable film sheets through laser beam or electronic beam recorders. Scale corrections and the removal of geometric distortions are routine parts of the same process. Superior quality products are routinely generated.

Performance of SAR is a function of the following factors:

1. *Resolution.* High resolution is of prime importance in any imaging system used for resource analysis and environmental monitoring: SAR systems can now achieve a resolution of 12 to 30 m in range and of 10 to 30 m in the along-track direction, providing from 8000 to 10 000 picture elements (pixels) per km².

2. *Dynamic range.* The ability of an imaging system to display correctly a variety of shades is called its dynamic range. Black-and-white photographic systems are limited to a total grey scale range of the order of 20 to 60 shades, of which the human eye perceives only 16 to 20. The SAR returns from the terrain may exhibit dynamic variations over a range of several thousand discrete values, and it is vital that environmental monitoring SAR systems retain this wide range of signals in some form. The only appropriate storage media now available are either high-quality coherent signals or high-

density digital storage units. The critical point is that the signal data should not be lost during processing or storage, because as technology advances improved methods of producing SAR imagery will become available which can then be used on any of the SAR data already in existence.

3. *Geometric accuracy.* Scale variations in the along-track direction are caused by the limited accuracy of airborne navigation systems and the characteristics of the orbital path of satellites. They cannot be avoided during initial data collection. If the SAR data are collected on film, these variations can be corrected optically. Within certain limits, both the optical system itself and the data film speed can be adjusted to comply with a desired correction curve and produce final imagery corrected to the curve. This process provides a continuous image with a resolution, dynamic range, and local distortion, which are operationally acceptable. Similar techniques can be used to correct digital data.

4. *Image uniformity.* Uniformity in the image reconstitution process is vital to the consistency of interpretation. The same operations which permit the correction of variations in along-track geometric scale also permit the correction of secondary changes in signal level and the resulting variations in grey levels in SAR imagery.

It should be noted that further distortions are introduced by the Earth's rotation, and SAR data must, and can be, corrected for this factor. However, SAR also tends to distort apparent slopes, because it is essentially viewing them at an angle. It also tends to introduce meaningless shadow effects in high-relief areas. These distortions cannot be corrected.

4.6.5. SAR availability

Keeping a complete SAR system, its aircraft, and its crew ready for operation on short notice is costly and very few systems are yet available for commercial operations.

4.6.6. SAR monitoring applications

Synthetic aperture radar produces imagery which requires careful interpretation. Major features are easily identifiable once they have been correlated with what is known to exist on the ground, and once the observer has acquired experience in analysing SAR images. Most features are presented in the form of subtle textural and tonal variations. The latter reflect surface roughness, surface slope and the dielectrical properties of the surface material. The first and last of these provide distinctive signals for vegetative cover. Considerable training may be required to enable observers to interpret SAR imagery correctly. The process is complicated by the fact that SAR imagery includes pronounced shadow effects in high-relief areas (which have no information content) and geometric distortions, which have not always been corrected for. In fact, the interpretation difficulties and errors associated with SAR are considerably more serious than were the initial problems encountered with Landsat images.

The value of SAR as a monitoring tool is readily apparent from the conclusions and recommendations issued by a number of groups, both in the United States and in Europe. World-wide vegetation classification, investigations of the world carbon budget and the modelling of soil moisture on a regional scale are quoted in those studies as applications for which SAR data may be useful. These are major environmental monitoring objectives of the 1980s. To help define what can already be obtained in the monitoring field with SAR, four specific areas will be examined: agriculture, forests, rangelands, and wetlands.

4.6.6.1. SAR in agriculture Data obtained by SAR have a unique role to play in soil moisture evaluation, assessment of the state of vegetation cover and the monitoring of saline seep. Within the temperate zone, SAR also has an important supplementary role in cover identification and soil mapping. Crop type is an important variable influencing SAR returns from multifrequency SAR. Secondary residual influences in SAR returns within a single crop are related to crop height, ground cover density, and vegetation moisture.

Experience gained with SAR in tropical agriculture has also been valuable but in rather different areas. For example, agricultural potential maps based on SAR have been produced routinely for permanently cloud-covered areas as part of Project Radam in Brazil (see Fig. 4.12). The maps are providing information which is helping to determine which of two different agricultural management options, traditional or technologically advanced, should be employed in different areas.

4.6.6.2. SAR in forested land Increased importance is now being given to making a precise model of the world carbon budget. The cloud-covered tropical forests play an important though little understood role in the carbon cycle. Obviously, only active microwave systems are capable of monitoring significant changes in these timber stands. SAR data are providing information on living and dead timber ratios, and may allow the extent of residual saleable timber to be evaluated in damaged areas.

Reconnaissance-level, phytoecological maps of the Amazon River basin were produced as part of Project Radam. Nine broad vegetation classes were defined and outlined in the SAR imagery, three of which are forest types further subdivided into twenty-eight categories.

Fig. 4.12. Photo-map produced from Projecto RADAM, Brazil. Scale 1:250 000.

Enlarged SAR imagery at 1:250 000 and 1:100 000 scale is near the optimum for forest inventories of large cloud-covered areas.

4.6.6.3. SAR in rangelands Pre-operational demonstrations of SAR capabilities in rangelands are rare, because most airborne SAR data have been acquired at the expense of the mineral resources industry, and directed at features within the tropical cloud belt in which natural rangelands are the exception and tropical forest is the dominant vegetation.

Incentives to develop SAR techniques for rangelands have thus been minimal. A noticeable exception is again Project Radam and its reconnaissance phytoecology map at 1:250 000 in which four major classes of potential land-use are defined and the corresponding areas outlined. Among those, areas capable of sustained rangeland exploitation are singled out.

The classification of rangeland and vegetation is possible with single-frequency SAR imagery, when combined with fieldwork and/or low-flying aircraft. Combination of multispectral Landsat data and SAR data is certainly worth further investigation, although its cost is high. However, differing textures on SAR images can be used to distinguish different plant types to a degree which is not possible with Landsat images. Furthermore, the important parameter of soil moisture can be deduced from SAR data on rangelands; currently, the operational way of obtaining most data on soil moisture is through fieldwork.

4.6.6.4. SAR in wetlands Waters with a surface roughness less than the SAR wavelength do not reflect microwave energy, and thus appear black in SAR imagery. That property makes SAR a most valuable tool for detecting water areas and water/land interfaces. Floating vegetation produces very conspicuous anomalies in SAR images, making SAR a useful tool for studies of wetlands (see Fig. 4.13). In this way, eutrophication can be monitored. Anomalous SAR returns occurring in Seasat imagery of forested wetlands have been interpreted as standing water beneath a partial canopy of vegetation. More research is still needed on the complex ways in which vegetation on or over surface water affects SAR imagery.

4.6.7. Spaceborne SAR

Seasat, a spaceborne synthetic aperture system, was successfully flown by NASA for 106 active days in the autumn of 1978, at a nominal altitude of 800 km in near-polar orbit. About 100 million km² of North and Central America, Western Europe, and North Africa were covered in 2500 min of data collection, which was powered by solar cells on the spacecraft. Efforts to involve receiving stations in Nigeria and in Kenya failed due to lack of time. The antenna beam illuminated a 100-km swath

Fig. 4.13. An SAR enlargement at approx. 1:50 000. Texas Gulf area. Illumination angle accents low relief surface features and vegetation. Note vegetation in the pond, right upper corner.

of the Earth's surface located from 240 km to 340 km to the right of the spacecraft. In the 23.5 cm spectral region, SAR returns are dependent chiefly on surface physical properties (average slope and small-scale roughness) and on the surface/near-surface dielectric constant, a function of surface composition, cover, and moisture content.

Optical Seasat imagery suffers from scale inconsistency and numerous artefacts introduced by the processor. Digital Seasat imagery suffers from the reduced dynamic range, but was nevertheless found useful in enlarged formats up to 1:50 000. Several more years will be required to process and analyse all the data gathered.

Since Seasat, two more experimental SAR spaceborne systems, called SIR-A and SIR-B, have been flown on NASA space shuttles, with encouraging results. However, a number of problems remain to be solved, among the most important of which are providing SAR spacecraft with enough solar cells and storage capacity to continue functioning when they are in the Earth's shadow. Major improvements in the cost and quality of processing SAR data – both optically and digitally – are likely to make SAR an operational tool of the late 1980s.

Some indication of the potential importance of SAR is revealed by the success of the SIR-A experiment carried on the third US space shuttle. During revolution 27, the shuttle provided SAR data on what is probably the Earth's most arid region, in north-east Africa, where rainfall is currently estimated to occur only once every 30–50 years. Consequently, there are no superficial signs of stream or river beds at all. The area is one of severe wind erosion and there are extensive windblown sand deposits.

The SAR imagery, however, was able to look below this superficial sand sheet to reveal an intricate pattern of ancient river valleys which must once have given this area of the Arabian desert in north-west Sudan a very different character. These climatic conditions, as revealed by SIR-A, probably date back to the late Tertiary.

Mapping of this area and other areas in Egypt's Western Desert using SIR-A is expected to continue on future shuttle missions, and to lead to further important revelations. SIR-A and other SAR systems using even longer wavelengths were theoretically expected to be able to penetrate dry sand and soil to the depths attained in this pass over Africa. However, the results were not expected to be of much practical interest. That they have been is encouraging for the future exploration of other poorly mapped and inaccessible areas, such as the Arabian Peninsula, coastal Peru and the Namibian Desert in south-west Africa. Earth scientists have become excited by the new potential which now exists to map ancient drainage patterns and, by inference, to locate potential sources of near-surface ground water.

Several more spaceborne SAR systems are planned for the 1980s, notably from the European Space Agency, Canada, Japan, France and the United States. In the longer term, during 1990–2000, substantial advances are expected. Resolution should increase to 5 m by 1990, and to 3 m by the end of the century, should there be a need for such high resolution. Over this period, progress in computer technology is likely to reduce the costs of processing and storing SAR data by several orders of magnitude. In the early 1980s, computer and processor technology took 6 to 10 h to pre-process a 100×100 km scene digitally.

4.6.8. Conclusions

Major changes are likely to occur in our ability to monitor the Earth's resources and environment with remote sensing by the mid- to late 1980s. Those changes are likely to have an impact comparable to those which Landsat produced in the early 1970s. There are, however, three major differences:

1. The resources devoted to unclassified research and development on SAR have been very small, probably less than a fraction of 1 per cent of those devoted to remote sensing in the visible and infrared regions.

2. Few managers and decision-makers have ever seen SAR data and few of their technical staff have had any analytical experience with it. With Landsat, however, there was general awareness of the technique and its potential, at least in the industrialized countries, before Landsat imagery became widely available.

3. The evidence in favour of SAR as a useful and cost-effective monitoring technique is positive but confined at present to a few specific industrial situations.

The case for spaceborne SAR would have gained wide acceptance many years ago had there been a wider range of potential users and a more substantial SAR data base from which to work. This situation will undoubtedly change during the late 1980s, particularly if costs begin to fall. Even now, however, a case can be made for including a specialist on SAR interpretation within an ecological monitoring unit (EMU). For example, published data suggest that an appropriate annual operating cost for an EMU amounts to about US$1400/100 km^2. The addition of a SAR specialist to a team of five people might increase this cost by only about 30 per cent, to around US$2000/1000 km^2. To this must be added the cost of acquiring data which currently amounts to US$5–15/km^2, according to the amount of data acquired, for airborne SAR. Spaceborne SAR could become cost competitive for areas of 10 million km^2 or more.

In the future, however, it is possible that an international system for the acquisition of spaceborne SAR data, perhaps akin to that co-ordinated by the World Meteorological Organization for meteorological information from space, may emerge. When it does, SAR will finally take its place alongside other established techniques as a vital component of ecological monitoring.

4.7. Space systems useful for ecological monitoring

Ecological monitoring can be carried out at virtually any scale, from that of the ecology of a termite mound or microbe colony to global ecology. The preceding sections have described the main components of habitat monitoring and examined the types of ground measurements which are useful for monitoring activities. The use of aircraft to obtain data over larger areas has been discussed, and the use of sampling in this context has also been examined.

Remote sensing expands the gathering of data from visual observations to include parts of the spectrum beyond visible light. The sensor systems which gather such data and the ranges of electromagnetic energy which are of particular value in ecological monitoring have also been discussed. In all cases, the principles embodied in these discussions apply directly to data gathered by space systems and the concepts which relate satellite and aircraft systems to each other are the concepts of scale, regional homogeneity, and nature of the boundaries between ecosystems, habitats, or other components.

The concept of scale is relatively easily understood. Scales of more than 1:1 are usually referred to as magnifications and the principle of using a magnifying lens has been widely accepted in the biological sciences for many years. Increasing magnification using electron microscopes, in fact, applies the principles of remote sensing in the widely accepted technique of enlargement for detailed study. Although the electron microscope does not permit direct observation of molecular structure it can, by scanning, create electron-beam records which can be reconstituted as images and used for detailed analysis and measurement.

Exactly the same principles can be applied in creating data at scales of less than 1:1. Such scales are often considered less 'scientific' than enlargements. In ecological studies, products with scales of less than 1:1 are usually maps showing spatial relationships between the major components of an environment, or photographs illustrating these relationships. Maps at scales of 1:50 000 are routinely used in examining ecological regions, and often national mapping agencies produce soil maps, geological maps, and vegetation maps at these scales. These are compiled on base maps which are topographic maps on a 1:50 000 scale. In order to view larger areas (such as countries or climatic regions), information compiled at 1:50 000 scale is generalized to scales of 1:250 000 or 1:1 000 000. This generalization was often achieved by the subjective action of cartographers grouping mapping units together and often grouping subclasses of data together, thus 'generalizing' in the sense of reducing spatial detail and often reducing the precision of thematic classes in the data as well.

Because this generalization process is from one cartographic product to another, the precision with which the boundary lines are drawn is in each case the same but the accuracy of the boundaries decreases as the boundaries become more generalized. Thus, the final map product is a series of boundaries defining regions which need not of themselves be the major influences of habitat nor necessarily the major components of the regional ecology. Historically, in order to overcome this deficiency each discipline compiled its own maps. From the individual field surveys of each scientist, a cartographic product emerged. These products were variously defined and included such themes as geology, vegetation cover, agricultural type, and land-use. Some of these formed an input to subsequent studies which synthesized this information into thematic maps; for example, of habitat, land capability and suitability for wildlife.

Aerial photographs provided a new dimension in this work. The air photo is a record of conditions at a point in time and it can be examined many times. Thus, the same data can be examined by interpreters from different disciplines; however, if the need is for a map of a large area at a small scale many air photographs are required, the exact number depending on their scale. The scale of air photographs is determined by the focal length of the camera lens and the altitude of the camera above the Earth. Thus, the principles of scale are, for a fixed focal length lens, a series of relationships which, for a given focal length, are as follows:

(i) increasing altitude gives increasing area of coverage;

(ii) increasing altitude gives decreasing scale; and

(iii) increasing altitude gives decreasing detail (increasing generalization).

In the case of space systems, altitude reaches an extreme. Thus, space systems give large area coverage, small scale, and generalized data. For space systems, the extreme case of area covered is the image of the illuminated hemisphere and the scale is then solely a function of the format and sensor characteristics used to record this. The characteristics of the sensor define the detail recorded.

Space systems operate above the Earth's atmosphere. They are not subject to disturbance by weather systems, do not require large amounts of power to combat air resistance and gravity and, with relatively little cost, can repeat precisely calculated orbit paths many times. Consequently, they are suitable for collecting repetitive data on Earth resources. They are thus a valuable system for monitoring the Earth's surface environment. Systems at lower altitudes have a greater tendency to orbit decay than those at higher altitudes and therefore require more energy and support than the high-altitude craft.

The launch of a space system represents a major cost, and this must be amortized against a long productive operation of the sensor systems if a cost-effective programme is to be mounted. This type of philosophy exists in the Landsat programme where individual satellites have operated for up to six years before going out of service. It is possible to use spacecraft to meet specific needs by launching low-orbit space capsules, either manned or unmanned, to gather data and in the case of certain projects a rocket with a sensor package can gather data at a specific site, the sensor package returning to earth by parachute. In the case of rockets or low-orbit capsules, however, the benefits derived from the data must be sufficiently high to justify the launch and recovery costs of a 'one-shot' operation.

In most ecological monitoring programmes, the only data from space which are used are those which originate from the spacecraft operated by the major space agencies. Thus, data from the US and Soviet spacecraft form the major source of information currently available. India operates its own programme using satellites, and France has announced details of a new Earth-resources satellite programme named SPOT. Meteorological satellites are operated as part of the world-wide meteorological system by the United States, France, and Japan. The use of data from these systems is discussed below.

4.7.1. Automatic satellites

Understanding the role and function of satellites requires some clarification of the terminology. Objects which orbit the Earth under the influence of its gravitational field are known as satellites. The orbit of these objects is elliptical. Assuming the satellite is not powered or assisted, its orbit will decay so that the object is eventually drawn into the upper layers of the atmosphere where it burns up.

Satellite size varies greatly and so does the altitude of orbit. Very few artificial satellites have been manned. Most operate automatically, responding to control signals from earth and fulfilling various data-gathering or signal-retransmission functions. It is useful to distinguish between two functions of satellite systems: the engineering functions which are required to maintain the satellite in orbit; and the systems which perform some other purpose. The latter are usually referred to as the 'payload' and the former as 'housekeeping' systems.

The successful operation of any satellite requires a successful launch and efficient functioning of the housekeeping systems. Together the launching and controlling systems should establish a platform in space behaving in a predictable and controlled manner. Communication links with the ground stations should permit aberrations in performance to be corrected. Once such conditions can be routinely met it is possible to use satellites for a variety of purposes.

Typical uses of satellites in the 1970s included communications relay, meteorological observations, observations of earth surface temperature, sea state, and ground cover. Ecological monitoring is able to take advantage of all these functions. It is important to understand that all these systems are remote from the Earth, operate only by remote control and thus, when providing data about the Earth's surface, they are performing 'remote sensing'.

Automatic satellites, unlike aircraft systems, do not require return to earth, although recent successful space shuttle missions indicate that satellite repair and retrieval may soon be routine. Thus, actual photographs created by a camera exposing light on to a film are of no use on automatic Earth-resources satellites. All data currently gathered by Earth-resources automatic satellites are transmitted to Earth as an electronic signal, and so any pictures subsequently produced are comparable to television images in that they are built up by individual scan lines in a raster system. Consequently, with the present state of technology, satellite remote sensing of the Earth does not regularly produce photographs from unmanned satellites for ecological purposes. All 'photographic' products from Landsat have been compiled from electronic data. The data from multispectral scanners are not conventional photographs in their geometry and perspective. Unlike photographs, the limit of enlargement is not the grain of the emulsion of the originally exposed film but the element for which an electronic record has been made. This picture element is referred to as a 'pixel' (a contraction of *pic*ture and *el*ement).

4.7.1.1. Landsat: the programme The United States began to develop the use of satellites for Earth resources in the 1970s when the US Geological Survey established the Earth Resources Observation Satellite (EROS) programme specifically for this purpose. The work of EROS led to the Earth Resources Technology programme developed by NASA which included the first Earth-resources satellite, ERTS-1, which was launched on 23 July 1972. The second satellite in the series was launched on 22 January 1975 and when launched was named Landsat-2. Simultaneously, ERTS-1 was renamed Landsat-1. Landsat-3, the third satellite in the series, was launched on 5 March 1978. Landsats 4 and 5, launched on 16 July 1982 and 1 March 1984 respectively, were of a different configuration with a more advanced sensor. All of the Landsat satellites have been equipped with a multispectral scanner system (MSS) recording four areas of the spectrum, two in visible light and two in the photographic infra-red (see 7.1.2. below). A summary of the satellite launch dates and operational life as at August 1985 follows:

Landsat satellites launched and operated

Landsat-1   Launched 23 July 1972 (as ERTS-1)
                Renamed Landsat-1 on 22 January 1975
                Ceased operation on 6 January 1978.

Landsat-2   Launched 22 January 1975
                Ceased operation 27 July 1983.

Landsat-3   Launched 5 March 1978
                Ceased operation 7 September 1983.

(Throughout the life of this satellite there were problems with the data flow. The thermal sensor only worked at half resolution for a few months. The MSS system lost the first 25–30 per cent of the data because of a line start identification problem.)

Landsat-4 Launched 16 July 1982
MSS system still operating
TM shut down since 14 February 1983.

(This satellite has no tape recorder system and has had power supply problems since late 1982.)

Landsat-5 Launched 1 March 1984
Operating normally

(This satellite has no tape recorder system.)

The Landsat Spacecraft

Landsats 1, 2, and 3

Size: 3 m high 1.5 m basal diameter
                    4 m width (with solar panels extended)
Weight: 815 kg
Launched by: Long tank Delta rocket
Stabilization: 3-axis stabilization system using flywheels, rate gyros, horizon scanners, and reaction jets accurate to 0.4 degrees for pitch and roll 0.6 degrees for yaw.
Orbit control: Propulsion system controlled from the ground.

Landsats 4 and 5

Size: 4 m long, 2 m wide with a 3.7 m high mast carrying a 1.8 m diameter antenna.
Weight: 2000 kg
Launched by: Delta 3920 booster rocket
Stabilization: 3-axis angular displacement sensor, inertial gyros and reaction jets accurate to 0.01 degrees, stability accurate to 0.0000001 degrees/second.
Orbit control: Hydrazine propulsion system controlled from the ground.

Landsat-1 and -2 both carried the same systems for observing Earth resources. The payload carried by Landsat-3 differed from the earlier payloads. All three were launched into a sun synchronous orbit at an altitude of 900–950 km. The orbit is of particular significance in ecological monitoring because it provides for the following:

Time for one complete orbit: 104 minutes
Number of orbits per 24 hours: 14

Time to complete orbit pattern and repeat original track: 18 days
Inclination of orbit to polar axis: 99°
Orbital coverage: 82°N to 82°S

The satellites therefore offered the possibility of viewing each point of the Earth's surface between 82°N and 82°S every 18 days. This possibility is frustrated by clouds, and lack of receiving equipment. However, the opportunity to view the majority of the Earth 20 times each year was a new dimension in studies of Earth resources and added a new element to traditional thinking. Landsat-1, -2, and -3 are no longer in operation. However the data they gathered are still being analysed and form a valuable base for studies of change.

Landsat-4 and -5 both carry a more advanced system for observing the Earth, as well as one scanner system similar to that carried on Landsats -1, -2, and -3. These two Landsats are a second generation Earth resources observation satellite system and provide more detailed data. They are to be followed by two further satellites of this same type, which will be known as Landsat-6 and -7. Data from these satellites should continue to be available into the next decade, an important point for any monitoring system which utilizes Landsat data. Landsat-4 and -5 orbit the earth at a nominal altitude of 705 km. This orbit has the following characteristics:

Time for one complete orbit: 98.9 minutes
Number of orbits per 24 hours: 14.5
Time to complete orbit pattern and repeat original track: 16 days
Inclination of orbit to polar axis: 98.2°
Orbital coverage: 83°N to 83°S

These Landsat satellites therefore offer the possibility of viewing each point on the Earth's surface between 83°N and 83°S every 16 days. The orbits of Landsat-1, -2, and -3 provided for a sidelap of 14 per cent between adjacent observations at the equator whereas Landsat-4 and -5 only permit a 7.6 per cent sidelap at the equator, thus requiring fewer orbits to view the whole area of coverage. Landsat-4 and -5 offer 22 opportunities to view the majority of the Earth each year. However, the sensors are unable to gather good data when there is cloud cover, and the data are only collected when the satellite is within a range of a suitable receiving station or is transmitting data via a data relay satellite. This latter service is costly and subject to available time on the relay satellites.

The nature of the data on Earth resources gathered by the Landsat satellites determines their usefulness in ecological monitoring. Data gathered by Landsat are always reconstituted from electronic signals into some form the human investigator can accept. This can be done instantaneously as the signal is received, thus creating a television-type image from the satellite signal. Such systems are operational and the first regular supply of such data was from the Canadian receiving station. The product available as photographic prints is marketed as 'quicklook' data. Such a product can be available within minutes of the satellite pass and can be transmitted by various facsimile devices to remote locations within hours of receipt. It was therefore possible to use Landsat data as an instant update on an 18-day monitoring cycle, and currently a 16-day cycle is possible.

Most users, however, have to accept the fact that several weeks elapse between data collection and data product generation. Thus, most Landsat data are currently used as records of past states of the Earth's resources. The data most often used are the 'picture products' created on photographic film from the information provided by the multispectral scanner system. Other data gathered by the return beam vidicon camera system are also used. The information from the data-collection system was used in a smaller number of investigations and this system required the operation of ground-based data collection platforms. These systems are described below.

4.7.1.2. Landsat: the multispectral scanner system (MSS) Landsats-1, 2, 3, 4, and 5 each carried a multispectral scanner system. The important characteristics of this system are that it records data in four parts of the spectrum and digitizes this information for transmission to earth. Thus, the signal received from the satellite is a four-part statement of the energy reflected by the Earth's surface. The four parts are the bands of the electromagnetic spectrum precisely defined as follows:

	Wavelength	Description
Band 4 [*This is band 1 on Landsats 4 and 5.*]	500–600 nm (0.5–0.6 µm)	Green/yellow visible light
Band 5 [*This is band 2 on Landsats 4 and 5.*]	600–700 nm (0.6–0.7 µm)	Orange/red visible light
Band 6 [*This is band 3 on Landsats 4 and 5.*]	700–800 nm (0.7–0.8 µm)	Invisible reflected infra-red energy 'near infra-red'
Band 7 [*This is band 4 on Landsats 4 and 5.*]	800–1100 nm (0.8–1.1 µm)	Invisible reflected infra-red 'near infra-red'
Band 8 [*This was only on Landsat 3 and did not function satisfactorily.*]	10 500–12 400 nm (10.5–12.4 µm)	Heat (thermal radiation)

These bands of energy were not chosen at random. They represent attempts to define the Earth's surface features with appropriate clarity. Visible light exists in the wavelength range 400–700 nm (0.4–0.7 μm). At the lower wavelengths, violet to blue/green light is scattered by the atmosphere. It is for this reason that photographers often use 'minus blue' filters on their cameras when taking scenic views in vegetated regions. From space, this scattering takes the form of a blue-green fogginess. However, green/yellow light is less scattered and red light is the least scattered of the visible spectrum so that these two (represented by bands 4 and 5) provide a 'clearer view' of the Earth's surface using visible light. Band 6, the first near infra-red band, is an energy band reflected by active chlorophyll. There is some debate about the exact details of the reflectance mechanisms but in general this portion of the spectrum is reflected by healthy green vegetation. Band 7 is a broader band of the spectrum than the others. The wavelengths of band 7 are absorbed by water and also reflected by healthy green vegetation.

Bands 6 and 7 are reflected infra-red and not thermal infra-red bands of the spectrum. The scanners on Landsat-1 and -2, therefore, are entirely dependent upon reflected solar radiation and so are not effective at night. They do not record emitted thermal radiation or heat. Only on Landsat-3 did the scanner have an additional band 8, a thermal band operating in the 10.5–12.4-μm range of the spectrum (10 500–12 400 nm) which detected heat energy radiated from the Earth; band 8 data were also collected at night. However, the thermal band operated for a brief period with only one of two parts of the system functioning before it ceased operation entirely.

In the operation of the multispectral scanner on Landsat the effective ground trace is 185 km across the direction of satellite travel. Over this distance, the sensors in the satellite are sampled 3240 times, giving an effective ground width to each sample element of about 57 m. The 185-km ground trace is simultaneously recorded by six units, and the effective ground width of this group is 474 m. Each scan of the sensors therefore views a 474 m × 185 km swath of the Earth's surface in a direction from 9° N. of W. to 9° S. of E. at 0940 local solar time.

Each sampling of the reflected solar energy detected is digitized and relates to an effective ground area of 57 × 79 m. Such an area, referred to as a pixel, is the basic unit of scanner data. For each pixel, the scanner provides four values which represent the energy in each of bands 4, 5, 6, and 7.

The data from Landsat scanners are recorded on a high-density digital (magnetic) tape. These are then converted into either photographic form or tapes compatible with computer systems – these being known as computer-compatible tapes. In both cases, the satellite data are assembled into a format equivalent to a 185 × 185 km portion of the

Earth's surface. Each such product is equivalent to 2340 scan lines of data with 3240 units per line or a format of 2340×3240 pixels, giving a total of 7 581 600 pixels recording information over 34.225 km². For each pixel there are digitized values of reflectance for four spectral bands, so that a Landsat 'scene' consists of 30 326 400 pieces of information for 185×185 km of the Earth's surface. The satellite gathers this information in approximately 25 seconds.

A computer compatible tape of a Landsat scene contains all this information. The photographic product does not. Photographic products are typically available in 70-mm format at a scale of 1:3 369 000, in 9 in × 9 in format with a scale of 1:1 000 000, in 15-in format with a scale of 1:500 000, and in 30-in format with a scale of 1:250 000. The black-and-white standard photo-product is one spectral band only. The grey tones in the image correspond to the digitized reflectance values for one band as transmitted by the satellite. Colour products are created using the three-colour process and the standard product is created using band 4 data as blue, band 5 as green, and band 7 as red. This standard product is similar to the standard aircraft colour infra-red photograph which exposes reflected infra-red energy onto the red dye of the film. As a result, green vegetation with healthy chlorophyll activity shows as bright red and magenta colours.

Because our eyes cannot see reflected infra-red energy, there is no 'real' colour for it. Therefore, if we are to view the results of the scanners' record of infra-red energy we must give it some colour, but that colour is a false-colour and the standard technique used is to record green/yellow light as blue, orange/red light as green, and invisible reflected infra-red as red. Thus, we have a false-colour composite created from the data. In the case of Landsat, the standard false-colour product relates to the sensors as follows.

	Wavelength	Description	Colour used in false-colour composite
band 4	500/600 nm	green/yellow light	blue
band 5	600/700 nm	orange/red light	green
band 6	700/800 nm	invisible reflected infra-red (*Not* thermal energy)	not used
band 7	800/1100 nm	invisible reflected infra-red (*Not* thermal energy)	red

The value of these data in ecological monitoring is that a standard false-colour composite may be obtained for different occasions and comparisons made between these occasions to determine change, especially in vegetation cover and vegetation vigour. A further advantage is that non-standard composites may be created to define various items of interest. Finally, combinations of data from different dates can be put together to create time-change composites, now possible over the period July 1972 to the present. Thus, multispectral scanner data from satellites appear to offer considerable benefits to regional ecological monitoring programmes.

4.7.1.3. Landsat-1 and -2: the return beam vidicon system A return beam vidicon (RBV) camera is a television camera system in which the image is focused onto a screen and scanned by an electron beam. The electron beam is measured on its return and this measurement is transmitted as the television signal. In the case of Landsat, the measurement is digitized before transmission to Earth. On Landsat-1 and -2, the RBV system consisted of three television-type cameras mounted together, so that all three viewed the same scene. Each system was a modified design so that the scene was focused through a camera lens onto a phosphorescent plate and the plate retained an image for at least 12.5 s. The plate itself was scanned by the electron beam. One of the most significant differences from the MSS system is that the RBV system used a shutter and a whole Landsat scene (185×185 km) was exposed on the phosphorescent plate instantaneously. This differs from the MSS system, which continuously acquires data with each scan. Once the scene was exposed the phosphorescent plate was scanned with a return beam system and the digitized signal was transmitted to Earth. Each of the three cameras was fitted with different filters, so the three cameras each recorded a different part of the spectrum. These were:

	Wavelength	Description
band 1	475–575 nm (0.475–0.575 µm)	green/yellow light
band 2	580–680 nm (0.58–0.68 µm)	orange/red light
band 3	690–830 nm (0.69–0.83 µm)	red light/near-infra-red energy

The products from this system can be treated exactly as the products from the MSS system in the creation of false-colour composites. Because the RBV system used a lens focused onto an object plane, the principles of photogrammetry apply. The reseau marks (small crosses) engraved on the phosphorescent screen appear in the image product. They permit accurate scaling of the image and precise calculations of geometric distortions. The intended ground resolution of the RBV system was better than the 57 × 79 m unit of the MSS. In theory, a 45-m resolution is possible, but contrast is important and calibration tests showed that low-contrast scenes gave an effective resolution of only 82 m.

In general, RBV data from Landsats-1 and -2 have not been widely used because of the operational problems. Early in the Landsat-1 operation, the RBV cameras malfunctioned and were turned off. Similar problems were experienced with the RBV system on Landsat-2. For Landsat-3, a redesigned system was installed with quite different characteristics.

4.7.1.4. Landsat-3: the return beam vidicon system The RBV system on Landsat-3 consists of two cameras mounted alonside each other so that their fields of view overlap by 14 per cent. The width of their *combined* field of view is 185 km but each views a 9 km square with the overlap vertically below the satellite. The design was intended to create an image pair from these cameras and when operated twice they provide a 4-scene set which covers the area of a standard MSS scene.

The two cameras both gather data in the 500–750-nm wavelengths of the spectrum and can, for ease of comprehension, be considered equivalent to 'panchromatic', or black-and-white systems. The photographic product has an effective resolution of twice that of the MSS system, giving a ground resolution of 40 m or less. Note that the data gathered are primarily in the visible spectrum and, being gathered as only a single record of total brightness of each element, they *cannot* provide colour products. The value of Landsat-3 RBV data to ecological studies is that they provide a more detailed view of the Earth than has been available from earlier Landsat systems and so provide better locational information and feature definition.

4.7.1.5. The data-collection system Landsat satellites (and others) operated a system which links ground measurement to satellite capabilities through a data retransmission service. Because of its altitude Landsat is able to receive signals from a wide area of the Earth's surface. It can immediately retransmit these data to a receiving station. This is, in effect, a data-relay system which is made more efficient over large areas by the operation of the satellite.

The system operates on a very simple basis. Instrumented platforms transmit data to the satellite which retransmits them to ground stations. The requirement is that a suitable measuring device be interfaced to a transmitter. The assembly, including power source, transmitter antenna, and measuring device, is referred to as a data-collection platform. Applications of this system are virtually unlimited. Stations can be installed in remote areas or hazardous regions and remain there, unmanned, providing valuable data. Examples are such things as seismic devices in volcanic areas or stream gauges in remote arctic or mountain areas. Rain gauges, thermistors, and evaporation pans can all be linked to the transmitter and data collection points can, with appropriate interfacing, provide data about any major environmental parameter which can be monitored or measured automatically.

4.7.1.6. The Thematic Mapper (TM) Landsat-4 and -5 Improved definition of spectral signatures can result from more precise measurement of narrow bands of the spectrum, and smaller features can be detected if the sensors have a smaller resolution element. Both these advantages are incorporated in the improved scanner system known as the thematic mapper carried on Landsat-4 and -5. The TM has an effective ground resolution of approximately 30 m, and records seven parts of the electro-magnetic spectrum. The seven spectral bands are defined as follows:

	Wavelength	Description
Band 1	450–520 nm (0.45–0.50 μm)	Blue/green light (visible)
Band 2	520–600 nm (0.52–0.60 μm)	Green/yellow light (visible)
Band 3	630–690 nm (0.63–0.69 μm)	Red light (visible)
Band 4	760–900 nm (0.76–0.90 μm)	Reflected infra-red energy (near IR) (invisible)
Band 5	1550–1750 nm (1.55–1.75 μm)	Infra-red energy (invisible)
Band 6	10 400–12 500 nm (10.4–12.5 μm)	Thermal infra-red energy (Thermal IR) (invisible)
Band 7	2080–2350 nm (2.0–2.35 μm)	Infra-red energy (invisible)

These spectral bands were chosen specifically for the following purposes:

Band 1: Designed for water body penetration making it useful for coastal water mapping. Also useful for differentiation of soil from vegetation and deciduous from coniferous flora.

Band 2: Designed to measure visible green reflectance peak of vegetation for vigour assessment.

Band 3: A chlorophyll absorption band important for vegetation discrimination.

Band 4: Useful for determining biomass content and for delineation of water bodies.

Band 5: An indicator of vegetation moisture content and soil moisture. Also useful for differentiation of snow from clouds.

Band 6: A thermal infra-red band of use in vegetation stress analysis, soil moisture discrimination and thermal mapping.

Band 7: A band selected for its potential for discriminating rock types and for hydrothermal mapping.

Such a large number of bands offers the potential to combine any three from seven in a colour composite. Using bands 1 or 2 in blue, band 3 in green, and band 4 in red produces a false colour composite which has the appearance of the standard colour infra-red product. Since any band may be chosen to appear in any of the additive colours and the intensity may be varied for each colour there is the potential for an almost unlimited number of renditions of TM data in colour. Effective use of this capability is slowly emerging from the current research and at present the intended purpose of each band offers a reasonable guide to composite construction.

Standard processing currently available for TM data is limited as composites are restricted to a use of blue, green, and red in that sequence for three bands which must be in correct numerical sequence. Because the data for band 6 have a ground resolution of 120 metres they tend to produce a generalizing effect when registered with other bands. All bands are quantified on a 256 scale of energy levels which exceeds the ability of the human eye to discriminate on conventional film. These levels, from the 8 bit signal which is received from the satellites, contain valuable information, which is often only accessible by analysing the computer compatible tapes directly. Such an analysis permits the user to identify the more significant areas of the data distribution and to combine these in an appropriate balance to optimise feature definition in a final colour product. Once this has been achieved the hard copy photographic transparency produced can be enlarged to scale, matched to a map, and printed for use in the field.

The detail in a TM scene is excellent when the area of coverage is also considered. For ecological monitoring purposes the problem is to reduce the data flow to manageable levels. The total data content of a TM scene exceeds 200 000 000 individual values distributed over the 30 000 000 data points which comprise the spatial network of the standard scene. Whilst this data set can be processed by the available computer systems, the majority of ecologists still have difficulty in comprehending the extent to which such a data set can be manipulated and the appropriate levels at which it can be used. Consequently the value of TM data in ecological studies is still to be realized.

4.7.1.7. Landsats and ecological monitoring The value of reflected solar radiation for Earth-resources monitoring arises from the use of scientific observations in which ecologists record visible changes or characteristics. Most ecologists create their records using reflected solar-energy detectors usually referred to as 'eyes', which function in that self-defined spectral region called visible light. Visible light is the 400–700 nm wavelength range of electromagnetic energy.

For many purposes, this energy range will define the nature of Earth resources; water, trees, rock, and soil can generally be distinguished by the human eye and hence detected by a discriminating human. The precise measurement of electromagnetic energy reflected in each case can be used to define the object. Such a measurement is spoken of as the spectral signature of the object. Spectral signatures are usually shown as a two-dimensional plot with per cent reflectance on the ordinate (*y*-axis) and wavelength on the abscissa (*x*-axis).

However, there are greater differences between vegetation and other substances beyond the range of visible light. It is therefore easily possible to discriminate between vegetation and other Earth surface materials if information from the infra-red portion of the spectrum is included. Many different types of vegetation cover may also be detected in this way and for ecological monitoring purposes this fact is of great importance.

However, ecological monitoring requires more information than the separation of some vegetation types. Ecological monitoring is usually undertaken by amassing observations over time. These observations are rarely on one variable. Items such as the crop calendar need to be compiled. Usually, observations are of more than one vegetation type and flowering and fruiting are recorded. Animal movements, climatic events, and the procession of changes in ecosystems following seasonal cycles, or patterns of stress, are often important items in monitoring.

The same multivariate approach is provided by the satellite system itself. A combination of the orbit and the sensor systems permits a view of the Earth's surface, in a given spectral region (or combinations of spectral regions), during different times of the year. In the same way that different parts of the spectrum give better separation of vegetation types, so do different times of the year manifest differences in separability of vegetation communities. The most obvious examples are the separation between the evergreen (coniferous) and deciduous forests in North America and the separation between the productive season and the dry season in rangelands.

Other ecological changes are vividly apparent, such as the advent of winter snow in higher altitudes and the progress of the subsequent thaw. The seasonal cycle can be recorded by Landsat in considerable detail for temperate climates, and the wet/dry cycle of arid lands and the ephemeral wet periods in desert lands can all be recorded in Landsat data. Overall the Landsat satellites provide multitemporal, multispectral, regional-scale data about the Earth's surface. These data can be used to great effect in monitoring major regions of the earth. In the 1970s, mankind was able, for the first time, to begin to view the temporal component of ecological regions of the Earth's surface. Landsat data provided integrated views of the Earth's surface which revealed regional patterns of geology, vegetation, water resources, and land-use for the first time. As the Landsat programme progresses and other systems are launched into space, the resolution of the data will increase and the utility of data from satellite platforms will increase.

4.7.1.8. SPOT (Système Probatoire d'Observation de la Terre) The French earth resources satellite, SPOT, will provide another advance in data collection and potential ecological monitoring ability. SPOT will orbit at an altitude of 822 km in a near circular orbit inclined at 98.7°. The orbit will be sun-synchronous with an equatorial crossing time of 1030 hours. The orbital period will be 101 minutes and the orbital cycle will repeat every 26 days. An important innovation is the system's ability to use a movable mirror to gather data off nadir. This ability to look to the side of the orbit path by as much as 26° provides both the increased opportunity to gather data and the potential to gather stereographic pairs of images.

The satellite will gather data in two distinct modes, the panchromatic mode and the multi-spectral mode. In the panchromatic mode the satellite will have an effective ground resolution of 10 metres and will gather data in the 500 to 900 nm range of the spectrum. (0.5 to 0.9 μm). Multispectral data will be gathered with a ground resolution of 20 metres and will be a three band system using 500–590 nm (0.5–0.59 μm) which is green/yellow light, 610–690 nm (0.61–0.69 μm) which is red light, and 790–900 nm (0.79–0.90 μm) which is near infra-red energy invisible to the human eye. This system will be far superior to the Landsat system in ground resolution and should provide a greatly improved view of many variables important to ecologists. Because the mirror system permits the satellite to view as much as 400 km to the side of its orbit path there is the opportunity to view the same place up to 112 times each year at the equator and more frequently at higher latitudes.

When operating with a vertical view the satellite will gather data for a swath 60 km wide with each of two sensors, to give a total cover across a 120 km strip of the Earth's surface. Simulation data gathered in the experimental stages of this project provide a detailed look at the Earth's surface with spectral resolution giving a good false colour (colour infra-red) composite image. By providing new types of data SPOT will increase the resources available to the ecologist interested in monitoring and will provide a data source complementary to the Landsat data. Used together these data types could form an exciting new resource for monitoring ecological regions.

4.7.2. Meteorological satellites

A series of meteorological satellites has been operating since 1960, and since 1966 at least one weather satellite has been in operation at any given time. In 1984, there were two major types of systems in operation: orbiting satellites, providing views of a continuous strip of the Earth's atmosphere as they pass overhead, and geostationary satellites, which orbit so that they remain over the same point on the Earth's surface. The geostationary satellites provide data about the disc of the earth viewed by the sensors. One such, the Geostationary Operational Environmental Satellite (GOES), is capable of providing an image of the Earth every 20 min. Such images, in both visible and infra-red portions of the spectrum, permit the monitoring of cloud cover and atmospheric circulation. Global temperatures can be monitored and certain processing of the data yields images of global humidity or water-vapour patterns.

The first of these satellites, launched by the United States, was positioned over the mouth of the Amazon; a second was positioned over the Pacific ocean; and a third, launched by the European Space Agency, (Meteosat) was positioned over the Gulf of Guinea. Data from these satellites are used for atmospheric monitoring and the development of local and regional weather forecasting and the tracking of major storms. In addition, they are also used as relay satellites so that meteorological data collected by ground stations can be rapidly and reliably transmitted via these satellites to a data-processing headquarters which can analyse data and distribute the results to interested, contributing parties.

The various satellites which have operated on a low orbit with a repeat period of 12 h give both visible and thermal infra-red data for the Earth's surface. These data are processed for various environmental applications including the monitoring of sea-ice in high latitudes and the analysis of the extent and duration of snow cover.

4.7.3. Manned satellites

The other major category of spaceborne systems of potential use in ecological monitoring are manned systems. Skylab, the first manned laboratory in space, was used for a series of Earth-resources experiments and was able to gather conventional photographs and return the film to earth for processing. The data from Skylab demonstrate the potential uses of an orbiting laboratory for global environmental monitoring. Data from the Gemini and Apollo programmes have also demonstrated the potential use of manned systems for monitoring. So far, however, the data gathered have not provided a substantive source of material for monitoring.

The space shuttle system came into operation during the 1980s. Comprising a reusable manned spacecraft capable of being flown back to earth and landing on a runway, the craft is launched into orbit by a rocket system which falls away leaving the spacecraft to operate under the control of its crew. The spacecraft can carry any payload of appropriate size and, on its second mission in 1981, it carried a series of Earth-resources sensors and gathered data on large areas of the Earth's surface.

Because the spacecraft returns to earth, conventional photographic systems can be used. The European Space Agency has used the shuttle to carry a series of mapping cameras in a mission named Spacelab flown later in 1984. The shuttle system also allows the spacecraft to operate as a repair and maintenance vehicle as the shuttle can be manoeuvred alongside satellites to retrieve them for repair (as was done in 1984); if necessary, it can even bring them back to earth for maintenance or refurbishing.

A blend of products is possible because this system can now gather conventional photographs or use other man-operated devices which can be returned to earth. It permits space systems to include many types of sensors in the future and thus open up a new range of possibilities for ecological monitoring.

4.7.4. Applications

Data gathered from space can be used in ecological monitoring in many different ways. Ecological monitoring, like many other kinds of scientific work, is concerned with observed or detected changes in the environment. Observed changes are those which can be detected by the human eye and which occur in the visible region of the spectrum. Detection of changes in other parts of the spectrum, such as the infra-red and thermal regions, needs different sensors.

Applications are therefore based on observed or detected changes, or a combination of the two. Because most scientists ultimately need to 'see' proof, an essential part of monitoring is presenting data so that it can be clearly viewed and thus made accessible to the human eye and brain for evaluation. Remote sensing is an integral part of this approach which, in diagrammatic form, can occur in the following ways:

CASE A: Observer present, may or may not be machine- assisted	Visible changes			Monitor reacts
CASE B: Observer not continuously present but has access to machine	Visible or invisible change	Machine receives/ records data	Monitor compares data with normal case	Monitor reacts
CASE C: Observer remote from event and machine	Visible or invisible change	Machine receives/ records data, transmits it	Data received translated to human read- able form, compared with normal case	Monitor reacts

Typical of case A is the system of observation towers used in the monitoring of the Canadian commercial coniferous forests. Here, the observer is the monitor and may observe smoke or fire, report it, and direct fire-fighting equipment to the fire. Monitoring the fire-fighting effort results in a continuous interaction between the observer and the fire-fighters until the fire is extinguished.

Typical of case B is the monitoring of climate using automatic weather stations, and the monitoring of stream or lake levels using hydrographs. In these cases, measurements are taken at a point and are recorded as print outs in anaologue or digital form. These products are then examined and any changes assessed for significance. The monitoring function is exercised and, in the case of meteorological data, the responsive actions – such as issuing storm warnings – are put into effect. In the case of the hydrograph, the responsive action may be to control sluices on dams to permit more or less water to flow, or to impose water-use restrictions in times of drought.

Typical of case C is most remote sensing activity. Because the machines are remote from the observer, the function of observer is taken over by the operation of the machine. In many ways, the machine is superior to the human observer because it can gather data beyond the range of the human senses. However, once these data are gathered they must be translated into some form which humans can assimilate. It is this step which is the area of most intensive research in remote sensing and it is this area which causes the greatest misunderstandings.

A remote sensing unit includes the following units: the sensor, which determines the type of data gathered; the platform, which determines the scale and repeatability of data; and the data-recovery system, which takes sensor output to a prime processor. Secondary processing systems further translate the data into forms required by the user.

In effect, the sensor plus platform constitute the data-gathering step. The data recovery and prime processing constitute the data-delivery step. And the secondary processing, leading to an end product, constitutes the interpretation step. Monitoring involves the evaluation of these products to decide upon reactions in response to deviations from a norm.

Most users enter the system after the data have been gathered and processed. What is ultimately delivered may be a single item or a range of standard products. It is at this point that the user may begin to interpret the data.

4.7.4.1. Processing the data Three spectral bands (4, 5, and 7) of the Nile Delta area in Egypt, together with a colour composite of the three bands, are shown in Plate II. Note that the image area is a parallelogram, not a square, because of the earth's rotation during the 28 s it takes the satellite to travel from the top of the scene to the bottom. The three bands shown in this figure were digitally processed at the Egyptian Remote Sensing Center to produce optimum contrast in the land area.

Individual Landsat MSS images have an annotation strip with useful information on the side of the image. For example, the following list explains the annotation strip for the images in Plate III.

16-Oct-75	Date image was acquired
N31-39/E034-14	Geographical centrepoint of the image, in degrees–minutes
N31-39/E034-18	Nadir of the spacecraft
MSS	Multispectral scanner image
4, 5, 7	MSS spectral bands in the colour composite
Sun El. 41	Sun elevation in degrees clockwise from north
AZ 141	Sun azimuth in degrees clockwise from north
190	Spacecraft heading in degrees
3717	Orbit revolution number
2267-07352	The unique frame identification number composed as follows:
2	Landsat
267	Days since launch
07	GMT hour at time of observation
35	Minutes
2	Tens of seconds

Landsat images are now often subjected to electronic processing so that they yield more information. An image can be restored by eliminating or reducing distortions; it can be enhanced, so that the apparent contrast between certain features is increased; and it can be classified and categorized, either by computer alone or by computer under the supervision of an operator if information is to hand as to the likely meanings of certain features. In both the latter processes, each pixel of information is evaluated and assigned an information category.

Plate IIIa shows a 1:1 000 000 colour composite scene of the Eastern Sinai Peninsula (channels 4, 5, and 7). Figure 4.27(b) shows one 1:250 000 sector of the same scene produced directly by computer processing, with special enhancement and contrast stretching. This image shows much more detail than in the original 1:1 000 000 scene. One interesting feature is the tonal contrast on either side of the line that represents the pre-1967 borders between Egypt and Israel. This phenomenon is worth investigating, since it is attributed by some interpreters to differences in land-use and grazing patterns on different sides of the line. It indicates the sensitivity and value of the Landsat MSS in environmental monitoring.

Typical colour signatures on these and other Landsat colour composite images are as follows:

Green vegetation	Red
Water	Dark blue to black
Suspended sediment in water	White to light blue
Red beds	Yellow
Bare soil	Blue
Eolian sand	Yellow
Cities	Dark blue
Clouds	White

Plate IV is an example of a categorized image using supervised classification. It shows the same area of the Nile Delta as Plate II but classified for cultivated and non-cultivated land-use activities. Various colours assigned to the scene by computer designate areas covered with cultivation, areas prepared for cultivation but not covered with vegetation at time of coverage, and areas of non-agricultural use (such as urban areas). It demonstrates at a glance the size of the urban encroachment problem on the settled agricultural areas of the Nile Delta.

An example for the potential use of categorized MSS data in monitoring water quality is shown in Plate V. This scene shows the various levels of sedimentation in the Aswan Dam Lake at the specified date of coverage. Quantitative data were collected at various locations in the lake and were used to typify each of the desired levels of sedimentation at specific locations in the image. These data were used as training sets for the computer which scanned every pixel in the scene and assigned the shown categories of sedimentation levels. The same approach was used to produce categorized images for the same areas of the lake showing chlorophyll distribution. Landsat images have been similarly used to study the growth of algal blooms and the movement of islands of floating vegetation, principally of water fern and papyrus, in tropical lakes in Africa.

Another example is illustrated in Plate VI, where numerical values for water depth at specific locations off the shores of Qatar Peninsula were used to computer classify the area. In this case, the computer assigned black to all land areas above water level, and various other colours for water depth, with deepest water showing dark blue. The island at the upper left corner of the image is the State of Bahrain. Such an image can be of great value to marine scientists.

Bibliography

Abdel Hady, M., El Shazly, E. M., and Myers, V. (1979). Monitoring of Desertification elements in Egypt by Remote Sensing techniques. In: Seminar on Remote Sensing Applications and Technology, *Transfer for International Development.* Ann Arbor, Michigan.

Aboul Eid, H. Z., Khodair, M. M., Abdel Samie, A. E., and Abdel Hady, M. (1974). Spectral reflectance and photographic studies on some healthy and nematode infected cotton and corn plant in Egypt. *Proc. 40th Annual Meeting,* pp. 126–51. American Society of Photogrammetry, St. Louis, Missouri.

Allison, L. J., Wexler, R., Laughlin, C. R., and Bandeen, W. R. (1977). Remote sensing of the atmosphere from environmental satellites, Report No. X-901-77-132. NASA Goddard Space Flight Center.

American Society of Photogrammetry (1960). *Manual of photographic interpretation.*

—— (1968). *Manual of photogrammetry.*

—— (1968). *Manual of color aerial photography.*

—— (1975). *Manual of remote sensing,* Vol. 1. Falls Church, Virginia.

Anson, A. (1966). Color photo comparison. *Photogramm. Engng* **32**(2), 286–97.

—— (1970). Color aerial photos in the reconnaissance of soils and rocks. *Photogramm. Engng* **36**(4), 343–54.

Anuta, P. E. (1970). Spatial registration of multispectral and multitemporal digital imagery using fast fourier transform techniques, *IEEE Trans. Geosci. Electron.* GE**8**(4), 353–68.

Badgley, P. C. and Vest, W. L. (1966). Orbital remote sensing and natural resources, *Photogramm. Engng* **32**(5), 780–90.

——, Childs, L. and Vest, W. L. (1967). The application of remote sensing instruments in Earth resource surveys, *J. Geophys.* **32**(4), 583–601.

Barbe, D. F. (1975). Imaging devices using the charge-coupled concept, *Proc. IEEE* **63**, 38–67.

Barr, D. J. (1969). *Use of side-looking airborne radar (SLAR) imagery for engineering studies.* US Army Engineer Topographic Laboratories, Tech. Report 46 TR, Fort Belvoir, Virginia.

—— and Miles, R. D. (1970). SLAR Imagery and site selection, *Photogramm. Engng* **36**, 1155–70.

Barrett, E. C. and Curtis, L. E. (1976). *Introduction to environmental remote sensing.* Chapman & Hall, London.

Barringer, A. R. (1968). The remote sensing of spectral signatures applied to pollution measurements and fish detection. In: *Proc. 9th Meeting Ad Hoc Spacecraft Oceanography Advisory Group.* (Abstract.) January. Spacecraft Oceanography Project, NAVOCEANO, Maryland.

——, Newbury, B. C., and Moffat, A. J. (1968). Surveillance of air pollution from airborne and space platforms. In: *Proc. 5th Int. Symp. on Remote Sensing of the Environment,* pp. 123–55. University of Michigan, Ann Arbor.

—— (1970*a*). Remote sensing techniques for mineral discovery. In: *Proc. 9th Commonwealth Mining & Metallurgical Congr 1969,* Vol. 2, *Mining and Petroleum Geology,* pp. 649–90. London.

——, Davies, J. H., and Moffat, A. J. (1970*b*). The problems and potential in monitoring pollution from satellites, Paper No. 70-305. Earth Resources Observations and Information Systems Meeting, American Institute of Aeronautics and Astronautics, New York.

Beckmann, P. and Spizzichino, A. (1963). *The scattering of electromagnetic waves from rough surfaces.* Pergamon Press, New York.

Beilock, M. M., Wilson, C., and Zaitzeff, E. (1969). Design considerations of aerospace multispectral scanning systems. In: *Symp. on Information Processing II,* pp. 658–71. Purdue University, West Lafayette, Indiana.

Billingsley, F. E. (1970). Applications of digital image processing. *Appl. Optics* **9**(2), 289–99.

Blythe, R. and Kurath, E. (1967). Infrared and natural subject. *Appl. Optics* **7**(9), 772–7.

—— —— (1968). Infrared and natural subject. *Appl. Optics* **7**(9), 1769–77.

Brandli, H. W. (1978), The night eye in the sky. *Photogramm. Engng remote Sens.* **44**(4), 503–5.

Brock, G. C. (1967). *The physical aspects of aerial photography.* Dover Publications, New York.

Brown, W. M. and Porcello, L. J. (1969). An introduction to synthetic aperture radar, *IEEE Spectrum* **6**(9), 52–62.

Buettner, K. J., Kern, C. D. and Cronin, J. F. (1965). The consequences of terrestrial surface infrared emmissivity. In: *Proc. 3rd int. Symp. on Remote Sensing of the Environment,* pp. 549–61. University of Michigan, Ann Arbor.

Colwell, R. N. (1961). Some practical applications of multiband spectral reconnaissance. *Am. Scient.* **49**(3), 9–36.

Conrod, A. C., Kelly, M. G., and Boersma, A. (1968). Aerial photography for shallow water studies on the west edge of the Bahama Banks, Report RE-42. Mass. Inst. of Tech., Experimental Astronomy Lab., Cambridge, Mass.

Condit, H. R. (1969). Spectral reflectance of soil and sand. In: *New horizons in aerial color photography,* pp. 3–15. American Society of Photogrammetry, Falls Church, Virginia.

Cook, J. J. and Erickson, J. D. (1974). Remote sensing of earth resources, fundamental principles, data collections, sensors and information extraction techniques. *Proc. UN/FAO Regional Seminar on Remote Sensing,* Cairo, Egypt.

Corsi, C. (1975). Infrared detector arrays by new technologies. *Proc. IEEE* **63**, 14–26.

Coulson, K. L. (1966). Effects of reflection properties of natural surfaces in aerial reconnaissance. *Appl. Optics* **5**(6), 905–17.

Cronin, J. F. (1967). *Terrestrial multispectral photography.* Special Report No. 56, Air Force Cambridge Research Laboratory, Bedford, Mass.

Dellwig, L. F., Macdonald, H. C., and Kirk, J. N. (1968). The potential of radar in geological exploration. In: *Proc. 5th int. Symp. on Remote Sensing of the Environment* 747–63. University of Michigan, Ann Arbor.

Doyle, F. J. (1979). A large format camera for shuttle. *Photogramm. Engng. remote Sens.* **45**, 73.

Eastman, Kodak Co. (1970). *Wratten filters,* Pub. No. B-3. Eastman Kodak, Rochester, N.Y.

—— (1972*a*). *Color as seen and photographed,* 2nd edn. Eastman Kodak, Rochester, N. Y.

—— (1972*b*). *Kodak aerial filters for scientific and technical uses.* Eastman Kodak, Rochester, N.Y.

—— (1972*c*). *Kodak aerial films and photographic plates.* Eastman Kodak, Rochester, N.Y.

—— (1977). *Applied infrared photography.* Eastman Kodak, Rochester, N.Y.

Eden, R. C. (1975). Heterojunction III-V alloy photodetectors for high sensitivity 1.06 μm optical receivers, *Proc. IEEE* **63**, 32–7.

El Shazly, E. M. and Apdel Hady, M. A. (1977). Landsat satellite mapping in Egypt and its possible applications in petroleum and natural gas exploration. Tenth Arab Petroleum Congress, Tripoli, Libya.

——, ——, and El Shazly, M. M. (1977). Groundwater studies in arid areas in Egypt using Landsat satellite images. *Proc. 11th int. Symp. Remote Sensing of the Environment.* Michigan, Ann Arbor.

——, ——, and Morsy, M. A. (1974). Geologic interpretation of infrared thermal images in East Qatrani area, Western Desert, Egypt. *Proc. 9th int. Symp. on Remote Sensing of the Environment.* pp. 1877–89. Michigan, Ann Arbor.

——, ——, El Ghawaby, M. A. and Khawasik, S. M. (1977). Application of Landsat satellite imagery for iron ore prospecting in the Western Desert of Egypt. *Proc. 11th int. Symp. on Remote Sensing of the Environment.* Michigan, Ann Arbor.

——, ——, El Kassas, I. A., and El Ghawaby, M. A. (1974). Geologic interpretation of ERTS-1 satellite images for West Aswan area, Egypt. *Proc. 9th int. Symp. on Remote Sensing of the Environment,* pp. 119–31. Michigan, Ann Arbor.

——, ——, El Ghawaby, M. A., El Kassas, I. A., and El Shazly, M. M. (1979). Mapping of Sinai Peninsula by Landsat-1 satellite imagery interpretation. *Proc. 13th int. Symp. on Remote Sensing of the Environment.* Ann Arbor, Michigan.

——, ——, ——, Khawasik, S. M., and El Shazly, M. M. (1977). Application of Landsat satellilte imagery in assessing the regional, geological, structural, environmental and groundwater conditions in the Qattara Depression area, Egypt. *Proc. 28th int. Astron. Congr.,* Prague.

——, ——, Abdel Hafez, M. A., Salman, A. B., Morsy, M. A., El Rakaiby, M. A., El Aassy, I. E., and Kamel, A. F. (1977). Interpretation of multispectral and infrared thermal surveys of the Suez Canal Zone, Egypt. *Proc. 11th int. Symp. on Remote Sensing of the Environment,* Michigan, Ann Arbor.

——, ——, El Shazly, M. M., El Ghawaby, M. A., Salman, A. B., El Kassas, I. A., Khawasik, S. M., El Rakaiby, M. M., and El Amin, H. (1978). Jonglei Canal Project, Sudan, A Landsat imagery approach. *Proc. 12th int. Symp. on Remote Sensing of the Environment,* Manila, Philippines.

Feder, A. M. (1960). Interpreting natural terrain from radar displays. *Photogramm. Engng* **26**(4), 618–30.

Fischer, W. A. (ed.) (1975). History of remote sensing. In: *Manual of remote sensing* (ed. R. G. Reeves) Chapter 2, pp. 27–50. American Society of Photogrammetry, Falls Church, Virginia.

Fritz, N. L. (1967). Optimum methods for using infrared sensitive color films. *Photogramm. Engng* **33**(10), 1128–38.

—— (1977). Filters: an aid in color-infrared photography. *Photogramm. Engng and remote Sens.* **43**(1), 61–72.

Gausman, H. W. (1974). Leaf reflectance of near-infrared. *Photogramm. Engng* **40**(2), 183–91.

Griggs, M. (1968). Emissivities of natural surfaces in the 8- to 14-micron spectral region, *J. Geophys. Res.* **73**(24), 7545–51.

Harger, R. O. (1970). Synthetic aperture radar systems, theory and design. Academic Press, New York.

Holter, M. R. (1970). *Imaging with nonphotographic sensors, in remote sensing with special reference to agriculture and forestry* (ed. National Acad. Sciences), pp. 73–163. Washington, D.C.

Hudson, R. D. Jr. and Hudson, J. W. (1974). *Infrared detectors.* Dowden, Hutchinson & Ross, Stroudsburg, Pennsylvania.

——, —— (1975). The military applications of remote sensing by infrared, *Proc. IEEE* **63**, 104–28.

Hayt, W. H. (1967). *Engineering electromagnetics.* McGraw-Hill, New York.

Janza, F. J. (ed.) (1975). *Interaction mechanics, Manual of remote sensing.* American Society of Photogrammetry, Falls Church, Virginia.

Jensen, H., Graham, L. C., Porcello, L. J., and Leith, E. N. (1977). Side looking airborne radar. *Scient. Am.* **237**(4), 84–95.

Karbs, H. and Abdel Hady, M. A. (1971). Depth to groundwater by remote sensing techniques. *J. Irrig. Drain. Div. Am. Soc. Civil Engrs* **97**, IR3.

——, ——, and Abdel Hafez, M. (1970). Subsurface drainage mapping by infrared imagery techniques. *Proc. Oklahoma Acad. Sci.,* **50**, 10–18.

Kenney, G. P. and Demel, K. J. (1975). Skylab Program, Earth resources experiment package, sensor performance evaluation. Final Report, Vol. 1 (S190A), NASA-CR-144563.

Kennedy, C. A., Kinden, K. J., and Soderman, D. A. (1975). High performance 8–14μm Pb 1-x Smx Te phogodiodes. *Proc. IEEE* **63**, 27–32.

Kruse, P. W., McGlauchlin, L. D., and McQuistan, R. B. (1962). *Elements of infrared technology.* John Wiley, New York.

Landen, D. (1952). History of photogrammetry in the United States. *Photogr. Engng* **18**, 854–98.

Lewis, A. J. (ed.) (1976). Geoscience applications of imaging radar systems. *Remote sensing of the electromagnetic spectrum,* Vol. 3, No. 3.

Lillesand, T. M. and Kiefer, R. W. (1979). *Remote sensing and image interpretation.* John Wiley, New York.

Lintz, J., Jr. and Simonett, D. S. (1976). *Remote sensing of environment.* Addison-Wesley, London.

Lond, M. W. (1975). Radar reflectivity of land and sea. Lexington Books, Lexington, Mass.

Lowman, P. D. Jr. (1965). Space photography. A review. *Photogramm. Engng* **31**(1), 76–86.

—— (1969). Apollo 9 multispectral photography; geological analysis; Goddard Space Flight Center, X-644-69-423.

——, McDivitt, J. A., and White, E. H., II. (1967). Terrain photography on the Gemini IV mission, preliminary report. NASA Technical Note D-3982.

—— and Tiedemann, H. A. (1971). *Terrain photography from Gemini spacecraft.* Final geologic report: NASA Report X-644-71-15.

Ludlum, R. and Van Lopik, J. R. (1966). *A remote sensor survey of areas in central coastal LA.* Report prepared for Office of Naval Research, Geography Branch, Dept. of Navy, Washington, D.C. (AD 808 904).

McEwen, R. B. (1971). Geometric calibration of the RBV system for ERTS. *Proc. 7th int. Symp. on Remote Sensing of the Environment,* pp. 791–807, University of Michigan, Ann Arbor.

McLerran, J. H. and Morgan, J. O. (1964). Thermal mapping of Yellowstone National Park, *Proc. 3rd int. Symp. on Remote Sensing of the Environment,* pp. 517–30. University of Michigan, Ann Arbor.

—— (1968). Infrared sensing of soils and rocks, *Mater. Res. & Stand.* **8**(2), 17–21.

Miller, V. C. (1961). *Photography,* 248 p. McGraw-Hill, New York.

Molineux, C. E. (1964). Aerial reconnaissance of surface features with the multiband spectral system. *Proc. 3rd int. Symp. on Remote Sensing of the Environment,* pp. 339–421. University of Michigan, Ann Arbor.

—— (1965). Multiband spectral system for reconnaissance, *Photogramm. Engng* **31**, 131–43.

Moore, R. K., Waite, W. P., Lundien, J. R., and Masenthin, H. W. (1968). Radar scatterometer data analysis techniques. *Proc. 5th int. Symp. on Remote Sensing of the Environment,* pp. 765–77, University of Michigan, Ann Arbor, Michigan.

National Aeronautics and Space Administration (NASA) (1972). ERTS-1 *Data user's handbook.* Goddard Space Center, Greenbelt, Maryland.

—— (1973). *Advanced scanners and imaging systems for Earth observations,* NASA SP-335. Superintendent of Documents, US Government Printing Office, Washington, D.C.

—— (1974). *Skylab Earth Resources Data Catalog.* No. 3300-00586, US Government Printing Office, Washington, D.C.

—— (1976). *Landsat data users handbook,* Document No. 76SD4258. Goddard Space Flight Center, Greenbelt, Maryland.

National Academy of Sciencies (1970). *Remote Sensing with special reference to agriculture and forestry.* Washington, D.C.

Orr, D. G. (1968). Multiband-color photography. In: *Manual of color aerial photography* (ed. J. T. Smith) pp. 441–50. American Society of Photogrammetry and Remote Sensing, Falls Church, Virginia.

Ory, T. R. (1964). Line-scanning reconnaissance systems in land utilization and terrain studies. *Proc. 3rd int. Symp. on Remote Sensing of the Environment,* pp. 393–8. University of Michigan, Ann Arbor.

Pease, R. W. (1971). Mapping terrestrial radiation emission with a scanning radiometer. *Proc. 7th int. Symp. on Remote Sensing of the Environment,* pp. 501–21. University of Michigan, Ann Arbor.

Ray, R. G. (1960). *Aerial photographs in geologic interpretation and mapping.* US Geological Survey Professional Paper 373, 230 p.

Raytheon Autometric Operations (1971). *Remote sensing and its applications to environmental and resources management.* Raytheon Co., Virginia.

Rempel, R. C. and Parker, A. K. (1964). An information note on an airborne laser terrain profiler for micro-relief studies. *Proc. 3rd int. Symp. on Remote Sensing of the Environment.* University of Michigan, Ann Arbor.

Richardson, A. J., Torline, R. J., and Allen, W. A. (1971). Computer identification of ground pattern from aerial photographs. *Proc. 7th int. Symp. on Remote Sensing of the Environment.* 2, pp. 1357–76. University of Michigan, Ann Arbor.

Rohde, R. B. and McCall, F. H. (1971). *Photography.* Macmillan, New York.

Sabins, F. F. (1969). Thermal infrared imagery and its applications to structural mapping in Southern California, *Geol. Soc. Am. Bull.* **80**(3), 397–404.

—— (1973). *Engineering geology, Applications of remote sensing in geology, seismicity and environmental impact.* Association of Engineering Geologists Special Publication, pp. 141–55.

—— (1976). *Remote sensing handbook.* Chevron Oil Field Research Co. Research Report RR76000200, Part 1 of 2, 257 p.

—— (1978). *Remote sensing – Principles and interpretation.* Freeman, San Francisco.

Seyrafi, K. (1975). Performance-cost analysis of electro-optical systems. *Proc. IEEE* **63**, 176–89.

Short, N. M., Lowman, P. D., Jr., Freden, S. C., and Finch, W. A. (1976). *Mission to Earth: Landsat views the world.* SP.360, NASA Scientific and Technological Information Office, Washington, D.C.

Simonett, D. S. (ed.) (1970). *The utility of space photography, high altitude aerial photography, radar imagery and other remote sensor imagery in thematic land use mapping.* Final Report, U.S.G.S. Contract 14-08-0001-12077. University of Kansas, Lawrence.

Skolnik, M. I. (1962). *Introduction to radar systems.* McGraw-Hill, New York.

Slater, P. N. (1980). *Remote sensing optics and optical systems.* Addison-Wesley, London.

Smedes, H. W. (1971). Automatic computer mapping of terrain, *Proc. int. Workshop on Earth Resources Survey Systems,* Vol. 2, pp. 344–406. University of Michigan. Ann Arbor.

Smith, R. A., Jones, F. E., and Chasmar, R. P. (1957). *The detection and measurement of infrared radiation.* Clarendon Press, Oxford.

Society of Photographic Scientists and Engineers (1973). *Color: theory and imaging systems.* Washington, D.C.

Staeilin, D. H. (1969). Passive remote sensing at microwave wavelengths. *Proc. ICCC* **57**(4), 427–39.

Steiner, D. (1963). Technical aspects of air photographic interpretation in the USSR. *Photogramm. Engng* **29**, 988–97.

Stratton, J. (1941). *Electromagnetic theory.* McGraw-Hill, New York.

Swain, P. H. and Davis, S. M. (eds.) (1978). *Remote sensing – The quantitative approach.* McGraw-Hill, New York.

Taranik, J. V. (1978). *Characteristics of the Landsat multispectral data system.* US Geological Survey *Open File Report* 78–187, Sioux Falls, South Dakota.

Tawfik, F. M., Khodair, M. M., Abdel Samie, A. G., and Abdel Hady, M. A. (1974). Spectral reflectance and photographic studies on healthy and fungus-infected cotton and corn plants in Egypt. *Proc. 40th Annual Meeting,* pp. 152–174. American Society of Photogrammetry. St. Louis, Missouri.

Thomas, V. L. (1975). *Generation and physical characteristics of the Landsat 1 and 2 MSS computer compatible tapes.* Doc. No. X-563-75-223, Goddard Space Flight Center, Greenbelt, Maryland.

Thomson, F. J., Erickson, J. P., Nalepka, R. F., and Webber, J. D. (1974). *Multi-spectral scanner data application evaluation.* Tech. Report 102000-40F. Environmental Research Inst. of Michigan, Ann Arbor.

Thompson, L. L. (1979). Remote sensing using solid state array technology. *Photogramm. Engng remote sens.* **45**, 47.

Thompson, W. I., III (1971). Atmospheric transmission handbook (NASA-CR-117173). US Department of Transportation, Transportation Systems Center, Cambridge, Mass.

US Government Printing Office (1963). *Military standards,* 150A, Washington, D.C.

van Lopik, J. (1968). Infrared mapping – Basic technology and geoscience applications. *Geoscience News.* **407** (Jan–Feb), 24–31.

Wallace, R. E. and Moxham, R. M. (1967). *Use of infrared imagery of the San Andreas Fault system, California.* US Geological Survey Professional Paper 575D. d147-D156.

Wolfe, W. L. (ed.) (1965). *Handbook of military infrared technology.* Office of Naval Research, Washington, D.C.

—— and Zissis, G. (eds.) (1979). *The infrared handbook.* US Government Printing Office, Washington, D.C.

Yost, E. and Wenderoth, S. (1967). Multispectral color aerial photography. *Photogramm. Engng* **33**, 1020–33.

——, —— (1968). *Additive color aerial photography: Manual of color aerial photography* pp. 451–71. American Society of Photogrammetry.

5. Postscript
GRID: a tool for environmental management

5.1. National, regional, and global environmental data

Ecological monitoring, of the kind described in this book, is only one way of gathering environmental data. Most countries regularly monitor several environmental variables, particularly those relating to climate. National surveys of geology, land-form, and soil type are continually being improved. National maps of vegetation and forest cover exist in all developed countries, and in many developing ones.

Census data also exist almost everywhere. Most countries have reasonably reliable data on the geographical distribution of crops, livestock, and wildlife, size, and location of smallholdings and farms, and incomes and employment of local populations.

Similar information is also gathered and stored on a regional and global basis. The World Meteorological Organization, for example, monitors and publishes global meteorological data; Unesco has published a series of global Vegetation Maps; and FAO has produced a Map of World Soils.

The international community also produces a number of more specialized data bases. In 1979, for example, FAO, UNEP, and Unesco began a joint programme to develop a methodology for the assessment of soil degradation risks and rates. The chemical, biological and physical properties of soils in the Near East and Africa north of the equator were assessed from field testing, laboratory analysis, and satellite imagery. This work enabled the degree of present degradation and future risk to be determined. Maps were then published of areas at risk to wind and water erosion. They showed, for example, that in some countries 75 per cent of the land was prone to wind erosion, and that water erosion was an equally serious threat elsewhere.

These data are of sufficiently high resolution and quality to provide useful guidance in national planning – for example, in planning the routes of new railways or roads, or in siting new dams. In all cases, however, the information is sufficient only to identify those areas in which it would be inadvisable to site new infrastructure unless specific plans to combat erosion were also included. More detailed surveying is needed to test viable alternatives.

During the late 1970s, a GEMS project executed by FAO developed techniques for monitoring forest cover in three West African tropical countries. These techniques are suitable for use elsewhere in developing countries, and are based on the combined use of data from the interpretation of satellite and aerial photographs, aerial observations, and ground surveys. This work should eventually lead to a global network based on national monitoring projects. In conjunction with FAO, UNEP produced an assessment of the current state of tropical forest resources in 76 countries, which was published in 1981. It includes information on natural forest, the various forms of logged and cleared forest, and replacement forests. It is intended to produce regular assessments every five years, which will eventually form the basis of a tropical forest resource data bank.

The work of FAO on agroecological zones is also of interest to planners. By combining data on soil structure and climate, FAO – in cooperation with UNEP and the International Institute for Applied Analysis in Vienna – has been able to demarcate the principal growing areas for 15 of the world's major crops. This work has now been extended to provide regional estimates of the population-carrying capacities of land, based on a number of assumptions about the sophistication of the agriculture in use.

The methodology developed in the agroecological zones project is capable of more detailed use on a national or regional basis. In 1985, about a dozen countries were involved in more detailed studies of the ability of their agriculture to support future populations. Such information can be important in land-use planning because it exposes the boundary conditions for agricultural development.

The Global Environment Monitoring System (GEMS) of UNEP plays an important role in co-ordinating and promoting global monitoring in five major areas: climate, the long-range transport of pollutants, health-related monitoring, ocean monitoring and monitoring of renewable resources. As a result, knowledge of such important environmental phenomena as atmospheric pollution, the world climatic system, the build-up of carbon dioxide in the atmosphere, acid rain, water quality, deforestation, and the state of the world's soils is continually being improved. Large quantities of data are collected every year, and stored in data banks. Some are published in map or tabular form, and some are used to make major assessments of the state of the world environment.

5.2. Utility of existing environmental data

Numerous environmental variables are thus being regularly monitored, and the results published in a number of different forms. However, cross-analysis and correlation between data in different data sets are either difficult or impossible. Environmental decision-makers who need information are thus faced with a number of problems. The first is that their decisions usually concern a specific area of land, about which they need to know as much as possible. While existing data bases may provide them with information on specific environmental variables, such as water quality or forest cover, these data will not be comparable. The information is stored in different ways in different data bases, and is geo-referenced in different ways. Hence it cannot be overlaid in a meaningful manner. To cite a specific example, copious data exist over many different years on atmospheric pollution and forest cover. But these data are not available in a form which would allow researchers to investigate their mutual interaction, and hence to determine the role of atmospheric pollution in forest destruction.

A second problem is that environmental managers must treat their subject as an interactive system which amounts to more than the sum of its component parts. Ecosystems are complex; they are easily misunderstood if they are persistently regarded as no more than a collection of discrete variables. A better and more integrated method of analysing environmental data is urgently needed.

5.3. Towards a global data base for the environment

The need for a data base which incorporates different environmental data sets – for example, on soils, forests, vegetation, land-use, climate, pollution, and socio-economic variables – was foreseen by GEMS several years ago. An initial scheme was proposed by UNEP consultants in 1981. Between October 1982 and July 1984, the idea was presented and discussed at ten international meetings. These meetings concluded that the system was feasible, identified several suitable software systems for the data base, and spelt out ten important tasks which the system should be able to undertake.

The project is known as the Global Resource Information Database (GRID). Its pilot phase was begun in March 1985. By that time, GRID had received substantial backing both nationally and internationally. Running costs for the pilot phase were supplied by UNEP's Environment Fund, and contributions in kind had been received from the Environmental Systems Research Institute, the National Aeronautics and Space Administration, and the Prime Computer Corporation in the United States, and from the Swiss Confederation, the Canton of Geneva, and the University of Geneva in Switzerland and the Governments of Canada and Norway.

When fully operational, GRID will provide decision-makers and environmental managers with convenient access to the information they need. They will be able, for example, to specify any particular area of the world, and then call up data for that area on such variables as soil type, forest cover, water resources, roads and other infrastructure, human, livestock and wildlife populations, climate, pollution, vegetation cover, and even the numbers of cows or cars per inhabitant.

But GRID's real strength will go far beyond this. GRID will be a powerful tool for environmental modelling and analysis. Those using it will be able to ask detailed and specific questions which involve over-laying information from many different data sets. An example of such a question might be how many lakes are there in northern Ghana which are within 10 km of a major road, which have acidity levels of pH 6.0 or less, are larger than 5 km^2, and are surrounded by soils suitable for growing maize?

5.3.1. The organization of GRID

The idea behind GRID is to get environmental information out to those who need it, wherever they may be, quickly, conveniently and in a form which will allow cross-comparison of different types of data. Initially, there will be two GRID centres: a control unit in Nairobi, headquarters of UNEP, and a processing unit in Geneva, where data will be entered, updated, and analysed. As the idea develops, other national and inter-national GRID centres will be created.

In this way, GRID will become an information network, with environ-mental data dispersed among the different national and international centres: for example, soils data may be stored at the FAO GRID centre, and meteorological data at the WMO GRID centre. National census data, national data on infrastructure and land-form, and data derived from national ecological monitoring projects, will be stored at national GRID centres.

These centres will be linked by telecommunications. Thus, each centre will have access to the data stored elsewhere. Users of the system will be able to input, extract, and analyse data at each GRID centre. Strict rules will govern which centre has responsibility for modifying and updating each data base.

A further sophistication will enable users who do not have access to one of these centres to benefit from the system. These users will be provided with a microcomputer, enabling them to make use of GRID data and software. These microcomputers will be able to run suit-ably modified versions of the GRID software; they will also have access to the complete range of GRID data, though only selected packages of the data could be handled by the microcomputer at any one time.

5.3.2. The functions of GRID

The GRID system has two basic functions: the assessment and the analysis of environmental data. As Table 5.1 shows, the tasks which can be performed in these two areas cover a wide range of activities, from improving national or global data bases to testing the effectiveness of proposed environmental policies.

Table 5.1. Functions and tasks of GRID.

Function	Task	Example
Assessment	Data supply	Supply information on numbers of elephant in northern Kenya
	Inventory management	Improved data on global soils
	Status reporting	Periodic assessment of state of environmental pollution
	Monitoring change	Reports on change in forest cover
Analysis	Research support	Analysis of causes of desertification
	Forecasting	Prediction of locust swarms or climate change
	Improved management	Use of GRID data to decide when to move cattle in drought-affected areas
	Policy development	Testing of effectiveness of alternative environmental policies
	Aid allocation	Identification of areas in which development support is critical
	Project evaluation	Analysis of environmental impact of introduction of irrigation to an arid area

5.3.3. How GRID will work

5.3.3.1. The hardware Specialized hardware for GRID's pilot phase will be provided on loan from NASA. It will consist primarily of a Perkin Elmer 3241 32-bit computer with four megabytes of memory, backed by four CRT terminals, three CDC 300 megabyte disc drives and two tape drives.

In addition, the Prime Computer Corporation has agreed to donate two mini-computers to the system: a six megabyte Prime 750 and a 2.0 megabyte Prime 2250, together with associated consoles, printers, disc and tape drives.

The success of the system will be highly dependent on the peripheral devices. A high-resolution digitizer, for example, will be used to enter cartographic information quickly and easily. An image processor will help generate visual output displays and, in conjunction with a light-pen, will be used for entering or editing existing data. High-quality monitors, printers and plotters will also be used to provide users with outputs in the most convenient form such as coloured maps, on film or paper, displays on a colour monitor, or tables, graphs, and listings.

5.3.3.2. The software Two major software suites have been donated to GRID: NASA's Earth Resources Laboratory Applications Software (ELAS) and the Environmental Systems Research Institute's ARC/INFO system.

The ELAS Suite has been specially developed for processing environmental data from satellite imagery and other sources to aid in resource management. It contains about 200 modules, each of which can be accessed separately. It was originally developed to overcome problems of data incompatibility, and hence is ideal for GRID. Data from different sources, such as satellite imagery or existing data banks, can be entered into the system using a series of programs, each developed specifically for individual applications (such as entering Landsat or Seasat data).

The ELAS Suite incorporates sophisticated means of generating overlays of different data sets, so that environmental changes can be monitored over time, or the incidence of specific variables such as erosion, correlated with other variables such as soil type. The kinds of analysis that can be carried out are sufficiently detailed, for example, to allow a national institution to search through the data to find areas with a specific kind of vegetation cover, as identified by a spectral signature from satellite imagery, in a specific watershed, on a specific soil type, with a given slope, and between specified elevations. This means that the software can be used at the micro-level as well as in the investigation of national or global trends.

The ARC/INFO system is for managing geographic information, and it is easy to use. It is ideal, for example, in any application which requires the overlaying of two or more maps, and it includes provision for editing and labelling the resulting map. Portions of the map can then be enlarged for more detailed display, and produced on colour film or plotters. New data can be entered by a reverse procedure, in which information from a new map is input via the digitizer. The software then automatically makes the appropriate modifications to the existing data base.

5.4. The future of environmental data management

As GRID develops and expands, decision-makers in both developed and developing countries will find themselves in possession of a powerful new tool. For the first time, they will be able to call up the data they need to make informed decisions about environmental management.

Of course, GRID will not eliminate the need for further research. Nor will it eliminate the need for ecological monitoring of the type described in this book. But it will make the task a great deal easier. In the future, the first step in any ecological monitoring project will be to interrogate GRID for the existence of relevant data in the area concerned. The second step will be a preliminary analysis of these data to see if they can provide the answers required. Where the data are insufficient, GRID interactions will provide detailed specifications of data gaps, and in effect will play a key role in the design of new monitoring projects. This should produce dramatic savings in cost and time.

A further advantage will be that it will be possible to store the results of ecological monitoring projects in GRID. They will therefore be accessible to GRID users. Project managers will thus be able to make enquiries about previous projects and to assess the relevance of results obtained from them. This will also help streamline the design of new monitoring projects.

Index

active systems, remote sensing 223
aerial livestock surveys 174–5
aerial photographs 257
  and design of ecological monitoring
      programmes 31
  and landslides 54
  and preparation of medium-scale maps 39
  and rill and gully erosion 55
aerial photographs (vertical) and vegetation
      survey 63
aerial photography
  black-and-white panchromatic 230–1
  the early days 223–5
aerial survey data-base
  applications for resource inventories
      210–11
  applications for thematic mapping 210
  collation and integration of ancillary data
      203–5
  data-base analyses 211–12
  data manipulation 205–7
  data transformation 205
  structure of 201, 203
  survey estimates 207–8
    precision of 208–10
aerial surveys 9–13
  history of 4
  major applications 142–65
  operational procedures for 166–219
  selection of data variables 169–76
  sources of ancillary data 170
  and vegetation monitoring 62–3
Africa (North East) and SIR–A experiment
      254
ageing animals (LMH) 108–10
agricultural aerial surveys and survey
      planning 177
agricultural land-use, and aerial survey 174
agriculture and SAR 250, 251 (fig.)
agroecological zones and FAO 284
aircraft (light), use of in aerial monitoring
      141–219
aircraft and equipment for aerial surveys
      and monitoring 166–8
aircraft operation and bias 213–14
air humidity 26
air temperature 26
Amboseli Ecological Monitoring Programme,
      Kenya 144
animal abundance (LMH), estimation of
      82–3

animal counts
  counting biases 85–6
  per unit area 83
  quadrat (block) counts 83–4
  transect counting 84–5
animal numbers, monitoring of 142–3
animal populations, long-term monitoring of
      142–7
annotation strip, Landsat MSS images 274
Apollo programme 272
  and space photography 227
Apollo–Soyuz programme 228
ARC/INFO system 288
area data 148–9, 200
Arizona, University of (Office of Arid Land
      Studies), long-term monitoring of arid
      rangelands 146–7
automatic satellites 258–71
Automatic Weather Station (AWS) (UK
      Institute of Hydrology) 24
average percentage slope, obtained from
      topographic maps 45

base maps, preparation of 29–31
basin sediment yield, annual 48–9
bedload samplers 50–1
bedload transport measurements 51
bias
  control of in aerial surveys 212–18
  counting bias in ground monitoring 85–6
biological activity (process studies) 54–5
biomass 71
  and productivity measures 73–5
  reduction of by selective feeding
      (LMS) 103
biomass death and tissue movement 74–5
biomass (def.) 73
biomass (green), air survey of 74
block counting 164
  and SRF 141
body condition, free-living LMH 104–5
  fat and protein reserves 106–7
  general condition 105–6
Braun–Blanquet method, classification of
      vegetation types 63–4
burrowing and erosion 55

Camargue horses, dietary study 97–101

cameras
  35-mm 167, 194, 196–7
  large-format 234
  metric 228–9
  use of two 198–9
Canadian International Development Agency
  and KREMU 4–5, 143
canopy interception and sampling biomass
  and standing dead 73–4
capture–recapture method, estimate of small
  populations 89
catchment (drainage-basin) studies 48–9
catchment (drainage-basin) studies,
  experimental design 53
catch per unit effort (CPUE) 87
catena 33–4, 39
cation exchange capacity of soil 37
climate, data sources 170, 172
climate measurements 23–9
cluster analysis, dietary study of Camargue
  horses 99–101
colour additive viewers 233–4
colour film 231
colour infra-red film 231–2
colour video tape recorders (VTR) 10–11
community composition data, summary and
  analysis 72
community involvement in surveys 127–8
comparative index and density estimation 88
computer interpretation, SIS raingauge 25
computerized data analysis of
  questionnaires 129–30
computer processing of images, development
  of 225
computer programs and aerial survey
  data 12
computing, advances in, and climatic
  analysis 276
concentrate feeders (ruminants) 80
continuous monitoring, value of 2
continuous strata 206
contour-flying 185, 198
correspondence analysis, dietary study of
  Camargue horses 97–8, 99
count data 148, 199–200
counting biases, occurrence of in ground
  monitoring 85–6
counting bias, influenced by ground speed
  186
counting (sampling) strip
  defined 193
  observations 193
  recording and transcribing (rear-seat
    observer) 194–6
crew duties, aerial survey 168–9
crop potentials, aerial survey data-base 211
crop production, aerial survey data-base 211
CSIRO (Australia), land systems and land
  units 42

data
  digital, Landsat 14
  plotting of 12
data analysis, social and economic surveys
  129–30
data analysis, SRF data set 150–9
data bases, specialized, produced by
  international community 283
data collection, integration and analysis,
  stratified random sampling 161
data-collection system, Landsat (and other)
  satellites 266–7
data-gathering techniques, social and
  economic surveys 117–23
data integration, SRF survey 149–50
data recombination and creation of new
  variables, SRF and ancillary data 150
data record 203
data transformation, aerial survey 205
dietary protein and herbivores 79
diet components, herbivore diets 91
  use made of dietary components 92–101
diet (LMH), nutritional value of 107–8
  protein-energy nutrition 108
difference method and diet data (LMH) 93
differential digestion, effects and problems of
  95, 96
direct observation and diet data (LMH)
  93–4
discontinuous strata 206
distribution maps 162
dynamic range, SAR 248–9

Earth-resource asssessment satellites 4
Earth Resources Experiment Package
  (EREP) 228
Earth Resources Observation Satellite
  (EROS) 259
Earth Resources Technology Satellite
  programme 228
Earth terrain camera 228
East Africa and SGS monitoring transects
  8–9
ecological information and base maps 29–31
ecological monitoring
  advantages of a global system 20–1
  costs of 16–20
  development of programme for 18–19
    (*fig.*), 20
  and the environment 1–2
  history of 3–4
  and Landsats 269–70
    usefulness of Landsat data 261–2
  need for 111
  and permanent study plots 75–6
  techniques described 2–3
  uses of 3
ecological monitoring data 6–7

ecological monitoring unit (EMU) 15–16
ecological problems and historical decisions 112
ecological research, morphometric indices used for hypothesis testing 45
economic/social data 7
ecosystems, changing 1–2
ELAS suite (NASA) 288
EMU (ecological monitoring unit) 15–16
 and SAR 255
enumerators (interviewers)
 choice of 123–4
 supervision of 128–9
 training of 124–7
environmental constraints to cultivation, aerial survey data-base 211
environmental data management, future of 288–9
environmental data, problems of cross-analysis and correlation 284–5
environmental gradients and sampling transects 179–80
environmental impact assessment and aerial survey 145–6
environmental stress, shown by intensity gradients 158
erosion, and aerial survey 173
erosion linked to land-use patterns, surveys for 177
erosion pedestals and measurement of surface erosion 56–7
erosion-pins (stakes) 58
erosion rates 54
erosion-related topics 48
ERS (Japan) satellite 15
ERTS-1, *see* Landsat-1
evaporation devices 25–6
evaporation and transpiration 25–6
exclosures, value of in plant species studies 103–4

faecal analysis 96
faecal pellet group (FPG) counts 83
 and LMH densities 89–90
false-colour film, *see* colour infra-red film
false colour, need for 264–5
FAO 283, 284
fat reserves in LMH 106
fauna surveys 6–7
feasibility studies and large-scale maps 39
fecundity rate (LMH) 110
film and processing for aerial survey 197
film resolving power 229–30
film, types of 230–2
filters used in photography 234
flight lines (transects) to cut across important gradients 179–80, 182–3
flushing distance, as transect width 85

foraging, selectivity in 101–2, 103
forest cover (W. Africa) monitored—GEMS project 284
forested land and SAR 250, 252

Gemini programme 272
 and space photography 227
GEMS (Global Environmental Monitoring System) 1, 284
geometric accuracy, SAR 249
Geostationary Operational Environmental Satellite (GOES) 271
geostationary satellites (meteorological) 271
global data base for the environment, need for 285–8
Global Resource Information Database (GRID) 283–9
GNS (global navigation system) 166–7, 186
 and bias 213–14
gradient analyses, aerial survey data-base 211
GRID 283–9
 functions of 286–7
 organization of 286
 working of 287–8
grid cell maps 151–2
grid cells (UTM) uses in SRF survey 148
grid cell (UTM) data 204
grid data, SRF survey 149
grid system and monitoring 2
ground monitoring 7–9
 climate measurements 23–9
 and land-form classification 40–7
 large mammal herbivores (LMH) 77–104
  nutrition and population dynamics 104–11
 preparation of a base map 29–31
 reasons for 22
 social and economic surveys 111–31
 soil erosion and sediment yields 48–60
 soil mapping and interpretation 31–40
 vegetation monitoring 60–77
ground resolution distance (GRD) 230
ground sampling techniques, importance of 7–8
ground slope and bias 215–16
ground speed, control of 185–6
ground speed control and bias 213–14
ground studies, origins of 3–4
ground surveys 9
group interviews, social and economic surveys 120–1
group size and density 86
Guidelines for soil description, FAO 35–6
Guide to hydrological practice, WMO 25
Guide to hydrometeorological practices, WMO 27

habitat attributes assessable by ecological
    monitoring 8 (*table*)
habitat survey, ecological monitoring data
    6–7
height control and radar altimeter 185
helicopter survey 200
Helley-Smith (bedload) sampler 51
herbivore diets 91–104
    analysis of 96–101
hillslope transects, surveys along 46–7
holographic storage and SAR imagery
    247–8
hydrology, data sources 172–3

image resolution and detectability,
    recognizability and identifiability 230
image restoration and enhancement 275
image uniformity, SAR 249
imaging with non-photographic sensors
    optical–mechanical scanners 237–8
    thermal infra-red scanners 238–42
    TV cameras or image tubes 235–6
index calibration 87–8
information (data)-gathering techniques
    structured survey 119
    unstructured interviews 118–19
infra-red film, advantages of 231
infra-red imagery 238–9
infra-red photography 238–9
intensity gradients, value of 158
intercept methods, vegetation sampling
    69–71
interpreters and questionnaires 126

Jonglei Canal, S. Sudan, and SRF surveys
    145

Kelker's method (estimation of absolute
    numbers of animals) 87, 88–9
Kenya 5, 6, 155; *see also* KREMU
Kenya Rangeland Ecological Monitoring
    Unit, *see* KREMU
kidney fat index (KFI) 106
Kipp solarimeter (AWS) 26
KREMU 4–5, 15, 16
    costs of 20
    rangeland monitoring 143

land-budgets, aerial survey data-base 211
land-form classification and ground
    monitoring 40–7
land-form parameters, classification of 44
    (*table*)
land-form, data sources 170

land-forms, vagueness of descriptions 44
Landsat-1 (ERTS-1) 4, 228, 259
Landsat
    data-collection system 266–7
    and ecological monitoring 269–70
    multispectral scanner (MSS) imagery 63
    multispectral scanner (MSS) system 244,
        259–60, 262–5
    the programme 63, 228, 259–62
    return beam vidicon (RBV) system 236,
        265–6
    thematic mapper (TM) 14, 267–8
Landsat data, frequency of 14
Landsat data, integrated view of Earth's
    surface 270
Landsat images and electronic processing
    274–5
Landsat scene and computer compatible tape
    264
Landsat viewing of Earth 260–1
landscape morphometry 44–6
landslides and debris flows (process studies)
    54
land suitability from SRF-generated data,
    value of 158–9
land system classifications 42–4
land system (def.) 42
land-use changes, monitoring of 147
land-use development, planning of 2
land-use patterns and stratification 160
large-format camera 234
large mammal herbivores (LMH)
    diet 91–104
    monogastric 78
    nutrition and population dynamics
        104–11
    population ranges and use of vegetation
        types 82–91
    ruminants 79
    seasonal requirements 79–80
    selective feeding 80–1
    use of primary production by 81–2
large mammal herbivores (LMH), ground
    monitoring of 77–111
leaching 32–3
line-intercept method, vegetation sampling
    70
line-scanners 237–8
livestock densities and stratification 182
live weight as measure of condition (LMH)
    105
LMH, *see* large mammal herbivores

manned satellites 271–2
man as a soil-forming factor 34
manual data analysis of questionnaires 129

map scale related to soil survey field methods 38–40
maps for survey planning 176
marrow fat index (MFI), as indicator of prolonged malnutrition 106
Mercury programme 226–7
meteorological and hydrological stations, siting of 24
meteorological methods and equipment, climate measurement 23–4
meteorological satellites 271
Meteosat 271
metric camera 228–9
micro-computers and survey data analysis 129
microwave systems, active
  history of 245
  principles of 245–7
  radar resolution 247
  SAR systems 247–55
mineral deficiencies (LMH) 107
mortality rates, variations in 110–11
multiband photography 232–4
multispectral cameras 233
multispectral data and SPOT 270
multispectral images (Landsat) and annotation strip 274
multispectral photography, concept of 225
multispectral scanner data
  potential use of categorized 275–6
  processing of 244
multispectral scanners (MSS) 243–4
  and Landsat satellites 244, 259–60, 262–4
multi-stage sampling, use of 116–17

natural mortality and density estimates 88
nearest-neighbour method, vegetation sampling 71
nitrogen concentrations, measurement of 108
Njaramau land system 43 (*fig.*)
NOAA satellites 4, 14
  and climatic data 170, 172
nodes and remoteness indices 204
nutrient deficiencies in LMH 80–1
nutritional value of diet (LMH) 107–8
nutrition and population dynamics (LMH) 104–11

observed and detected changes and application of remote sensing data 272
observer counting bias 214
observer records, aerial survey 191–3

oesophageal fistulation and diet data (LMH) 94–5, 96
OMEGA/VLF navigation system 148, 166, 176, 186–8
  guidelines for use 188–9
optical–mechanical scanners 237–8
orbital multispectral photographs 227
orbital photography 226–7
orbiting satellites (meteorological) 271

paired-basin studies, catchment (drainage basin) studies 53
parasitism 110
passive systems, remote sensing 223
pastoral populations and aerial survey 176
people–environment interaction, related factors 112
percentage base saturation (soil) 37–8
permanent study plots 75–6
phenology, aerial survey data on 174
photogeology 224
photogrammetry 223–4
photographic images, Landsat 14, 15 (*table*)
photographic resolution 229–30
photographic sensors and applications 228–34
photography, vertical 35-mm 196–201
  count and area data 148–9
photo-interpretation 199
  interpretation procedures 200–1
photo-interpretation and bias 216–18
photo-interpreters, consistency of 216–18
photo-scale bias 214–15
photo-scales and aerial survey 197–8
piloting and navigation, aerial survey 185–91
plant material, utility to herbivores 78
plant size
  measurement of for biomass estimate 73
  methods of measurement 68
plotless sampling, vegetation sampling 71–2
plot (quadrat-transect) sampling 67–9
point data, SRF survey 149
point gauge measurements, surface lowering 58
point-intercept method, vegetation sampling 70–1
point-quarter method, vegetation sampling 71–2
polygon data 204
polygon maps 152–4
polygons, SRF survey data 149–50
population, aerial survey data-base analyses 211
population dynamics (LMH), analysis of 108–11
population (human) and natural resources 1
population structure, monitoring of 144

potential evaporation, estimate of 26
pre-reconnaissance survey 200
pre-survey flights, importance of 184–5
primary data gathered from primary sources 119–20
primary production and off-take in rangeland, aerial survey data-base 212
primary production, selectivity of LMH 81–2
principal and preferred resources 91
probability theory in climatic analysis 26–7
process studies 53–60
project Radam (Brazil) and SAR 250, 251 (*fig.*) 252
protein-energy deficiency, free-living LMH 104–5
protein-energy nutrition (LMH) 108
protein reserves (LMH) 106–7

quadrats, nested 69
quadrat-transect (plot) sampling 67–9
questionnaire
    construction of 121–3, 125
    familiarization with 125–6
    in local language 126
questionnaire interview 121
quota sampling, population estimation 116, 117

radar altimeter 166, 185, 198
radar, used for rainfall measurement 23–4
rainfall
    measured by radar 23–4
    measurement of 23
rainfall and soil 32–3
rain-gauge distribution and type 25
rain-gauge network design: a case study 28–9
random-number tables, and vegetation monitoring 65–7
random sampling
    estimating population characteristics 115–17
    simple 115–16
    vegetation 65
rangelands (arid), importance of aerial survey data 173
rangelands and SAR 252
recombinant data variables 206–7
relative density data, use of 83
relief, influence on soil formation 33
remoteness indices 204–5
remote sensing
    active microwave systems 245–55
    history of 223–8
    imaging with non-photographic sensors 235–42

multispectral scanners 243–4
photographic sensors and applications 228–34
principles of 222–3
space systems useful for ecological monitoring 255–76
remote sensing data
    presentation for evaluation 272–4
    processing of 274–6
remote sensing and expansion in data gathering 256
remote sensing from space 226–8
remote sensing unit 274
reproduction (LMH) 110
    limited by diet 107
reproductive costs, LMH 79–80
reservoir design and surveys 52
reservoir sedimentation surveys 51–2
resolution and SAR 248
resource inventories 154–6
    aerial survey 210–11
    from SRF-generated data 162
    regional 144–5
resource partitioning among ruminants 80
respondents (sampling units), careful choice of 114
return beam vidicon (RBV) system 236
    and Landsat satellites 265–6
rill and gully erosion (process studies) 55–6
    monitoring of 59–60
rills 55–6
river channel pattern, descriptions of 46
river studies 46
rocket photographs 226
roughage feeders (ruminants) 80

sample intensity 180
sample points 203
    and data manipulation 205–6
sampler, depth-integrating 49
sample size, determination of 65–6
sampling effort and areas of importance 181–2
sampling intensity, and stratification 183
sampling methods, social and economic surveys 114–17
SAR imagery, interpretation of 249–50
SAR (synthetic aperture radar) systems
    availability of 249
    monitoring applications 249–52
    performance of 247–9
    spaceborne SR 252–4, 255
satellite imagery for climatic data 170, 172
satellite information, value of 14–15
satellite systems and multispectral scanners (MSS) 243

Saudi Arabia, aerial photography 6
scale, concept of 256
Seasat (spaceborne SAR) 252–4
sector summary 210
  resource inventories 154
sediment yield, annual 50
Selous Game Reserve, Tanzania, and SRF
  surveys 146
Serengeti National Park, Tanzania
  monitoring of animal numbers 142
  monitoring seasonal movements with SRF
    143–4
service networks, aerial survey data-
  base 211
settlement-site distribution (Kenya) 47
settlements and population, value of aerial
  survey 175–6
shifting cultivation, beneficial effects of 33
Simple Instrument System (SIS) Raingauge
  (Institute of Hydrology) 25
SIR-A and SIR-B (spaceborne SAR) 254
skeletal size, index of 105–6
Skylab 228, 271–2
SLAR (side-looking radar) systems 246, 247
smallholder cultivation and aerial survey 174
social and economic surveys 111–31
  data analysis 129–30
  data-gathering techniques 117–23
  organization of 123–9
  sampling methods 114–17
  survey design 113–14
software suites donated to GRID 288
soil analysis 37–8
soil catena 33–4, 39
soil consistency 36
soil cores and biomass 73
soil erosion and sediment yields 48–9
soil formation
  affected by environment 31–4
  and climate past and present 32
soil-forming factors 31–2
soil mapping and interpretation 31–40
soil maps as base maps 30
soil moisture holding capacity 37
soil organic matter content 37
soil pH 37
  and percentage base saturation 38
soil pores 36
soil profile 32, 34–5
  described 35–6
  soil sampling 36–7
soil salinity or alkalinity 37
soil sampling 36–7
soil structure 36
soil surveys
  and combined map scales 39–40
  field methods in 38–40
  and soil sampling 36–7

soil texture 32, 37
soil weathering 32
solarimeter (pyrheliometer) 26
solar radiation 26
  reflected, value of for Earth-resources
    monitoring 269
solum 35
spaceborne SAR 252–4
space shuttle system 272
space systems useful for ecological
  monitoring 255–76
  automatic satellites 258–71
  data applications 272–6
  manned satellites 271–2
  meteorological satellites 271
space systems, value versus cost 257–8
spectral bands, thematic mapper 267–8
spectral data, Landsat 14
spectral signatures 269
SPOT (France), Earth-resources satellite
  15, 258, 270–1
SRF data set and integration of ancillary data
  149
SRF method, when appropriate 163
SRF programme, information available from
  12–13
SRF surveys
  Kenya 144, 146, 157 (*table*), 158 (*table*),
    159 (*table*), 182, 183
  Tanzania 143–4, 145–6
SRF (systematic reconnaissance flight) 9–13,
  16, 141, 147–59
  costs of 17
  data analyses, relevance to development
    planners 156–9
  general concepts 147–8
  a sampling technique 147
standing crop (def.) 73
standing dead (def.) 73
stationary scanners 242
statistical techniques, climate measurements
  26–7
step-count method, vegetation sampling 70
stomach analysis and diet data (LMH) 95
stratification
  concept of 159–60
  process of 160–1
stratification, survey planning 182–3
stratified random sampling 159–64
  animal numbers 143
  lack of flexibility 162–3
  population estimation 116, 117
  and SRF 141
  vegetation 65
  when appropriate 163
stratum profile 210–11
  resource inventories 154–5
streambank erosion, monitoring of 59–60

subunits 203
  geo-referencing of 190–1
  systematic and random sampling 183–4
surface erosion (process studies) 56–7
  monitoring of 57–9
survey
  implementation of 127–9
  timing of 128
survey design
  and bias 212–13
  socio-economic study 113–14
survey organization, social and economic
    surveys 123–9
survey planning, aerial surveys 176–85
surveys along hillslope transects 46–7
suspended load, monitoring of 49
Systematic Ground Survey (SGS) 8
systematic sample, design of 177–82
systematic sampling and bias 212–13
systematic sampling (distribution
    patterns) 143
systematic sampling (SRF method) and
    stratified sampling compared 145,
    161–4

Tanzania (Rukwa region), air survey and
    land-use plan 5–6
teeth and ageing of animals 109
thematic mapper (TM) data, limitations of
    standard processing 268
thematic mapper (TM), Landsat
    satellites 14, 267–8
thematic mapping 210
thematic maps 150, 162, 257
thermal imagery, uses of 239–40
thermal images, interpretation of 239,
    241–2
thermal infra-red scanners 238–42
thermal scanning missions, planning of 241
topographic maps and preparation of base
    maps 30
topography and stratification 182
total counting 164
transect counting 84–5, 164
trap efficiency of lakes 52
tree-throw mounds 54–5
troughs, measurement of surface erosion 59
Turkanaland, Kenya, and SRF surveys 144,
    146, 157 (*table*), 159 (*table*), 182, 183
TV cameras or image tubes 235–6

UNEP (United Nations Environment
    Programme) 1, 283, 284
  and GRID 285
United Nations Food and Agricultural
    Organization (FAO) and KREMU 5
US Soil Taxonomy, analyses needed 38
UTM grid system 148, 203, 204
  used for thematic units 210

variance and survey estimates 208–10
vegetation
  and aerial survey 173–4
  impact of LMH on 91–2, 102–4
  influence on soil 33
  most frequently described properties of 60
  and stratification 182
vegetation (background) and survey planning
    177
vegetation monitoring 60–77, 146–7
vegetation monitoring programmes and
    standardized data collection 76–7
vegetation sampling 65–7
  intercept methods 69–71
  plotless sampling 71–2
  plot methods 67–9
  stratified random sampling (arbitrary and
    subjective) 65
  systematic sampling 65
vegetation sampling, field measurements
    data 69
vegetation survey 6, 62–4
vegetation types and infra-red film 232
Very Low Frequency navigation system,
    accuracy of 10
visual observations, SRF survey 148

weathering 48
  chemical 32
  and climate 32
weather and survey planning 177
wetlands and SAR 252
wind speed 26
world carbon budget, precise model and
    SAR 250
World Meteorological Organization
    (WMO) 283
  and standard equipment 24

T
THE B
OF DISEASE

Abridged Edition

by

J. H. TILDEN, M.D.

•

AN ANTIDOTE TO FEAR, FRENZY
AND THE POPULAR MANIA OF
CHASING AFTER SO-CALLED CURES

•

Presenting: The true interpretation
of the cause of disease and how
healing is accomplished. . . .

•

NATURAL HYGIENE PRESS
A Division of
AMERICAN NATURAL HYGIENE SOCIETY, INC.
1920 Irving Park Road
Chicago, Illinois 60613
A Not for Profit Educational Organization

TOXEMIA EXPLAINED
First printing, June 1974
by American Natural Hygiene Society

Library of Congress Number: 74-82367

Natural Hygiene Press
a division of:
The American Natural Hygiene Society, Inc.
1920 Irving Park Road
Chicago, Illinois, 60613

ISBN-0-914532-07-3

TABLE OF CONTENTS

                                                        Page
Preface   1
Editor's Preface   4
Author's Preface   6

Chapter

    1   Introduction to Toxemia............. 15
    2   Toxemia Explained 25
    3   Enervation is General 61
    4   Poise 69
    5   The Causes of Enervation 87

Appendix

    A   Retrospection 105
    B   A Few Suggestions 107
    C   Dr. Tilden's Tensing Exercises.......109
        Index 115

A Prefatory Suggestion

WHAT more can be asked of a health system
than that it simplifies the cause of disease,
making it understandable to all open-minded
lay minds?

TOXEMIA EXPLAINED does this very thing. If the
reader will read or study this book as he must
study a public school book in order to understand it, he can know what causes disease, and
knowing the cause, it will be an easy matter
to avoid developing disease; but if imprudence
brings on disease, he has the knowledge of
how to overcome it.

                                          J. H. TILDEN

Preface

Dr. John H. Tilden, the son of a physician, was born in Van Burenburg, Illinois, on January 21, 1851. He received his medical education at the Eclectic Medical Institute, Cincinnati, Ohio, a medical school founded in 1830 as a protest against the allopathic and homeopathic schools of medicine of that time. He was graduated in 1872 with the degree of doctor of medicine. From the best information we can obtain, his father was a Dr. Joseph G. Tilden, who came from Vermont in 1837 to Kentucky, in which state he married.

Dr. John H. Tilden started the practice of medicine at Nokomis, Illinois, then for a year at St. Louis, Missouri, and then at Litchfield, Illinois, until 1890, when he moved to Denver, Colorado. In Denver he located in the downtown business section in an office with other doctors. Later he established a sanitarium in an outer section of the city. This sanitarium and school he conducted until 1924 when he sold the Institution, for about half of what he had plowed back into its development, to a Dr. Arthur Voss of Cincinnati, Ohio, intending to devote himself to writing and lecturing. However, he soon became discontented without his school and after a period he bought two residences on Pennsylvania Avenue, in Denver, united them into one and opened a new sanitarium and school, having to borrow from a friend a part of the money with which to make the purchases. This prob-

1

ably was in 1926. This school continued until the Doctor's death on September 1, 1940.

It was during the early years of his practice in Illinois that Dr. Tilden began to question the use of medicine to remedy illness. His extensive reading, especially of medical studies from European medical schools, and his own thinking led him to the conclusion that there should be some way to live so as not to build disease, and in this period his thoughts on toxemia began to formulate and materially develop. From the beginning of his practice in Denver the Doctor used no medicine but practiced his theory of clearing the body of toxic matters and then allowing inherent healing powers to restore health, teaching his patients how to live so as not to create a toxic condition and thus retain a healthy body free of disease. An uncompromising realist and a strict disciplinarian, the Doctor wasted no time on those who would not relinquish regenerating habits, but to his patients and disciples he was both friends and mentor.

In 1900 he began the publication of a monthly magazine called "The Stuffed Club," which continued until 1915 when he changed the name to "The Philosophy of Health," and in 1926 the name was changed to "Health Review and Critique." His writing for his publication was almost entirely done in the early morning hours from three until seven. The purpose of the publication was not to make money but to spread knowledge of the Doctor's teachings. In time it attained a wide circulation not only in this country but also abroad, even in Australia. It never produced revenue for the Doctor refused to make it an advertising medium, as often urged to do by advertising firms. As his death revealed, after sixty-eight years of practice, the Doctor had accumulated only an exceedingly modest estate. His life was pre-eminently one of self-sacrifice and of devotion to service, searching after truth with an indomitable will and with an intense fortitude to adhere to the truth when discovered. In his day the Doctor's thoughts received no support from the established medical profession but brought the strongest of opposition and condemnation.

Frederic N. Gilbert

Editor's Preface

Of such timeless value is Dr. John H. Tilden's *Toxemia Explained* that the American Natural Hygiene Society through its Natural Hygiene Press takes great pride in republishing it as one of the great classics of health literature. In Dr. Tilden's immortal contribution is embodied the delineation of the physiological principles that are the bases for disease and healing.

Neither Dr. Tilden's *toxemia theory of disease causation* nor his prescribed course of patient care were new to Hygienic Practitioners. The pioneers of Natural Hygiene had anticipated him by the better part of a century, but none had so succinctly and correctly formulated the course of disease in humans from inception to correction as did Dr. Tilden.

Had not Dr. Tilden had such an observant and inquiring mind of great insight with the overweening drive to be of genuine help to his patients, the world might not today be endowed with this health masterpiece. Although Dr. Tilden was indebted to his Hygienic predecessors in renouncing the medical system and in employing many Hygienic measures in the care of his patients, he was possessed of much native ability and creativity. But there can be little doubt that he constructed this masterly treatise on the causation and correction of disease upon the existing edifice of Natural Hygienic health science.

It must be kept in mind that Dr. Tilden and most

of the early Natural Hygienic Practitioners were M.D.s who deserted the medical system. And, although Dr. Tilden observed the fundamental practices of Natural Hygiene in the care of the sick, notably in the employment of the fast, ample rest, relaxation and sleep, adequate sunshine, exercise and certain other factors truly conducive to health, he continued to employ some medical modalities and he did not employ the science of nutrition at the high level to which hygienists such as Dr. Herbert M. Shelton have brought it today. His patients fared well under the Hydienic measures he *did* observe and his procedures did have the virtue of removing most of the causes his patients' problems, i.e., medical treatments and their injurious habits and indulgences. Further, he taught his patients to observe many beneficial Hygienic practices in their daily lives.

In this revised modern edition of *Toxemia Explained* some of its language has been changed to more clearly reflect the Hygienic outlook and, wherever feasible, non-hygienic procedures Dr. Tilden recommended have been deleted. Even though such alterations have been made, great care has been exercised to insure that the essential contribution of Dr. Tilden to health science remains intact.

T. C. FRY

Preface

FROM time immemorial man has looked for a savior; and, when not looking for a savior, he is looking for a cure. He believes in paternalism. He is looking to get something for nothing, not knowing that the highest price we ever pay for anything is to have it given to us.

Instead of accepting salvation, it is better to deserve it. Instead of buying, begging or stealing a cure, it is better to stop building disease. Disease is of man's own building, and one worse thing than the stupidity of buying a cure is to remain so ignorant as to believe in cures.

The false theories of salvation and cures have built man into a mental mendicant when he could be the arbiter of his own salvation and certainly his own doctor instead of being a slave to a profession that has neither worked out its own salvation from disease nor discovered a single cure in all the age long period of man's existence on earth.

We hear of diet cures, dietitians, balanced rations, meat diets, vegetable diets and other diets—chemically prepared foods of all kinds. The reading public is bewildered with hundreds of health magazines and thousands of health ideas. There are thousands writing on health who would not recognize it if they should meet it on the street. Fanaticism, bigotry, stupidity and commercialism are the principal elements in the dietetic complex that is now belaboring the public.

Cures are what the people want and cures are what physicians and cultists affect to make; but at most only relief is given.

The periodicity which characterizes all functional derangements of the body lends color to the claims of cure-mongers that their remedy has cured their patients, when the truth is that the so-called disease "ran its course." The truth is that the so-called disease was a toxemic crisis, and when the toxin was eliminated below the toleration point, the sickness passed—automatically health returned. But the disease was not cured; for the cause (enervating habits) is continued, toxin still accumulates, and in due course of time another crisis appears. Unless the cause of toxemia is discovered and removed, crises will recur until functional derangements will give way to organic disease.

The entire medical profession is engaged in treating crises of toxemia—curing (?) and curing (?) until their patients are overtaken with chronic disease of whatever organ was the seat of the toxin crisis.

THERE ARE NO CURES

Nature returns to normal when enervating habits are given up. There are no cures in the sense generally understood. If one has a tobacco heart, what is the remedy? Stop the use of tobacco, of course. If the heart is worn out from shock, as we see it among gamblers or among men who, plunging in the stock

7

market, what will cure? Drugs? No! Removing the cause.

Every so-called disease is built within the mind and body by enervating habits. The food and dietetic insanity that constitutes the headliner on the medical stage just now is causing the people to demand a diet that will cure them of their peculiar maladies. The idea prevails that some peculiar diet will cure rheumatism or any other disease. Diet or food *will not cure any disease.*

A fast, rest in bed and the giving-up of enervating habits, mental and physical, will allow nature to eliminate the accumulated toxin; then, if enervating habits are given up, and rational living habits adopted, health will come back to stay, if the one HEALED will "stay put." This applies to any so-called disease. Yes, it fits your disease—you who write to find out if the Tilden system of healing applies to your case. Yes; cannot you realize that law and order pervades the universe? And it is the same from nebula to stone, from stone to plant, from plant to animal, from animal to man, from man to mind, and from mind to super-mind—God. To use a blanket expression: Law and order pervades the universe, the same yesterday, today and forever, and is the same from star-dust to mind—from electron to mind. Toxemia explains how the universal law operates in health and disease. One disease is the same as another; one man the same as another; one flower the same as another; the carbon in bread, sugar, coal and the diamond is the same. Yes, one disease can be healed the same as another unless the organ acted on by toxemic crises is destroyed.

8

For example: If wrong eating is persisted in, the acid fermentation first irritates the mucous membrane of the stomach; the irritation becomes inflammation, then ulceration, then thickening and hardening, which ends in cancer at last. The medical world is struggling to find the cause of cancer. It is the distal end of an inflammatory process whose proximal beginning may be any irritation. The end is degeneration from a lack of oxygen and nutriment and, in degenerating the septic material enters the circulation, setting up chronic septic poisoning called cancer cachexia.

Disease is a common expression of universal enervation (nervous exhaustion). An understanding of physiology and pathology necessitates a firm grip on evolution as expressed in biology; or reasoning will go astray occasionally.

Modern "cures" and "immunization" are vanity and vexation; they are founded on the foolish principle of reasoning from effect, which is disease, to cause. The organ which is suffering from many crises of toxemia is discovered—it may be ulcer of the stomach, then the ulcer is cut out; it may be gallstone, then the stone is cut out; it may be fibroid tumor of the womb, then the tumor or womb is cut out. The same may be said of other effects—the medical armament is turned loose on a lot of effects. This is accepted by the public mind as efficient treatment of disease when, in fact, it is a stupid removing of effects. And that is not the worst of such blundering. The operators have not the slightest idea of the cause of the effects they so skillfully remove.

In other derangements the same lack of knowledge of cause prevails. In the treatment of deficiency disease the lacking element is supplied from the laboratory but nothing is done in the line of restoring the organ to normalcy. Why? Because medical science has

9

not discovered why organs fail to function properly; and until this discovery is made, scientific blundering will continue.

The World Needs the Science of Surgery

If mutilation (unnecessary surgery) is required in nine hundred and ninety-nine cases to perfect the skill required in the thousandth case, the question of the need of high-class surgery must be answered by the mutilated or vandalized class.

Is war necessary? What would be the answer of the 7,485,000 who were killed in the First World War if the question were submitted to them? Estimate $5,000 as the manpower loss for each man; then the world lost $37,425,000,000 in this one item alone. Surgery costs the world in vandalizing the bodies of men, women and children as much per year. Is it worth that much for all the real good it does? Why is so much surgery thought to be necessary? Because of the ignorance of the people, egged on by a science-mad or selfish profession. It is more spectacular to operate than to teach people how to live to avoid chronic disease and operations.

Are Palliatives Ever Necessary?

It is doubtful the palliation which physicians and cultist give is worth the disadvantage that the sick habit taught the patients by their physician brings back.

The drug habit taught the thousands certainly overbalances any relief given. Drugs to relieve pain are never necessary. Twenty-five years in which I used

10

drugs and forty-two in which I have not used drugs should make my conviction that drugs are unnecessary and in most cases injurious, worth something to those who care to know the truth.

Yes, Venereal Diseases Can Be Overcome Without Drugs

I make no exception of syphilis and stand ready to demonstrate the truth of what I say at any time and anywhere to a committee of physicians.

Nature heals—nature can eliminate syphilis or any type of infection if all enervating habits are given up and a rational mode of living adopted.

Stimulants Are Subtly Undermining Of Health

So insidious of their action are all stimulants that the unwary are surprised by finding themselves more or less slaves to them when they are not conscious of using them to excess.

The coffee headache is an example. A time comes when it is not convenient to get the usual breakfast up. A dullness or languid feeling appears three or four hours after breakfast that cannot be accounted for until some friend suggests that perhaps it is due to missing the coffee, but the victim is not convinced until he proves it true by trying it out several times. Some develop a headache and still others are troubled with gaping or yawning and a feeling of oppression due to heart enervation brought on from the use of coffee.

11

At first stimulants gently remove awareness—remove tiredness and actuate the mind and body. It should be obvious to reasoning minds that borrowed activity must be paid for sooner or later.

Using nerve energy in excess of normal production brings on enervation. Few people waste nerve energy in one way only. Food is a stimulant. Overeating is overstimulating. Add to this excess one or two other stimulants—coffee or tobacco—excessive venery, overwork and worry, and one subject to that amount of drain of nerve energy will become decidedly enervated. Elimination falls far short of requirements; consequently, toxic matters accumulate in the body. This adds pronounced self-intoxication stimulation to that coming from overstimulating habits and completes a vicious circle. This complex stands for a disease-producing *toxemia* which will be permanent except as toxin crises—so-called acute diseases—lower the amount of toxin, again to accumulate and continue until the habits that keep the body enervated are controlled. Perfect health cannot be established until all enervating habits have been eliminated.

DEFINITION of toxemia *and crises of* toxemia:—
In the process of tissue building—metabolism—
there is cell building—anabolism—and cell destruc-
tion—catabolism. The broken down tissue is toxic
and in health—when nerve energy is normal—it is
eliminated from the blood as fast as evolved.
When nerve energy is dissipated from any cause—
physical or mental excitement or bad habits—the
body becomes enervated. When enervated elimi-
nation is checked, causing a retention of toxin in
the blood, or toxemia. *This accumulation of toxin*
when once established will continue until nerve
energy is restored by removing the causes. So-
called disease is nature's effort at eliminating the
toxin from the blood. All so-called diseases are
crises of toxemia.

CHAPTER I

INTRODUCTION TO TOXEMIA

THE medical world has built an infinite literature without any (except erroneous and vacillating) idea of cause. Medicine is rich in science, but now, as well as in the past, it suffers from a dearth of practical ideas. The average doctor is often educated out of all the common sense he was born with. This, however, is not his fault. It is the fault of the medical system. He is an educated automaton. He has facts—scientific facts galore—without ideas. Ford has mechanical facts—not more, perhaps, than thousands of other mechanics, but he joined them in an idea that made him a multimillionaire. Millions have facts, but no ideas. Thousands of doctors have all the scientific data needed, but they have not harnessed their science to common sense and philosophy.

Without a clear conception of cause, disease must remain the riddle that it is.

The late Sir James Mackenzie—while living, the greatest clinician in the world—declared: "In medical research the object is mainly the prevention and cure

15

of disease." If cause is not known, how is prevention or correction possible—as, for example, by producing a mild form of smallpox or other so-called disease by poisoning a healthy person by introducing into his body the pathological products of said disease? Certainly only pathological thinking can arrive at such conclusions. Vaccines and autogenous remedies are made from the products of disease, and the idea that disease can be made to cure itself is an end-product of pathological thinking. This statement is not so incongruous after we consider the fact that all search and research work by medical scientists to find cause has been made in dead and dying people. As ridiculous as it may appear medical science has gone and is still going to the dead and dying to find cause.

If prevention and cure mean producing disease, surely prevention and "cure" are not desirable. If prevention can be accomplished, then cures will not be needed.

At the time of his death Mackenzie was laboring to discover prevention. A more worthy work cannot be imagined. But the tragedy of his life was that he died from a preventable and correctible disease; and he could have survived this disease that killed him if his conception of cause had been in line with the *Truth* of *Toxemia*—the primary cause of all disease.

In spite of Mackenzie's ambition to put the profession in possession of truth concerning pervention and cure, he died without a correct idea of even in what direction to look for this desirable knowledge, as evidenced by such statements as: "Our problems being the prevention of disease, we require a complete knowledge of disease in all its aspects before we can take steps to prevent its occurrence." There is the crux of the whole subject. It is not disease; it is cause "in all its aspects" that we need to know before we can take steps to prevent "disease." Mackenzie stated the following concerning diagnosis:

But it appears to be unlikely that in the present state of medicine there would be any great dissimilarity in the proportions of diagnosed and undiagnosed cases in many series of investigations such as we have made. The proportion depends, not on the skill or training of individual practitioners, but on the unsatisfactory state of all medical knowledge. The similarity of the statistical records from the institute and from private practice goes far to support this view. In spite of the additional time given at the institute to the examination of cases which are undiagnosable in general practice, and the assistance given by the special departments—clinical groups—in their investigation, they remain profoundly obscure, although we know that it is from among them that there will gradually emerge the cases of advanced organic disease and the end-results which form so large a proportion of the inmates of hospital wards. And the tragedy is that many of them suffer from no serious disabilities, and might, but for our ignorance, be checked on their downward course.

Isn't that about as sharp a criticism of medical inefficiency as Tilden has ever made?

This brings vividly to mind the statement made only a short time ago by Dr. Cabot, of Boston, that he himself was mistaken in his diagnoses about fifty per cent of the time—that he had proved it by post-mortems. Such a statement as this, coming from a man of his standing, means much. To me it means that diagnosis is a meaningless term; for, as used, it means discovering what pathological effects—what changes—have been brought about by an undiscovered cause. Diagnosis means, in a few words, discovering effects which, when found, throw no light whatever on cause.

17

Again I quote Mackenzie: "The knowledge of disease is so incomplete that we do not yet even know what steps should be taken to advance our knowledge." This being true, there is little excuse for laws to shut out or prevent cults from practicing less harmful palliations. How many reputable physicians have the honesty of Sir James Mackenzie?

In spite of Mackenzie's high and worthy ambitions he could not get away from the profession's stereotyped thinking. The early symptoms of disease he declared held the secret of their cause, and he believed an intense study of them would give the facts. But functional derangements are of the same nature and from the same universal cause that ends in all so-called organic diseases. All so-called diseases are from beginning to end the same evolutionary process.

The study of pathology—the study of disease—has engaged the best minds in the profession always, and it surely appears that the last word must have been spoken on the subject; but the great Englishman believed, as all research workers believe, that a more intense and minute study of the early symptoms of disease will reveal the cause. There is, however, one great reason why it cannot, and that is that all symptom-complexes—diseases—from their initiation to their ending are effects and the most intense of any phrase or stage of their progress will not throw any light on the cause.

Cause is constant, ever present and always the same. Only effects and the object on which cause acts change, and the change is most inconstant. To illustrate: A catarrh of the stomach presents first irritation, then inflammation, then ulceration, and finally induration and cancer. Not all cases run true to form; only a small percentage evolve to ulcer, and fewer still reach the cancer stage. More exit by way of acute "food" poisoning or acute indigestion than by chronic diseases.

In the early stages of this evolution there are all kinds of discomforts: more or less attacks of indigestion, frequent attacks of gastritis—upset stomach and vomiting. No two cases are alike. Nervous people suffer most and some present all kinds of nervous symptoms—insomnia, headaches, etc. Women have painful menstruation and hysterical symptoms—some are morose and others have epilepsy. As the more chronic symptoms appear, those of the lymphatic temperament do not suffer so much. As the disease progresses, a few become pallid and develop pernicious anemia due to gastric or intestinal ulceration and putrid protein infection; in others the first appearance of ulcer is manifested by a severe hemorrhage; others have a cachexia and a retention of food in the stomach, which is vomited every two or three days, caused by a partial closing of the pylorus. These are usually malignant cases.

To look upon any of these symptom-complexes as a distinct disease requiring a distinct treatment, is to fall into the diagnostic maze that now bewilders the profession and renders treatment chaotic.

It should be known to all discerning physicians that the earliest stage of organic disease is purely functional, evanescent and never autogenerated so far as the affected organ is concerned but is invariably due to an extraneous irritation (stimulation, if you please, augmented by *toxemia*. When the irritation is not continuous and toxin is eliminated as fast as developed to the toleration point, normal functioning is resumed between the intervals of irritation and toxin excess.

19

For example: a simple coryza (running at the nose—cold in the head), gastritis or colonitis. At first these colds, catarrhs or inflammations are periodic and functional; but, as the exciting cause or causes—local irritation and *toxemia*—become more intense and continuous, the mucous membranes of these organs take on organic changes, which are given various names, such as irritation, inflammation, ulceration and cancer. The pathology (organic change) may be studied until doomsday without throwing any light on the cause; for from the first irritation to the extreme ending—cachexia—which may be given the blanket term of tuberculosis, syphilis or cancer, the whole pathologic panorama is one continuous evolution of intensifying effects.

Germs and other so-called causes may be discovered in the course of pathological development, but they are accidental, coincidental or at most auxiliary—or, to use the vernacular of law, *obiter dicta*.

The proper way to study disease is to study health and every influence favorable or not to its continuance. Disease is vitiated health. Any influence that lowers nerve energy becomes disease producing. Disease cannot be its own cause; it has antecedent cause.

After years of wandering in the jungle of medical diagnosis—the usual guesswork of cause and effect and the worse-than-guesswork of treatment and becoming more confounded all the time—I resolved either to quit the profession or to find the cause of disease. To do this it was necessary to exile myself from physicians and medical conventions; for I could not think for myself while listening to the babblings of babeldom. I took the advice found in Matthew 6:6.

According to prevailing opinion, unless a physician spends much time in medical societies and in the society of other physicians, takes postgraduate work, travels, etc., he cannot keep abreast of advancement.

This opinion would be true if the sciences of medicine were fitted to a truthful etiology (efficient cause) of disease. But, since they are founded on no cause or at most speculative and spectacular causes, as unstable as the sands of the sea, the physician who cannot brook the bewilderment of vacillation is compelled to hide away from the voices of mistaken pedants and knowing blather-skites until stabilized. By that time ostracism will have overtaken him and his fate, metaphorically speaking, will be that of the son of Zacharias.

An honest search after truth too often, if not always, leads to the rack, stake, cross or the blessed privilege of recanting; but the victim by this time decides as did the diving Jew: "Not My will, but Thine, be done;" or, as Patrick Henry declared: "Give me liberty or give me death!" The dying words of another great Irishman, Emmet, is the wish, no doubt, of every lover of freedom and truth:

That no man write my epitaph; for, as no man who knows my motives dares now vindicate them, let not prejudice or ignorance asperse them. Let them and me rest in peace, and my tomb remain uninscribed, and my memory in oblivion, until other times and other men can do justice to my character. When my country takes her place among the nations of the earth, then, and not until then, let my epitaph be written.

The truth is larger than any man and until it is established the memory of its advocate is not important. In the last analysis is not truth the only immortality?

Man is an incident. If he discovers a truth it benefits all who accept it. Truth too often must pray to be delivered from its friends.

I must acknowledge that I have not been very courteous to indifferent convention; and the truth I have discovered has suffered thereby. It has always appeared to me that the attention of fallacy-mongers cannot be attracted except by the use of a club of shillalah; and possibly my style of presenting my facts has caused too great a shock and the desired effect has been lost in the reaction.

That I have discovered the true cause of disease cannot be successfully disputed. This being true, my earnestness in presenting this great truth is justifiable.

When I think back over my life and remember the struggle I had with myself in supplanting my old beliefs with the new—the thousands of times I have doubted my own sanity—I then cannot be surprised at the opposition I have met and am meeting.

My discovery of the truth that *toxemia* is the cause of all so-called diseases came about slowly, step by step, with many dangerous skids.

At first I believed that enervation must be the general cause of disease; then I decided that simple enervation is not disease, that disease must be due to poison, and that poison, to be the general cause of disease, must be autogenerated; and if disease is due to autogenerated poison, what is the cause of that autogeneration? I dallied long in endeavoring to trace disease back to poison taken into the system, such as food eaten after putrescence had begun, or from poisoning due to the development of putrescence after ingestion. In time I decided that poisoning per se is not disease. I observed where poisoning did not kill; some cases reacted and were soon in full

22

health while others remained in a state of semi-invalidism. I found the same thing true of injuries and mental shock. It took a long time to develop the thought that a poisoned or injured body, when not overwhelmed by *toxemia*, would speedily return to the normal; and when it did not, there was a sick habit—a derangement of some kind—that required some such contingency to bring it within sense perception.

To illustrate: An injury to a point is often complicated with rheumatism; the rheumatism previous to the injury was potentially in the blood.

Just what change has taken place in the organism which, under stress of injury or shock of any kind, would cause a reaction with fever, I could not understand until the *toxemic theory* suggested itself to my mind, after which the cause of disease unfolded before me in an easy and natural manner. And now the theory is a proved fact.

After years of perplexing thought and "watchful waiting," I learned that all disease, of whatever nature, was of slow development; that without systemic preparation even so-called acute systemic disease could not manifest.

In a few words: Without *toxemia* there can be no disease. I knew that the waste products of metabolism were toxic and that the only reason why we were not poisoned by them was because they were removed from the organism as fast as produced. Then I decided that the toxin was retained in the blood when there was a checking of elimination. Then the cause of the checking had to be determined. In time I thought out the cause. I knew that, when we had normal nerve energy, organic functioning was normal. Then

23

came the thought that enervation caused a checking of elimination. Eureka! The cause of all so-called diseases is found! Enervation checks elimination of the waste products of metabolism. Thus retention of metabolic toxin is the first and only cause of disease!

Those who would be freed from the bondage of medical superstition should study "*Toxemia Explained.*"

CHAPTER II

TOXEMIA EXPLAINED

No ONE outside of the medical profession knows so well as physicians themselves the great need of more knowledge of what disease really is. Never in the history of so-called medical science has there been so much research work done as in the past decade; but with every new discovery there follows very closely on its heels the stark and stalking nemesis that chills the honest and earnest researchers to the bone—the inevitable word *failure*. Why inevitable? Because back in the beginning of man's reasoning on the subject of his discomforts, his pains and his sickness he made the monstrous mistake that something outside of himself—outside of his own volition—had wished him harm. Man being a religious animal, he early thought he had in some manner offended one of his many deities. The history of how man evolved the idea of disease being an entity is too long to do more than allude to it in a book of this kind. Any of the old mythologies may be referred to by those who are curious enough to look the matter up. That man is still saturated with centuries of mythological inheritance was brought out vividly when the germ theory was introduced. It answered the instinctive call for demoniacal possession! At last man's search for the demon—the author of all his woes—had been re-warded, and a satisfactory apology could be made to his conscience for all his apparent shortcomings. However, eighty years of vicarious atonement for man's sins by the demon germ are waning and reason be praised if the microbe is the last excuse that man can make for his sins of omission and commission before the throne of his own reason!

Medical science is founded on a false premise—namely, that disease is caused by extraneous influences and that drugs are something that "cures" or palliates discomfort. The term "medical" means pertaining to medicine or the practice of medicine. Anything used intended in a remedial way carries the idea of curing, healing, correcting or affording relief; thereapeutics are all administered without any clear understanding of cause.

The words *medical, medicine, disease,* and *cure* have become concrete in our understanding and shape our thoughts and beliefs. So arbitrary are these beliefs that new schools and cults are forced to the conventional understanding. They may declare that an impinged nerve is the cause of any pathology. But they do not trouble themselves to find why one impinged nerve creates a pathology and another does not.

The psychologist does not trouble himself to explain why worry in one subject causes disease and in another it does not; why hope in one subject heals and in another it does not; why negation does not always heal; why faith does not always heal; begging the question by declaring that there was not faith enough, etc. No fool is a bigger fool than the fool who fools himself.

Why should not all new schools of thought be found harking back to their mother thought—I say why not? So long as the idea that disease is a reality, an individuality, an entity, is firmly fixed in the mind, even those in research work will be controlled and directed in their labors by the conventional understanding. That is why every wonderful discovery soon proves a mistaken belief.

There is no hope that medical science will ever be a science; for the whole structure is built around the idea that there is an entity—disease—that can be exorcised when the right drug is found.

It is my intention to portray the common, every day foibles of scientific medicine so that the people may see the absurdities concerning disease and cure which they are and have been hood-winked into believing by the blare of science. Then I shall describe the only worked out rational explanation of the cause of so-called diseases, hoping by contrasting the old and new, to start a few to thinking and building new brain cells which in time may supersede the old and conventional.

Until *toxemia* was discovered and elaborated by myself into a philosophy, there was no real light shed upon disease, its causation and purpose. The cause and correction of disease is and has been a medley of guesswork and speculation which has confounded the best and most industrious medical minds in every generation.

Today, as never before, the brightest minds in the profession are delving into research work endeavoring to find the efficient cause of disease. But they are doomed to disappointment; for they fail at their beginning. Why? Because all the work that has ever been done in searching for cause has been along the line of critical study and examination of effects; and certainly reasoning minds cannot believe that an effect can be its own cause. No one believes in spontaneous generation. The remnant of this belief was annihilated by Pasteur's discovery of germs as the cause of fermentation—a discovery so profound that it created a frenzy in the medical world; and, as in every epidemic of frenzy, mental poise was lost. The importance of the germ as a primary or efficient cause of disease was accepted *nolens volens,* willy-nilly. Everyone was swept off his feet. As in all sudden gushes in change of belief, it was dangerous not to agree with the mob spirit; hence opposing or conservative voices were suppressed or ostracized.

The germ frenzy was fierce for two or three decades; but now it is a thing of the past and will soon be, if not now, a dead letter.

Cause of disease is being looked for everywhere, and no less a personage than the late Sir James Mackenzie in *Reports of the St. Andrews Institute for Clinical Research,* Volume I, declared: "The knowledge of disease is so incomplete that we do not yet even know what steps should be taken to advance our knowledge." At another time he wrote: "Disease is made manifest to us only by the symptoms which it produces; the first object in the examination of a patient is the detection of symptoms, and therefore the symptoms of disease form one of the main objects of our study."

THE VALUE OF SYMPTOMATOLOGY

Sir James, when living, was probably the greatest clinician of the English-speaking world; yet he had not outlived the medical superstition that disease is a positive entity and that the way to find disease is to trace symptoms to their source. But if a symptom is traced to its source, what of it? A pain is traced to its source and we find that it comes from the head. The head does not cause the pain. Then we find that there are symptoms of hyperemia—too much blood in the head. The pressure from too much blood in the head causes the pain. Then pressure must be the disease? No. Then too much blood is the disease—hyperemia? Certainly; too much blood in the head was a cause. What is it that causes congestion? We find that pain is a symptom. Pressure causes pain; it, too, is a symptom. Too much blood in the head causes pressure; it also is a symptom. Pain, pressure, hyperemia are all three symptoms. In time the walls of the blood-vessels weaken and the pressure ruptures one of the vessels. Hemorrhage into the brain causes death from apoplexy. Is the ruptured blood-vessel the disease? No. Is hemorrhage into the brain disease? No; it is a symptom. Is death from hemorrhage the disease?

If the hemorrhage is not severe enough to cause death but does produce some form of paralysis—and there can be many kinds—is paralysis a disease? Haven't we been traveling along a chain of symptoms from headache to paralysis? We have not found anything to which all these symptoms point as disease; and, according to the requirements of Sir James Mackenzie, disease is made manifest to us only by symptoms. Here we have a chain of symptoms beginning with pain, ending in hemorrhage and death or paralysis without giving us any indication whatever of cause as understood. Any other chain, namely, stomach symptoms, ending in pyloric cancer, will not give any more indication of disease at the various stages than the foregoing illustration.

The first symptom we have of any chain of symptoms is discomfort or pain. In any stomach derangement we have pain, more or less aggravated by food. Catarrh follows or, more often, precedes it—or what we call inflammation or gastritis. Gastritis continues with a thickening of the mucous membrane. A time comes when there is ulceration. This will be called a disease and is recognized as ulcer of the stomach; but it is only a continuation of the primary symptoms of catarrh and pain. The ulcer is removed but the symptom of inflammation and pain continues and other ulcers will follow. This state eventually emerges into induration or hardening of the pyloric orifice of the stomach. When this develops, there is more or less obstruction to the outlet causing occasional vomiting and on thorough examination cancer is found.

If we analyze the symptoms from the first pain and catarrh in the stomach, we shall find the chain of symptoms running along. The first symptom to be noticed is pain. On examination we find a catarrhal condition of the stomach; and this catarrhal condition is not a disease—it is a symptom. Catarrhal inflammation continues with the thickening of the mucous membrane, which finally ends in ulceration. Ulceration is not the disease; it is only a continuation of the inflammatory symptom. If the ulcer is removed it does not remove the disease; it only removes a symptom. These symptoms continue until there is a thickening and induration of the pyloris, which is called cancer. And yet we have not discovered anything but symptoms from beginning to end.

By removing the cancer, the question of what the disease is has not been answered. Cancer being the end symptom, it cannot be the cause of the first symptom.

Any other so-called disease can be worked out in the same way. Pain and catarrh are the first symptoms, as a rule, that call a physician's or a patient's attention to anything being wrong; and pain and catarrh are not the disease. When the cause of the pain is found, it too will be found a symptom and not a disease. And this will be true to the end.

It is no wonder that diagnosticians become perplexed in their search after disease, because they have confounded symptoms and disease. The fact of the matter is, it is impossible to put the finger on any ending of a chain of symptoms and say: "This is the disease." In the beginning of this analysis we showed that headache, or pain in the head, is not a disease; and when we had finished we found that hemorrhage or apoplexy is not a disease—it is only a continuation of the primary symptoms.

"Disease is made manifest to us only by symptoms which it produces." This statement tacitly infers that there are diseases and symptoms and that through symptoms we may find disease. When we undertake to trace symptoms to disease we are in the dilemma of a mountain climber who, on reaching the top of one mountain, finds other peak and higher ones farther on and on.

That Mackenzie had been baffled in his search for fixed disease is indicated in the following, which I quote from the reports mentioned before:

Many diseases are considered to be of a dangerous nature, and many attempts are made to combat the danger, with, however, no perception of its nature. This is particularly the case with epidemic diseases, such as measles, influenza, scarlet fever, and diphtheria. As a consequence, proposals have at different times been put forward to treat individuals who suffer from these diseases upon some general plan, without consideration of the peculiarities of the individual case—and thus we get that rule-of-thumb treatment which is shown in the indiscriminate use of a serum or vaccine.

During influenza epidemics there is always a cry for a universal method of treatment, and attempts are made to meet this cry in the shape of so-called specifics and vaccines.

When a great authority declares that dangerous diseases are combated without any perception of their nature—and that, too, in spite of the germ theory—it should be obvious to thinking minds that the germ theory has been weighed and found wanting. Yet when something must be done and nothing better has been discovered, "serums and vaccines may be used indiscriminately."

That the "rule of thumb" is the rule governing all thinking concerning symptoms, the cause and treatment of diseases are so obvious that anyone possessing a reasoning mind, not camouflaged by scientific buncombe, should readily see on the run.

Medicine rests on a sound scientific foundation. Anatomy, physiology, biology, chemistry and all collateral sciences that have a bearing on the science of man, are advanced to great perfection. But the so-called sciences of symptomatology, disease, diagnosis, etiology and the treatment of disease go back to superstition for their foundation. We see the incongruity of jumbling real science with delusion and superstition. Disease is believed to be an entity; and this idea is necessarily followed by another as absurd—namely, cure. Around these two old assumptions has grown an infinite literature that confounds its builders.

32

When a man's knowledge is not in order, the more of it he has, the greater will be his confusion.—Herbert Spencer.

Confusion worse confounded is the only explanation that can be given of the theory and practice of medicine. Of course it is hoary with age and is one of the learned professions. With much just pride can the rank and file point to its aristocracy—its long list of famous dead as well as living physicians. What has made most of them famous? The same that has made others famous in and out of the professions—namely, personal worth and education. Franklin was not a physician; yet he was as great as any and could use his gray manner in advising the sick as well as those not sick. He appeared to have a sense perception for truth; and I would say that his discrimination is the leading, if not the distinguishing, trait that has divided and always will divide the really great from the mediocre majority. They are the leaven that leaven the whole herd of humanity—the quality of character that could not be found in all Sodom and Gomorrah.

There was another discriminating mind in the eighteenth century—another Benjamin, who also was a signer of the Declaration of Independence—Benjamin Rush, a physician, a luminary that brought distinction to medical science. He was larger than his profession. He left seeds of thought which, if acted upon by the profession, would have organized medical thought and prevented the present day confusion. He left on record such golden nuggets as:

Much mischief has been done by the nosological arrangement of diseases. . . . Disease is as much a unit as fever. . . .

Its different seats and degrees should no more be multiplied into different diseases than the numerous and different effects of heat and light upon our globe should be multiplied into a plurality of suns.

The whole materia medica is infected with the baneful consequences of the nomenclature of disease; for every article in it is pointed only against their name. . . . By the rejection of the artificial arrangement of diseases, a revolution must follow in medicine. . . . The road to knowledge in medicine by this means will likewise be shortened; so that a young man will be able to qualify himself to practice physic at a much less expense of time and labor than formerly, as a child would learn to read and write by the help of the Roman alphabet, instead of Chinese characters.

Science has much to deplore from the multiplication of diseases. It is repugnant to truth in medicine as polytheism is to truth in religion. The physician who considers every different affection of the different parts of the same system as distinct diseases, when they arise from one cause, resembles the Indian or African savage who considers water, dew, ice, frost, and snow as distinct essences; while the physician who considers the morbid affections of every part of the body, however diversified they may be in their form or degrees, as derived from one cause, resembles the philosopher who considers dew, ice, frost, and snow as different modifications of water, and as derived simply from the absence of heat.

Humanity has likewise much to deplore from this paganism in medicine. The sword will probably be sheathed forever, as an instrument of death, before physicians will cease to add to the mortality of mankind by prescribing for the names of diseases.

There is but one remote cause of disease. . . . These remarks are of extensive application, and, if duly attended to, would deliver us from a mass of error which has been accumulating for ages in medicine; I mean the nomenclature of disease from their remote causes. It is the most offensive and injurious part of the rubbish of our science.

The physician who can cure one disease by a knowledge of its principles may by the same means cure all the diseases of the human body; for their causes are the same.

There is the same difference between the knowldge of a physician who prescribes for diseases as limited by genera and species, and of one who prescribes under the direction of just principles, that there is between the knowledge we obtain of the nature and extent of the sky, by viewing a few feet of it from the bottom of a well, and viewing from the top of a mountain the whole canopy of heaven.

I would as soon believe that ratafia was intended by the Author of Nature to be the only drink of man, instead of water, as believe that the knowledge of what relates to the health and lives of a whole city, or nation, should be confined to one, and that a small or a privileged, order of men.

From a short review of these facts, reason and humanity awake from their long repose in medicine, and unite in proclaiming that it is time to take the cure of pestilential epidemics out of the hands of physicians, and to place it in the hands of the people.

Dissections daily convince us of our ignorance of the seats of disease, and cause us to blush at our prescriptions. . . . What mischief have we done under the belief of false facts, if I may be allowed the expression, and false theories! We have assisted in multiplying disease. We have done more—we have increased their mortality.

I shall not pause to beg pardon of the faculty for acknowledging, in this public manner, the weakness of our profession. I am pursuing Truth, and while I can keep my eye fixed upon my guide, I am indifferent whither I am led, provided she is my leader.

Oliver W. Holmes, M.D., was a man who gave dignity and respectibility to the profession. He was a literary man and from his beginning to his end was always larger than his profession. He once said: "I firmly believe that, if the whole materia medica could be sunk to the bottom of the sea, it would be all the better for mankind and all the worse for the fishes." *Breakfast-Table Series* will be read by the intelligent people of the future, who will know nothing of Holmes' fight for women against the dirty hands of herd-doctors and their consequences—puerperal fever.

Aequanimitas will keep Osler in the minds of intelligent people when Osler's *Practice of Medicine* will be found only in the shops of bibliomaniacs. Such men as Osler keep the dead weight of mediocre medicine from sinking to oblivion by embellishing medical fallacies with their superb personalities and their literary polish.

Throughout all the ages the finest minds have sensed the truth concerning the cause of disease—and this has bulked large against medical insanities and inanities.

A very striking picture of the medical herd was made by "Anonymous" in his essay on "Medicine" in "Civilization in the United States."

It has been remarked above that one of the chief causes of the unscientific nature of medicine and the antiscientific character of physicians lies in their innate credulity and inability to think independently. This contention is supported by the report on the intelligence of physicians recently published by the National Research Council. They are found by more or less trustworthy psychologic tests to be lowest in intelligence of all professional men, excepting only dentists and vetinarians. Dentists and vetinarians are ten per cent less intelligent. But since the quantitative methods employed certainly carry an experimental error of ten per cent or even higher, it is not certain that the members of the two more humble professions have not equal or even greater intellectual ability. It is significant that engineers head the list in intelligence. In fact, they are rated sixty per cent higher than physicians.

This inside disparity leads to a temptation to interesting psychological probings. Is not the lamentable lack of intelligence of the physician due to lack of necessity for rigid intellectual discipline? Many conditions conspire to make him an intellectual cheat. Fortunately for us, most diseases are self-limiting. But it is natural for the physician to turn this dispensation of nature to his advantage and to intimate that he cured John Smith, when actually nature has done the trick. On the contrary, should Smith die, the good physician can assume a pious expression and suggest that, despite his own incredible skill and tremendous effort, it was God's (or nature's) will that John should pass beyond. Now, the engineer is open to no such temptation. He builds a bridge or erects a building, and disaster is sure to follow any misstep in calculation or fault in construction. Should such a calamity occur, he is presently disqualified and disappears from view. Thus he is held up to a high mark of intellectual rigor and discipline that is utterly unknown in the world the physician inhabits.

The critic appears to think that "one of the chief causes of the antiscientific character of physicians lies in their innate credulity and inability to think independently." I presume he means that the physicians cannot think independently; for if medicine, scientific or unscientific, could think at all, it might have thought itself out of its present day muddle.

The only thing that saves all physicians from the above indictment is that they are not examined on the cause and treatment of disease. If average physicians pass low on "trustworthy psychological tests," it does not speak very well for the higher education which put so many medical students out of business a few years ago. But these psychological tests may be fitted to educational standards which are assembled with intelligence left out. Intelligence, like the *cause* of *disease*, is a force in nature that can be used under the proper environments; but it cannot be monopolized to the exclusion of all mankind. Gladstone in youth was passed upon by the psychological test of his teacher and pronounced incorrigible; yet at eighty-six he was wielding an ax and translating Virgil.

SCIENTIFIC TESTS

People should not take too seriously to heart verdicts resting on scientific tests, where a very large part of the integral is scientific assumption and presumption. The New York Life Insurance Company turned me down more than fifty years ago.

"Anonymous," whoever he is, writes well, and as that of an iconoclast, his style is quite fetching. But, to save his bacon, it was well that he criticized from ambush; for he would make an excellent target. From my point of view I find him as vulnerable as any Standard A type of professional men.

He shows his medical length and breadth when he says: "Of all the dreadful afflictions that plague us a few may be cured or ameliorated by the administration of remedies." That was said by medical men now one and two hundred years dead and with no more aplomb than that of the physicians of today in the literary class of our "Anonymous."

"Dreadful afflictions" do not "plague us." If we are plagued by disease, it is of our own building; and all we need to do to get back to comfort and health is to quit building disease; then our subconscious self gets busy cleaning house.

38

"Anonymous" could not have made a statement that would have been more perfectly one hundred per cent fallacy. He says: "A few may be cured." That is a mild statement coming from one of the ambushed Caesars of scientific medicine. I presume he means that there is a contingent possibility that a few can be "cured." This is false; for "afflictions" or disease cannot be "cured." Nature—our subconsciousness—has a full monopoly on the power to heal. Healing is nature's prerogative and she cannot, if she would, delegate it to physicians or to the academies of medical science.

What a glorious legacy vouchsafed by the powers that be! What a sad plight humanity would be in if medical commercialism had a monopoly on healing or "curing" the sick! It does very well, however, as it is vending its camouflage "cures" of all kinds. But when mankind awakens to a full realization of the truth that for all the past time it has been buying a pretense of power of which it alone possesses a monopoly, old hoary-headed Aesculapius will be unfrocked and thrown out of business—staff, snake, and all.

"Anonymous," fearing that the statement, "A few may be cured," was too strong, added the modifying phrase "or ameliorated;" which, in medical parlance, means palliated, relieved, etc. This in reality is the whole truth concerning so-called remedies or "cures." And when the truth is known that healing, or the power to throw off disease and get well, is wholly within the subconscious and is personal, we will know that curing and palliating by the administration of remedies—drugs, serums, vaccines, surgery, feeding to keep up the strength, etc.—are superfluous, meddlesome, and on the order of throwing a monkey wrench into the machinery.

39

After criticizing "Anonymous" for what we know, inferentially, that he stands for, we will quote the remainder of what he says concerning the treatment of the "dreadful afflictions that plague us." He further declares:

And an equally small number improved or were abolished by surgical interference. But in spite of the relatively few diseases to which surgery is beneficial, the number of surgeons that flourished in the land is enormous. The fundamental discoveries of Pasteur and their brilliant application by Lister were quickly seized upon in America. The names of Bull, Halstead, Murphy, the brothers Mayo, Cushing and Finney are to be ranked with those of the best surgeons of any nation. In fact, we may be said to lead the world—to use an apt Americanism—in the production of surgeons (and surgical plants), just as we do in that of automobiles, baby-carriages and antique furniture.

"A few diseases may be cured or ameliorated." I say never "cured," and amelioration is a form of building disease.

A delicate woman became my patient after suffering from megrim for twenty-two years and taking more or less palliatives from twenty-two different physicians—a few widely known, one a neurologist of more than national fame; the majority of whom told her that there was no cure, but that, when she changed life, the headaches would cease. This was a "bum" guess; for she declared that her suffering had been greater the past two years, since her menstruation had ceased, than ever before. Just how much the psychological suggestion, made by fifteen or twenty physicians, that she would not get well for a given time, had to do with prolonging her headaches, no one can tell. Drug palliation is always inclined to enervate and build *toxemia*. This woman had been relieved by hypodermics of morphine—a fiendish treatment. There should be a law against such malpractice. But the majority never handicap themselves with prohibitory laws.

My prescription was: No more smoking in the home (the husband being an inveterate smoker); stay in bed; fast until a paroxysm of headache had been missed.

The paroxysms had been coming weekly, beginning on Tuesday and leaving her prostrate until Friday. The patient had only one paroxysm after becoming my patient. The husband became very enthusiastic over the fact that his wife had been relieved of her pain without drugs for the first time in twenty-two years. My comment on his outburst of rejoicing was: "Your smoking and the drugging were responsible for her unnecessary suffering during nearly a quarter of a century."

Drugging pain of any kind checks elimination and prevents the human organism from cleaning house. In this case of megrim, every time an eliminating crisis developed, the physician slammed the doors of egress shut and barred them with morphine. My prescription reversed the order: it opened all the doors with the result that she never had another headache. Of course, I tinkered with her eating and other habits afterwards. People are never sick who have no bad habits.

About the same time I advised another woman who had suffered weekly from paroxysms of megrim for sixteen years. Like the first case she had been medicated by many physicians and told she need not expect relief until after the change of life. This woman, too, had one paroxysm after giving up her drug palliation and making a few changes in her daily habits.

41

Here were two patients with a "dreadful affliction," which was kept "dreadful" by a senseless and criminal medication—and that, too, by physicians holding degrees from class A colleges.

I refer to these two cases to illustrate what "Anonymous" means by saying: "Few diseases may be cured or ameliorated." Megrim is not cured; and if doping, as these two cases were doped, is ameliorating, some other name should be used to designate the procedure.

CRISES

According to the toxin philosophy every so-called disease is a crisis of toxemia; which means that toxin has accumulated in the blood above the toleration point, and the crisis, the so-called disease—call it cold, "flu," pneumonia, headache or typhoid fever— is a vicarious elimination. Nature is endeavoring to rid the body of toxin. Any treatment that obstructs this effort at elimination baffles nature in her effort at self-healing.

Drugs, feeding, fear and keeping at work prevent elimination. A cold is driven into chronic catarrh; "flu" may be forced to take on an infected state; pneumonia may end fatally if secretions are checked by drugs; we already know what becomes of headaches; typhoid will be forced into a septic state and greatly prolonged if the patient is not killed.

The above illustrates how "a few cases may be cured or ameliorated." But the story is different when the attending physician *knows* that every so-called disease is a complex of symptoms signifying a crisis of *toxemia*—nature's house cleaning. And she—nature— can succeed admirably if not interferred with by venders of poison, who are endeavoring to destroy an imaginary entity lurking somewhere in the system, which is mightily increased and intensified by the vender's "cures" or amelioratives.

It is a real pleasure for the physician who knows that he cannot "cure" anything to watch nature throw off all these symptoms by elimination if he is willing to do a little "watchful waiting" and "keep hands off." The patient will be comfortable most of the time and will say when asked how he is: "I feel all right; I am comfortable." Patients never answer in that way when drugged and fed. Yes, when nature is not hindered by officious professional meddling, sick people can truthfully say when well over a crisis of house cleaning: "I had a very comfortable sickness." Nature is not revengeful. Great suffering, chronic and fatal maladies are built by the incorrigibleness of patients and the well-meaning but belligerent efforts of the physicians who fight the imaginary foe without ceasing. The people are so saturated with the idea that disease must be fought to a finish that they are not satisfied with conservative treatment. Something must be done even if they pay for it with their lives as tens of thousands do every year. This willingness to die on the altar of medical superstition is one very great reason why no real improvement is made in fundamental medical science. When the people demand education—not medication, vaccination and immunization—they will get it.

Is there nothing for a physician to do? Yes, of course! He should enter the sick room with a smile and a cheerful word, free from odors and neat and clean; be natural and free from affectations. He should not tell at how many confinements he officiated the night before or how many thousands he has had in

43

the past ten years. Professional lobbying is not appropriate in the sickroom. Patients should have confidence in their physician; and if he does a lot of medico-political lying, the patient will know it, and it sloughs confidence.

He should advise something warm to the feet; perfect quiet; no food, liquid or solid, and positively no drugs but all the water desired; a warm bath at night and as often as necessary to secure comfort. Rest, warmth, fresh air and quiet are conducive to healing. Then the physician should educate his patient into proper living habits so as to avoid future crises of *toxemia*.

When the regime is carried out and nature is allowed full control, the pessimistic statement of "Anonymous" that "a few diseases may be cured or ameliorated" can be changed to read: "All acute so-called diseases will get well and will stay well if patients will practice self-control concerning the enervating habits that brought on the crisis of *toxemia*. Where this plan is carried out faithfully, so-called chronic diseases will never be built.

All Diseases Once Innocent

Cancer, tuberculosis, Bright's disease and all chronic diseases were once innocent colds "ameliorated" and which returned and were "ameliorated" again and again; each time accompanied by a greater constitutional enervation and a greater constitutional toleration for toxin-poisoning, requiring a greater requisition of mucous and submucous tissue through which to eliminate the toxin.

Research is being carried on vigorously in an attempt to find the cause of disease, the conception of disease being that it is an entity. All the so-called diseases are increasing symptom complexes due to repeated crises of toxemia. They have no independent existence. As soon as *toxemia* is controlled they disappear, unless an organ has been forced by innumerable crises to degenerate. Even organic change, when the organ is not destroyed, will be overcome by correcting the life and getting rid of the cause—crises of *toxemia.*

To find the cause of cancer start with colds and catarrh and watch the pathology as it travels from irritation, catarrh, inflammation, induration, ulceration to cancer.

As well try to find the cause of man by ignoring his conception, embryonic life, childhood, manhood, etc.

All symptoms of all so-called diseases have one origin. All diseases are one. Unity in all things is nature's plan. Polytheism is gone, and overything pertaining to it and coming out of it must go.

HERD BELIEFS

Few realize man's possibilities if his handicaps are removed—handicaps which are old beliefs and herd instincts.

The *toxemic philosophy* is founded on the truth that there is no such thing as cure. In this it differs from all the so-called curing systems. Every pretense or promise of cure in all lines of therapeutics is false. This cannot be grasped by all minds until time for thinking has allowed the idea to soak in. Convention and superstition have the floor and they are unwilling to sit down and listen to the other side. Many learn slowly, others not at all and still others are put to sleep mentally by truth.

There are ox-cart minds in every generation. The well-known episode at Dayton, Tennessee, should quell the enthusiasm of those who think the world has outgrown superstition. I have buckled up against medical superstition of all kinds all my life and I know that clear-thinking minds are as scarce as hens' teeth. Many compliment me on my clear reasoning on medical subjects; but the moment I cross the border-line into their ethical, moral and theological preserves, they remind me of my trespassing in no uncertain terms. Even my own profession is quick to ink the waters of my reasoning by declaring that I am an infidel—a word that fills the elect with abhorrence. Who is an infidel? One who rejects a senseless convention. Didn't Christ repudiate the Jehovistic cult?

The average mind prefers the old intepretation of words to the "new-fangled" definitions. Until the world agrees on one dictionary, one Bible and one God, the tempest in the teapot of misunderstanding will continue to ebullate, sending the atomized fundamentalists heavenward and the unatomized modernists hellward.

Of course God made man. He made everything. But why not find out just how He made him? Surely there is as much "glory to God" in discovering just how He did it as in accepting an infantile interpretation which up to date has got us nowhere. When we know how man is made, we shall understand the laws of his being; and it will not be necessary for him to die of apoplexy, stone in the gall bladder or kidney, hardening of the arteries or any other so-called disease caused by breaking the laws of his body and mind.

46

If we do our duty to our children, shall we teach them the laws of their being and how to respect them or shall we go on in the same old way, and when they get sick from breaking the laws of their being and ruin their health, call a surgeon who will cut out God's mistakes? Think it over; or, if you're too fanatical or bigoted to think, pay a surgeon to cut out the effects of wrong living and continue the cause.

LET US REASON TOGETHER!

Let us do a little homely reasoning. We are inclined to be awed by the word *infinite*. The *infinite* is limitless to our limited comprehension—it is a relative term and ambiguous; but as we grow in experience, our once limited comprehensions take one extended dimensions. Each person's infinite is personal and varies from every other person's comprehension. We cannot think in terms of the limitless and we should not try; for if we know the analysis of an atom of salt, we know the analysis of the infinite amount there is in the world. This is true of all elements. If we know the analysis of a pound of butter, we know the analysis of the infinite amount contained in the world. If we know all about a man, we know all about all men. If we know what finite love is, we know that infinite love is of the same character.

We should keep our feet on the ground—stay on earth—and be satisfied that all worlds are like our world.

HOW TO MEASURE THE INFINITE

We know all by an intensive study of a part. If we know all about one disease, we know all about all diseases.

We shall tell the reader all about *toxemia* and then he should know all about all diseases for *toxemia* is the basic cause of all diseases.

Instead of beginning at the top of any subject, we should begin at the bottom and work up. The usual way for our finite minds is to accept the infinite on faith; then to us the comprehensible does not agree with our preconception, our faith is shocked, our house of belief is divided against itself and we fall. This is the parting of the ways; and we must reconcile our faith and knowledge by transferring our faith to the belief that the road to all knowledge is by way of the comprehensible. We must either do this or live in doubt concerning the knowable and accept unknowable on faith.

Every truth squares itself with every other truth; every department of science and reason blends into a unit. The laws of life are those of the cosmos; the laws of the universe are the laws of God. The road to an understanding of God is from rock to man and through man to God. Every step must be a block of truth or God, the goal, will be sidestepped. Behold the head-on collision of the Christian world and the wholesale massacre that took place during the First World War—all due to undigested truth. The world is full of truth; but mental undigestion, due to wrong food combinations, is universal.

Many think they know what I mean when I use the word *toxemia,* having referred to the dictionary for its definition.

TOXEMIA, THE BASAL CAUSE OF ALL SO-CALLED DISEASES

Toxin Poisoning.—Toxin: Any of a class of poisonous compounds of animal, bacterial and vegetable origin—and poisonous ptomaine—Standard Dictionary.

There are so many ways for the blood to become poisoned that, unless what I mean by *toxemia* is thoroughly comprehended, there must be a confused understanding. This explanation is made necessary because even professional men have said to me: "Oh, yes; I believe in the poisoning resulting from retained excretions (constipation) and ptomaine (food) poisoning."

As stated before, a ptomaine poisoning resulting from the ingestion of food that has taken on a state of putrescence, or a poisoning resulting from this change taking place in food after it has been eaten, and which is generally called autotoxemia, is not an autogenerated poisoning. Both of these poisons are generated on the outside of the body and must be absorbed before the blood can be poisoned. Food or poison in the intestines is still on the outside of the body. A suppurating wound, ulcer or chancre is on the outside of the body, and if it causes septic (blood) poisoning, it will be because the waste products are not allowed to drain—to escape. The discharge being obstructed, it becomes septic and its forced absorption poisons the blood. Even vaccinia fails to produce septic poisoning because its poison is discharged on the surface—on the outside of the body. Occasionally the waste products are forced to enter the blood because of faulty dressings; then septic poisoning with death follows.

The Deadly Germ

It should not be forgotten that unobstructed free

49

drainage from wounds, ulcers, canals, ducts, keeps them non-poisonous. The *deadly germ* on the hands, lips, drinking cups, hanging straps of street cars—in fact, found anywhere and everywhere—is not deadly until it gets mixed up with man's deadly dirty, filthy physical and mental habits. There are people who cannot be taught cleanliness; they either scrub their bodies raw or neglect them overtime. It is an art to wear clothes and maintain a state of cleanliness conducive to health. Venereal and skin diseases, including the eruptive fevers, are fostered by clothes. There is something more than prejudice, fanaticism and partisanship in my reiterated allusions to the congeneric relationship of syphilis, vaccination and smallpox. The kinship would have been settled long ago if vaccine and vaccinia were not commercialized. Will those with millions invested and turning out large dividends willingly be convinced that they are engaged in the wholesale syphilization of the people? It is not in keeping with our commercialized religion.

The *deadly germ* must be mixed with retained, pent-up waste products before it becomes metamorphosed into its deadly toxic state. The dog or other animal licks it out of his wound. When the "deadly germ" is asculated into the mouth and from there into the stomach, it is digested. The normal secretions of the body, on the outside as well as on the inside are more than enough to do away with all the "deadly germs" allotted to each person.

Normal persons are deadly to all germs and parasites peculiar to the human habitat.

Normal people have no need of heaven or hell; these are the conjurations of ignorance and filth in

50

a search for artificial immunization. Truth immunizes the germ fallacy.

"Cures" and immunization are the products of a civilization that does not civilize. Creedal religion is a "cure" and an immunization for those who would be good if evil did not betide them.

Self-control and a knowledge of the limitations of privileges bring to us the best in life; then, if we are contented to live one world at a time, we shall have the best preparation for the tomorrows as they come. If we live well today—live for health of mind and body today—we need not worry about the germs that come tomorrow.

Those who preach fear of germs today are the mental offspring of those who have preached fear of God, devil, hell and heaven in the past. They do not know that the fear which they inculcate is more to be dreaded than the object of their warning. Fear does a thousand times more harm than any other one cause of *toxemia*.

Nature goes her limit in the prevention of absorption of any and all poisons. The indurated wall built at the base of ulceration is a conservative measure—it is to prevent absorption. In the matter of prevention nature sometimes goes too far and builds tumors and indurations so dense as to obstruct the circulation; then degeneration takes place with slow absorption of the septic matter. This poisoning takes place very insidiously. It is called cachexia and the names, given to this pathology are syphilis or cancer; or, if of the lungs, it is called tuberculosis.

This may be thought a very great digression from the subject of *toxemia*; but as all pathological roads lead to Rome—the unity of all diseases—an apology is not necessary.

The medical world has been looking for a remedy to cure disease, notwithstanding the obvious fact that nature needs no remedy—she needs only an opportunity to exercise her own prerogative of self-healing.

A few years ago a sick doctor offered a million dollars for a cure for cancer. If he had known the cause of disease instead of being scientifically educated, he would not have died believing in the possibility of a cure after nature had passed her eternal fiat of unfitness in his case. Cancer is the culmination of years of abuse of nutrition and years of *toxemia* from faulty elimination. Forcing the bowels to move is an old and conventional method of so-called elimination which gets rid of the accumulation in the bowels, causing an extra amount of water to be thrown out by the kidneys and bowels; but this forcing measure adds to enervation by its overstimulation and further inhibits elimination proper—elimination of waste products in the blood, the source of all disease producing toxins. The most powerful eliminant is a fast. In other words, give nature rest and she needs no so-called cures. Rest means: Stay in bed, poised mind and body and fast. Nature then works without handicaps unless fear is created by all the old fear-mongers, professional and lay, sending to the patient the warning: "It is dangerous to fast; you may never live through it." These wiseacres do not know that there is a vast difference between fasting and starving.

Here is a hint for those kill-joys who are afraid to allow their patients to fast: You know, or think you do, that people who are forced to stay in bed from injury never do well, and this is especially true of old people. Why? Because they are overfed.

Germs as a cause of disease is a dying fallacy. The bacteriological deadmarch is on and those with their ears to the ground can hear it. Intuition is forcing the active medical minds to fortify against the coming revulsion; they are buckling on the armor of endocrinology. Endocrinology, focal infection, autogenous and synthetic remedies, vaccine and serum immunization are some of the high points in the science of medicine today; but there is a lack of fundamental unity to the system and nature abhors chaos as she does a vacuum.

Toxemia accepts the germ (organized ferment) as it does the enzyme (unorganized ferment). Both are necessary to health.

My theories have received but little attention except from plagiarists. A few, a very few, physicians know what I stand for. Those few, however, are enthusiastic and have proved to their own satisfaction that the theory has a universal application. Many attempt to work *toxemia* along with some little two-by-four pet curing system—it means petting a little personal pride; but it will not work. *Toxemia* is big enough for the best in any man.

What more can be asked by any physician than a philosophy of cause that gives a perfect understanding of the cause of all so-called diseases? To know cause supplies even the laymen with a dependable course of correction and an "immunization" that truly immunizes. Dependable knowledge is man's salvation; and when it can be had with as little effort as that required for a thorough understanding of the *philosophy* of *toxemia* there is little excuse for any man, lay or professional, to hazard ignorance of it.

Toxin—the designating poison in toxemia—is a product of metabolism. It is a constant, being constantly generated; and when nerve energy is normal it it as constantly eliminated as fast as produced.

The body is strong or weak, as the case may be, depending entirely on whether the nerve energy is strong or weak. And it should be remembered that the functions of the body are carried on well or badly according to the amount of energy generated.

IMPORTANCE OF NERVE ENERGY

Without nerve energy the functions of the various organs of the body cannot be carried on. Secretions are necessary for preparing the building-up material to take the place of worn out tissue. The worn out tissue must be removed—eliminated—from the blood as fast as it it formed or it accumulates and, as it is toxic, the system will be poisoned. This becomes a source of enervation.

Elimination of the waste products of tissue building is just as necessary as the building-up process. As these two important functions depend on each other and as both depend on the proper amount of nerve energy to do their work well, it behooves all people who would enjoy life and health to the full to understand in what way they may be frugal in using nerve energy so that they may learn how to live conservatively or prudently, thereby enjoying the greatest mental and physical efficiency, and also the longest life. (See chapter on "Enervating Habits.")

To the ignorant, thoughtless and sensual such suggestion and advice will seem unnecessary or perhaps the whims or preachments of a crochety person or the qualms of a sated sensualist; but it is the writer's belief that the more sober and thoughtful will welcome a knowledge that will help them to become masters of themselves. So far the masses have trusted their health and life to a profession that has failed to make good. I say this advisedly; for now the supposed masters in the pofession are looking for the causes of disease and it should be obvious to any thinking mind that until the cause of disease is found, certainly no dependable advice can be given as to how to avoid disease.

Sixty-seven years of independent thinking, unbiased by sect or creed, have enabled me to discover the true cause of disease; and it is so simple that even a child can learn to protect itself against the said-to-be "diseases peculiar to children."

"These are the times that try men's souls." If Tom Paine were here now, he would change the wording of that line to read, "These are the times that try men's nerves." Nerve energy and good money are the commodities that are spent very rapidly these days. Chasing the dollar causes great waste of energy; and the dollar has been chased so much that it has developed wanderlust. Wanderlust is developed to such a degree that men enervate themselves catching up with a few dollars and prostrate themselves upon the altar of money. There are many ways to use up nerve energy. It should be the ambition of everybody to conserve all the nerve energy possible for the extraordinary amount required to keep the speeding up necessary to adjust humanity to the automobile pace. This will come in time.

Man adjusted himself to the change from the ox cart. Dobbin the flea-bitten, string-halt, and blind and the steamboats on which our forefathers took their honeymoon trips to the "steam-cars" and high-stepping bays and family carriage.

Many will go into the hands of the receiver before the nervous system becomes adjusted to highpower automobiles and flying machines.

Without nerve energy the functions of the body cannot be carried on properly. The present day strenuousness causes enervation which checks elimination, and the retained toxins bring on *toxemia.*

Everything that acts on the body uses up energy. Cold and heat require the expenditure of nerve-energy to adjust the body to the changes.

After middle life those who would keep well and live to be old must have a care concerning keeping warm and avoid chilling of the body. They must let up on table pleasures and practice self-restraint in all ways. Allowing the feet to be cold for any length of time—allowing the body to chill when a topcoat would prevent—is using up nerve energy very fast.

Work with worry will soon end in flagging energy—evervation.

As no provision is made for the demand of an extra supply of energy at a given time, it is necessary, very necessary, to know how to conserve what we have and build more.

CONSERVATION OF ENERGY THE GREATEST STEP TO HEALTH RECOVERY

Now that I have found that enervation is the source of the cause of the only disease (*toxemia*) to which mankind is heir, it is easy to see that the so-called science of medicine, as practiced, is an ally extraordinary of all the causes of enervation and becomes a builder of disease instead of correcting or ameliorating man's sufferings. Every so-called cure in its very nature causes enervation. Even the drugs used to relieve pain end in making a greater pain and sometimes kill. The drugs to relieve cough in pneumonia sometimes kill the patient. Removing stones from the gallbladder does not remove the cause and more stones form.

Rest from habits that enervate is the only way to put nature in line for healing. Sleep and rest of body and mind are necessary to keep a sufficient supply of energy. Few people in active life rest enough.

WHY ENERVATION IS THE CAUSE AND NOT THE DISEASE

Enervation *per se* is not disease. Weakness or lost power is not disease; but, by causing a flagging of the elimination of tissue waste, which is toxic, the blood becomes charged with toxin and this we call *toxemia* —poison in the blood. This is disease and when the toxin accumulates beyond the toleration point, a crisis takes place; which means that the poison is being eliminated. This we call disease, but it is not. The only disease is *toxemia*, and what we call diseases are the symptoms produced by a forced vicarious elimination of toxin through the mucous membrane.

When the elimination takes place through the mucous membrane of the nose, it is called a cold—catarrh of the nose; and where these crises are repeated for years, the mucous membrane thickens and ulcerates and the bones enlarge, closing the passage, etc. At this stage hay fever or hay asthma develops. When the throat and tonsils or any of the respiratory passages become the seat of the crises of *toxemia,* we have croup, tonsilitis, pharyngitis, laryngitis, bronchitis, pneumonia, etc. What is in a name? All are symptoms of the expulsion of toxin from the blood at the different points named and are essentially of the same character and evolving from the one cause—namely, *toxemia*—crises of *toxemia.*

This description can be extended to every organ of the body; for any organ that is enervated below the average standard from stress or habit, from work or worry, from injury or from whatever cause may become the location of crises of *toxemia.* The symptoms presented differ with each organ affected; and that gives color to the belief that every symptom-complex is a separate and distinct disease. But thanks to the new light shed upon nomenclature (naming disease) by the *philosophy* of *toxemia,* every symptom-complex goes back to the one and the only cause of all so-called diseases—namely, *toxemia.*

The symptoms that are called gastritis (catarrh of the stomach) are very unlike the symptoms of cystitis (catarrh of the urinary bladder); yet both are caused by crises of *toxemia*—both become the locations for the vicarious elimination of toxin from the blood.

It should be obvious to the discerning how extraordinarily illogical it is to treat catarrh of the nose as a local disease; or, when crises are repeated until ulceration takes places and the mucous membrane becomes so sensitive that rust and pollen cause sneezing and watering of the eyes—symptoms called hay fever—to treat these symptoms as a distinct disease caused by pollen. Rest and total abstinence from food, liquid and solid, and reforming all enervating habits will restore nerve energy; the elimination of toxin through the natural channels will take place and full health will return. This state will remain permanently if the erstwhile victim of hay fever or any other so-called disease will "stay put."

The first elimination of toxin through the nose is called a cold. When this elimination is continuous, with exacerbation—toxin crises (fresh colds)—occasionally, ulceration takes place, bony spurs form and hay-fever develops. These are symptoms of toxin elimination. The cause is the same from the first cold to hay fever. The catarrhal discharge that continues throughout the interims of fresh colds (crises of *toxemia*) is chronic catarrh, named such in medical nomenclatures and treated locally as though it were an independant, fiendish entity; when the truth is that the victim of so-called *chronic catarrh* keeps his systems enervated by tobacco, alcohol, sugar and sweets of all kinds, coffee, tea, excessive eating of butter and bread, too much rich cooking, excessive eating of all foods, excess of sensual pleasures, etc.

Keeping the system enervated prevents the reestablishment in full of elimination through the normal excretory organs. The organism as time runs on becomes more tolerant of toxin and the "catching-cold habit" shows fewer (colds) crises of *toxemia*. A greater number of the mucous membranes are requisitioned to carry out vicarious elimination. The whole organism begins to show deterioration. The so-called chronic diseases begin to manifest. In catarrh of the stomach the mucous membrane takes on thickening, hardening, ulceration and cancer—all described in the nomenclature of medical science as so many distinctive diseases. But they are no more distinctive than President Washington was distinct from the boy George who cut down his father's cherry tree. Cancer was once the symptom-complex of a so-called cold; but, according to the *philosophy of toxemia*, it is the end of many crises of *toxemia*. As the crises continued, symptoms changed in accordance with the organic degeneration caused by the crises of *toxemia*.

Every so-called disease has the same inception, evolution and maturity, differing only as the organic structure involved differs.

Treating the various symptom-complexes as distinct entities is fully as scientific as salving the end of a dog's tail for its sore ear.

All diseases are the same fundamentally.

The cause travels back to *toxemia*, caused by enervation, which checked elimination; and enervating habits of body and mind are the primary causes of lost resistance—enervation.

Every chronic disease starts with *toxemia* and a toxemic crisis. The crises are repeated until organic changes take place. The chain of symptoms range from cold to catarrh to Bright's disease, tuberculosis, cancer, syphilis, ataxia and other so-called diseases; all from beginning to end symptoms of the cumulative effects of crises of *toxemia*.

CHAPTER III

ENERVATION IS GENERAL

EVERYBODY was surprised at the large percentage of our young manhood found unfit by the medical examining boards during the First World War. To that surprise add the one which the *philosophy of toxemia* adds and thinking people should be appalled.

The examining boards passed all young men who did not show a developed pathology; which meant all who did not show some change of organ or tissue—structural change.

When it is known that functional derangements precede structural changes by months and even years, it should be quite obvious that there were more young men passed by the Boards who were potentially ill or unable to carry on than were unfit. Time has proven this generally unknown fact true for before the war was over ninety-five per cent of the American army had received hospital attention for sickness, other than injury, from one to five times. And the boys who did not get over to France died by the thousands from the "flu."

What does this mean? It means that life as it is lived causes the people generally to be enervated. And when nerve energy drops below normal, the elimination of toxin—a natural product of metabolism —is checked and it is retained in the blood, bringing on *toxemia*—the first, last *and only efficient* cause of all so-called diseases.

It should be obvious to discerning minds that the amount of toxin in the blood must vary with each individual and that the degree of resistance also must vary with each individual. An amount that would cause a toxemic crisis in one would apparently have no effect on another. An enervating cause — the usual immunization — that would scarcely produce a reaction at one time in a given subject might send the same subject to a hospital at another time or even be fatal instanter. *Active anaphylaxis is the alibi or apology of the pro-vaccinators;* but it does not change the fact that vaccines are poisons even if they are "pure," regardless of the iterated and reiterated process that they are innocent and harmless.

The amounts of harm done the army by vaccination and re-vaccination will never be known. No words can describe the harm that immunizing with vaccines and serums has done and is doing except wholesale vandalism.

The average doctor cannot think and the others do not dare to think except conventionally out loud. I do not know where to place the men of the medical profession who are capable of thinking but who refuse to allow reason to guide them in their thinking in the matter of so-called immunization. Can class-consciousness or class-bigotry explain? Surely knavishness is unfit. It has been said of me because of my stand against the germ theory and vaccination that I have "peculiar views;" by some, that I am "an ignoramus." If I am, it is strange that fundamentally I find my thoughts and beliefs running parallel with one of the greatest thinkers of the nineteenth century—the famous English philosopher, Herbert Spencer. I was browsing in my library a few days ago and picked up

Facts and Comments. I returned to "Vaccination" and in it found more worthwhile, constructive thought in a short essay of less than three pages than can be found in all medical literature on the same subject. I have decided to quote the whole essay and I shall be pleased if others get the mental kick out of it that I have enjoyed.

"When once you interfere with the order of nature, there is no knowing where the results will end," was the remark made in my presence by a distinguished biologist. There immediately escaped from him an expression of vexation at his lack of reticence; for he saw the various uses I might make of the admission.

Jenner and his disciples have assumed that when the vaccine virus has passed through a patient's system he is safe, or comparatively safe, against smallpox, and that there the matter ends. I will not here say anything for or against this assumption.* I merely propose to show that there the matter does *not* end. The interference with the order of nature has various sequences other than that counted upon. Some have been made known.

A Parliamentary Return issued in 1880 (No. 392) shows that, comparing the quinquennial periods 1847-1851 and 1874-1878, there was in the latter a diminution in the deaths from all causes of infants under one year old of 6,600 per million births per annum; while the mortality caused by eight specified diseases, either directly communicable or exacerbated by the effects of vaccination, increased from 20,524 to 41,353

----

*Except, indeed, by quoting the statement of a well-known man, Mr. Kegan Paul, the publisher, respecting his own experience. In his "Memoirs" (pp. 260-61) he says, respecting his smallpox when adult: "I had had smallpox when a child, in spite of vaccination, and had been vaccinated but a short time before. I am the third of my immediate family who have had smallpox twice, and with whom vaccination has always taken."

per million births per annum—more than double. It is clear that far more were killed by these other diseases than were saved from smallpox.*

To the communication of diseases thus demonstrated must be added accompanying effects. It is held that the immunity produced by vaccination implies some change in the components of the body—a necessary assumption. But now, if the substances composing the body, solid or liquid or both, have been so modified as to leave them no longer liable to smallpox, is the modification otherwise inoperative? Will anyone dare to say that it produces no further effect than that of shielding the patient from a particular disease? You cannot change the constitution in relation to one invading agent and leave it unchanged in regard to all other invading agents. What must the change be? These are cases of unhealthy persons in whom a serious disease, as typhoid fever, is followed by improved health. But these are not normal cases; if they were, a healthy person would become more healthy by having a succession of diseases.† Hence, as a constitution modified by vaccination is not made more able to resist perturbing influences in general, it must be made less able. Heat and cold and wet and atmospheric changes tend ever to disturb the balance, as do also various foods, excessive exertion, mental strain. We have no means of measuring alterations in

---

*This was in the days of arm-to-arm vaccination, when medical men were certain that other diseases (syphilis, for instance) could not be communicated through the vaccine virus. Anyone who looks into the Transactions of the Epidemiological Society of some thirty years ago will find that they were suddenly convinced to the contrary by a dreadful case of wholesale syphilization. In these days of self-lymph vaccination, such dangers are excluded; not that of bovine tuberculosis, however. But I name the fact as showing what amount of faith is to be placed in medical opinion.

†*Toxemia* explains this phenomenon.—Ed.

resisting power, and hence they commonly pass unremarked. There are, however, evidences of a general relative debility. Measles is a severer disease than it used to be, and deaths from it are very numerous. Influenza yields proof. Sixty years ago, when at long untervals an epidemic occurred, it seized but few, was not severe, and left no serious sequel; now it it permanently established, affects multitudes in ex- treme forms, and often leaves damaged constitutions. The disease is the same, but there is less ability to withstand it.

There are other significant facts. It is a familiar bio- logical truth that the organs of sense and the teeth arise out of the dermal layer of the embryo. Hence ab- normalities affect all of them; blue-eyed cats are deaf, and hairless dogs have imperfect teeth. ("Origin of Species," Chap. 1.) The like holds of constitutional abnormalities caused by disease. Syphilis in its earlier stages is a skin disease. When it is inherited the ef- fects are malformation of teeth, and in later years iri- tis (inflamation of the iris.) Kindred relations hold with other skin diseases; instance the fact that scarlet fever is often accompanied by loosening the teeth, and the fact that with measles often go disorders— sometimes temporary, sometimes permanent—of both eyes and ears. May it not be thus with another skin disease—that which vaccination gives? If so, we have an explanation of the frightful degeneracy of teeth among young people in recent times; and we need not wonder at the prevalence of weak and defective eyes among them. Be these suggestions true or not, one thing is certain: The assumption that vaccination changes the constitution in relation to smallpox, and does not otherwise change it, is sheer folly.

"When once you interfere with the order of nature, there is no knowing where the results will end."

Interfering with the order of nature is a vast subject—one without end; but nature "comes smiling through" except when overwhelmed. Health—good health—is a greater force than bad—than every interference—and can correct every evil effect that is not fatal if the influence is removed.

Stimulants, continued over a long period, cause a gradual deterioration and finally, unless the habit is stopped, a fatal end. Toxin is a stimulant and a natural product of metabolism. When the body is normal, the toxin is removed as fast as generated; but when any enervating habit is practiced beyond the power of recuperation, the toxin accumulates, and *toxemia* is established—which means that the body has lost its protecting power. Now, if vaccine or any infection gains entrance into the blood, "there is no knowing where the effects will end."

Toxemia throws light on this perplexing point. When an infection takes place in a person with normal resistance, creating a vaccinia—a local skin inflammation—and pus formation occurs, it usually ends with the healing of the abscess. If inoculation of small-pox virus is made in the Jennerian way by inserting the virus subcutaneously—splitting the skin and rubbing it in—violent septic infection takes place, causing death in many cases. Laws were passed in England many years ago prohibiting this practice.

In toxemic subjects a local infection set up by the virus of sepsis from any source—vaccination, a badly cared for injury, a wound that fails to drain, an infected tooth, sinus, etc.—causes a septic fever of a malignant type which is liable to end in death or in invalidism. A system badly enervated and toxemic has little power to resist; and when the blood is very tox-

66

emic, it is very vulnerable to the influence of any infection.

Where the infection is not so malignant as to overwhelm the system, due to the virulence of the infecting agent or to the enervation and toxemic state being so great as to have destroyed resistance, the patient may rally from the crisis and get well under proper management. If, however, the management is bad, the patient may linger in a state of semi-invalidism for a few months or years and finally die.

Theodore Roosevelt's illness and death at least twenty-five years too soon was a pronounced type of such derangement. The great and forceful man was pronouncedly toxemic. He was injured, as everybody knows, on one of his trips into the jungles. Infection took place, which probably would have killed a less robust man. He returned home and continued his enervating habits, preventing his fine body from cleaning house.

Such cases can be brought back to the normal, but never under conventional treatment.

When toxemic subjects are infected, the infection will never be eliminated entirely until enervation and *toxemia* are overcome. Unless patients of this character are put to bed and fasted until elimination is completed, then fed properly and taught how to eat within their limitations, and unless they are willing to give up all enervating habits, there is no hope of their ever getting-well. These subjects often develop tuberculosis, Bright's disease and other lingering so-called diseases. Our federal hospitals are full of young men who will never get well; for *toxemia* is developed faster than it is thrown off. Scientific medicine is helpless.

Nature's order is interfered with by enervating habits until *toxemia* is established; then a vaccination, or an infection from any source, acts sooner or later as a firebrand in causing the most vulnerable organ to take an organic change. The organ, however, has nothing to do with cause and directing treatment to the organ is compounding fallacy. Types of such nonsense are blood transfusion for pernicious anemia; gland treatment for gland impotence; cutting out stones, ulcers, tumors, etc.

There is no question but that one of the most pernicious practices in vogue today is treating so-called disease with disease and immunizing with the products of disease.

One of the first things to do to get rid of any so-called disease is to get rid of *toxemia* for it is this state of the blood that makes disease possible. Infection, drug and food poisoning may kill; but if they do not, they will be short-lived in a subject free from enervation and *toxemia*. Conversely, the poisoning will linger in the system until *toxemia* is overcome; then elimination will remove all traces of infection.

Syphilitic infection in a pronouncedly toxemic subject is thrown into great virulency by conventional treatment. The infection is the least offender of the trio. Add fear and wrong eating and we have a formidable symptom-complex, justifying all the professional syphilomaniacs say and write about the disease. Remove *toxemia*, drugging, fear and vile eating, and there is little left. What there is can easily be thrown out by nature.

WE are builders of tomorrow and we need not pay a fortune-teller—a doctor, lawyer, preacher, banker—to tell us what will happen to us tomorrow.

Nothing will happen. The inevitable will come. We shall inherit the fruits of today's sowing.

CHAPTER IV

POISE

The state or quality of being balanced. Figuratively, equanimity; repose. Equanimity—Evenness of mind or temper; composure, calmness. Standard Dictionary

I PRESUME that, to be technically poised, we should be anatomically, physiologically and chemically balanced; but as asymmetry is the rule, we cannot hope to be balanced. We can, however, strive for equanimity—evenness of mind and temper.

Contentment comes with striving, not with possession. Apparently this is not always true for we see people very dissatisfied and unhappy who are busy.

Someone has said: "Blessed is the man who has found his work." This means that he is fully occupied and contented with his work, not its emoluments. No man is satisfied with work that has nothing in it but the dollars he gets out of it. Nothing but creative work satisfies the mind.

What is there in it? Advancement, self-development and a chance in the future to do good are about as little as will satisfy ambition.

To make for contentment, the work must occupy and satisfy the mind. Idle minds are dissatisfied

69

minds. If asked what prescription I would give children to secure their future happiness, I would say: Teach them to love work! work! work! We have overworked the old saying: "All work and no play makes Jack a dull boy." Now it is reversed to: "All play and no work makes Jack a bandit."

If parents cannot keep children busy, the city, county or state should furnish work—not in industrial schools, but the work that is best suited to each child. A child must be busy. Christ got busy at twelve years of age and earlier. We must be busy.

As I said, contentment comes with striving, not with possession. This is a law of psychology as well as of physics. We should be happy that we are not contented; for, if we were, we should not have anything to overcome—no reason for striving—and, of course, fail to enjoy the work and labor of attaining.

Man never is, but always to be blest.—Pope.

Because Pope made that statement it should not be taken too seriously. I have found many people blest who did not know it. There are more blessings in disguise than are found in the limelight. One of the commonest blessings of mankind is that about ninety-nine per cent of our wants we never realize. If most people could cutout time as often as they wish, their lives would be greatly shortened: "I wish it were this time next year." "I wish now were ten years from now; I should then be through college and established in business."

The disposition of most people is to seek abridgment. Nature abhors a vacuum, and that is what abridgments are: "Get-Rich-Quick Wallingford" is the ideal of all.

Short cuts to success: a salesmanship that means

coercing the vacillating—those of weak will, those who can be persuaded to buy prematurely, those who do not know their own minds; in short, inducing people to buy what they do not need and cannot afford is called salesmanship. What is the matter with the people today? General indebtedness. The sales people have made more than they know how to spend wisely on themselves—they do not know how to fill their vacuums. Those who have been persuaded to run in high when they should have stayed in low—or, what would have been better, continued to ride a bicycle or remained on foot—are distressed because of premature supply. Both extremes lack poise and build restlessness and dissatisfaction. The automobile is a necessity; but it has been forced into a luxury that has far outrun necessity. It has built great fortunes at one end, and marked poverty at the other end that will create a financial disease called panic unless remedied soon. Panic is another name for a vacuum which will be filled with much unhappiness.

Getting through school without filling in the time well, by short cuts, ponies and favoritism, builds vacuity. Time and honest labor are necessary for building character, education and ability in any and all lines. In the physical as well as in the mental world the old Latin apothegm applies: *Cito maturum, cito putridum*—"Soon ripe, soon rotten." Athletes die early. Why? Development is forced. Excessive use of the muscular system forces an extra supply of blood to the muscles. This in turn forces an extra supply of food to meet the demand of waste and supply. Overstimulation enervates and the toxin fails to be carried out as rapidly as formed; hence *toxemia* is established which gradually brings on degeneration of heart and blood vessels. "No chain is stronger than its weakest link."

71

In athletics the strongest links are in constant use for all the strength they have. The stability that youth gives is rapidly aging with the result that the athlete dies of senility in youth. Fitzsimmons was called the "grand old man of the ring" at thirty-five. In this saying, which was meant to be a compliment to the king of athletes, was an expression of scientific knowledge beyond understanding in the sporting world—subconsciously better than they knew; for in reality he had aged himself by stressing his body.

Youth wants to move faster than good, substantial growth justifies. Young professional men are in hot haste to succeed their predecessors, always confident that they can do more than fill their places.

Today inexperience is hotfooting civilization to a quick maturity and obviously to a premature end. Hot haste has ill prepared even those with age to be safe advisers. Knowledge not seasoned by time, experience and poise never matures.

Poise and equanimity have become meaningless terms in this age. The elements of success which make for ideal maturity are lacking the welding influence of time and experience. The present day mind is athletic; it is prematurely aged at the expense of time which is required for stabilizing. Hospitals, penitentiaries and insane asylums cannot be built fast enough to accommodate the prematurely senile. That is what disease is—old age tissues outrunning the supply of new.

Too many abridgments, from the kindergarten to the high school and on through college, leave vacuums to be filled by the lies of civilization and the disease and unhappiness that false knowledge and immature judgment bring.

Personal peculiarities, affectations and petty habits

of all kinds are boomerangs that return to poison life's sweet dreams.

Nature smiles on those who are natural; but those who persist in grimacing, mentally or physically, she joins in a conspiracy to distort them at their pleasure. We can be happy and contented or we can be unhappy and discontented. We can make our choice and nature will do the rest.

I just came from a drug store into which I had stepped to purchase a tube of camphor ice. The druggist fumbled and, being self-conscious, his self-pity made it necessary for him to say that he was feeling bad and had been lying down most of the afternoon. He accompanied his remarks with a sick grimace of his features and a bodily expression of weakness. He no doubt would have enjoyed discussing his discomforts with me, but I ignored the subject and passed out. He is cultivating a sick habit that will spoil his life and make of him a bore to all except those who frequent his shop hunting cures. "Misery loves company." People with the sick habit flock together and never appear to tire of recounting and comparing their discomforts. The most insignificant symptoms are retained in memory for years. Self-pity causes them to exaggerate and in time they believe the worst possible about themselves. Such a life is ruined unless complete reformation is made. This state of mind brings on enervation and *toxemia*. The symptoms are a general nervousness, indigestion, constipation, coated tongue, anxiety concerning cancer or some other malady that may prove fatal. The muscular system is more or less tensed. The constipation is accompanied by an abnormal contraction of the rectum. The entire body is abnormally tense. Such patients have difficulty in going to sleep, and when they are about to drop off to sleep they are awakened with a jerk—a violent contraction of all the muscles. These people are light sleepers and complain that they do not sleep at all. A few complain of headache and nausea. They are imitators and often develop new symptoms after reading about disease or listening to others relating their symptoms.

Many of these cases of neurosis are operated upon for various supposed abdominal derangements. Too often physicians treat such people for what they say is the matter with them. Occasionally we find self-sacrificing, amiable women who are never robust but who live and work beyond their strength for others. These mothers in early life had ambitions for a career, and the disappointment brought on a profound enervation, permanently impairing nutrition; for the one great sorrow prevented a full return to normal. Fortunately, surcease was found in doing for others; and in time making others happy became a vicarious tranquilizer so perfect that those whom they soothed with their sweet smiles and cheering words often said: "Aunt Mary, you must have lived a charmed life in which no sorrow ever entered." The answer would be more smiles and encouragement.

Those who find a life of service to take the place of ambition's jilts have made no mistake in the selection of the Great Physician; but those who seek cures outside of self are hunting cures in a fool's paradise.

Cures! There are no cures. The subconscious builds health or disease according to our order. If we send impulses of irritation, discontent, unhappiness, complaining, hate, envy, selfishness, greed, lust, etc., the subconscious builds us in the image of our order.

If we send sensual impulses to the subconscious, our order is returned to us blear-eyed with swollen features, headaches, bad breath, pain here, pain there, blurred intellect, carelessness in business, of friends and of self. We interpret our state as disease and send for a physician who finds albumin in the urine, rheumatism in the joints, a leaky heart, threatened apoplexy, dropsy, *et alii*. We take his dope, his operations, his immunizations; but we continue to send sensual impulses—big dinners, strong cigars, lascivious indulgences. The physician does no good. Another and another is sent for. Skillful examinations are given. Syphilis is found. Synthetic drugs are prescribed. Other physicians examine who find tuberculosis. And at least real skill is discovered in a physician who finds *cancer*. But all the time our orders are going to the subconscious and the returns are made faithfully in the image of their maker.

The truth is that we are not needing a physician at all. We need a teacher who can effect a reconciliation between our subconscious maker and ourselves. What we need is to be taught self-control, poise, equanimity and repose. And when these impulses are sent over the sympathetic nerves to our subconscious maker, we shall begin to receive images of a more ideal man until an approach to physical perfection is attained.

Self-control, with an ideal of just the kind of person we should like to be, held before the subconscious all the time, will be returned to us just as we order. We are made in the image of the ideal we hold before our maker—the subconscious. We must live it, however. Simply holding an ideal will not get us anywhere. If our ideal is for sobriety, getting drunk will not bring our dreams true. If our ideal is for perfect health, we certainly cannot expect a sensual life to build it.

We may have an ideal image, but if we do not live it, a distortion will be created.

75

A disgruntled, complaining habit builds that kind of an individual.

If we refuse to be composed, poised and relaxed, we become tense and build discomfort. A contracted brow builds headache. A tense, fixed state of the muscular system brings on muscular fatigue, which may be treated as neuralgia, neuritis or rheumatism. A slight injury on any part of the body, coddled, nursed and kept without motion may start a fixation of the muscles, causing more pain from muscular fatigue than from the injury.

Enough neurotics have been relieved and cured of muscular fatigue to put two schools of spine manipulators in good standing with the people.

All through the ages mountebanks, magnetic healers and various cults of "laying on of hands" have worked among people who had time to nurse a slight injury into a very large fatigue disease. Fortunes have been made out of vile-smelling liniments because of the supposed cures made by rubbing the dope on sprained backs and joints. The same cures could have been made by simply rubbing the parts; but the minds that go with spineless people, who have time to wait for miraculous cures, could not be made to believe that a cure could be effected without that mysterious healing property associated with evil-looking and vile-smelling medicamentums.

A sensitive, insignificant pile tumor set up such a tense state of the entire muscular system as to render the subject a confirmed invalid. Such a case became a patient of mine a few weeks ago. On examination I found an extreme contraction of the sphincter muscles. His entire body was tense, and, of course, he had muscular fatigue, which caused him to believe that he was a very sick man. I had him lie down and I taught him how to relax; then I introduced a finger into his rectum—very slowly, to avoid giving pain as much as possible. I was about thirty minutes bringing relaxation of the anal muscles. While manipulating, I was advising relaxation of his body. Before he left my office he declared that he felt better than he had for two years, notwithstanding the fact he had been in a hospital and otherwise treated most of that time. I gave him instructions on how to poise, how to manipulate the rectum and anus.

All his stomach troubles, and discomforts generally, passed away in a week.

I have seen many invalids of nervous type who had been treated by many physicians and for many diseases. Tension of the entire body was one of the pronounced symptoms and health could not be brought back until this habit was overcome.

The discomforts complained of by those who have tumor of the womb, goiter, cystitis, stomach and bowel derangements rest largely on a basis of nervous tension which must be overcome before comfort and full health will return.

Position in standing, walking, sitting and lying down may be such as to cause tension. We have occupational diseases and emotional diseases; and lack of poise complicates all of these so-called diseases and brings on tension.

Children are prone to become nervous and excited when tired. When allowed to eat heartily, when excited and tired, they have indigestion. Extreme cases develop convulsions. Fear and anxiety are two elements that lead on to chorea.

Poise of mind and body should receive attention early as well as late in life.

Good health late in life indicates self-control, moderation in all things, and equanimity—poise.

Moderation does not mean the same to all people. Some men call three to six cigars a day moderate indulgence; others believe that one to six a month is temperate. Those who have an irritable heart and stomach are immoderate when they use tobacco at all.

Fortunate is the person who knows his limitations and respects them. Of such a person it may be said that he is poised.

IMMUNIZATION

Wouldn't it be incongruous if in the evolution of man such an important element as auto-immunization should be left out? No animal has been forgotten in the great scheme of creation. Powers of offense and defense have been wisely provided, and to suppose that the king of all animals—man—should be left defenseless is most absurd. No, man is provided with a nervous system, at the head of which is a brain capable of thinking and which can come to the aid of a flagging nervous system and help to renew it.

When the nervous system is normal—when there is full nerve energy—man is normal and immune to disease. Disease begins to manifest only when environments and personal habits use up energy faster than it is renewed. This contingency the properly educated mind begins to remedy at once by removing or overcoming all enervating influences.

Man's immunization to disease requires a life so well ordered that his nerve energy is kept at or near normal. When nerve energy is prodigally squandered, he is forced into a state of enervation; then elimination of the waste products is checked, leaving waste—toxin—in the blood, causing *toxemia* or self-poisoning—the first, last and only true disease that man is heir to. All other poisons are accidental and evanescent and without *toxemia* can have no entree to the system. Poisons may be swallowed, injected or inoculated into the body and poison or even kill; but such an experience is not to be classed as disease any more than a broken leg or a gunshot wound.

Toxin is a normal, natural product of the system, always present. Being a constant, it answers every requirement for a universal cause of all so-called diseases. All the different symptom-complexes, which are given special names, take their names from the organs involved in the toxin crisis; but they are not individual—they are only symptoms of vicarious elimination. For example: Tonsilitis, gastritis, bronchitis, pneumonia, colonitis, are each and every one *toxemic* crises, differing only in location and symptoms. So-called diseases are just so many different locations where toxin is being eliminated. All are different manifestations of one disease—*toxemia*.

Toxemia is the only explanation of why so many young men were refused by the examining boards in tle First World War. Many were sent over to France who soon found the hospital for they were near the limit of their toxin-toleration. The excitement used up their nerve energy. The enervation was quickly followed by *toxemia*. Their sicknesses were given names but the truth was that they had *toxemia*, and their diseases were crises of *toxemia*, which means vicarious elimination.

After the numerous vaccinations to which the boys were subjected on entering the army, probably fear or apprehension was next in order of enervating influences.

79

Diagnosis according to *modern medical science* is a scheme of symptomatology that means nothing except a guide in discovering organic change—pathological change; and if no change or pathology is found, the case is sent home with the advice to return again in a few months; or perhaps it will be kept under observation for a while. Even cases presenting pathological changes, such as we see in rheumatic arthritis, I have known of being sent home for six months because no point of infection could be found. The patient would be sent away with the statement: "After a thorough examination, we cannot find the cause of your disease. Come back in about six months and it may be showing up in that time." So much for the influence that focal infection has on the mind of the profession. Suppose infected teeth were found, or sinus infection, what of it? What causes the teeth and sinuses to be infected? Why is rheumatism a symptom of infection and the focal infections not a symptom of rheumatism?

The truth is that rheumatism, infected teeth and sinus infections, as well as every other pathology found in the body, are effects. Symptoms without lesions represent functional derangements which have not been repeated long enough or often enough to cause organic change. If, as diagnosis goes, the cause is to be found in the disease, at what stage are we to look for it? Is it at the beginning or in the fully developed organic change or in the dead man? Mackenzie believed that it should be looked for at the very beginning, which meant with him the earliest change. He believed that an intensive study at this stage would discover cause. This was a mistaken idea of his, which is proved by the fact that the cause of rheumatism and cancer cannot be found early or late and that those who believe germs cause disease cannot find them until pathology is found. It appears to me, after being in the game for over sixty years, that a plan which has received so much labor without reward should be abandoned.

Diagnosis is so fraught with the element of uncertainty that no reliance can be placed upon it.

Research occupies an army of laboratory experts in hunting the cause of disease and also cures. They are doomed to fail; for how is it possible to find cause in effects?

The specialist is so limited in his knowledge of the philosophy of health and disease that he becomes deluded on the subject; and his delusion often causes him to see meningitis, appendicitis, ovaritis—or any disease that happens to be the subject of his speciality—in every case brought to him. As a matter of fact, most "attacks" of disease of any and all kinds get well, whether treated do not, if they have not passed from functional to organic.

This statement needs a little explanation. It is said that eighty per cent who fall sick get well or could get well without the aid of a physician. All so-called attacks of disease of whatever kind are crises of *toxemia*, which means vicarious elimination of toxin that has accumulated above the saturation (toleration) point. These crises may be symptoms which we call cold, "flu," tonsilitis, gastritis, headache or some other light malady. They come today and are gone in a few days. If treated, we say they are cured. If they are not treated, we say they got well without treatment. The truth is that the surplus toxin—the amount accumulated above the point which can be maintained with comfort—is eliminated and comfort returns. This is not a cure; it is one of nature's palliations. When the cause or causes of enervation are discovered and removed, the nerve energy returns to normal. Elimination removes toxin as fast as developed by metabolism. This is health—this is all there is to any cure. In a few words: Stop all enervating habits; stop eating; rest until nerve energy is restored to normal. When this is accomplished, the patient is "cured." A short or long fast is beneficial to most sick people. Those who are afraid of fasting should not fast. All other so-called cures are a delusion and at the most a passing palliation; but enough such cures performed daily to keep a large army of physicians and cultists in bread, butter and a degree of respectability. The "cured" patients, however, glacier-like, move steadily down to the river Styx—thousands and thousands of them years before their time, many even before their prime and all maintaining a false belief concerning what disease is and a more foolish notion concerning cures.

Toxemia Simplifies the Understanding of Disease

When a child shows symptoms of high fever, pain and vomiting, what is the disease? It may be indigestion from overeating or eating improper food. It may be the beginning of gastritis, scarlet fever, diptheria, meningitis, infantile paralysis, or some other so-called disease. The treatment, according to the *philosophy of toxemia,* may be positive and given with confidence. There need be no waiting for developments, no guessing, no mistakes. What is done is the correct treatment for any so-called disease, named or not named. Get rid of the exciting causes, whatever they are. Provide plenty of fresh air and water and keep the patient quiet. See to it that nothing but water goes into the stomach until the fever and discomfort are entirely overcome; then give very light food at first.

A child that is given meat and eggs and an excess of milk is liable to develop putrefactive diseases. It is doubtful (and I believe impossible) if any child brought up on fruit, nuts and vegetables can ever evolve diphtheria, scarlet fever, or smallpox or develop septic fever—typhoid.

The methods of the regular practice of medicine are in keeping with the habits of body and mind that lead to malignant disease, epidemics, etc. As a man thinketh, so is he.

The regular profession believes in antitoxin, vaccine and autogenous remedies; and these remedies fit the psychology of a mode of living that leads to vicious types of disease.

Most people are in sympathy with impossible cures—cures without removing causes.

All so-called cures will some day be proved a delusion. Remember that children will not be sick if they are not toxemic. Let the local manifestations be what they may, the basic cause is always the same— *toxemia* plus septic infection; and if this state is not added to by food, cases treated in this way will be aborted—jugulated, if you please. Physicians who have seen only regular practice will declare that the cases recovering in this manner are irregular and lacking in intensity. Of course they are not typical; for they have not been complicated with fear and disease-building treatment.

Physicians will say: "Suppose it is a case of diptheria? Antitoxin should be used for it is a specific."

What is diptheria? A toxemic subject with gastro-intestinal catarrh becomes infected from decomposition of animal food eaten in excess of digestive power. The symptoms are those of tonsilitis, showing a grayish exudate covering the tonsils or other parts of the throat, accompanied by a disagreeable, pungent, fetid breath. There is great prostration. Subjects developing these symptoms have been living haphazardly. Their eating has been too largely of animal foods and starch—the conventional mixtures—and devoid of raw vegetables and fruit. The only animal food may be milk and the patient a young child. There have been running before, for a longer or shorter term, gastric irritation, constipation, perhaps several gastric attacks—acute indigestion.

In some cases the physical state is so vicious that a severe development of gastro-intestinal putrefaction may end fatally in from one to three days. These are the cases supposed to be overwhelmed by the diptheria toxin, which means an acute protein poisoning—intestinal putrefaction—in a subject already greatly enervated and toxemic.

ACUTE MALIGNANCY DEFINED

Malignancy occurs in toxemic subjects who have been carrying continuously a state of gastro-intestinal indigestion from a surfeit of food, in which animal substances, possibly only milk, predominated. The entire organism is more or less infected by the protein decomposition. A feast day comes along; an excess produces a crisis; and the organism, which is enervated and toxemic to the point of no resistance, is overwhelmed by septic poisoning. The disease may be chicken pox!

84

Fatal cases in all epidemics are food drunkards who are very much enervated, toxemic and infected from putrescence in the bowels.

It is a crime to feed anything to the sick. No food should be given until all symptoms are gone; then fruit and vegetable juices (never any animal foods). All epidemic diseases are wholesale food-poisoning among people who are pronouncedly enervated and toxemic. The poisoning by food is on the order of poisoning by chemicals. Those who have least resistance (are most enervated and toxemic) suffer most and succumb the easiest for the poisoning brings on a crisis of *toxemia*; the two nerve-destroying influences; overwhelm the reduced resistance; and may end in death unless wisely treated. All acute diseases are gastro-intestinal infections acting on toxemic subjects. The more enervated and toxemic the subject the more severe the crisis. Certainly anyone with intelligence should see the danger in giving food when the exciting cause of the disease is food poisoning.

Keep the patient warm and quiet and in good air. More treatment is meddlesome. Getting rid of putrefaction is most important. Such diseases develop only in those of pronounced enervation and toxemia and those of very bad eating habits.

To Sum Up

To sum up briefly the difference between the *toxemic* method and "regular medicine": *Toxemia* is a system based on the true cause of disease—namely *toxemia*. Before *toxemia* is developed, natural immunization protects from germs, parasites and all physical vicissitudes.

Toxin is a by-product as constant and necessary as life itself. When the organism is normal, it is produced and eliminated as fast as produced. From the point of production to the point of elimination, it is carried by the blood; hence at no time is the organism free from toxin in the blood. In a normal amount it is gently stimulating; but when the organism is enervated, elimination is checked. Then the amount retained becomes overstimulating—toxic—ranging from a slight excess to an amount so profound as to overwhelm life.

The treatment is so simple that it staggers those who believe in curing. Heroic treatment is disease-building. Find in what way nerve energy is wasted and stop it—stop all nerve energy losses. Then returning to normal is a matter of time in which nature attends to all repairs herself. And she resents "help"—medical officiousness.

In writing and giving advice, I often make the mistake of taking for granted that the consultant understands what I have in mind. Why should he when I have not given oral or written expression to my meaning?

In the matter of stopping nerve leaks it is easy for me to say: "Find out in what way nerve energy is wasted, and stop it—stop all nerve energy losses," etc. I am appalled at my stupidity in saying to a patient to stop enervating himself and allowing the matter to end by naming one or two gross enervating habits; for example: stop worry; stop smoking; stop stimulants; control your temper; stop eating too rapidly; stop allowing yourself to become excited. Stopping one enervating habit benefits, but dependable health brooks no enervating habits at all.

CHAPTER V

THE CAUSES OF ENERVATION

To UNDERSTAND disease, it is necessary to know cause; and, as *toxemia is the cause* of all disease and as enervation—an enervated body and mind—is the cause of *toxemia* it behooves those who are sick and want to get well, and who want to know how to stay well, to know what causes enervation.

A normal, healthy person is one who is poised (self-controlled) and who has no nerve-destroying habits. A self-controlled man is a man who is not controlled, kicked, cuffed or driven by habits.

Man is either the master of himself or his appetite and sensual pleasures master him. If the former, he enjoys health until worn out; and he should go down at from ninety to one hundred and fifty years of age. If he is inclined to the latter, yet has his habits more or less under control he may live from six to ninety years. But if he is a sensualist—is controlled by habits and passions, sits up after bedtime to take a last smoke or eat a lunch, or gets up in the night and smokes (I know a celebrated physician who used tobacco to secure sleep; he died at fifty-four years of age), or takes a drink to quiet his nerves and make him sleep or goes the limit venereally—he becomes irritable, grouchy and dies prematurely.

Excess transforms a man into a disgusting brute. The word *brute* is used here to express the state of one being devoid of self-control. Those of fine constitutions are often converted into neurotics who have left health and comfort far behind. Many know comfort only for short periods and then by the influence of drugs or stimulants.

The youths of our country are fast developing a state of multi-inebriety—jazz, tobacco, alcohol and petting parties; are developing a sex neurosis that will be followed by a generation of paralytics, epileptics, insane, morons, idiots and monstrostities, embracing all who do not die of acute disease.

This class lives from thirty until the chloroforming age—sixty years. The majority die early in life. We are fast coming to an age of impotence. I knew one of superior mind who died of ataxia at thirty-five. I quote a few lines from his own writings concerning his state the last year of his life:

Could I but crystalize these midnight tears
    And gather from their beaded bitterness
    A rosary for burning lips to press,
Some pain-born token of these joyless years,
To teach the faith that saves, the hope that cheers;
    Then would I bid these fountains of distress
    Flow fast and free if their sad floods could bless
Or murmur peace in some poor sufferer's ears.

* * *

My world has shrunk at last to this small room
    Where, like a prisoner, I must now remain.
I'd rather be a captive in the gloom
    Of some damp dungeon, tearing at my chain;
    For then, perchance, my freedom I might gain.

Ah God! to think that I must languish here
   Fettered by sickness and subdued by pain,
To die a living death from year to year,
Joy banished from my breast and Sorrow brooding there.

*　*　*

I often think how once these stumbling feet,
   That now can scarcely bear me to my bed,
Were swift to follow, as wind is fleet,
   That baleful beam that to destruction led.

*　*　*

Thou domineering power, or love, or lust,
   Or passion, or whatever else thou art,
How have thy crimson roses turned to dust
   And strewn their withered leaves upon this heart!
   Though through my vitals now thy venomed dart
Strikes like an adder's sting, yet still I feel
   From Egypt's fleshpots it is hard to part;
   And my weak, wandering glances often steal
Back to sweet sinful things until my senses reel.

*　*　*

Still one retreat is left, to which I flee:
   Dear dreamy draught, in which I often steep
Body and soul, I turn again to thee
   And drift down Lethe's stream out on Oblivion's sea.

Thirty-five years is a short life for a brain to live
that can conjure the English language as the above
snatches indicate. Thousands pay the price that this
man paid, but very few can win so much admiration
and sympathy with their swan songs. Few people can
read the psychology of swan songs. Often they are an
epitome of a lifetime.

ENERVATING HABITS
BABIES

Babies should not be trundled about too much,
should not sleep in their mothers' arms, should not be

exposed to bright lights, loud talking, noises, too much heat or cold; should not be jolted about in baby-buggies, automobiles, trains, street cars.

The very young are made sick by too much excitement of all kinds. Very young children should be kept quiet enough to favor sleep all the time except when bathed and when clothes are changed. They should not be taken up every time they do any fretting. All that is needed is to make them dry and change their positions.

Young children should not be fed oftener than every four hours and not that often unless they are awake. To awaken a child for food is very unnecessary and harmful.

A human being is a cerebro-spinal dynamo and should be kept as much as possible in a static state, conserving nerve energy for future use. Poise or self-control—teaching a child to be contented alone—must be started at birth.

Children need no entertainment. When left alone, they find entertainment in becoming acquainted with themselves.

Children that are coddled in the matter of being entertained—dancing attendance on them—develop discontent and bring on enervation, which favors "the diseases peculiar to children."

CHILDREN

Children of school age are enervated by being urged in school work, exercise and all kinds of excitement. Play should be limited. When hysteria shows up, stop the play.

Much study, examinations, exercise without desire

and competitive examinations of all kinds cause a capricious craving for food. When a growing child is forced to the limit of its nervous capacity, nature must conserve in some way; and as there is no way to sidestep convention's eternal grind, the normal desire for food is lost.

Forced Feeding to Increase Weight. — The whole system of school feeding is one of destroying health by enervating if not killing the child.

The federal government is ruining thousands of our young men, teaching them the sick habit. The government should give them a pension and turn them loose. The present coddling is pernicious, not only for the ex-soldier, but also for those who are interested in keeping their hospital jobs.

Physicians must be able to detect cunning and craft. The sick habit often starts as a joke, an experiment—just to see how those interested will take it—and ends in deceiving the deceiver.

A common habit, and one that often leads to a sick habit, is self pity—being sorry for one's self. Children are inclined to play sick to buy what they want.

Giving even school lunches enervates by building dissatisfaction. It is disease-building. Children must be given an independant spirit—pride will save the world. Then, to add to all this routine of nerve-destroying customs of our schools, teeth must be straightened; which means pressure on nerve and more or less irritation. The tonsils and appendix must be removed. This is a pernicious medical fad. Feed right and there will be no excuse for operations.

Vaccines and serums must be used to immunize from disease that results from the enervation brought on from all preceding causes. This is another sense-less fad, besides it is disease-building.

People are sick from wrong living. Operations remove effects. Stop the cause and disease goes away. Nature heals when allowed to do so, by removing the cause of enervation.

Children Pampered and Spoiled.—This brings on the bad and enervating habits of irritability wilfulness, overeating, improper eating and temper. Many of the older children use tobacco, coffee and an excessive amount of sweets and pastry. Self-abuse begins early in many and is the cause of stomach symptoms. Adolescence comes with excessive dancing, loss of sleep, smoking, drinking, lasciviousness, venereal disease and the fear springing from the contemplation of the consequences. Irritable children are hard to do anything for. The reason they are irritable is because they are pampered and not made to mind.

It is a crime not to control children. They should be compelled to obey. But do not wait until they are sick. A cranky irritability will help bring on disease and keep a child sick.

Fear.—Fear is the greatest of all causes of enervation. Children are subject to many fears. They are educated to fear the dark, bogy man and punishment. Parents often keep children in a state of fear by irritably cuffing them for the slightest excuse. There are many parents who do their "scrapping" before their children. It is a dreadfully common thing to do.

Outlawry begins at home and at the breast of the mother. A child that cannot respect its parents will not respect the laws of the state or nation. No parent is respected who is not obeyed at once and without capitulation. Unconditional surrender is the discipline necessary for character-building. But children will not obey laws that parents disregard.

In domestic infelicity are born disease and crime, and no amount of treatment by practitioners of medicine, law and theology can restore health for none of them remove the cause. Those who die of chronic disease have no self-control.

There is much fear and anxiety in a child's life. No child can thrive living in a state of fear in home, school or church. Discipline taught by respected parents brings love and not fear.

Longevity has increased since hell fire and brimstone have ceased to be taught and to build fear. A morality kept intact by fear is not health-imparting and is not a morality at all. Remove the fear and mob license succeeds it. Fear and love are antidotal. Man has been taught to fear God and at the same time love Him. Where the fear is real, the love is fictitious. Love being the basis on which ethics is built, a love founded on fear builds humbug ethics; and this is the foundation of all the conventional lies of our civilization.

Fear in all lines concerning children, from their conception to their birth, and on through school life, social life and marriage, leads to enervation. The dearth of worthwhile knowledge of how to feed and otherwise care for children keeps up on unnecessary worry with parents concerning their health. How to teach the young to avoid breaking their health and handicapping their minds by excesses in play, eating, drinking, in controlling tempers and emotions and in self-pollution is a knowledge sadly lacking in nearly all homes. Disease follows these excesses in the young. There is not a habit so self-destructive and so generally practiced as a venereal excitement; and there is no habit receiving so little attention from parents.

Ataxia is supposed to be caused by syphilis, but in

fact, it is caused by cerebro-spinal enervation, brought on from sensuality in all forms—particularly venereal. Subjects of this disease usually begin onanism early in life. Parents should teach children to avoid destroying habits. I have had locomotor ataxia cases confess to me that they began their self-pollution as early as eight years of age. Ten to fifteen are the years when active pollution begins. Unless a physician is very tactful, youths will not confess. I will say that very few boys have been untruthful to me. The practice is not quite so common with the opposite sex.

The physical abuse in this line is not nearly so enervating as allowing the mind to dwell on sex subjects. Lascivious dreaming debauches the victim as much as excess venery. Early pollution, followed by excessive venery, often commonizes a mind that would shine in the forum and in intellectual pursuits. There is a difference, however, in garrulity and garrulous parroting and giving a feast of reason. Bright intellects at twenty and twenty-five often degenerate into mediocrity at forty-five because of brain enervation due to venereal excess. Add to sex-abuse, tobacco, coffee, tea, alcohol and excessive or wrong eating and no wonder man at sixty is fit for little else than chloroforming if nature has not already administered euthanasia.

ADULTS

Adults, too, have much fear in their lives. The bread-and-butter problem gives anxiety; but when enough has been accumulated, so that fear along this line is unnecessary, fear is felt that something may happen that will put them back in the breadline. Why? There is no confidence in business ethics— there is no God in business.

Business Worries. — Business worries are a source of enervation. Business—any business—is not the cause of worry. A work well done is a delight and anything that delights is character-building. A work slovenly carried on dissatisfies, but the worrier never looks within to find the cause. This life brings enervation in time and disease as a sequel; then more worries looking for a cure. Business is what a man makes of it. A thorough understanding of business with honesty and industry removes all worries and saves nerve energy. Worry does not build efficiency; neither is inefficiency removed by worrying. Worry, lack of control over emotions, improper eating, stimulants, all build disease.

Nothing is so conducive to poise as a thorough understanding of one's personal habits and occupation. Bluff and bluster may put the idea of efficiency "across" to the people for a time; but, as surely as chickens come home to roost, the truth will out. Worry, even though presenting a smooth exterior, will break through; the worker will break down—disease will be his lot. Housewives who carry a burden of worry become enervated and lose health. The cause of their worry is lack of control of eating, lack of control of the emotions, lack of care of the body and lack of efficiency. Instead of resolutely going to work to remove all the defects, they are drowned by them. An uncontrollable temper must be downed or it will down the one who gives way to it. Gossip is not an admirable quality and, unless overcome, it will in time drive friends away. Envy and jealously are cancers that eat the soul out of those who indulge them. What is left to love when the soul is gone?

When anyone, from indolence and health-destroying habits, allows himself to gravitate below the standards expected of him by his friends, he must not be surprised when they run away from him.

Who are the old people who are left alone? Those who have lived selfish lives—who have demanded entertainment when they should have been entertaining themselves. Happiness and entertainment must come from within—from a love of service, work and books. If this fountain of youth and pleasure is not found before old age creeps over us, we shall find ourselves alone. Even in the midst of a throng we shall be alone, forever alone. What could be more pathetic?

Self-Indulgence.—Self-indulgence is contrary to ethics and brings its condemnation. What about the ethics of gluttons—what about their religion? Excess in everything follows on the heels of abnormal selfish indulgence. Coming under this head are self-pity and a desire for cure. Extravagant habits, even if there is an inexhaustable supply, build a self-destructive morale, on the heels of which, like a nemesis, runs the trail to premature death. The causes are called heart disease, apoplexy, paralysis, kidney disease, suicide, etc. but what is in a name? Names are all misleading; for the cause—first, last and all the time—is a selfish body and mind—destructive self-indulgence.

A study of nature reveals the fact that man must live for service; not giving alms, but helping others to help themselves.

Self-indulgence in the use of stimulants, even in moderation, is a constant drain on the nervous system; and a time comes when the last cigar, the last cup of coffee, the last hearty meal snaps the vital cord; and the contingency is always unexpected and a surprise.

Overwork is said to enervate but this is an excuse behind which are hidden many bad habits that kill rather than the work. Work without pleasure in the work is enervating and disease-building; an unsatisfied mind—a desire to engage in some other work before efficiency has been attained in the work engaged in; more desire for pay than to do good work. A work is never well done until it takes on the individuality of the worker. We should work with the creative instinct. Our work should be created in the image of its creator—love of the creator—of the work not the emoluments.

Dissatisfaction and overworked emotions are enervating. Worry, fear, grief, anger, passion, temper, overjoy, depression, dissatisfaction, self-pity, pride, egotism, envy, jealousy, gossip, lying, dishonesty, failing to meet obligations and appointments, taking advantage of misunderstandings, abusing the credulity of friends, abusing the confidence of those who confide in us—all enervate and in time build chronic disease.

Grief.—Grief is enervating. Those who are very enervated and toxemic will be prostrated by grief and, unless put to bed and kept warm and quiet and without food may die. Food eaten under such circumstances will not digest but acts as a poison. Some people are made invalids for life by a great grief.

Shock—Shock, mental or physical, may enervate so greatly as to kill by heart failure or be followed by permanent nervousness. Wrong eating or overeating may prevent a return to health.

The shell shock that many soldiers suffered during the First World War was converted into permanent invalidism by tobacco and other enervating habits. Certainly overeating prevents a return to health.

Anger.—Anger is very enervating. A daily shock of

anger will build profound enervation. A temper that flies at the slightest provocation ruins digestion and builds nervousness. Unless controlled, epilepsy may evolve and cancer may end life. The chronic grouch is liable to build ulcer or cancer of the stomach. Those who cannot control their temper often build rheumatic arthritis, hard arteries, gall-stones and early old age.

Egotism. — Because of self-love, selfishness, misanthrophy and distrust the egotist sees unfriendliness in all the acts of others—every hand is against him. This causes enervation and *toxemia* which lead on to many nervous derangements and even insanity. A misanthrope loves self above everything and everybody. The moment the nearest and dearest friend is separated, the friend's head comes off figuratively. The egotist hates all who fail to feed his vanity. Hate and anger are always on tap but draped with a mocking smile when finesse or stratagem demands. Friendship, honor, honesty and veracity must go when self-interest is being impinged upon or neglected. Men of this type have no gratitude. They demand everything and give nothing without an ulterior motive. Where egotism is mild it may not go beyond a disagreeable, overbearing selfishness.

Selfishness. — A selfish nature always looks after self first. A common type of selfishness is interpreted as love of children. But when a son or daughter marries against the father's wish, disinheritance follows. Why? Because ambition is piqued. Love is oftener a selfish ambition than affection. Selfishness leads on to enervation and *Toxemia*.

Ambition.—Ambition of a selfish type brings on ill health for it meets with so many disappointments. When successful, it enables the one who succeeds to gratify his sensual nature, resulting in all the so-called diseases following in the wake of selfish gratification. A *noble ambition* goes with self-control and service to mankind and health and long life are two of the rewards. Ambition for display, ostentation, gives an evanescent gratification but it costs more in wasted nervous energy than it is worth.

Thousands of semi-invalid women bring on toxemic crises as their reward for giving dinners and displaying dress, homes and furnishings.

Women gratify silly, stupid ambitions and pay for their thrills in broken health.

Many waste more energy at an afternoon card party than they can renew in a week.

Envy.—Envy of a low and disease-producing type is a begrudging nature. The man possessing this kind of envy is a vandal. He will slip a monkey wrench into the machinery of those whom he envies. He will poison reputations by innuendo.

> Who steals my purse steals trash: 'tis something, nothing;
> 'Twas mine, 'tis his, and has been slave to thousands;
> But he who filches from me my good name
> Robs me of that which not enriches him,
> And makes me poor indeed.—Shakespeare.

When safe, such a person will go the limit in doing even bodily harm to those whose merits tower over his. Laudable envy is that of a desire to equal in success the one envied. To rejoice in the success of others and try to equal them, where the success has been achieved on merit, builds a healthy mind and body.

Love and Jealousy. — According to Solomon:

"Love is strong as death; jealousy is cruel as the grave." Solomon should have known.

99

Shakespeare knew about everything worth knowing up to his time. He said:

> How many fools serve maddened jealousy!
> The venomed clamors of a jealous woman
> Poison more deadly than a mad dog's tooth.

The systematic poisoning of overwrought emotions has been known since reasoning began; but, aside from knowing that "a poison is generated in the system" from great anger, jealously, hate and grief, just what the poison is and the *modus operandi* of its production have never been satisfactorily explained until made clear by the *philosophy of toxemia*. The pathology of jealousy Shakespeare knew well as evidenced by the words he put into the mouths of some of his characters.

Excessive emotion—jealousy, for example, or great anger—precipitates a profound enervation which inhibits elimination. This floods the blood with toxin and brings on a malignant *toxemia* in the form of toxin drunkenness, which in people of a belligerent nature causes them to *run amuck*. Murder, several murders, are sometimes committed. In those with more consideration for others—those with less self-love—suicide ends the psychological storm.

Jealousy and unrequited love, when not malignant—developing in a vicious, unmoral subject—in time undermine the constitution by keeping up a gradually increasing state of enervation and *toxemia*. Catarrhal inflammations and ulcerations get better and worse with no hope of final recovery until the causes of enervation are overcome—namely, enervating habits of mind and body, of which jealousy is chief.

Overeating.—Overeating is a common and universal enervating habit; eating too much fat—cream, butter, fat meats, oils, rich pastries, sweets; eating too often, eating between meals and checking digestion with water-drinking between meals.

Food inebriety is more common than alcolhol-inebriety. The subconscious is as busy as a hive of bees substituting, antidoting, and in reparation work; substituting one stimulating excess for another—demanding whiskey, tobacco, opium, etc., for gluttonous eating; thrills, shocks, sensual excesses for food poisoning. Ungratified sense demands are appeased by food excesses or other stimulants; and when nature is balked in her demands, the victim runs amuck.

A French sheep-herder's daughter, being opposed by her father in marrying a lover, killed the parent while he slept by their campfire. A short time after the tragedy some men came upon the camp and discovered the girl eating her father's heart, which she had cut out and roasted in the fire. When discovered at her cannibalistic feast, she held up what was left of the heart and with a sardonic laugh declared: "He broke my heart and I am eating his."

Only a short time ago the overwrought nerves of a jazz- and alcolhol-crazed girl forced her to kill her mother because the latter undertook to oppose her in the gratification of her subconscious demands for more stimulation.

When enervation and *toxemia* have reached the stage of inebriety seen in the two girls mentioned above, civil and moral laws have abdicated to the subconscious laws which, like cosmic law and order, are unmoral but run true to necessity. Psychological, like physical, cyclones are out of the regular order; yet they are obeying the laws of their nature. They have no scruples to gainsay but tear through order as ruthlessly as fiends.

101

Every human being should know that such phenomena are potential to him and that the road to such catastrophes is enervating habits.

Prohibition is a beautiful ideal, but it is palliating one social disease while it is building a greater.

What mother would not rather have her son brought home from the corner grogshop drunk than see him escorted to jail handcuffed to an officer?

Enervation and *toxemia* focused on the brain bring out neurotic states with all kinds of symptom complexes. Drunkenness substitutes for bank robbery and other outlawry. So long as food drunkenness retains its prestige with the professions—prescribed by doctors; babbled to us Sundays and deciding our brawls on Monday—it will take more than statutes to enforce law and order. Most of our laws are made while the lawmakers are drunk on food and tobacco.

Drunkenness and crime of all kinds are vicarious toxin eliminations—crises of *toxemia*. Enforcing temperance and control of crime must fail in its object—namely, causing people to be temperate and law-abiding. The reason should be obvious to the student of nature. Our wants are based on our subconscious needs; sentiment and ethics have nothing to do with it. Our subconscious is not moral nor immoral; it belongs to the Great Cosmos, which is systematic, perfect in order, but unmoral. Intemperance of any kind establishes a want which, if not satisfied in the usual way, will turn to other ways of being satisfied. The surgeon, laws and anodynes perhaps relieve effects, but health restoration is based on removing causes. Legislatures are quack doctors. Self-control is the only remedy. To develop self-control the need must be understood.

The gluttonous build putrefaction in the bowels. Nerve energy is used up in resisting systemic infection. The supply of blood to the surface of the body for the purposes of warmth—radiation—resisting cold and heat, is called to the mucous membrane of the gastro-intestinal canal to neutralize the septic material that is about to enter the system through the asorbents. The mucous membrane becomes turgid with blood, establishing a mucorrhea (excessive secretion of mucus.) This is what we call catarrh. This secretion mechanically obstructs absorption of putrescence and also antidotes the poison by bringing the antibodies from the blood.

A battle royal is on all the time in the intestines of the gluttonous. The subconscious musters all the help possible, and when the system is drained of autogenerated antidotes, the victim is sent by his subconscious to find alcolhol, tobacco, coffee, tea, condiments and more food. Moral preachments and prohibitory laws passed by solons drunk on toxin, bowel putrescence and tobacco, like all monstrosities, are perversions of nutrition.

Insatiable desire for food and stimulants means an enervated state of the body brought on from overindulgence—overstimulation.

A driving desire for food three times a day means enervation; trouble is only a little farther on. The wise will get busy and correct appetites.

Perverted appetites are built by overeating; eating rich food until enjoyment is lost for staple or plain foods; use of stimulants—alcohol, tobacco, coffee, tea; use of butter, salt, pepper and rich dressings; eating without a real hunger (real hunger will take the plainest foods with a relish); eating when sick or uncomfortable; eating at off hours or between meals; eating until uncomfortable.

Gossips are always slanderers and slanderers are always and forever potential liars. If they do not know that they are broadcasting lies, they are criminally careless in not endeavoring to find whether the tale they gossip is true or not. *Gossip enervates the gossiper.*

Gossips are always enervated for they live in fear of being discovered. Their secretions are always acid. They are inclined to develop pyorrhea and mucous membrane infections. They are slow to recover from catarrhal crisis of *toxemia.*

Gossips are empty-headed slaves to their habits of slander and spite; they are malignant parasites that feed upon carrion. They are the lowest types of criminal; hell monsters that kill with their breath. They often die of cancer.

Sycophancy.—Flatterers look like friends, as wolves like dogs (Byron). He hurts me most who lavishly commends Churchill).

A real sycophant, like all people who are not honest, lives a life that enervates and which nature condemns early.

Dishonesty. — Dishonesty eventually hardens the arteries and cancer ends a miserable existence.

Religiosity.—Morbidly *pious,* yet practicing the foregoing habits and ending in premature death.

A saving religion, Christian, Jewish or Mohamedan, is one free from mental and physical habits that overstimulate, enervate and intoxicate.

If *toxemic,* get rid of enervating habits. *Cures*—prayers, drugs, surgery—all honest or dishonest cures—will not remove cause. Get rid of cause and stay rid of it, then health returns and abides perpetually.

RETROSPECTION

MORE might have been said and no doubt better said about how we human beings vandalize our minds and bodies; but enough has been told for open-minded people to see that the only nemesis on our heels is our habits. O. W. Holmes, in his *The Autocrat of the Breakfast Table*, had this to say concerning habit.

Habit is the approximation of the animal system of the organic. It is a confession of failure in the highest function of being, which involves a perpetual self-determination in full view of all existing circumstances.

Autonomy or self-government is met at the threshold of life by all the conventional superstitions and educated into a lot of habits, such as trying to cure without removing cause. This, combined with man's inclination to hedonism (the doctrine that pleasure is the only good), leads to a life of failure in spite of man's potential desire to rise above the forces that hold him down. *Toxemia Explained* will help all who study it carefully to understand what disease is and how it is brought on. This knowledge will help the wise and self-controlled to sidestep disease and the medical octopus that unwittingly vandalizes the sick.

The profession is made up of an army of educated men; and I believe the majority are gentlemen and are endeavoring to serve humanity. Education and ethics, when established on fallacy and given the prestige of numbers—given an overwhelming majority—can make the fallacy true so far as the herd is concerned.

All I ask of laymen or the profession is honestly to put my *Philosophy of toxemia* to the acid test. Yes, prove, if possible, that I am mistaken and then give me what is coming to me!

Man makes his own diseases. This book tells how he does it. And he is the one who can bring back health. He and his subconsciousness alone can bring about health. Physicians cannot *cure*. Only very rarely is surgical vandalism a *dernier ressort* unless bad treatment forces unnecessary emergencies.

THE body is strong or weak, as the case may be, depending entirely on whether the nerve energy is strong or weak. And it should be remembered that the functions of the body are carried on well or badly according to the amount of energy generated.

A FEW SUGGESTIONS

THE following suggestions may be of assistance to those who wish to maintain a state of good health or help them to bring themselves from a state of impaired health to that of good health. Those who are badly handicapped and who wish more detailed information will have to have the advice fitted to their particular cases through individual instructions.

The first thing on awakening in the morning, the Tilden system of tensing exercises should be practiced for from fifteen to thirty minutes.* Following the exercises, go to the bathroom and, while standing in warm water, take a quick, warm sponge bath. Then follow this with plenty of dry-towel or friction-mitten rubbing. At night before retiring give the body a thorough friction rubbing again. If not convenient to take the warm sponge bath in the morning, use the dry rub in the morning and the warm sponge bath at night before retiring.

Never eat more than three meals a day; do not eat nor drink between meals. Use the following rules to guide you in "when to eat, when not to eat, and how to eat:"

*(See appendix C)

Rule No. 1—Never eat unless you are absolutely comfortable in mind and body from the previous mealtime.

Rule No. 2—Thoroughly masticate and insalivate every mouthful of starchy food and give the rest of your food a reasonable amount of chewing.

Rule No. 3—Never eat without a keen relish.

DR. TILDEN'S TENSING EXERCISES

BEGIN by tensing the leg muscles from the toes to the body as follows: First extend the toes as far as you can; then grip, as it were, by forcing the toes forward toward the heels, and at the same time make the muscles of the legs hard to the body. Completely relax. Do not repeat the tension again until the muscles are soft; then tense again, repeating the contraction and extension.

Tense the hands and arms in the same way. Extend the fingers as far as possible, making the muscles hard to the shoulders; then grip the fingers and shut the fist, hardening the muscles to the shoulders. Do this five times; then tense the legs five times; then the hands and arms again.

Fold a pillow and put under the shoulders so that when the head drops back it will not touch anything. Lift the head forward, the chin to the chest; drop the head back again as far as it will go, then lift. Do this four or five times. Then, with the pillow still under the shoulders, lock the fingers under the head, allowing the head to rest in the hands. Swing the head from side to side, up and down, and rotate, carrying each movement as far as possible.

Then push the folded pillow down under the hips and go through the leg movements of riding a bicycle. Then, with legs extended in the air, move each leg from side to side, allowing one to pass the other, scissors-fashion; changing however, each time they pass, having first one leg forward and then the other.

Tense the abdomen, making the muscles as hard as possible and at the same time kneading the muscles with the hands. This exercise will strengthen the abdominal muscles and help overcome constipation. In women the uterine ligaments will be strengthened, lifting and overcoming fallen and misplaced positions of the womb. The muscles of the bladder and rectum will be improved by these exercises. Piles—prolapsus of the rectal mucous membrane—will be overcome. An irritable bladder and prostrate enlargements will be benefited by these exercises.

Then sit up and turn the face to the right as far as possible; then to the left as far as possible; then allow the head to drop over so as to bring the ear close to the shoulder and then carry it over to the opposite shoulder.

These movements of the head and neck are necessary to remove toxic deposits that may have taken place between the vetebrae and in grooves and openings in bones where the nerves and arteries pass. If the hearing is bad these movements will improve it. If the sense of smell is not so acute as it should be, by keeping up the exercises the olfactory nerve will be freed and the power of smell will be improved. The taste, too, will be bettered. All the nerves of special sense will be invigorated. The pneumogastric nerve and all the vital nerves controlling vital organs are invigorated by this exercise. When nerves are pressed upon by organic deposits, the movements above described will cause the deposits to be absorbed. The muscles of the neck will develop; the muscles of the face will develop; one will grow to look and feel younger.

These exercises must be gone through with, not only before getting up, but every three or four hours during the day. You may think that this is very laborious, but it is the price you must pay to get well. So begin at once, and be faithful!

Sit on the edge of the bed and sway the body from side to side as far as possible; then follow with a twisting movement, attempting to look behind over the shoulders. Sit up in bed and sway backward and forward, compelling the spine to bend from the small of the back up to the head, forward and backward. This loosens up the spine and invigorates the nerves that are sent off to the lower part of the body. All body parts are improved by their exercised usage.

Get on the knees and elbows; then push the body forward as far as possible without falling upon the abdomen; then push back as far as possible. Go back and forth, while in this position until tired; then drop on either the left or right shoulder while the hips are highly elevated. This is called the knee-shoulder position. The knee and elbow position, with the movements described, I call the "Irish Mail movements." It is necessary to practice both these movements and positions in overcoming constipation, prolapsus of the bowels, rectum, or womb, and piles.

Place the forefinger over the closed eyes and rub gently from side to side. Then remove the fingers and rotate the eyeballs, reversing the movement to relieve the tire.

Place the forefingers on the wings of the nose; press together and move from side to side.

When the weather is nice, it is well to walk in the open air as often as possible.

111

J. H. TILDEN, M.D.

NOTES AND COMMENTS
by DR. HARRY CLEMENTS

THE RETENTIONAL THEORY OF DISEASE CAUSATION
Based on the Teachings of Dr. J. H. Tilden

Dr. Tilden was born in 1851 and graduated in medicine in 1872. Practiced in Missouri and Illinois until 1890 when he moved to Denver, Colorado, where he repudiated the conventional treatment of disease, formulated his theory of toxemia and founded his school of health. There he carried on his practice without the use of medicines for nearly half a century, dying in his ninetieth year.

The following diagram puts in proper sequence the events leading to disease as propounded by Dr. Tilden in his theory of toxemia and its significance as an important factor in health and impaired health. It is important to bear in mind this sequence if we are to understand the theory and not to misinterpret it as is so often done today. Some people, including practitioners and Nature Cure writers have said that they do not believe that toxemia is the cause of disease; one recently wrote that to cure disease we must aim at detoxication as if those sentiments expressed Dr. Tilden's views. If the diagram is examined, it will be seen that Dr. Tilden did not believe that toxemia was the cause of disease, nor did he hold that detoxifying methods equated the removal of causative factors, which lay in faulty habits of living and eating. If properly interpreted the theory *includes all forms of stress as causative factors, environmental, physical, mental and emotional.*

The diagram will help the reader to understand the line of thought pursued by Dr. Tilden which emphasizes the contention that *there is no single cause of disease and stresses the point that diet is not, as so many people think, the only factor to be considered in the maintenance of health and the management of disease.*

STRESS
ENVIRONMENTAL—DAILY HABITS

↓

STRAIN
PHYSICAL—MENTAL—EMOTIONAL
ENVIRONMENTAL

↓

ENERVATION

↓

INEFFICIENT ELIMINATION
LUNGS—BOWEL—KIDNEYS—SKIN

↓

RETENTION OF WASTE PRODUCTS

↓

TOXEMIA

↓

DISEASE REACTIONS
ACUTE CRISES
CHRONIC AND DEGENERATIVE
CONDITIONS

↓

NATURE OF DISEASE DETERMINED
BY INDIVIDUAL PREDISPOSITION
OR DIATHESIS AND EFFECTS OF
MEDICINAL TREATMENT

Dr. Tilden summed up his theory as follows: "In the process of tissue building—metabolism—there is cell building—
anabolism—and cell destruction—catabolism. The broken
down tissue is toxic and in health when nerve energy is
normal, it is eliminated from the blood as fast as evolved.
When nerve energy is dissipated from any cause, physical,
mental or bad habits, the body becomes enervated. When
enervated, elimination is checked, causing a retention of
toxins within the blood and tissues which we name toxemia. This accumulation of toxin when once established
will continue until nerve energy is restored. Diseases, so-
called, are Nature's efforts at eliminating the toxins from
the body. Such disease reactions are crises of toxemia."

Index

A

Acute disease, cannot manifest without cause, 23, 85
Acute malignancy, defined, 83
Adults, enervating habits in, 94ff.
Alcohol, enervating, 59, 88, 94, 102, 103
Ambition, sefish, enervating, 98
Anemia, pernicious, 19
  blood transfusion for, 68
Anger, enervating, 97-98
Apoplexy, 29, 31, 46, 75, 96
Appendix, removal of, 91
Arteries, hardening of, 46, 98
Asthma, 57
Ataxia, locomotor, 60, 88, 93-94
Athletes, die early, 71
Autogenerated poison, cause of disease, 22, 49
Auto-immunization, 78

B

Babies, habits in, 89-90
Bathing, proper, 107
Blood, ruptured vessels, 29
  amount of toxin in varies, 62
  transfusion in pernicious anemia, 68
  degeneration of vessels, 71
  state of, makes disease possible, 68, 79
Bowels, derangement of, 77
Brain, hemorrhage in, 29, 31
Bright's disease, 44, 60, 67
Bronchitis, 58, 79
Business worry, 95

C

Cabot, Dr., on diagnosis, 17
Cachexia, 19, 20

Cancer, 9, 18-19, 20, 30, 44, 45, 51, 60, 75, 81, 98
Care. *See* Treatment.
Catarrh, 20, 30, 42, 45, 57, 58, 60
Cause, of disease, 7, 12, 16, 18, 20, 22, 24, 27, 47, 53, 60, 62, 78, 83, 86, 87
  of enervation, 87ff.
Children, diseases peculiar to, 55
  must be busy, 70
  fever in, 82
  not sick unless toxemic, 83
  enervating habits in, 90ff.
Chorea, 77
Clothes and cleanliness, 50
Coffee, enervating, 59, 94, 103
Coffee headache, 11
Colds, 20, 42, 45, 57, 60, 81
  catching habit, 59
Colonitis, 20, 79
Conservation of nerve energy, greatest step to health recovery, 56
Constipation, 49, 73
Contentment, necessary, 69
Convulsions, 77
Crisis of toxemia, is disease, 7, 42, 57, 58, 59, 60, 79, 81, 102
Croup, 58
Cure, man looking for, 6
  there is none, 7, 27, 32, 38, 39, 43, 45, 51, 57, 74, 81, 83
Cystitis, 58, 77

D

Diagnosis, Mackenzie on, 17
  Cabot on, 17
  medical delusion, 20, 32, 80
Diets, too many, 6, 8
Diphtheria, 31, 82, 83
Disease, cause of, 7, 12, 13, 16, 18, 20, 22, 24, 27, 45, 47, 60, 62, 78, 83, 86, 87

man's own building, 6, 8, 38
toxemic crisis, 7, 42, 57, 58, 59, 60, 79, 81, 102
not an entity, 25, 27, 29, 32, 59, 60
a common expression of universal enervation, 9
early stages, 19
extraneous influence not cause of, 26
and symptoms confounded, 31
Mackenzie on, 31
unity of all, 45, 51, 60
germs as cause of, 53
peculiar to children, 55, 91
Dishonesty, enervating, 104
Dropsy, 75
Drug habit, 10
Drugs, effects of, 40, 41, 42, 57, 68
venereal disease healed without, 11
and medical science, 26

E

Eating, excessive, 59
wrong, effect of, 68
three meals only, 107
See also Food, Overeating
Egotism, enervating, 98
Elimination, checked by drugs, 41, 42
faulty, effect of, 12, 23, 24, 42, 52, 57, 59, 61, 67, 68
of waste products of tissue building, 54
normal, 19, 82
Emotion, excessive, enervating, 100
Energy. See Nerve energy.
Enervating habits, if continued, build disease, 7, 8, 59
must be removed, 12, 86
defined, 89ff.
Enervation, cause of, 12, 13, 40, 54, 55, 56, 82, 87ff.
effect of, 22, 24, 44, 56, 59, 61, 78
cause, and not disease, 57
general, 61ff.
prevents elimination of infection, 67
Envy, enervating, 95, 99
Epidemics, 83, 85

Epilepsy, 19, 98
Exercise, excessive, enervating, 71
tensing, 107, 109-111

F

Fast, most powerful eliminant, 52
fear of, 82
Fatality, what causes, 85
Fear, prevents elimination, 42
effect of, 51, 68, 77, 93
in children, 92
in adults, 94
Feet, cold, harmful, 56
Fever, septic, 66
scarlet, 82
Focal infection, 53, 80
Food, in intestines, on outside of body, 49
poisoning, 19, 49, 85
proper for children, 83, 90, 91
effect of wrong, 68
drunkards produce fatal cases, 85
inebriety, enervating, 101
driving desire for, 103
when to take, 107

G

Gall bladder, stone in, 9, 46, 57, 98
Gastritis, 19, 20, 30, 58, 79, 81, 82
Germs, accidental, 20
as cause of fermentation, 28
and disease, 32, 53
deadly, 49ff.
Gland, impotency, 68
Goiter, 77
Gossip, enervating, 103-04
Grief, enervating 97

H

Hardening of arteries. See Arteries.
Hay fever, 57, 59
Headache, 11, 19, 31, 42, 76, 81
Health, should be studied, 20
good, greater force than bad, 66
defined, 82
Heart, degeneration of, 71
leaky, 75
disease, 96

Hemorrhage, of stomach, 19
    in brain, 29, 31
Holmes, Oliver W., quotation
    from, 35-37, 105
Hyperemia, symptoms, of, 29

I

Idleness brings discontent, 69
Indigestion, 73, 77
Infantile paralysis, 82
Infection, protein, 19
    focal, 53, 80
    of sinus, 80
    of teeth, 80
Infinite, defined, 47-48
Influenza, 31, 42, 81
Immunity to disease, a myth, 78
Immunization, 78
    product of civilization, 51
    harm of, 62
    auto, 78
    See also Vaccines.
Insomnia, 19

J

Jazz, enervating, 88, 101
Jealousy, enervating, 95, 99-100

K

Kidneys, overworking, 52
    disease of, 96
Knowledge, man's salvation, 53
    seasoned by time, necessary, 72

L

Laryngitis, 58
Longevity, increasing, 93

M

Mackenzie, Sir James, on cure, 15
    on diagnosis, 17
    on symptoms, 18, 28
    on disease, 31-32
Malignant disease, 83
Malignancy, acute, defined, 84
Malignant septic fever, 66
Mastication, thorough, necessary, 108
Measles, 31, 65

Medical Science founded on false
    premise, 26
Medicine, lacks ideas, 15
    rest on sound scientific founda-
    tion, 32
Megrim, 40-41
Meningitis, 82
Menstruation, painful, 19
Metabolism, toxin, waste product
    of, 23, 54, 61, 66
Moderation, defined, 78
Muscle fatigue, 76

N

Nature, effect of interfering with,
    63
    heals when so allowed, 11, 39,
    43, 51, 52, 81, 82, 92
Nerve energy, waste of, 12, 20, 86
    normal, effect of, 13, 23, 56, 78,
    82
    importance of, 54-55
    conservation of, necessary, 86,
    106
Nerves, impinged, 26
Neuralgia, 76
Neuritis, 76
Neurosis, 74

O

Onanism, 93
Operations, unnecessary, 9, 10, 39,
    68, 91
Organic disease. *See* Disease.
Osler, opinion of, 36
Overeating, is overstimulating, 12
    is enervating, 100ff.
    See also Eating; Food

P

Pain, usually first symptom, 29,
    30, 31
Palliatives, are they ever neces-
    sary, 10
    most "cures" are, 81-82
Paralysis, 29, 96
    infantile, 82
Pasteur, discoverer of cause of fer-
    mentation, 28, 40
Pathology, study of, 18, 20, 45
Pernicious anemia. *See Anemia.*

117

Pharyngitis, 58
Physicians, cannot cure anything, 7, 25, 43, 75, 106
  duty of, 43
Piles, 76
Pneumonia, 42, 58, 79
Poison, disease indirectly due to, 22
  per se, not disease, 22, 79
  autogenerated, 22
  ptomaine, 49
Prohibition, 102
Protein, infection, 19
Psychologists, work of, 26
Ptomaine poisoning, 49

Q

Quiet, necessary, during sickness, 44, 83, 85
  necessary in children, 90

R

Religiosity, enervating, 104
Rest, necessary for cure, 8, 44, 52, 67, 85
Rheumatic arthritis, 98
Rheumatism, 8, 23, 75, 76, 80, 81
Roosevelt, Theodore, cause of death, 67
Rush, Benjamin, thought from, 33-35

S

Scarlet fever, 31, 65, 82, 83
Scientific tests, 38ff.
Secretions of body, overcome germs, 50
Self-abuse, 92, 94
Self-control brings best in life, 51, 75, 102
Self-indulgence, enervating, 96-97
Self-pity, enervating, 73
Selfishness, enervating, 98
Septic fever, cause of, 66, 83
Septic poisoning, 9, 49, 51
  following vaccination, 66
Shock, enervating, 97
Sick habit, 73, 91
Sinus, infected, 80
Smallpox, 16, 66, 83
Smoking, enervating, 86

Spencer, Herbert, on vaccination 62-63
Stimulants, subtly undermining, 1
  remove awareness, 12
  continues use of, 66, 86
  See also Alcohol; Coffee; Tea
Stone in gall bladder. See Gall bladder.
Subconscious, influence of, 39 74-75
  not moral nor immoral, 102
  alone, can cure, 106
Surgery, unnecessary, 9, 10, 39 68, 91
Sycophancy, enervating, 104
Symptomatology, value of, 28ff. 32
Symptoms, Sir James Mackenzie on, 18, 28
  chain of, 29, 31
  and disease, confounded, 31, 32
  pain, first, 30, 31
  complex of signifies crisis of toxemia, 42, 43, 45, 57, 60, 68, 79
  all have same origin, 45, 80
  vary, 58
Syphilis, 20, 50, 51, 60, 65, 75, 93
  healed without drugs, 11

T

Tea, enervating, 59, 94, 103
Teeth, infected, cause of, 80
Temper, enervating, 86
Tensing, exercises, 107, 109-111
Tension, cause of, 77
Tilden philosophy applies to all disease, 8, 27, 58
Tissue, worn out must be removed, 54
Tobacco, enervating, 12, 41, 88, 92, 94, 97, 103
Tobacco heart, remedy for, 7
Tonsilitis, 58, 79, 81, 84
Tonsils, removal of, 91
Treatment, proper, 43-44, 52, 67, 77, 85
  for megrim, 40-41
  of tense muscles, 77
  of children, 82-83
Tuberculosis, 20, 44, 51, 60, 67, 75
Tumors, 9, 51, 77
Typhoid fever, 42, 64, 83

U

Ulcer of stomach, 9, 18, 19, 20, 30, 45, 98
Universal law rules in health and disease, 8
Urine, albumin in, 75

V

Vaccination, Herbert Spencer on, 63
Vaccines, 32, 39, 49
  made from products of disease, 16
  are poisons, 62
  effect of, 39, 50, 64, 65, 66

use of in children, 91
  See also Immunization.
Venereal disease. *See* Syphilis.
Venereal excitement, effect of, 94

W

Warmth, bodily, necessary, 56, 85
Womb, tumor in, 77
Work, brings contentment, 69, 70
Worry, enervating, 12, 86, 95
Wound, suppurating, 49

Y

Youth, desires speed, 72
  developing multi-inebriety, 88

HISTORICAL BACKGROUND

Natural Hygiene Press, the publisher of this book, is a division of the American Natural Hygiene Society. The Society is a non-profit, tax exempt membership organization founded in 1949 for the primary purpose of public education in *Natural Hygiene,* which is a system, based on biology and physiology, for preserving and recovering health through natural living habits.

Natural Hygiene came on the American scene as an educational movement in 1830 through the lectures of Sylvester Graham in New York, Rochester, Providence, Buffalo and other eastern cities. Modern dietary science is said to have had its beginning with Graham, who stressed the value of fresh fruits and vegetables as the best foods for man. He wrote books and articles on healthful living for 21 years and his greatest work is the *Science of Human Life,* published in 1839.

Graham pioneered in this country in advocating the teaching of physiology in the public schools and in expounding the value of regular physical exercise, fresh air and well ventilated homes, rest and sleep, sunbathing, emotional control and clothing reform for women from the tight waists, corsets and high heeled pointed toed shoes of the day.

Graham was joined in his work of health education by prominent medical people of the time such as Isaac Jennings, M.D., William Alcott, M.D., Russell Thacker Trall, M.D., Thomas Low Nichols, M.D., Susanna Dodds, M.D., James Caleb Jackson, M.D., George H. Taylor, M.D., and later by Robert Walker, M.D., John H Tilden, M.D.

Many of these pioneers of the *Natural Hygiene* System had suffered serious illness during their early years which became a strong motivating force in seeking the solution to the disease problem. They came to see in wrong living the true cause of disease and sought to induce mankind to return to a normal way of life by adopting good living habits. They wrote prodigiously in books and magazines and some founded colleges to train students in caring for people through hygienic means, rather than drugs and medicines. Many graduates of *Hygienic Colleges* served as doctors in the Civil War and helped their patients recover more quickly by their hygienic methods.

The American Natural Hygiene Society now carries on the educational work of the movement through distribution of books published by its press and other publishers, pamphlets, annual public conventions and seminars and a chapter structure which functions in many large cities through the membership, dispensing *Natural Hygiene* education to the local people. Future goals of the Society are the establishment of colleges to train practitioners in the Hygienic System of health maintenance, institutes to care for the sick the hygienic way, and community centers for family living on an educational, social and recreational basis along *Natural Hygienic* lines.

NOTICE TO THE READER

If after reading this book, you feel the vital knowledge which it contains deserves to be made widely known, you are urged to become a member of the American Natural Hygiene Society and help to contribute to this worthy cause for the benefit of mankind. (Contributions are tax exempt.)

As a membership bonus, we will send a free copy of this book to anyone of your choice. Fill out the application below and mail with your remittance of $7.00, which includes the annual membership and the bonus book.

AMERICAN NATURAL HYGIENE SOCIETY
1920 IRVING PARK ROAD, CHICAGO, ILL. 60613

Please enroll me as a member of your worthy cause. Enclosed is $7.00 for the Annual Membership and the bonus book.*

Name_____
            (please print)

Address_____

City, State, Zip_____

Phone No._____Age_____

**** PLEASE SEND BONUS BOOK TO ****

Name_____
            (please print)

Address_____

City, State, Zip_____

Phone No._____Age_____

*Outside U.S.A. add $1.00 to cover   I
added postage costs and handling.*

BOOK ORDER FORM

☐	FASTING FOR RENEWAL OF LIFE	$2.25
☐	TOXEMIA: The Basic Cause of All Disease	$1.50
☐	PROGRAM FOR DYNAMIC HEALTH	$1.00
☐	FASTING CAN SAVE YOUR LIFE	$1.45
☐	YOU DON'T HAVE TO BE SICK!	$1.45
☐	HEALTH FOR THE MILLIONS	$1.45
☐	HYGIENIC CARE OF CHILDREN	$1.95
☐	EXERCISE!	$1.95
☐	THE GREATEST HEALTH DISCOVERY	$1.75
☐	DICTIONARY OF MAN'S FOODS	$2.25
☐	SUPERIOR NUTRITION	$2.25
☐	INTRODUCTION TO NATURAL HYGIENE	$1.75
☐	FOOD COMBINING MADE EASY	$1.00
☐	RUBIES IN THE SAND	$4.50
☐	SYPHILIS: The Werewolf of Medicine	$4.00
☐	LIVING LIFE TO LIVE IT LONGER	$2.00
☐	HYGIENIC SYSTEM, Vol. 2	$5.50
☐	HYGIENIC SYSTEM, Vol. 3	$5.50
☐	NATURAL HYGIENE: Man's Pristine Way of Life	$6.50
☐	FASTING FOR HEALTH AND LONG LIFE	$3.00
☐	HUMAN BEAUTY: ITS CULTURE AND HYGIENE	$10.00

Add 20¢ to each book for postage

Illinois residents add 5% state sales tax.

☐	DR. SHELTON'S HYGIENIC REVIEW (yearly subscription) **Foreign $8.00**	$7.50
☐	FIT FOOD FOR MAN	$.50

American Natural Hygiene Society
1920 Irving Park Road, Chicago, Ill. 60613

Please ship books checked above. Enclosed is $_____

Name_____

Address_____

City, State, Zip_____

Recommended Reading List

FASTING FOR RENEWAL OF LIFE   **$2.25**
(1974) Herbert M. Shelton. 320 pages. Paperback. Everything you need to know about how fasting improves health.

TOXEMIA—The Basic Cause of All Disease   **$1.50**
(reprinted 1974) John H. Tilden, M.D. 125 pages. Paperback. An eminent medical doctor tells how to get well and stay well the drugless way.

PROGRAM FOR DYNAMIC HEALTH   **$1.00**
(1974) Compiled by T. C. Fry. 125 pages. The do-it-yourself way to top fitness in harmony with nature.

DICTIONARY OF MAN'S FOODS   **$2.25**
(1972) William L. Esser. 179 pages. Paperback. Descriptive alphabetical guide to fruits and vegetables and how to combine each for good digestion; tables of food composition and their nutritional values; seed sprouting instructions; food combining chart; listing of food classifications; suggested menus for every day of the week. Separate chapters on fruits, vegetables, nuts, conservative cooking, the kitchen on a budget, best methods of storing. Special color section shows varieties of breakfasts, lunches and dinners.

THE GREATEST HEALTH DISCOVERY   **$1.75**
(1972) Natural Hygiene and Its Evolution, Past, Present, Future. From the works of Sylvester Graham, Dr. R. T. Trall, Herbert M. Shelton and others. 241 pages. Paperback. The health care revolution which started in 19th century America and solved the problem of disease and premature death. Contains portraits of the pioneers who were mostly medical practitioners; 18 picture pages of the Hygienic way of life through the medium of a traditional Natural Hygiene convention. Presents a practical plan for bringing health unlimited on a community level.

EXERCISE!   **$1.95**
(1971) H. M. Shelton. 378 pages. Paperback. The history and role of formal exercise in maintaining good body functioning; how exercise aids in existing impairments by correcting weakened structural faults and muscles; profuse illustrations show how the exercises are done. Reprinted from Volume 4 of The Hygienic System.

HYGIENIC CARE OF CHILDREN   **$1.95**
(1970) H. M. Shelton. Over 400 pages. Paperback. The parents' comprehensive guide to rearing healthy children and insuring a healthful pregnancy. Gives facts about inoculations and their harmful effects.

NATURAL HYGIENE: Man's Pristine Way of Life   **$6.50**
(1968) H. M. Shelton. 638 pages. A complete book on the requirements of the body for recovering and maintaining health. Historical background of the hygienic movement.

HEALTH FOR THE MILLIONS   **$1.45**
(1968) H. M. Shelton. 320 pages. Paperback. 41 chapters on how the body functions, what it needs and what is harmful to it. Presenting Natural Hygiene in a nutshell!

YOU DON'T HAVE TO BE SICK   **$1.45**
(1967) Jack Dunn Trop. 231 pages. Paperback. Gives a step by step routine for putting a healthful living program into effect. Sample menus and party foods.

INTRODUCTION TO NATURAL HYGIENE   **$1.75**
   H. M. Shelton. 92 pages. Soft covers. Basic reading for
   understanding the principles underlying the Natural Hygiene
   system of health maintenance and recovery.

THE HYGIENIC SYSTEM, Vol. II   **$5.50**
   H. M. Shelton. 591 pages. A complete guide on correct food
   and feeding from infancy on.

THE HYGIENIC SYSTEM, Vol. III   **$5.50**
   H. M. Shelton. 541 pages. The most comprehensive and
   authoritative book on fasting. One chapter on sunbathing and
   its role in wellbeing.

FASTING CAN SAVE YOUR LIFE   **$1.45**
   (1964) H. M. Shelton. 191 pages. Part 1: Fasting and weight
   loss. Part 2: How fasting can help keep you well. Paperback.

HUMAN BEAUTY: ITS CULTURE & HYGIENE   **$10.00**
   H. M. Shelton. 1039 pages. The important relationship between good functioning and beauty. Over 100 illustrations.
   Proper care of the various parts of the body and exercises
   for neck, shoulders, arms, chest, back muscles, etc.

FOOD COMBINING MADE EASY   **$1.00**
   H. M. Shelton. 71 pages. Everything you need to know to
   avoid discomfort after meals, such as heartburn, bloating,
   flatulence (gas), acid indigestion.

RUBIES IN THE SAND   **$4.50**
   H. M. Shelton. 331 pages. The history of man's change from a
   natural way of life to the adoption of poison habits.

SUPERIOR NUTRITION   **$2.25**
   H. M. Shelton. 197 pages. Soft covers. Condensed version of
   Vol. II of the Hygienic System. Menus.

LIVING LIFE TO LIVE IT LONGER   **$2.00**
   H. M. Shelton. 139 pages. Soft covers. How to live more
   joyfully and with fulfillment.

SYPHILIS, The Werewolf of Medicine   **$4.00**
   H. M. Shelton. 150 pages. Soft covers. Gives the true cause
   of this "disease" and shows why it is a myth.

FASTING FOR HEALTH AND LONG LIFE   **$3.00**
   H. M. Carrington. 151 pages. Soft covers. Facts about fasting
   in abbreviated form.

DR. SHELTON'S HYGIENIC REVIEW   **$7.50**
   A monthly magazine edited and published by Herbert M.
   Shelton. Vital articles on the cause of disease, how to main-
   tain health, errors of medical practices.

FIT FOOD FOR MAN   **$.50**
   Arthur Andrews. 16 pages. Explains why man functions best
   on a fruit, nut, and vegetable diet. Anatomical comparison
   chart shows how differences in various animal species (including human beings) determine what type of food they are
   constituted to eat.

AMERICAN NATURAL HYGIENE SOCIETY
1920 IRVING PARK ROAD
CHICAGO, ILLINOIS 60613